Mastering Azure Machine Learning

Second Edition

Execute large-scale end-to-end machine learning with Azure

Christoph Körner

Marcel Alsdorf

BIRMINGHAM—MUMBAI

Mastering Azure Machine Learning
Second Edition

Publishing Product Manager: Ali Abidi
Senior Editor: Nathanya Dias
Content Development Editor: Manikandan Kurup
Technical Editor: Devanshi Ayare
Copy Editor: Safis Editing
Project Coordinator: Aparna Ravikumar Nair
Proofreader: Safis Editing
Indexer: Rekha Nair
Production Designer: Aparna Bhagat
Marketing Coordinators: Abeer Dawe, Shifa Ansari

First published: March 2020
Second edition: May 2022

Production reference: 1220422

Published by Packt Publishing Ltd.
Livery Place
35 Livery Street
Birmingham
B3 2PB, UK.

ISBN 978-1-80323-241-6

www.packt.com

Contributors

About the authors

Christoph Körner previously worked as a cloud solution architect for Microsoft, specializing in Azure-based big data and machine learning solutions, where he was responsible for designing end-to-end machine learning and data science platforms. He currently works for a large cloud provider on highly scalable distributed in-memory database services. Christoph has authored four books: *Deep Learning in the Browser* for Bleeding Edge Press, as well as *Mastering Azure Machine Learning* (first edition), *Learning Responsive Data Visualization*, and *Data Visualization with D3 and AngularJS* for Packt Publishing.

Marcel Alsdorf is a cloud solution architect with 5 years of experience at Microsoft consulting various companies on their cloud strategy. In this role, he focuses on supporting companies in their move toward being data-driven by analyzing their requirements and designing their data infrastructure in the areas of IoT and event streaming, data warehousing, and machine learning. On the side, he shares his technical and business knowledge as a coach in hackathons, as a mentor for start-ups and peers, and as a university lecturer. Before his current role, he worked as an FPGA engineer for the LHC project at CERN and as a software engineer in the banking industry.

I would like to thank Anthony Pino for the use of his housing dataset, Stefanie Grois for her hands-on insight into ML on IoT edge devices, and Henry Kröger for always being there. Further, a huge thanks goes to my friend and co-author Christoph, who let me take over his book. Finally, thanks to everyone who survived being around me during the work on this book.

About the reviewers

Nirbhay Anand has a master's degree in computer application and is also a Microsoft Certified Technology Specialist with 16 years of industry experience in software product development. He has developed software in different domains such as investment banking, manufacturing, supply chains, power forecasting, and railroads. He was head of delivery for a cosmetic company while working with C3IT Solutions Pvt. Ltd. He is associated with CloudMoyo, a leading cloud and analytics partner for Microsoft. CloudMoyo brings together powerful BI capabilities using the Azure data platform to transform complex data into business insights. He is currently working on products as a tech program manager.

I would like to thank my wife, Vijeta, and kids, Navya and Nitrika, for their support. I thank my friends too for their never-ending support.

Alexey Bokov is an experienced Azure architect and has been a Microsoft technical evangelist since 2011. He works closely with Microsoft top-tier customers all around the world to develop applications based on the Azure cloud platform. Building cloud-based applications in the most challenging scenarios is his passion, as well as helping the development community to upskill and learn new things by working hands-on and hacking. He is a long-time contributor, as a coauthor and reviewer, to many Azure books and is an occasional speaker at Kubernetes events.

Table of Contents

3

Preparing the Azure Machine Learning Workspace

Section 2: Data Ingestion, Preparation, Feature Engineering, and Pipelining

4

Ingesting Data and Managing Datasets

5

Performing Data Analysis and Visualization

6

Feature Engineering and Labeling

7

Advanced Feature Extraction with NLP

8

Azure Machine Learning Pipelines

Section 3: The Training and Optimization of Machine Learning Models

9

Building ML Models Using Azure Machine Learning

10

Training Deep Neural Networks on Azure

11

Hyperparameter Tuning and Automated Machine Learning

12

Distributed Machine Learning on Azure

13

Building a Recommendation Engine in Azure

Section 4: Machine Learning Model Deployment and Operations

14
Model Deployment, Endpoints, and Operations

15

Model Interoperability, Hardware Optimization, and Integrations

16

Bringing Models into Production with MLOps

17
Preparing for a Successful ML Journey

Index

Other Books You May Enjoy

Preface

During the last decade, **machine learning** (**ML**) has grown from a niche concept worked on in scientific circles to an enterprise-grade toolset that can be used to improve business processes and build intelligent products and services. The main reason is the constant increase in the volume of data being generated globally, requiring distributed systems, powerful algorithms, and scalable cloud infrastructure to compute insights. This book will help you improve your knowledge of ML concepts, find the right models for your use cases, and will give you the skillset to run machine learning models and build end-to-end ML pipelines in the Azure cloud.

The book starts with an overview of every step in an end-to-end ML project and a guide on how to choose the right Azure service for different ML tasks. From there on out, it focuses on the Azure Machine Learning service and takes you through the important processes of data preparation and feature engineering. Following that, the book focuses on ML modeling techniques for different requirements, including advanced feature extraction techniques using **natural language processing** (**NLP**), classical ML techniques such as ensemble learning, and the secrets of both a great recommendation engine and a performant computer vision model using deep learning methods. In addition, the book explores how to train, optimize, and tune models using Azure automated machine learning and HyperDrive, and perform model training on distributed training clusters on Azure. Finally, the book covers the deployment of ML models to different target computes such as Azure Machine Learning clusters, Azure Kubernetes Service, and **Field Programmable Gate Arrays** (**FPGAs**), along with the setup of MLOps pipelines with Azure DevOps.

By the end of this book, you'll have the foundation to run a well-thought-out ML project from start to finish and will have mastered the tooling available in Azure to train, deploy, and operate ML models and pipelines.

Who this book is for

This book is written for machine learning engineers, data scientists, and machine learning developers who want to use the Microsoft Azure cloud to manage their datasets and machine learning experiments and build an enterprise-grade ML architecture using MLOps. Any reader interested in the topic of ML will learn the important steps of the ML process and how to use Azure Machine Learning to support them. This book will support anyone building powerful ML cloud applications. A basic understanding of Python and knowledge of ML are advised.

What this book covers

Chapter 1, Understanding the End-to-End Machine Learning Process, covers the history of ML, the scenarios in which to apply ML, the statistical knowledge necessary, and the steps and components required for running a custom end-to-end ML project. Its purpose is to bring every reader to the same foundational level. Due to that, some sections might be a recap for readers that are very knowledgeable about ML but still might hold some useful practical tips and guidelines for them. It is also designed to be the guide for the rest of the book, where every step in the ML process will point to the chapters covering them in detail.

Chapter 2, Choosing the Right Machine Learning Service in Azure, helps us understand and classify the available Azure services for ML. We will define the scenarios in which to use certain services and we will conclude that for building custom ML models, Azure Machine Learning is the best choice. From this chapter onward, we use the available tooling in the Azure Machine Learning service to perform all upcoming tasks in the ML process.

Chapter 3, Preparing the Azure Machine Learning Workspace, covers the setup of the Azure Machine Learning service and some initial hands-on ML training using the service. We will perform ML training experiments while learning how to track the experiments, plot metrics, and create snapshots of ML runs with the available tooling in Azure Machine Learning.

Chapter 4, Ingesting Data and Managing Datasets, covers the available Azure services to store our underlying data and how to set them up in Azure. Furthermore, we will understand how we can bring the required data to these services either manually or automatically through **Extract, Transform, and Load** (**ETL**) processes and how we can integrate other Azure data services with Azure Machine Learning. Finally, we will introduce the concepts of datastores and datasets in Azure Machine Learning and how to use them in our experiment runs.

Chapter 5, Performing Data Analysis and Visualization, covers the steps required to explore and preprocess an ML dataset. We will understand the difference between a tabular and a file dataset, and we will learn how to clean our dataset, correlate features, and use statistical properties and domain knowledge to get insight into our dataset. Using what we've learned, we will go hands-on on a real-life dataset to apply our knowledge. Finally, we will have a peek at some popular embedding techniques such as PCA, LDA, t-SNE, and UMAP.

Chapter 6, Feature Engineering and Labeling, covers the important process of creating or adapting features in our dataset and creating labels for supervised ML training. We will understand the reasons for changing our features and we will glance at a variety of available methods to create, transform, extract, and select features in a dataset, which we will then use on our real-life dataset. Furthermore, we will explore techniques to label different types of datasets and go hands-on with the Data Labeling tool in Azure Machine Learning.

Chapter 7, Advanced Feature Extraction with NLP, takes us one step further to extract features from textual and categorical data – a problem that users are faced with often when training ML models. This chapter will describe the foundations of feature extraction for **Natural Language Processing** (**NLP**). This will help us to create semantic embeddings from categorical and textual data using techniques including n-grams, Bag of Words, TF-IDF, Word2Vec, and more.

Chapter 8, Azure Machine Learning Pipelines, covers how we can incorporate what we have learned in an automated preprocessing and training pipeline using Azure Machine Learning pipelines. We will learn how to split our code into modular pipeline steps and how to parameterize and trigger pipelines through endpoints and scheduling. Finally, we will build a couple of training pipelines and learn how to integrate them into other Azure services.

Chapter 9, Building ML Models Using Azure Machine Learning, teaches you how to use ensembling techniques to build a traditional ML model in Azure. This chapter focuses on decision tree-based ensemble learning with popular state-of-the-art boosting and bagging techniques using LightGBM in Azure Machine Learning. This will help you to apply concepts of bagging and boosting on ML models.

Chapter 10, Training Deep Neural Networks on Azure, covers training more complex parametric models using deep learning for better generalization over large datasets. We will give a short and practical overview of which situations deep learning can be applied well to and how it differs from the more traditional ML approaches. After that, we will discuss rational and practical guidelines to finally train a **Convolutional Neural Network** (**CNN**) on Azure Machine Learning using Keras.

Chapter 11, Hyperparameter Tuning and Automated Machine Learning, covers the optimization of the ML training process and how to automate it to avoid human errors. These tuning tricks will help you to train models faster and more efficiently. Therefore, we will look at hyperparameter tuning (also called **HyperDrive** in Azure Machine Learning), a standard technique for optimizing all external parameters of an ML model. By evaluating different sampling techniques for hyperparameter tuning, such as random sampling, grid sampling, and Bayesian optimization, you will learn how to efficiently manage the trade-offs between runtime and model performance. Then, we will generalize from hyperparameter optimization to automating the complete end-to-end ML training process using **Azure automated machine learning**.

Chapter 12, Distributed Machine Learning on Azure, looks into distributed and parallel computing algorithms and frameworks for efficiently training ML models in parallel on GPUs. The goal of this chapter is to build an environment in Azure where you can speed up the training process of classical ML and deep learning models by adding more machines to your training environment and hence scaling out the cluster.

Chapter 13, Building a Recommendation Engine in Azure, dives into traditional and modern recommendation engines that often combine the technologies and techniques covered in the previous chapters. We will take a quick look at the different types of recommendation engines, what data is needed for each type, and what can be recommended using these different approaches, such as content-based recommendations and rating-based recommendation engines. We will combine both techniques into a single hybrid recommender and learn about state-of-the-art techniques for modern recommendation engines.

Chapter 14, Model Deployment, Endpoints, and Operations, finally covers how to bring our ML models into a production environment, by deploying them either to a batch cluster for offline scoring or as an endpoint for online scoring. To achieve that, we are going to package the model and execution runtime, register both in a model registry, and deploy them to an execution environment. We will auto-deploy models from Azure Machine Learning to **Azure Kubernetes Service** with only a few lines of code. Finally, you will learn how to monitor your target environments using out-of-the-box custom metrics.

Chapter 15, Model Interoperability, Hardware Optimization, and Integrations, covers methods to standardize deployment model formats using the **Open Neural Network eXchange (ONNX)**, what **Field Programmable Gate Arrays (FPGA)** are, and how to use them as a deployment target in Azure. Further, we will learn how to integrate Azure Machine Learning with other Microsoft services such as **Azure IoT Edge** and **Power BI**. Here, we will understand the fundamental differences between FPGAs and GPUs in terms of performance, cost, and efficiency and we will go hands-on in Power BI to integrate one of our previously deployed endpoints.

Chapter 16, Bringing Models into Production with MLOps, finally covers how we put data ingestion, data preparation, our ML training and deployment pipelines, and any required script into one end-to-end operation. This includes the creation of environments; starting, stopping, and scaling clusters; submitting experiments; performing parameter optimization; and deploying full-fledged scoring services on Kubernetes. We will reuse all the concepts we applied previously to build a version-controlled, reproducible, automated ML training and deployment process as a **Continuous Integration/Continuous Deployment (CI/CD)** pipeline in Azure DevOps.

Chapter 17, Preparing for a Successful ML Journey, ends the book by giving you a summary of the major concepts we learned throughout it and highlights what really matters when performing ML. We reiterate the importance of a clean base infrastructure, monitoring, and automation and discuss the ever-changing nature of ML and cloud-based services. Finally, we cover one of the most important topics, which we glanced over throughout the book, ethics in data processing. We will discuss your responsibility to have fair and explainable ML models and how Azure Machine Learning and open source tooling can help you achieve that.

To get the most out of this book

This book requires the use of Azure services and therefore an Azure subscription. You can create an Azure account for free and receive USD 200 of credits to use within 30 days using the sign-up page at `https://azure.microsoft.com/en-us/free/`.

To run the authoring code, you can either use a compute instance in the Azure Machine Learning workspace (typically a `Standard_DS3_v2` virtual machine), which gives you access to a Jupyter environment and all essential libraries preinstalled, or you can run it on your own local machine. To do so, you need a Python runtime with the Jupyter package installed and some additional libraries, which will be mentioned in the technical requirements of each chapter. We tested all the code with Python version 3.8 and the Azure ML Python SDK version 1.34.0 at the time of writing. If you want to work with a different setup, be sure to check the supported Python version for the Azure ML Python SDK (`https://pypi.org/project/azureml-sdk/`).

If you are using the digital version of this book, we advise you to type the code yourself or access the code from the book's GitHub repository (a link is available in the next section). Doing so will help you avoid any potential errors related to the copying and pasting of code.

Finally, to get the most out of this book, you should have experience in programming in Python and have a basic understanding of popular ML and data manipulation libraries such as TensorFlow, Keras, scikit-learn, and pandas.

Download the example code files

You can download the example code files for this book from GitHub at
`https://github.com/PacktPublishing/Mastering-Azure-Machine-Learning-Second-Edition`. If there's an update to the code, it will be updated
in the GitHub repository.

We also have other code bundles from our rich catalog of books and videos available at
`https://github.com/PacktPublishing/`. Check them out!

Download the color images

We also provide a PDF file that has color images of the screenshots and diagrams used
in this book. You can download it here: `https://static.packt-cdn.com/
downloads/9781803232416_ColorImages.pdf`.

Conventions used

There are a number of text conventions used throughout this book.

`Code in text`: Indicates code words in text, database table names, folder names,
filenames, file extensions, pathnames, dummy URLs, user input, and Twitter handles.
Here is an example: "The `score.py` script is a deployment file that needs to contain
an `init()` and `run(batch)` method."

A block of code is set as follows:

```
# increase display of all columns of rows for pandas datasets
pd.set_option('display.max_columns', None)
pd.set_option('display.max_rows', None)
# create pandas dataframe
raw_df = tabdf.to_pandas_dataframe()
raw_df.head()
```

When we wish to draw your attention to a particular part of a code block, the relevant
lines or items are set in bold:

```
df = df.drop(['Postcode'],axis=1)
df.head()
```

Any command-line input or output is written as follows:

```
$ pip install azure-cognitiveservices-personalizer
```

Bold: Indicates a new term, an important word, or words that you see onscreen. For instance, words in menus or dialog boxes appear in **bold**. Here is an example: "We can see that the dataset is passed as the **titanic** named input to the **Preprocessing** step."

> **Tips or Important Notes**
> Appear like this.

Get in touch

Feedback from our readers is always welcome.

General feedback: If you have questions about any aspect of this book, email us at customercare@packtpub.com and mention the book title in the subject of your message.

Errata: Although we have taken every care to ensure the accuracy of our content, mistakes do happen. If you have found a mistake in this book, we would be grateful if you would report this to us. Please visit www.packtpub.com/support/errata and fill in the form.

Piracy: If you come across any illegal copies of our works in any form on the internet, we would be grateful if you would provide us with the location address or website name. Please contact us at copyright@packt.com with a link to the material.

If you are interested in becoming an author: If there is a topic that you have expertise in and you are interested in either writing or contributing to a book, please visit authors.packtpub.com.

Share Your Thoughts

Once you've read *Mastering Azure Machine Learning*, we'd love to hear your thoughts! Scan the QR code below to go straight to the Amazon review page for this book and share your feedback.

https://packt.link/r/1-803-23241-2

Your review is important to us and the tech community and will help us make sure we're delivering excellent quality content.

Section 1: Introduction to Azure Machine Learning

In this section, we will learn about the history of **Machine Learning** (**ML**), the scenarios in which to apply ML, the statistical knowledge necessary, and the steps and components required for running a custom end-to-end ML project. We will have a look at the available Azure services for ML and we will learn about the scenarios they are best suited for. Finally, we will introduce Azure Machine Learning, the main service we will utilize throughout the rest of the book. We will understand how to deploy this service and use it to run our first ML experiments in the cloud.

This section comprises the following chapters:

- *Chapter 1, Understanding the End-to-End Machine Learning Process*
- *Chapter 2, Choosing the Right Machine Learning Service in Azure*
- *Chapter 3, Preparing the Azure Machine Learning Workspace*

1

Understanding the End-to-End Machine Learning Process

Welcome to the second edition of *Mastering Azure Machine Learning*. In this first chapter, we want to give you an understanding of what kinds of problems require the use of **machine learning** (**ML**), how the full ML process unfolds, and what knowledge is required to navigate this vast terrain. You can view it as an introduction to ML and an overview of the book itself, where for most topics we will provide you with a reference to upcoming chapters so that you can easily find your way around the book.

In the first section, we will ask ourselves what ML is, when we should use it, and where it comes from. In addition, we will reflect on how ML is just another form of programming.

In the second section, we will lay the mathematical groundwork you require to process data, and we will understand that the data you work with probably cannot be fully trusted. Further, we will look at different classes of ML algorithms, how they are defined, and how we can define the performance of a trained model.

Finally, in the third section, we will have a look at the end-to-end process of an ML project. We will understand where to get data from, how to preprocess data, how to choose a fitting model, and how to deploy this model into production environments. This will also get us into the topic of **ML operations**, known as **MLOps**.

In this chapter, we will cover the following topics:

- Grasping the idea behind ML
- Understanding the mathematical basis for statistical analysis and ML modeling
- Discovering the end-to-end ML process

Grasping the idea behind ML

The terms **artificial intelligence** (AI) and—partially—**ML** are omnipresent in today's world. However, a lot of what is found under the term *AI* is often nothing more than a containerized ML solution, and to make matters worse, ML is sometimes unnecessarily used to solve something extremely simple.

Therefore, in this first section, let's understand the class of problems ML tries to solve, in which scenarios to use ML, and when not to use it.

Problems and scenarios requiring ML

If you look for a definition of ML, you will often find a description such as this: *It is the study of self-improving machine algorithms using data.* ML is basically described as an algorithm we are trying to evolve, which in turn can be seen as one complex mathematical function.

Any computer process today follows the simple structure of the **input-process-output (IPO) model**. We define allowed inputs, we define a process working with those inputs, and we define an output through the type of results the process will show us. A simple example would be a word processing application, where every keystroke will result in a letter shown as the output on the screen. A completely different process might run in parallel to that one, having a time-based trigger to store the text file periodically to a hard disk.

All these processes or algorithms have one thing in common—they were manually written by someone using a **high-level programming language**. It is clear which actions need to be done when someone presses a letter in a word processing application. Therefore, we can easily build a process in which we implement which input values should create which output values.

Now, let's look at a more complex problem. Imagine we have a picture of a dog and want an application to just say: *This is a dog*. This sounds simple enough, as we know the input *picture of a dog* and the output value *dog*. Unfortunately, our brain (our own machine) is far superior to the machines we built, especially when it comes to pattern recognition. For a computer, a picture is just a square of $n \times m$ pixels, each containing three color channels defined by an 8-bit or 10-bit value. Therefore, an image is just a bunch of pixels made up of vectors for the computer, so in essence, a lot of numbers.

We could manually start writing an algorithm that maybe clusters groups of pixels, looks for edges and points of interest, and eventually, with a lot of effort, we might succeed in having an algorithm that finds dogs in pictures. That is when we get a picture of a cat.

It should be clear to you by now that we might run into a problem. Therefore, let's define one problem that ML solves, as follows:

Building the desired algorithm for a required solution programmatically is either extremely time-consuming, completely unfeasible, or impossible.

Taking this description, we can surely define good scenarios to use ML, be it finding objects in images and videos or understanding voices and extracting their intent from audio files. We will further understand what building ML solutions entails throughout this chapter (and the rest of the book, for that matter), but to make a simple statement, let's just acknowledge that building an ML model is also a time-consuming matter.

In that vein, it should be of utmost importance to avoid ML if we have the chance to do so. This might be an obvious statement, but as we (the authors) can attest, it is not for a lot of people. We have seen projects realized with ML where the output could be defined with a simple combination of `if` statements given some input vectors. In such scenarios, a solution could be obtained with a couple of hundred lines of code. Instead, months of training and testing an ML algorithm occurred, costing a lot of time and resources.

An example of this would be a company wanting to predict fraud (stolen money) committed by their own employees in a retail store. You might have heard that predicting fraud is a typical scenario for ML. Here, it was *not necessary* to use ML, as the company already knew the influencing factors (length of time the cashier was open, error codes on return receipts, and so on) and therefore wanted to be alerted when certain combinations of these factors occurred. As they knew the factors already, they could have just written the code and be done with it. But what does this scenario tell us about ML?

So far, we have looked at ML as a solution to solve a problem that, in essence, is too hard to code. Looking at the preceding scenario, you might understand another aspect or another class of problems that ML can solve. Therefore, let's add a second problem description, as follows:

Building the desired algorithm for a required solution is not feasible, as the influencing factors for the outcome of the desired outputs are only partially known or completely unknown.

Looking at this problem, you might now understand why ML relies so heavily on the field of statistics as, through the application of statistics, we can learn how data points influence one another, and therefore we might be able to solve such a problem. At the same time, we can build an algorithm that can find and predict the desired outcome.

In the previously mentioned scenario for detecting fraud, it might be prudent to still use ML, as it may be able to find a combination of influencing factors no one has thought about. But if this is not your set goal—as it was not in this case—you should not use ML for something that is easily written in code.

Now that we have discussed some of the problems solved by ML and have had a look at some scenarios for ML, let's have a look at how ML came to be.

The history of ML

To understand ML as a whole, we must first understand where it comes from. Therefore, let's delve into the history of ML. As with all events in history, different currents are happening simultaneously, adding pieces to the whole picture. We'll now look at a few important pillars that birthed the idea of ML as we know it today.

Learnings from neuroscience

A neuropsychologist named Donald O. Hebb published a book titled *The Organization of Behavior* in 1949. In this book, he described his theory of how **neurons** (neural cells) in our brain function, and how they contribute to what we understand as *learning*. This theory is known as **Hebbian learning**, and it makes the following proposition:

> *When an axon of cell A is near enough to excite cell B and repeatedly or persistently takes part in firing it, some growth process or metabolic change takes place in one or both cells such that A's efficiency, as one of the cells firing B, is increased.*

This basically describes that there is a process where one cell excites another repeatedly (the initiating cell) and maybe even the receiving cell is changed through a hidden process. This process is what we call learning.

To understand this a bit more visually, let's have a look at the biological structure of a neuron, as follows:

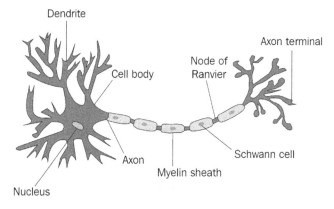

Figure 1.1 – Neuron in a biological neural network

What is visualized here? Firstly, on the left, we see the main body of the cell and its nucleus. The body receives input signals through dendrites that are connected to other neurons. In addition, there is a larger exit perturbing from the body called the axon, which connects the main body through a chain of Schwann cells to the so-called axon terminal, which in turn connects again to other neurons.

Looking at this structure with some creativity, it certainly resembles what a function or an algorithm might be. We have input signals coming from external neurons, we have some hidden process happening with these signals, and we have an output in the form of an axon terminal that connects the results to other neurons, and therefore other processes again.

It would take another decade again for someone to realize this connection.

Learnings from computer science

It is hard to talk about the history of ML in the context of computer science without mentioning one of the fathers of modern machines, Alan Turing. In a paper called *Computing Machinery and Intelligence* published in 1950, Turing defines a test called the **Imitation Game** (later called the **Turing test**) to evaluate whether a machine shows human behavior indistinguishable from a human. There are multiple iterations and variants of the test, but in essence, the idea is that a person would at no point in a conversation get the feeling they are not speaking with a human.

Certainly, this test is flawed, as there are ways to give relatively intelligent answers to questions while not being intelligent at all. If you want to learn more about this, have a look at **ELIZA** built by Joseph Weizenbaum, which passed the Turing test.

Nevertheless, this paper triggered one of the first discussions on what AI could be and what it means that a machine can learn.

Living in these exciting times, Arthur Samuel, a researcher working at **International Business Machines Corporation** (**IBM**) at that time, started developing a computer program that could make the right decisions in a game of checkers. In each move, he let the program evaluate a scoring function that tried to measure the chances of winning for each available move. Limited by the available resources at the time, it was not feasible to calculate all possible combinations of moves all the way to the end of the game.

This first step led to the definition of the so-called **minimax algorithm** and its accompanying **search tree**, which can commonly be used for any two-player adversarial game. Later, the **alpha-beta pruning** algorithm was added to automatically trim the tree from decisions that did not lead to better results than the ones already evaluated.

We are talking about Arthur Samuel, as it was he who coined the name *machine learning*, defining it as follows:

> *The field of study that gives computers the ability to learn*
> *without being explicitly programmed.*

Combining these first ideas of building an evaluation function for training a machine and the research done by Donald O. Hebb in neuroscience, Frank Rosenblatt, a researcher at the Cornell Aeronautical Laboratory, invented a new linear classifier that he called a **perceptron**. Even though his progress in building this perceptron into hardware was relatively short-lived and would not live up to its potential, its original definition is nowadays the basis for every neuron in an **artificial neural network** (**ANN**).

Therefore, let's now dive deeper into understanding how ANNs work and what we can deduce about the inner workings of an ML algorithm from them.

Understanding the inner workings of ML through the example of ANNs

ANNs, as we know them today, are defined by the following two major components, one of which we learned about already:

- **The neural network**: The base structure of the system. A perceptron is basically an NN with only one neuron. By now, this structure comes in multiple facets, often involving hidden layers of hundreds of neurons, in the case of **deep neural networks** (**DNNs**).

- **The backpropagation function**: A rule for the system to learn and evolve. An idea thought of in the 1970s came into appreciation through a paper called *Learning Representations by Back-Propagating Errors* by D. Rumelhart, Geoffrey E. Hinton, Ronald J. Williams in 1986.

To understand these two components and how they work in tandem with each other, let's have a deeper look at both.

The neural network

First, let's understand how a single neuron operates, which is very close to the idea of a perceptron defined by Rosenblatt. The following diagram shows the inner workings of such an artificial neuron:

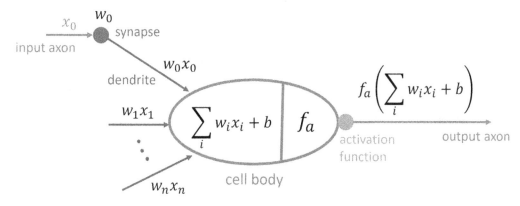

Figure 1.2 – Neuron in an ANN

We can clearly see the similarities to a real neuron. We get inputs from the connected neurons called x_i. Each of those inputs is weighted with a corresponding weight w_i, and then, in the neuron itself, they are all summed up, including a **bias** b. This is often referred to as the **net input function**.

As the final operation, a so-called **activation function** f_a is applied to this net input that decides how the output signal of the neuron should look. This function must be continuous and differentiable and should typically create results in the range of [0:1] or [-1:1] to keep results scaled. In addition, this function could be linear or non-linear in nature, even though using a linear activation function has its downfalls, as described next:

- You cannot learn a non-linear relationship presented in your data through a system of linear functions.
- A multilayered network made up of nodes with only linear activation functions can be broken down to just one layer of nodes with one linear activation function, making the network obsolete.

- You cannot use a linear activation function with backpropagation, as this requires calculating the derivative of this function, which we will discuss next.

Commonly used activation functions are **sigmoid, hyperbolic tangent (tanh), rectified linear unit (ReLU)**, and **softmax**. Keeping this in mind, let's have a look at how we connect neurons together to achieve an ANN. A whole network is typically defined by three types of layers, as outlined here:

- **Input layer**: Consists of neurons accepting singular input signals (not a weighted sum) to the network. Their weights might be constant or randomized depending on the application.

- **Hidden layer**: Consists of the types of neurons we described before. They are defined by an activation function and given weights to the weighted sum of the input signals. In DNNs, these layers typically represent specific transformation steps.

- **Output layer**: Consists of neurons performing the final transformation of the data. They can behave like neurons in hidden layers, but they do not have to.

These together result in a typical ANN, as shown in the following diagram:

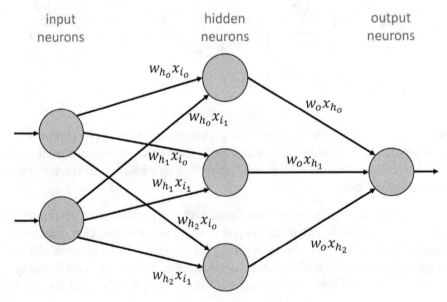

Figure 1.3 – ANN with one hidden layer

With this, we build a generic structure that can receive some input, realize some form of mathematical function through different layers of weights and activation functions, and in the end, hopefully show the correct output. This process of pushing information through the network from inputs to outputs is typically referred to as **forward propagation**. This, of course, only shows us what is happening with an input that passes through the network. The following question remains: *How does it learn the desired function in the first place?* The next section will answer this question.

The backpropagation function

The question that should have popped up in your mind by now is: *How do we define the correct output?* To have a way to change the behavior of the network, which mostly boils down to changing the values of the weights in the system, don't we need a way to quantize the error the system made?

Therefore, we need a function describing the error or loss, referred to as a **loss function** or **error function**. You might have even heard another name—a **cost function**. Let's define them next.

> **Loss Function versus Cost Function**
>
> A loss function (error function) computes the error for a single training example. A cost function, on the other hand, averages all loss function results for the entire training dataset.

This is the correct definition for those terms, but they are often used interchangeably. Just keep in mind that we are using some form of metric to measure the error we made or the distance we have from the correct results.

In classic backpropagation and other ML scenarios, the **mean squared error** (MSE) between the correct y_i and the computed $\hat{y}_i$ is used to define the error or loss of the operation. The obvious target is to now minimize this error. Therefore, the actual task to perform is to find the total minimum of this function in n-dimensional space.

To do this, we use something that is often referred to as an **optimizer**, defined next.

> **Optimizer (Objective Function)**
>
> An optimizer is a function that implements a specific way to reach the objective of minimizing the cost function.

One such optimizer is an iterative process called **gradient descent**. Its idea is visualized in the following screenshot:

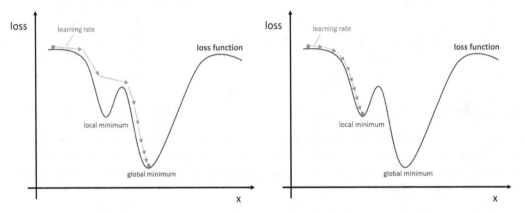

Figure 1.4 – Gradient descent with loss function influenced by only one input (left: finding global minimum, right: stuck in local minimum)

In gradient descent, we try to navigate an n-dimensional loss function by taking reasonably large enough steps, often defined by a *learning rate*, with the goal to find the global minimum, while avoiding getting stuck in a local minimum.

Keeping this in mind and without going into too much detail, let's finish this thought by going through the steps the backpropagation algorithm performs on the neural network. These are set out here:

1. Pass a pair (x_i, y_i) through the network (forward propagation).
2. Compute the loss between the expected y_i and the computed $\hat{y}_i$.
3. Compute all derivatives for all functions and weights throughout the layers using a mathematical chain rule.
4. Update all weights beginning from the back of the network to the front, with slightly changed weights defined by the optimizer.
5. Repeat until convergence is achieved (the weights are not receiving any meaningful updates anymore).

This is, in a nutshell, how an ANN learns. Be aware that it is vital to constantly change the pairs in *Step 1*, as otherwise, you might push the network too far into memorizing these couple of pairs you constantly showed it. We will discuss the phenomenon of **overfitting** and **underfitting** later in this chapter.

As a final step in this section, let's now bring together what we have learned so far about ML and what this means for building software solutions in the future.

ML and Software 2.0

What we learned so far is that ML seems to be defined by a base structure with various knobs and levers (settings and values) that can be changed. In the case of ANNs, that would be the structure of the network itself and the weights, bias, and activation function we can set in some regard.

Accompanying this base structure is some sort of rule or function as to how these knobs and levers should be transformed through a learning process. In the case of ANNs, this is defined through the backpropagation function, which combines a loss function with an optimizer and some math.

In 2017, Andrej Karpathy, the **chief technical officer** (**CTO**) of Tesla's AI division, proposed that the aforementioned idea could be just another way of programming, which he called **Software 2.0** (`https://karpathy.medium.com/software-2-0-a64152b37c35`).

Up to this point, writing software was about explaining to the machine precisely what it must do and what outcome it must produce through defining specific commands it had to follow. In this classical software development paradigm, we define algorithms by their code and let data run through it, typically written in a reasonably readable language.

Instead of doing that, another idea could be to define a program we build by a base structure, a way to evolve this structure, and the type of data it must process. In this case, we get something very human-unfriendly to understand (an ANN with weights, for example), but it might be much better to understand for a machine.

So, we leave you at the end of this section with the thought that Andrej wanted to convey. Perhaps ML is just another form of programming machines.

Keeping all this in mind, let's now talk about math.

Understanding the mathematical basis for statistical analysis and ML modeling

Looking at what we have learned so far, it becomes abundantly clear that ML requires an ample understanding of mathematics. We already came across multiple mathematical functions we have to handle. Think about the activation function of neurons and the optimizer and loss functions for training. On top of that, we have not talked about the second aspect of our new programming paradigm—the data!

To choose the right ML algorithm and derive a good metric for a loss function, we have to take apart the data points we work with. In addition, we need to bring in the data points in relation to the domain we are working with. Therefore, when defining the role of a data scientist, you will often find a visual like this one:

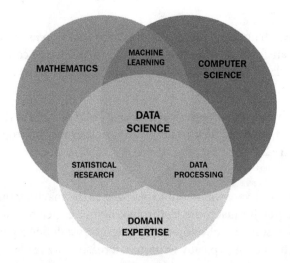

Figure 1.5 – Requirements for data scientists

In this section, we will concentrate on what is referred to in *Figure 1.5* as *statistical research*. We will understand why we need statistics and what base information we can derive from a given dataset, learn what bias is and ways to avoid that, mathematically classify possible ML algorithms, and finally, discuss how we choose useful metrics to define the performance of our trained models.

The case for statistics in ML

As we have seen, we require statistics to clean and analyze our given data. Therefore, let's start by asking: *What do we understand from the term "statistics"?*

> *Statistics is the science of collecting and analyzing a representative sample made up of a large quantity of numerical data with the purpose of inferring the statistical distribution of the underlying population.*

A typical example of something such as this would be the prediction for the results of an election you see during the campaign or shortly after voting booths close. At those points in time, we do not know the precise result of the full **population** but we can acquire a **sample**, sometimes referred to as an **observation**. We get that by asking people for responses through a questionnaire. Then, based on this subset, we make a sound prediction for the full population by applying statistical methods.

We learned that in ML, we are trying to let the machine figure out a mathematical function that fits our problem, such as this:

$$\vec{y} = f(\vec{x})$$

Thinking back to our ANN, $\vec{x}$ would be an input vector and $\vec{y}$ would be the resulting output vector. In ML jargon, they are known under a different name, as seen next.

> **Features and Labels**
>
> One element of the input vector x is called a feature; the full output vector is called the label. Often, we only deal with a **one-dimensional** label.

Now, to bring this together, when training an ML model, we typically only have a sample of the given world, and as with any other time you are dealing with only a sample or subset of reality, you want to pick highly representative features and samples of the underlying population.

So, what does this mean? Let's think of an example. Imagine you want to train a small little robot car to be able to automatically drive through a tunnel. First, we need to think about what our features and labels in this scenario are. As features, we probably need something that measures the distance from the edges of the car to the tunnel in each direction, as we probably do not want to drive into the sides of the tunnel. Let's assume we have some infrared sensors attached to the front, the sides, and the back of the vehicle. Then, the output of our program would probably control the steering and the speed of the vehicle, which would be our labels.

Given that, as a next step, we should think of a whole bunch of scenarios in which the vehicle could find itself. This might be a simple scenario of the vehicle sitting straight-facing in the tunnel, or it could be a bad scenario where the vehicle is nearly stuck in a corner and the tunnel is going left or right from that point on. In all these cases, we read out the values of our infrared sensors and then do the more complicated tasks of making an educated guess as to how the steering has to be changed and how the motor has to operate. Eventually, we end up with a bunch of example situations and corresponding actions to take, which would be our training dataset. This can then be used to train an ANN so that the small car can learn how to follow a tunnel.

If you ever get the opportunity, try to perform this training. If you pick very good examples, you will understand the full power of ML, as you will most likely see something exciting, which I can attest to. In my setup, even though we never had a sample where we would instruct the vehicle to drive backward, the optimal function the machine trained had values where the vehicle learned to do exactly that.

In an example such as that, we would do everything from scratch and hopefully take representative samples by ourselves. In most cases you will encounter, the dataset already exists, and you need to figure out whether it is representative or whether we need to introduce additional data to achieve an optimal training result.

Therefore, let's have a look at some statistical properties you should familiarize yourself with.

Basics of statistics

We now understand that we need to be able to analyze the statistical properties of single features, derive their distribution, and analyze their relationship with other features and labels in the dataset.

Let's start with the properties of single features and their distribution. All the following operations require numerical data. This means that if you work with categorical data or something such as media files, you need to transform them into some form of numerical representation to get such results.

The following screenshot shows the main statistical properties you are after, their importance, and how you can calculate them:

Name	Formula	Description
Count	n	The count is the number of samples. For a full population this is denoted as N.
Minimum	$min(x_i)$	The minimum is the minimal value among all samples.
Maximum	$max(x_i)$	The maximum is the maximum value among all samples.
Mean	$\bar{x} = \sum_{i=0}^{n-1} \frac{x_i}{n}$	The mean value of a group of samples. Mean value of population is donated as μ.
Median	$med = \left(\frac{n+1}{2}\right) th\ term$	The median is the value in the middle of n samples after ordering. If even, it is the two middle values divided by 2.
Mode	---	The mode is the value most frequent among all samples.
Variance (Samples)	$s^2 = \frac{\sum_{i=0}^{n-1}(x_i - \bar{x})^2}{n-1}$	The variance is the squared deviation. For a full population the denominator is N instead $(n-1)$ and it is denotated as σ^2.
Standard deviation (Samples)	$s = \sqrt{s^2}$	The standard deviation is the mean distance from the mean of the distribution. For a full population it is denoted as σ.
Skew	$skew = \frac{\sum_{i=0}^{n-1}(x_i - \bar{x})^3}{(n-1) * s^3}$	The skew is the degree of asymmetry in a probability distribution.

Figure 1.6 – List of major statistical properties

From here onward, we can make the reasonable assumption that the underlying stochastic process follows a **normal distribution**. Be aware that this must not be the case, and therefore you should make yourself comfortable with other distributions (see `https://www.itl.nist.gov/div898/handbook/eda/section3/eda36.htm`).

The following screenshot shows a visual representation of a standard normal distribution:

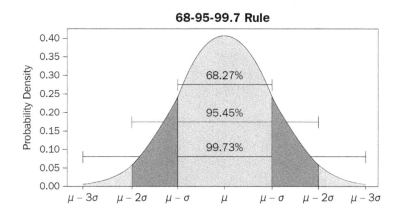

Figure 1.7 – Standard normal distribution and its properties

Now, the strength of this normal distribution is that, based on the mean μ and standard deviation σ, we can make assumptions for the probabilities of samples to be in a certain range. As shown in *Figure 1.7*, there is a probability of around **68.27%** for a value to have a distance from the mean of 1σ, **95.45%** for a distance of 2σ, and **99.73%** for a distance of 3σ. Based on this, we can ask questions such as this:

How probable is it to find a value with a distance of 5σ from the mean?

Through questions such as this, we can start assessing whether what we see in our data is a statistical anomaly of the distribution, is a value that is simply false, or whether our suspected distribution is incorrect. This is done through a process called **hypothesis testing**, defined next.

> **Hypothesis Testing (Definition)**
>
> This is a method of testing if the so-called null hypothesis H_0 is false, typically referring to the current suspected distribution. It means that the unlikely observation we encounter is pure chance. This hypothesis is rejected in favor of an alternative hypothesis H_a, if the probability falls below a predefined significance level (typically higher than 2σ/lower than 5%). The alternative hypothesis thus presumes that the observation we have is due to a real effect that is not taken into account in the initial distribution.

We will not go into further details on how to perform this test properly, but we urge you to familiarize yourself with this process thoroughly.

What we will talk about is the types of errors you can make in this process, as shown in the following screenshot:

Truth about Population

	H_a is true	H_o is true
Reject H_o	**True Positive** Correct Decision	**False Positive** Type I Error
Accept H_o	**False Negative** Type II Error	**True Negative** Correct Decision

Decision based on sample

Figure 1.8 – Type I and Type II errors

We define the errors you see in *Figure 1.8* as follows:

- **Type I error**: This denotes that we reject the hypothesis H_0 and the underlying distribution, even though it is correct. This is also referred to as a **false-positive** result or an **alpha error**.

- **Type II error**: This denotes that we do not reject the hypothesis H_0 and the underlying distribution, even though H_a is correct. This error is also referred to as a **false-negative** result or a **beta error**.

You might have heard the term *false positive* before. Often, it comes up when you take a medical test. A false positive would denote that you have a positive result from a test, even though you do not have the disease you are testing for. As a medical test is also a **stochastic process**, as with nearly everything else in our world, the term is correctly used in this scenario.

At the end of this section, when we talk about errors and metrics in ML model training, we will come back to these definitions. As a final step, let's discuss relationships among features and between features and labels. Such a relationship is referred to as a **correlation**.

There are multiple ways to calculate a correlation between two vectors $\vec{a}$ and $\vec{b}$, but what they all have in common is that their results will fall in the range of [-1,1]. The result of this operation can be broadly defined by the following three categories:

- **Negatively correlated**: The result leans toward -1. When the value of vector $\vec{a}$ rises, the values of vector $\vec{b}$ fall and vice versa.

- **Uncorrelated**: The result leans toward 0. There is no real interaction between vectors $\vec{a}$ and $\vec{b}$.

- **Positively correlated**: The result leans toward 1. When the value of vector $\vec{a}$ rises, the values of vector $\vec{b}$ rise and vice versa.

Through this, we can get an idea of relationships between data points, but please be aware of the differences between causation and correlation, as outlined next.

> **Causation versus Correlation**
>
> Even if two vectors are correlated with each other, it does not mean one of them is the cause of the other one—it simply means that one of them influences the other one. It is not causation as we probably don't see the full picture and every single influencing factor.

The mathematical theory we discussed so far should give you a good basis to build upon. In the next section, we will have a quick look at what kinds of errors we can make when taking samples, typically referred to as the bias in the data.

Understanding bias

At any stage of taking samples and when working with data, it is easily possible to introduce what is called **bias**. Typically, this influences the sampling quality and therefore has a big impact on any ML model we would like to fit to the data.

One example would be the *causation versus correlation* we just discussed. Seeing causation where none exists can have consequences in terms of the way you continue processing the data points. Other prominent biases that influence data are shown next:

- **Selection bias**: This bias happens when samples are taken that are not representative of the real-life distribution of data. This is the case when randomization is not properly done or when only a certain subgroup is selected for a study—for example, when a questionnaire about city planning is only given out to people in half of the neighborhoods of the city.

- **Funding bias**: This bias should be very well known and happens when a study or data project is funded by a sponsor and the results will therefore have a tendency toward the interests of the funding party.

- **Reporting bias**: This bias happens when only a selection of outcomes is represented in a dataset due to the fact that it is the tendency of people to underreport certain outcomes. Examples of this are given here: when you report bad weather events but not when there is sunshine; when you write negative reviews for a product but not positive reviews; when you only know about results written in your own language or from your own region but not from others.

- **Observer bias/confirmation bias**: This bias happens when someone favors results that confirm or support their own beliefs and values. Typically, this results in ignoring contrary information, not following the agreed guideline, or using ambiguous studies that support the existing preconceived opinion. The dangerous part here is that this can happen unconsciously.

- **Exclusion bias**: This bias happens when you remove data points during preprocessing that you consider irrelevant but are not. This includes removing null values, outliers, or other special data points. The removal might result in the loss of accuracy concerning the underlying real-life distribution.

- **Automation bias**: This bias happens when you favor results generated from automated systems over information taken from humans, even if they are correct.

- **Overgeneralization bias**: This bias happens when you project a property of your dataset toward the whole population. An example would be that you would assume that all cats have gray fur because in the large dataset you have, this is true.

- **Group attribution bias**: This bias happens when stereotypes are added as attributes to a whole group because of the actions of a few individuals within that group.

- **Survivorship bias**: This bias happens when you focus on successful examples while completely ignoring failures. An example would be that you study the competition of your company while ignoring all companies that failed, merged, or went bankrupt.

This list should give you a good understanding of problems that may arise when gathering and processing data. We can only urge you to read further into this topic while following these next guidelines.

> **Guidance for Handling Bias in Data**
>
> When using existing datasets, figure out the circumstances in which they were obtained to be able to judge their quality. When processing data either alone or in a team, define clear guidelines on how you define data and how you handle certain situations, and always reflect whether you are making assumptions based on your own predispositions.

To solidify your understanding that things are—most of the time—not as they seem, have a look at what is referred to as **Simpson's paradox** and the corresponding **University of California** (**UC**) Berkeley case (`http://corysimon.github.io/articles/simpsons-paradox/`).

Now that we have a good understanding of what to look out for when working with data, let's come back to the basics of ML.

Classifying ML algorithms

In the first section of this chapter, we got a glimpse into ANNs. These are special in the sense that they can be used in a so-called supervised or unsupervised training setup. To understand what is meant by this, let's define the current three major types of ML algorithms, as follows:

- **Supervised learning**: In supervised learning, models are trained with a so-called labeled dataset. That means besides knowing the input for the required algorithm, we also know the required output. This type of learning is split into two groups of problems—namely, **classification problems** and **regression problems**. Classification works with discrete results, where the output is a class or group, while regression works with continuous results, where the output would be a certain value. Examples of classification would be identifying fraud in money transactions or doing object detection in images. Examples of regression would be forecasting prices for houses or the stock market or predicting population growth. It is important to understand that this type of learning *requires* labels, which often results in the tedious task of labeling the whole dataset.

- **Unsupervised learning**: In unsupervised learning, models are trained on unlabeled data. This is basically self-organized learning to find patterns in data, referred to as **clustering**. Examples of this would be the filtering of spam emails in an inbox or the recommendation of movies or clothing a person might like to watch or purchase. Often, the learning algorithms are used in a real-time scenario where the data needs to be processed directly. The beauty of this type of learning is that we do not have to label the dataset.

- **Reinforcement learning**: In reinforcement learning, algorithms learn by reacting to a given environment on their own. The idea of this comes from how we as humans learn as we grow up. We did a certain action, and the outcome of that action was either good or bad or somewhere in between. We then either receive some sort of reward or we don't. Another similar example would be the way you would train a dog to behave. Technically, this is realized through a so-called *agent* that is guided by a *policy map*, deciding the probability to take actions when in a specific state. For the environment itself, we define a so-called *state-value function* that returns the *value* of being in a specific state. Good examples of this type of learning are training navigation control for a robot or an AI opponent for a game.

The following diagram provides an overview of the discussed ML types and the corresponding algorithms that are utilized in those areas:

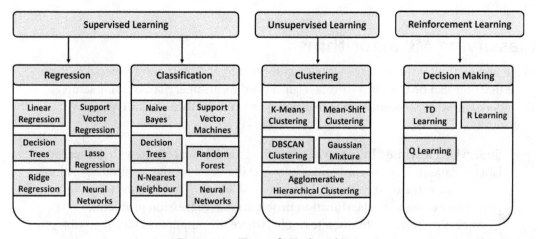

Figure 1.9 – Types of ML algorithms

A detailed overview of many of the prominent ML algorithms can be found on the *scikit-learn* web page (https://scikit-learn.org/stable/), which is one of the major Python libraries for ML.

Now that we have an idea of the types of training we can perform, let's have a short look at what types of results we get from a training run and how to interpret them.

Analyzing errors and the quality of results of model training

As we discussed in the first section of this chapter, we require a loss function that we can minimize to optimize our training results. Typically, this is defined through what is referred to in mathematics as a metric. We need to differentiate at this point between metrics that are used to define a loss function and therefore used in an optimizer to train the model, and metrics that can be calculated to give additional hints toward the performance of the trained model. We will have a look at both kinds in this section.

As we have seen when looking at types of ML algorithms, we might work with an output represented by continuous data (regression), or we might work with an output represented by discrete data (classification).

The most prominent loss functions used in regression are **MSE** and **root MSE** (**RMSE**). Imagine you try to determine a fitted line for a bunch of samples in linear regression. The distance between the line and the sample point in **two-dimensional** (**2D**) space is your error. To calculate the RMSE for all data points, you would take the expected values y_i and the predicted values $\hat{y}_i$ and calculate the following:

$$RMSE = \sqrt{\frac{\sum_{i=1}^{N}(y_i - \hat{y}_i)^2}{N}}$$

For classifications, this gets a little bit trickier. In most cases, the model can predict the correct class or cannot, making it a binary result. Further, we might have a binary classification problem (1 or 0—yes or no), or a multi-class problem (cat, dog, horse, and so on).

For both classification problems, there is a prominent loss function used called **cross-entropy loss**. To solve the problem of having a binary result, this loss function requires a model that outputs a probability p between 0 and 1 for a given data point x and a suggested prediction y. For a binary classification model, it is calculated as follows:

$$-\left(y * log\,p + (1-y) * log(1-p)\right)$$

For multi-class classification, we sum up this error for all classes C, as follows:

$$-\sum_{C=1}^{C} y_C \, log \, p_C$$

If you want to look further into this topic, consider other useful loss functions for regression, such as the **absolute error** loss and the **Huber loss** functions (used in **support vector machines**, or **SVMs**), useful loss functions for binary classification, such as the **hinge loss** function, and useful loss functions for multi-class classification, such as the **Kullback-Leibler divergence** (**KL-divergence**) function. The last one can also be used in RL as a metric to monitor the policy function during training.

Everything we have discussed so far requires something we can put into a mathematical formula. Imagine working with text files to build a model for **natural language processing** (**NLP**). In such a case, we do not have a useful mathematical representation for text besides something such as **Unicode**. We will learn in *Chapter 7, Advanced Feature Extraction with NLP*, how to represent it in a useful, vectorized manner. Having vectors, we can use a different kind of metric to calculate how similar vectors are, called the **cosine similarity** metric, which we will discuss in *Chapter 6, Feature Engineering and Labeling*.

So far, we have discussed how to calculate loss functions for a couple of scenarios, but how can we define the performance of our model overall?

For regression models, our loss function was defined over the whole corpus of our training set. The error of a single observation or prediction would be $(y - \hat{y})$. Therefore, RMSE is already a cost function and can be used by an optimizer to improve the model performance, so we can use it to judge the performance of the model.

For classification models, this gets a little bit more interesting. Cross-entropy can be used with an optimizer to train the model and can be used to judge the model, but besides that, we can define an additional metric to look out for.

Something obvious would be what is referred to as the **accuracy** of a model, calculated as follows:

$$accuracy = \frac{\#correct\ predictions}{\#all\ predictions}$$

Now, this looks about right. We just say that the quality of our model is the percentage of how often we guessed correctly, and the reality is that a lot of people agree with this statement. Remember when we defined **false positives** and **false negatives**? These now come into play. Let's look at an example.

Imagine a test that checks for a contagious virus. *Figure 1.10* shows the results for 100 people being tested for this virus, including the correctness of the results:

True Positive	False Positive
• Reality: infected with virus • Test result: infected with virus • **Number of TP results: 2**	• Reality: not infected • Test result: infected with virus • **Number of FP results: 1**
False Negative	**True Negative**
• Reality: infected with virus • Test result: not infected • **Number of FN results: 8**	• Reality: not infected • Test result: not infected • **Number of TN results: 89**

Figure 1.10 – Test results for a group of 100 people

Now, what would be the accuracy of this test given these results? Let's define it again using the values for true positive (TP), false positive (FP), false negative (FN), and true negative (TN) and calculate the results for our example, as follows:

$$accuracy = \frac{TP + TN}{TP + TN + FP + FN} = \frac{2 + 89}{2 + 89 + 1 + 8} = 0.92$$

This sounds like a good test. It gives accurate results in 92% of cases, but perhaps you see the problem here. Accuracy sees everything equally. Our test misclassifies someone having the virus eight times as someone being virus-free, which might have dire ramifications. That means it might be useful having performance metrics that put more emphasis on false-positive or false-negative outcomes. Therefore, let's define two additional metrics to calculate.

The first one we call **precision**, a value that defines how many positive identifications were correct. The formula is shown here:

$$precision = \frac{TP}{TP + FP} = \frac{2}{2 + 1} = 0.66$$

In our example, only in two out of three cases are we correct when we declare someone to be infected. A model with a precision value of 1 would have no false-positive results.

The second one we call **recall**, a value that defines how many positive results we identify correctly. The formula is shown here:

$$recall = \frac{TP}{TP + FN} = \frac{2}{2 + 8} = 0.2$$

This means in our example, we correctly identify 20% of all infected patients, which is a bad result. A model with a recall value of 1 would have no false-negative results.

To evaluate our test or classification correctly, we need to evaluate accuracy, precision, and recall. Be aware that, as mentioned when we talked about hypothesis testing, precision and recall can work against each other. Therefore, you often have to decide whether you prefer to be precise when saying "*You have the virus*" or whether you prefer to find everyone who has the virus. You might now understand why such tests are often designed toward recall.

With this, we conclude the section on the mathematical basis required to get better at building ML models and working with data. Based on what we have learned so far, you should take the next point with you.

> **Important Note**
> Never just use methods from ML libraries for data analysis and modeling; understand them mathematically.

In the next section, we will guide you through the structure of the end-to-end ML process and the structure of this book.

Discovering the end-to-end ML process

We have finally arrived at the main topic of this chapter. After reviewing the past and understanding the purpose of ML and how it takes its roots in mathematical data analysis, let's now get a clear picture of which steps need to be taken to create a high-quality ML model.

The following diagram shows an overview of the (sometimes recursive) steps from data to model to deployed model:

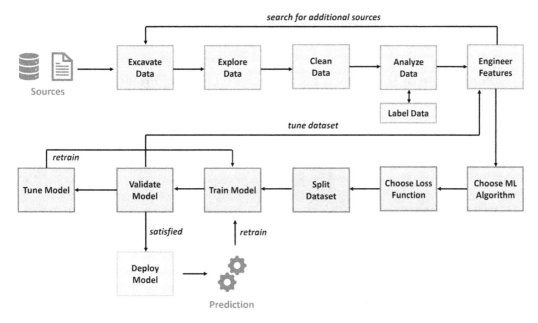

Figure 1.11 – End-to-end ML process

Looking at this flow, we can define the following distinct steps to take:

1. Excavating data and sources
2. Preparing and cleaning data
3. Defining labels and engineering features
4. Training models
5. Deploying models

These show the steps for running one single ML project. When you deal with a lot of projects and data, it becomes increasingly important to adopt some form of automation and operationalization, which is typically referred to as MLOps.

In this section, we will give an overview of each of these steps, including MLOps and its importance, and explain in which chapters we will delve deeper into the corresponding topic. Before we start going through those steps, reflect on the following question:

As a percentage, how much time would you put aside for each of those steps?

After you are done, have a look at the following screenshot, which shows you the typical time investment required for those tasks:

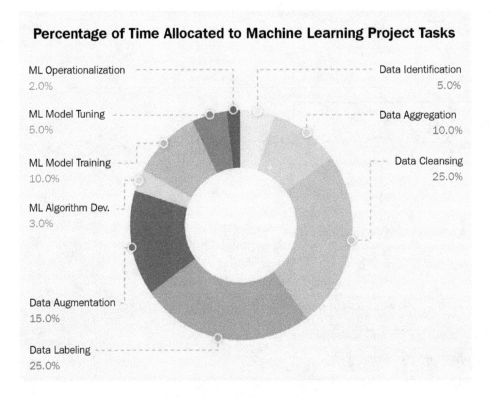

Percentage of Time Allocated to Machine Learning Project Tasks

ML Operationalization
2.0%

Data Identification
5.0%

ML Model Tuning
5.0%

Data Aggregation
10.0%

ML Model Training
10.0%

Data Cleansing
25.0%

ML Algorithm Dev.
3.0%

Data Augmentation
15.0%

Data Labeling
25.0%

Figure 1.12 – ML time invested

Was your guess reasonably close to this? You might be surprised that only 20% of the time, you will work on something that has to do with the actual training and deployment of ML models. Therefore, you should take the next point to heart.

> **Important Note**
> In an ML project, you should spend most of your time taking apart your datasets and finding other useful data sources.

Failure to do so will have ramifications on the quality of your model and its performance. Now, having said that, let's go through the steps one by one, starting with where to source your data from.

Excavating data and sources

When you start an ML project, you probably have some outcome in mind, and often, you have some form of existing dataset you or your company wants to start with. This is where you start familiarizing yourself with the given data, understanding what you have and what is missing by doing analysis, which we will come back to in the following steps.

At some point, you might realize that you are missing additional—but crucial—data points to increase the quality of your results. This highly depends on what you are missing—whether it is something you or your company can obtain or whether you need to find it somewhere else. To give you some ideas, let's have a look at the following options to acquire additional data and what you should be aware of:

- **In-house data sources**: If you are running this project in or with a company, the first point to look is internally. Advantages of this are that it is free of charge, it is often standardized, and you should be able to find a person that knows this data and how it was obtained. Depending on the project, it might also be the only place you can acquire the required data. Disadvantages of this option are that you might not find what you are looking for, that the data is poorly documented, and that the quality might be in question due to bias in the data.

- **Open data sources**: Another option is to use freely available datasets. Advantages of those are that they are typically gigantic in size (**terabytes (TB)** of data), they cover different time periods, and they are typically well structured and documented. Disadvantages are that some data fields might be hard to understand (and the creator is not available), the quality might also vary due to bias in the data, and often when used, they require you to publish your results. Examples of this would be the **National Oceanic and Atmospheric Administration (NOAA)** (`https://www.ncei.noaa.gov/weather-climate-links`) and the **European Union (EU)** Open Data Portal (`https://data.europa.eu/en`), among many others.

- **Data seller (data as a service, or DaaS)**: A final option would be to buy data from a data seller, either by purchasing an existing dataset or by requesting the creation of one. Advantages of this option are that it saves you time, it can give you access to an individualized dataset, and you might even get access to preprocessed data. Disadvantages are that this is expensive, you still need to do all the other following steps to make this data useful, and there might be questions concerning privacy and ethics.

Now that we have a good idea of where to get data initially or additionally, let's look at the next step: preparing and cleaning the data.

Preparing and cleaning data

As alluded to before, descriptive data exploration is without a doubt one of the most important steps in an ML project. If you want to clean data and build derived features or select an ML algorithm to predict a target variable in your dataset, then you need to understand your data first. Your data will define many of the necessary cleaning and preprocessing steps. It will define which algorithms you can choose, and it will ultimately define the performance of your predictive model.

The exploration should be done as a structured analytical process rather than a set of experimental tasks. Therefore, we will go through a checklist of data exploration tasks that you can perform as an initial step in every ML project, before starting any data cleaning, preprocessing, **feature engineering**, or model selection. By applying these steps, you will be able to understand the data and gain knowledge about the required preprocessing tasks.

Along with that, it will give you a good estimate of what kinds of difficulties you can expect in your prediction task, which is essential for judging the required algorithms and validation strategies. You will also gain an insight into which possible feature engineering methods could apply to your dataset and have a better understanding of how to select a good loss function.

Let's have a look at the required steps.

Storing and preparing data

Your data might come in a variety of different formats. You might work with tabular data stored in a **comma-separated values** (**CSV**) file; you might have images stored as **Joint Photographic Experts Group** (**JPEG**) or **Portable Network Graphics** (**PNG**) files, text stored in a **JavaScript Object Notation** (**JSON**) file, or audio files in **MP3** or **M4V** format. CSV can be a good format as it is human-readable and can be parsed efficiently. You can open and browse it using any text editor.

If you work on your own, you might just store this raw data in a folder on your system, but when you are working with a cloud infrastructure or even just a company infrastructure in general, you might need some form of cloud storage. Certainly, you can just upload your raw data by hand to such storage, but often, the data you work with is coming from a live system and needs to be extracted from there. This means it might be worthwhile having a look at so-called **extract-transform-load** (**ETL**) tools that can automate this process and bring the required raw data into cloud storage.

After all of the preprocessing steps are done, you will have some form of layered data in your storage, from raw to cleaned to labeled to processed datasets.

We will dive deeper into this topic in *Chapter 4, Ingesting Data and Managing Datasets*. For now, just understand that we will automate this process of making data available for processing.

Cleaning data

In this step, we have a look at inconsistency and structural errors in the data itself. This step is often required for tabular data and sometimes text files, but not so much for image or audio files. For the latter, we might be able to crop images and change their brightness or contrast, but it might be required to go back to the source to create better-quality samples. The same goes for audio files.

For tabular datasets, we have much more options for processing. Let's go through what to look out for, as follows:

- **Duplicates**: Through mistakes in copying data or due to a combination of different data sources, you might find duplicate samples. Typically, copies can be deleted. Just make sure that these are not two different samples that look the same.

- **Irrelevant information**: In most cases, you will have datasets with a lot of different features, some of which will be completely unnecessary for your project. The obvious ones you should just remove in the beginning; others you will be able to remove later after analyzing the data further.

- **Structural errors**: This refers to the values you can see in the samples. You might run into different entries with the same meaning (such as US and United States) or simply typos. These should be standardized or cleaned up. A good way to do this is by visualizing all available values of a feature.

- **Anomalies (outliers)**: This refers to very unlikely values for which you need to decide whether they are errors or actually true. This is typically done after analyzing the data when you know the distribution of a feature.

- **Missing values**: This refers to cells in your data that are either blank or have some generic value in them, such as NA or NaN. There are different ways to rectify this besides deleting entire samples. It is also prudent to wait until you have more insight from analyzing the data, as you might see better ways to replace them.

After this step, we can start analyzing the cleaned version of our dataset further.

Analyzing data

In this step, we apply our understanding of statistics to get some insights into our features and labels. This includes calculating statistical properties for each feature, visualizing them, finding correlated features, and measuring something that is called **feature importance**, which calculates the impact of a feature on the label, also referred to as the **target variable**.

Through these methods, we get ideas about relationships among features and between features and targets, which can help us to make a decision. In this decision-making process, we also start adding something vitally important—our **domain knowledge**. If you do not know what the data represents, you will have a hard time pruning it and choosing optimal features and samples for training.

There are a lot more techniques that can be applied in this step, including something called **dimensional reduction**. If you have thousands of features (a numerical representation of an image, for example), it gets very complicated for humans and even for ML processes to understand relationships. In such cases, it might be useful to map this high-dimensional sample to a two-dimensional or three-dimensional representation in the form of a vector. Through this, we can easily find similarities in different samples.

We will dive deeper into the topics of cleaning and analyzing data in *Chapter 5, Performing Data Analysis and Visualization.*

Having done all these steps, we will have a good understanding of the data we have at hand, and we might already know what we are missing. As the final step in preprocessing our data, we will have a look at creating and transforming features, typically referred to as **feature engineering**, and creating labels when missing.

Defining labels and engineering features

In the second part of the preprocessing of data, we will discuss the labeling of data and the actions we can perform on features. To perform these steps, we need the knowledge obtained through the exploratory steps we've discussed so far. Let's start by looking at labeling data.

Labeling

Let's start with a bummer: this process is very tedious. Labeling, also called **annotation**, is the least exciting part of an ML project yet one of the most important tasks in the whole process. The goal is to feed high-quality training data into the ML algorithms.

While proper labels greatly help to improve prediction performance, the labeling process will also help you to study the dataset in greater detail. Let me clarify that labeling data requires deep insight and understanding of the context of the dataset and the prediction process, which you should have acquired at this point. If we were, for example, aiming to predict breast cancer using **computerized tomography (CT)** scans, we would also need to understand how breast cancer can be detected in CT images to label the data.

Mislabeling the training data has a couple of consequences, such as **label noise**, which you want to avoid as it will affect the performance of every downstream process in the ML pipeline. In some cases, your labeling methodology is dependent on the chosen ML approach for a prediction problem. A good example is the difference between object detection and segmentation, both of which require completely differently labeled data.

There are some techniques and tooling available to speed up the labeling process that make use of the fact that we can use ML algorithms not only for the desired project but also to learn how to label our data. Such models start proposing labels during your manual annotation of the dataset.

Feature engineering

In a nutshell, in this step, we will start transforming the features or adding new features. Obviously, we are not doing such actions on a whim, but rather due to the knowledge we gathered in the previous steps. We might have understood, for example, that the full date and time are far too precise, and we need just the day of the week or the month. Whatever it might be, we will try to shape and extract what we need.

Typically, we will perform one of the following actions:

- **Feature creation**: Create new features from a given set of features or from additional information sources.

- **Feature transformation**: Transform single features to make them useful and stable for the utilized ML algorithm.

- **Feature extraction**: Create derived features from the original data.

- **Feature selection**: Choose the most prominent and predictive features.

We will dive deeper into labeling and the multitude of methods to apply to our features in *Chapter 6, Feature Engineering and Labeling*. In addition, we will have a detailed look at a more complex example of feature engineering when working with text data in an NLP project. You will find this in *Chapter 7, Advanced Feature Extraction with NLP*.

We conclude this step by reiterating how important the whole preprocessing data steps are and how much influence they have on the next step, where we will discuss model training. Further, we remember that we might need to come back to this after model training in case of lackluster performance of our model.

Training models

We finally reached the point where we can bring ML algorithms into play. As with data experimentation and preprocessing, training an ML model is an analytical, step-by-step process. Each step involves a thought process that evaluates the pros and cons of each algorithm according to the results of the experimentation phase. As in every other scientific process, it is recommended that you come up with a hypothesis first and verify whether this hypothesis is true afterward.

Let's look at the steps that define the process of training an ML model, as follows:

1. **Define your ML task**: First, we need to define the ML task we are facing, which most of the time is defined by the business decision behind your use case. Depending on the amount of labeled data, you can choose between unsupervised and supervised learning methods, as well as many other subcategories.

2. **Pick a suitable model**: Pick a suitable model for the chosen ML task. This might be a logistical regression, a gradient-boosted ensemble tree, or a DNN, just to name a few popular ML model choices. The choice is mainly dependent on the training (or production) infrastructure (such as Python, R, Julia, C, and so on) and the shape and type of the data.

3. **Pick or implement a loss function and an optimizer**: During the data experimentation phase, you should have already come up with a strategy on how to test your model performance. Hence, you should have picked a data split, loss function, and optimizer already. If you have not done so, you should at this point evaluate what you want to measure and optimize.

4. **Pick a dataset split**: Splitting your data into different sets—namely, training, validation, and test sets—gives you additional insights into the performance of your training and optimization process and helps you to avoid overfitting your model to your training data.

5. **Train a simple model using cross-validation**: When all the preceding choices are made, you can go ahead and train your ML model. Optimally, this is done as cross-validation on a training and validation set, without leaking training data into validation. After training a baseline model, it's time to interpret the error metric of the validation runs. Does it make sense? Is it as high or low as expected? Is it (hopefully) better than random and better than always predicting the most popular target?

6. **Tune the model**: Finally, you can either tune the outcome of the model by working with the so-called hyperparameters of a model, do model stacking or other advanced methods, or you might have to go back to the initial data and work on that before training the model again.

These are the base steps we perform when training our model. In the following section, we will give some more insights into the aforementioned steps, starting with how to choose a model.

Choosing a model

When it comes to choosing a good model for your data, it is recommended that you favor simple traditional models before going toward the more complex options. An example would be ensemble models, such as **gradient-boosted tree ensembles**, when training data is limited. These models perform well on a broad set of input values (ordinal, nominal, and numeric) as well as training efficiently, and they are understandable.

Tree-based ensemble models combine many weak learners into a single predictor based on decision trees. This greatly reduces the problem of the overfitting and instability aspects of a single decision tree. The output, after a few iterations using the default parameter, usually delivers great baseline results for many different applications.

In *Chapter 9*, *Building ML Models Using Azure Machine Learning*, we dedicate a complete section to training a gradient-boosted tree ensemble classifier using **LightGBM**, a popular tree ensemble library from Microsoft.

To capture the meaning of large amounts of complex training data, we need large parametric models. However, training parametric models with many hundreds of millions of parameters is no easy task, due to exploding and vanishing gradients, loss propagation through such a complex model, numerical instability, and normalization. In recent years, a branch of such high-parametric models achieved extremely good results through many complex tasks—namely, **deep learning** (**DL**).

DL basically spans up a multilayer ANN, where each layer is seen as a certain step in the data processing pipeline of the model.

In *Chapter 10*, *Training Deep Neural Networks on Azure*, and *Chapter 12*, *Distributed Machine Learning on Azure*, we will delve deeper into how to train large and complex DL models on single machines and on a distributed GPU cluster.

Finally, you might work with a completely different form of data, such as audio or text data. In such cases, there are specialized ways to preprocess and score this data. One of these fields would be **recommendation engines**, which we will discuss thoroughly in *Chapter 13*, *Building a Recommendation Engine in Azure*.

Choosing a loss function and an optimizer

As we discussed in the previous section, there are many metrics to choose from, depending on the type of training and model you want to use. After looking at the relationship between the feature and target dimensions, as well as the separability of the data, you should continue to evaluate which loss function and optimizer you will use to train your model.

Many ML practitioners don't value the importance of a proper error metric highly enough and just use what is easy, such as accuracy and RMSE. This choice is critical. Furthermore, it is useful to understand the baseline performance and the model's robustness to noise. The first can be achieved by computing the error metric using only the target variable with the highest occurrence as a prediction. This will be your baseline performance. The second can be done by modifying the random seed of your ML model and observing the changes to the error metric. This will show you which decimal place you can trust the error metric to.

Keep in mind that it is prudent to evaluate the chosen error metric and any additional metric you desire after training runs, and experiment whether others might be more beneficial.

As for the optimizer, it highly depends on the model you chose as to which options you have in this regard. Just remember the optimizer is how we get to the target, and the target is defined by the loss function.

Splitting the dataset

Once you have selected an ML model, a loss function, and an optimizer, you need to think about splitting your dataset for training. Optimally, the data should be split into three disjointed sets: a training, a validation, and a test dataset. We use multiple sets to ensure that the model generalizes well on unseen data and that the reported error metric can be trusted. Hence, you can see that dividing the data into representative sets is a task that should be performed as an analytical process. These sets are defined as follows:

- **Training dataset**: The subset of data used to fit/train the model.
- **Validation dataset**: The subset of data used to provide an evaluation during training to tune hyperparameters. The algorithm sees this data during training, but never learns from it. Therefore, it has an indirect influence on the model.
- **Test dataset**: The subset of data used to run an unbiased evaluation of the trained model after training.

If training data leaks into the validation or testing set, you risk overfitting the model and skewing the validation and testing results. Overfitting is a problem that you must handle besides underfitting the model. Both are defined as follows:

> **Underfitting versus Overfitting**
>
> An underfitted model performs purely on the data. The reasons for that are often that the model is too simplistic to understand the relationship between the features and the target variables, or that your initial data is lacking useful features. An overfitted model performs perfectly on the training dataset and purely on any other data. The reason for that is that it basically memorized the training data and is unable to generalize.

There are different discussions on what the size of these splits should be and many different further techniques to choose samples for each category, such as stratified splitting (sampling based on class distributions), temporal splitting, and group-based splitting. We will take a deeper look at these in *Chapter 9, Building ML Models Using Azure Machine Learning*.

Running the model training

In most cases, you will not build an ANN structure and an optimizer from scratch. You will use ready-made ML libraries, such as **scikit-learn**, **TensorFlow**, or **PyTorch**. Most of these frameworks and libraries are written in Python, which should therefore be the language of choice for your ML projects.

When writing your code for model training, it is a good idea to logically divide the required code into two files, as follows:

- **Authoring script (authoring environment)**: The script that defines the environment (libraries, training location, and so on) in which the ML training will take place and the one triggering the execution script

- **Execution script (execution environment)**: The script that only contains the actual ML training

By splitting your code in this way, you avoid updating the actual training script when your target environment changes. This will make code versioning and MLOps much cleaner.

To understand what types of class methods we might encounter in an ML library, let's have a look at a short code snippet from TensorFlow here:

```
model = tf.keras.models.Sequential([
    tf.keras.layers.Flatten(input_shape=(28, 28)),…])
```

```
model.compile(optimizer='adam',
              loss='sparse_categorical_crossentropy',
              metrics=['accuracy'])

model.fit(x_train, y_train, epochs=5)
model.evaluate(x_test, y_test)
```

Looking at this code, we see that we are using a model called `Sequential` that is a basic ANN defined by a sequential set of layers with one input and one output. We see in the model creation step that there are layers defined and some omitted other settings. In addition, in the `compile()` method, we define an optimizer, a loss function, and some additional metrics we are interested in. Finally, we see a method called `fit()` running on the training dataset and a method called `evaluate()` running on the test dataset. Now, what do these methods do exactly? Before we get to that, let's first define something.

Hyperparameters versus Parameters of a Model

There are two kinds of settings that are adjusted during model training. Settings such as the weights and the bias in an ANN are referred to as the parameters. They are changed during the training phase. Other settings—such as the activation functions and the number of layers in an ANN, the data split, the learning rate, or the chosen optimizer—are referred to as hyperparameters. Those are the meta settings we adjust before a training run.

Having this out of the way, let's define the typical methods you will encounter, as follows:

- **Hyperparameter methods**: These are methods used to define the characteristics of the model. They are often found in the constructor (as for the `Sequential` class), in a special function such as `compile()`, or they are part of the training method we discuss next.

- **Training method**: Often named `fit()` or `train()`, this is the main method that trains the parameter of the model based on the training dataset, the loss function, and the optimizer. These methods do not return any type of value—they just update the model object and its parameters.

- **Test method**: Often named `evaluate()`, `transform()`, `score()`, or `predict()`. In most cases, these return some form of result, as they are typically running the test dataset against the trained model.

This is the typical structure of methods you will encounter for a model in an ML library. Now that we have a good idea of how to set up our coding environment and use available ML libraries, let's look at how to tune the model after our initial training.

Tuning the model

After we have trained a simple ensemble model that performs reasonably better than the baseline model and achieves acceptable performance according to the expected performance estimated during data preparation, we can progress with optimization. This is a point we really want to emphasize. It's strongly discouraged to begin model optimization and stacking when a simple ensemble technique fails to deliver useful results. If this is the case, it would be much better to take a step back and dive deeper into data analysis and feature engineering.

Common ML optimization techniques—such as hyperparameter optimization, model stacking, and even **automated machine learning** (**AutoML**)—help you get the last 10% of performance boost out of your model.

Hyperparameter optimization concentrates on changing the initial settings of the model training to improve its final performance. Similarly, model stacking is a very common technique used to improve prediction performance by putting a combination of multiple *different* model types into a single stacked model. Hence, the output of each model is fed into a meta-model, which itself is trained through cross-validation and hyperparameter tuning. By combining significantly different models into a single stacked model, you can always outperform a single model.

If you decide to use any of those optimization techniques, it is advised to perform them in parallel and fully automated on a distributed cluster. After seeing too many ML practitioners manually parametrizing, tuning, and stacking models together, we want to raise this important message: *optimizing ML models is boring.*

It should rarely be done manually as it is much faster to perform it automatically as an end-to-end optimization process. Most of your time and effort should go into experimentation, data preparation, and feature engineering—that is, everything that cannot be easily automated and optimized using raw compute power. We will delve deeper into the topic of model tuning in *Chapter 11, Hyperparameter Tuning and Automated Machine Learning.*

This concludes all important topics to know about model training. Next, we will have a look at options for the deployment of ML models.

Deploying models

Once you have trained and optimized an ML model, it is ready for deployment. This step is typically referred to as **inferencing** or **scoring** a model. Many data science teams, in practice, stop here and move the model to production as a Docker image, often embedded in a **REpresentational State Transfer** (**REST**) **API** using Flask or similar frameworks. However, as you can imagine, this is not always the best solution, depending on your requirements. An ML or data engineer's responsibility doesn't stop here.

The deployment and operation of an ML pipeline can be best seen when testing the model on live data in production. A test is done to collect insights and data to continuously improve the model. Hence, collecting model performance over time is an essential step to guaranteeing and improving the performance of the model.

In general, we differentiate two main architectures for ML-scoring pipelines, as follows:

- **Batch scoring using pipelines**: An offline process where you evaluate an ML model against a batch of data. The result of this scoring technique is usually not time-critical, and the data to be scored is usually larger than the model.

- **Real-time scoring using a container-based web service endpoint**: This refers to a technique where we score single data inputs. This is very common in stream processing, where single events are scored in real time. It's obvious that this task is highly time-critical, and the execution is blocked until the resulting score is computed.

We will discuss these two architectures in more detail in *Chapter 14, Model Deployments, Endpoints, and Operations*. There, we will also investigate an efficient way of collecting runtimes, latency, and other operational metrics, as well as model performance.

The model files we create, and the previously mentioned options, are typically defined by a standard hardware architecture. As mentioned, we probably create a Docker image that is deployed to a **virtual machine** (**VM**) or a web service. What if we want to deploy our model to a highly specialized hardware environment, such as a GPU or a **field-programmable gate array** (**FPGA**)?

To explore this further, we will dive deeper into alternative deployment targets and methods in *Chapter 15, Model Interoperability, Hardware Optimization, and Integrations*. There, we will have a look at a framework called **Open Neural Network eXchange** (**ONNX**) that allows us to convert our model into a standardized model format to be deployed to virtually any environment. Additionally, we have a look at FPGAs and why they might be a good deployment target for ML, and finally, we will explore other Azure services such as **Azure IoT Edge** and **Power BI** for integration.

This step wraps up the end-to-end process for a single ML model. Next, we will see a short overview of how to make such ML projects operational in an enterprise-grade environment using MLOps.

Developing and operating enterprise-grade ML solutions

To operationalize ML projects requires the use of automated pipelines and **development-operations** (**DevOps**) methodologies such as **continuous integration** (**CI**) and **continuous delivery/continuous deployment** (**CD**). These combined are typically referred to as MLOps.

When looking at the steps we performed in an ML project, we can see that there are typically two major operations happening—the training of a model and the deployment of a model. As these can happen independently of one another, it is worthwhile defining two different automated pipelines, as follows:

- **Training pipeline**: This includes loading datasets (possibly even including an ETL pipeline), transformation, model training, and registering final models. This pipeline could be triggered by changes in the dataset or possible detected data drift in a deployed model.

- **Deployment pipeline**: This includes loading of models from the registry, creating and deploying Docker images, creating and deploying operational scripts, and the final deployment of the model to the target. This pipeline could be triggered by new versions of an ML model.

We will have a deep dive into ML pipelining with Azure Machine Learning in *Chapter 8, Azure Machine Learning Pipelines*.

Having these pipelines, we can then turn our eye on **Azure DevOps** besides other tooling. With that, we can build a life cycle for our ML projects defined by the following parts:

- **Creating or retraining a model**: Here, we use training pipelines to create or retrain our model while version-controlling the pipelines and the code.

- **Deploying the model and creating scoring files and dependencies**: Here, we use a deployment pipeline to deploy a specific model version while version-controlling the pipeline and the code.

- **Creating an audit trail**: Through CI/CD pipelines and version control, we create an audit trail for all assets ensuring integrity and compliance.

- **Monitoring model in production**: We monitor the performance and possible data drift, which might automatically trigger retraining of the model.

We will discuss these topics and others in more detail in *Chapter 16, Bringing Models into Production with MLOps*.

This concludes our discussion on the end-to-end ML process and this chapter. If you hadn't already, you should now have a good understanding of ML and what to expect in the rest of the book.

Summary

In this chapter, we learned in which situations we should use ML and where it is coming from, we understood basic concepts of statistics and the mathematical knowledge we require for ML, and we discovered the steps we need to go through to create a performing ML model. In addition, we had a first glimpse at what is required to operationalize ML projects. This should give a base idea of what ML is about and what we will dive into in this book.

As this book not only covers ML but also the cloud platform Azure, in the next two chapters, we will go deeper into a topic that we have not covered so far—we will speak about tooling for ML. Therefore, in the next chapter, we will discover what Azure has to offer in the form of tools and services for ML, and in the third chapter, we will use the most useful tool to run our first hands-on experimentation with ML on Azure.

2
Choosing the Right Machine Learning Service in Azure

In the previous chapter, we learned about the end-to-end ML process and all the required steps, from data exploration to data preprocessing, training, optimization, deployment, and operation. Understanding the whole process will better help us in choosing the right service for building cloud-based ML services.

In this chapter, we will help you navigate the different Azure AI services and show you how to select the right service for your ML task. First, we will classify the different services by service abstraction and application domain, and then look at the different trade-offs and benefits of the different services.

In the next section, we will focus on managed services and jump right into Azure Cognitive Services, multiple pre-trained ML services for general tasks and domains. We will then cover customized Cognitive Services, which is a way to fine-tune a Cognitive Service for a specific task or domain, and end the section by looking into applied AI services.

In the following section, we will discuss custom ML services in Azure, such as Azure Automated Machine Learning, Azure Machine Learning designer, and the Azure Machine Learning service – the service that we will use throughout this book.

In the last section, we will look into custom compute services, such as Azure Databricks, Azure Batch, and Data Science Virtual Machines, for building custom ML solutions.

At the end of this chapter, you will know how to navigate the Azure AI landscape and understand why Azure Machine Learning is the preferred service to build custom ML solutions.

The following topics will be covered in this chapter:

- Choosing an Azure service for ML
- Managed ML services
- Custom ML services
- Custom compute services for ML

Choosing an Azure service for ML

Azure provides more than 200 services, of which more than 30 services are targeted for building solutions for AI and ML. This vast number of services often makes it difficult for someone new to Azure to choose the right service for a specific task. Choosing the right service for your ML task is the most important decision you will have to make when starting with ML in Azure. In this section, we will provide clear guidance about how to choose the right ML and compute services in Azure.

The right service with the right layer of abstraction could save you months if not years of time to market your ML-based product or feature. It could help you avoid tedious time-consuming tasks such as improving model performance through transfer learning, re-training, managing, and re-deploying ML models, or monitoring, scaling, and operating inference services and endpoints.

Choosing the wrong service could mean that you start producing results quickly, but it might become impossible to improve model performance for a specific domain or extend a model for other tasks. Therefore, having a basic understanding of the different Azure AI and ML services will help you to make the right trade-offs and choose the right service for your use case. In the next section, we will help you navigate the many Azure services and Azure AI landscape to identify the right ML service for your use case.

Navigating the Azure AI landscape

For many cloud-based services, such as compute, storage, database, or analytics, the most important choice is the service level abstraction – **Infrastructure as a Service (IaaS)**, **Platform as a Service (PaaS)**, or **Software as a Service (SaaS)**. *Figure 2.1* shows the difference between the self-managed and managed parts of the application stack for cloud services:

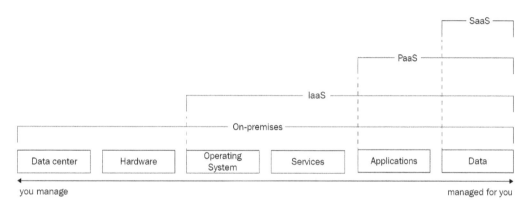

Figure 2.1 – An IaaS versus PaaS versus SaaS comparison for cloud services

Let's compare the different types of abstractions and responsibilities presented in the previous figure. The application stack is built from left to right, starting with a *data center* (building, cooling, power, and so on) that contains *hardware* (computers, disks, network cards, switches, and so on). Each machine is powered by an *operating system* (Linux or Windows) and runs specific *services* (web server, database, cache, and so on) and *applications* (for example, WordPress), which store and serve your *data* (for example, your custom website):

- With on-premises compute, you own and manage everything – from the building, cooling, power, physical servers, network connections, switches, and BIOS, up to the operating system, services, applications, and data. If a disk, network interface, or power connection fails, you need to get it changed.

- With *IaaS* services, you consume infrastructure from your cloud provider such as a **Virtual Machine (VM)**. You choose the number of CPUs, memory, disks, network interfaces, and so on, which will all be managed for you, but you need to manage the OS as well as all the services, applications, and data yourself. If there is an important kernel security update, you need to get it installed. IaaS services are the fundamental building blocks for all other services.

- *PaaS* services let you focus purely on your application. A typical example is so-called *serverless compute* such as Azure Functions. Here, you can choose your JVM version to deploy a Java-based application, but you don't need to worry about patching your operating system, your service runtime, or the underlying hardware. PaaS services often provide a good trade-off between ownership, customization, and cost. Most cloud services fall into this category.

- Lastly, *SaaS* services are whole applications that are designed, implemented, and managed by the cloud provider. You usually interact with these services through a website or API endpoint, without even knowing what operating system or service runtime is used or what the application code or data model looks like. SaaS services can be compared with popular web services that we use every day, such as Facebook, Netflix, Spotify, or YouTube. Cloud providers often build these services for specific use cases, such as IoT, genomics, computer vision, and others.

In conclusion, all Azure services can be placed somewhere on the IaaS, PaaS, and SaaS scale based on the level of service abstraction. We can use this scale to categorize all Azure AI services into three groups:

- Managed ML services (SaaS)

- Custom ML services (PaaS)

- Custom compute services for ML (IaaS)

Therefore, your first step in choosing an ML service in Azure is to determine the right service-level abstraction for your use case – by choosing the right trade-off between flexibility, ownership, skills, time, and cost.

However, choosing an ML service is a bit more nuanced than differentiating only between managed and custom services. Especially for managed ML services, we also need to compare the different application domains and levels of customization and specialization.

Azure provides many pre-trained domain-specific models and services, such as object detection, sentiment analysis, recommendation engines, and document parsing. Depending on your application domain, you could choose an ML service that includes a pre-trained model. For example, if you need a general face-recognition model, you could consume this as a managed service from Azure. This means that you don't need any training data at all for building such a feature. The decision of using a pre-trained model has a huge impact on your project timeline, as acquiring, cleaning, and labeling training data is one of the most tedious and time-consuming steps in the ML process.

However, many ML applications are built for highly specialized domains such as medical data analysis, forensic analysis, and the legal profession. If you are building ML-based applications or features for such a domain, a pre-trained model without any customization for the application domain might not be the right fit. In this case, you can choose a managed ML service that provides customization capabilities – a way to use training data to fine-tune a pre-trained model for a custom domain. This process is also referred to as transfer learning and supported by some managed Azure Machine Learning services.

Some domains or ML-based applications don't fit into this category and can't easily be fine-tuned for a different application domain. For example, it's not practical to pre-train a recommendation engine on someone else's ratings, transfer text-to-speech features to a generative model for classical music, or fine-tune a two-dimensional model with three-dimensional image data. In these cases, you have no other choice but to create your own models using your own training data.

Using the preceding examples, we can sub-divide the managed and custom ML services by the amount of required training data and application domain into the following groups:

- No training data required
- Some training data required for customization
- Training data required

Therefore, the second option to choose a managed or custom ML service is based on your application domain and requirements for training data and model specialization. Similar to service abstraction, the trade-off is between flexibility (customization), ownership, skills, time, and cost.

Let's compare these requirements and look at a similar IaaS, PaaS, and SaaS comparison specifically for cloud-based ML services in *Figure 2.2*:

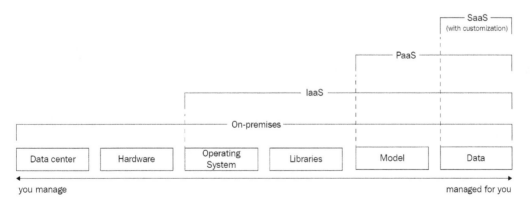

Figure 2.2 – An IaaS versus PaaS versus SaaS comparison for ML services

As you can see in the preceding figure, you can evaluate the preferred service abstraction for your ML service along similar dimensions as any other cloud service – depending on which part of the stack you want to manage yourself. The table contains a few adjustments specifically for ML applications, such as *libraries* (ML frameworks, tools, and runtimes) instead of services and a *model* instead of an application. SaaS services for ML can either allow customization, which means you can bring your own data, or don't allow customization, which means you don't have to provide any training data at all.

Armed with this knowledge about service abstractions (IaaS versus PaaS versus SaaS) as well as application domain and required training data (no training data versus data for customization through transfer learning versus training data), we can start dissecting the Azure Machine Learning landscape.

Consuming a managed AI service

Consuming a managed AI service through an API is the easiest and quickest way to build ML-based features or applications. It's simple because you don't have to clean the training data and train the model, you don't have to manage compute clusters for training or inferencing, and you don't have to monitor and scale your model deployment for making batch predictions.

For many managed AI services in Azure, all you need is to call a web service with your API key and your data, and the API will respond with the corresponding prediction, which is often a combination of multiple model scores. The Azure Cognitive Services API for understanding images, for example, will return predictions for object detection, image tagging, adult content classification, gory and racy classification, face detection, gender and age detection, image description, and more within a single API call.

If you are dealing with a general ML problem and a general domain – such as image tagging, text extraction, speech-to-text, and translation – you are lucky enough to be able to choose such a managed AI service for your application. Image analysis for general image domains (such as photos), text analysis, text-to-speech and speech-to-text, language, and translation services are common ML problems that can take advantage of an off-the-shelf ML solution. We will explore the different APIs and services for managed pre-trained AI services later, in the *Azure Cognitive Services* section.

A downside of managed AI services is that they all ship with pre-trained black-box models that we can't see, interpret, analyze, or optimize. This makes it infeasible to use these APIs for highly specific domains. If you work with MRI images for cancer detection, you won't find Azure's general object detection algorithm very useful.

For these specific cases – general ML problems with custom application domains – Azure provides customizable managed AI services. One such example is the Azure Custom Vision service, which lets you fine-tune a pre-trained model for common image recognition tasks. What sets these services apart is that you can provide your own training data to fine-tune a model for a custom application domain, while benefiting from the advantages of using a managed service.

Another such example is **Azure Form Recognizer**, a tool that allows you to extract printed and handwritten text from a structured document. It can be fine-tuned to detect custom text formats used in your application domain. We will take a look at all of these customizable managed services later, in the *Custom cognitive services* and *Azure applied services* sections.

However, if you need the flexibility of choosing a specific model or algorithm that is not supported as a service (for example, image segmentation), then you don't have a choice but to implement your own model and build your own AI solution. We will dive deeper into this topic in the next section.

Let's end this section with important advice for developing cloud- and ML-based features or applications – if possible, opt for a managed service with a pre-trained model over building a custom ML solution. Consuming a pre-trained model through an API is often magnitudes easier, faster, and cheaper than training, deploying, and operating your own ML service. Many practical applications can take advantage of generalized pre-trained models or fine-tuned customized models, and the list of provided models, services, and domains is constantly growing.

Throughout this book, we will help you to master the skill of building custom ML applications in Azure, to cover all use cases where consuming a managed AI service is not possible.

Building a custom AI service

If you can't consume a managed AI service either because there is no model or service available for your use case, or the fine-tuning capabilities are not sufficient for your application domain, you have no other choice but to build a custom AI solution.

You can choose either PaaS or IaaS services to build a custom AI solution in Azure. Both types of services will give you a similar flexibility in choosing your own ML ingredients, such as picking your preferred programming language and libraries for implementing and training ML models, choosing your own data sources and formats as training data, and choosing specific deployment strategies, such as optimization for batch prediction or low-latency on-device inferencing.

However, this flexibility comes at a cost, which is usually significantly higher than consuming a pre-trained or customized AI service. The higher costs are a result of the additional tasks, skills, and investments required for successfully building and operating an ML service. The most important differences for building a custom AI solution over consuming an AI service are the following:

- Collecting, preprocessing, and labeling training data
- Building infrastructure and automation for training and inferencing
- The modeling, training, and optimization of ML models
- Operating the ML service in production

It's easy to see that the additional complexity doesn't only come from training a custom model but from many other tasks in the end-to-end ML process. The availability of a sufficient amount of training data, the quality of the data and the availability of people for labeling this data are the major blockers to build a high-performing custom AI solutions. Therefore, you need to make sure that training data is available before the start of the project or can be acquired during the project.

The second most important additional cost and resources are related to infrastructure. Modeling, training, and optimizing is an ongoing iterative process for the lifetime of an ML service. After a deployment, we often collect more training data, record model metrics, measure the model drift, and repeat the whole process over and over. Therefore, even for smaller ML projects, investments in infrastructure are significant but essential for the long-term success of the project.

Larger companies even split these responsibilities into different teams to address the need for different skillsets for both areas – one for building and maintaining the ML infrastructure and one for ML modeling, training, and optimization. This clearly shows that both infrastructure and modeling are equally important for developing successful ML projects.

The best trade-off in terms of flexibility and ownership for building a cloud-based custom AI service is to choose a PaaS-based ML platform. Therefore, a great custom ML platform supports you with all these infrastructure setups and operations, facilitates your modeling and optimization tasks, provides abstractions to encapsulate repetitive workloads, and offers automation to minimize manual effort during the project life cycle. On top, a custom ML service provides you with the flexibility to choose any ML framework, any modeling technique and training algorithm, and any data source and format to build a fully custom AI solution.

Azure Machine Learning is a great example of a PaaS-based service for building custom ML solutions and for optimizing the whole end-to-end life cycle of ML projects. We will take a closer look at Azure Machine Learning and compare its capabilities with other custom ML services later, in the *Custom ML services* section, and cover it in much more detail in the subsequent chapters.

In this book, we will give you all the required skills to build your own custom ML service from start to finish, using Azure Machine Learning as your managed ML service of choice.

However, it's worth noting that in order to build custom AI services, you don't necessarily need a platform to register your models, to define your datasets, or to track your training scores. You can simply pick your favorite compute service (for example, Azure Kubernetes Service), your favorite storage service (for example, Azure Data Lake Storage), and your favorite database service (for example, Azure Cosmos DB) and build your own custom solution. In fact, you can use any compute service to build your custom IaaS-based ML application in Azure.

Choosing IaaS services to build your own ML applications gives you the most flexibility in terms of choosing any infrastructure component during your ML process. On the other hand, it also means that you need to manually set up, configure, and integrate these services as well as setting up identities, authentication, and access control, which results in a higher upfront investment, higher infrastructure development costs, and the need for a specific skillset.

Azure provides excellent IaaS compute services to build custom ML solutions. You can choose from simple VMs, VMs with pre-installed ML images, batch computation services and services for scalable distributed computing. We will see a few service examples later, in the *Custom compute services for ML* section.

What is the Azure Machine Learning service?

Before we start looking into the specific managed and custom ML services, we want to clear some confusion around the term **Azure Machine Learning**, which is not only prominent on the cover of this book but also a popular ML service in Azure, a workspace for other ML services, and a popular keyword across the internet, blogs, and books.

First and foremost, the term *Azure Machine Learning* stands for a popular Azure service (`https://docs.microsoft.com/en-us/azure/machine-learning/overview-what-is-azure-machine-learning`) that provides capabilities for building custom ML solutions. The service contains different components to manage resources (such as compute clusters and data storage) and assets (such as datasets, experiments, models, pipelines, Docker environments, and endpoints), as well as access to these resources and assets, all within the same workspace.

This is the service that we will use throughout this book to build an end-to-end pipeline for training, deploying, and operating custom ML models. You will start by creating your first Azure Machine Learning workspace in the next chapter.

In order to build custom ML models, you will create training clusters, track experiments, register data as datasets, store trained models, manage Docker images for training and inferencing, and configure endpoints, all within Azure Machine Learning.

Throughout this book, we will mostly use the Python APIs (`https://docs.microsoft.com/en-us/python/api/overview/azure/ml/?view=azure-ml-py`) to interact with Azure Machine Learning. However, you can also use a UI portal to access and manage the resources and assets, create experiments, submit training jobs, visualize training results, create Docker environments, and deploy inference clusters.

The UI to interact with Azure Machine Learning is called **Azure Machine Learning studio** (`https://docs.microsoft.com/en-us/azure/machine-learning/overview-what-is-machine-learning-studio`). This name is not to be confused with an older Azure service, Azure Machine Learning Studio – a GUI-based service to create and deploy ML services through a block-based drag-and-drop interface, which is now called **Azure Machine Learning Studio (classic)** (`https://studio.azureml.net/`).

The Azure Machine Learning service also provides access to other ML services that share the same resources and assets through the ML workspace. This includes services such as Azure Automated Machine Learner, the Azure Machine Learning designer – the new GUI-based experience for Azure Machine Learning, a data labeling tool, and an integrated notebook server for Azure Machine Learning (not to be confused with the discontinued `https://notebooks.azure.com/` experience), which all can be created within a workspace in Azure Machine Learning. Therefore, Azure Machine Learning is sometimes referred to as the Azure Machine Learning service or the Azure Machine Learning workspace (`https://docs.microsoft.com/en-us/azure/machine-learning/concept-workspace`).

Knowing these subtle differences about the different terms and services for Azure Machine Learning, you are ready to learn more about the different managed and custom ML services in Azure.

Managed ML services

If you are dealing with a well-defined general-purpose ML problem in the domain of text, image, video, language, or documents, then the chances are high that Azure already provides a managed ML service for this problem.

Managed ML services are very easy to use, quick to embed into an application, and usually don't require any operational overhead. This makes them perfect for creating AI-based applications or features without the need for collecting training data, training models, and operating model deployments in production. Most importantly, managed ML services don't require any ML expertise to build ML-based applications.

Some examples of well-defined ML problems are image classification, image tagging, object detection, face detection, handwriting recognition, speech-to-text and text-to-speech conversion, speaker recognition, translation, spell-checking, keywords and entity extraction, sentiment analysis, adult content filtering, and document parsing.

Managed ML services are usually used with pre-trained models that sometimes can be trained or fine-tuned for a specific application domain. Using customized models in managed ML services combines the benefits of managed services with the flexibility of custom application domains.

In this section, we will look into Azure Cognitive Services, customizable AI services, and Azure Applied AI Services.

Azure Cognitive Services

Let's start with Azure's most popular service for managed AI capabilities, Azure Cognitive Services. **Azure Cognitive Services** is a collection of APIs containing multiple pre-trained ML models for well-defined common problems across the following categories – vision, language, speech, and decision.

Azure Cognitive Services models are very easy to use and can be integrated by a single REST API call from within any programming language. This makes Cognitive Services a popular choice for adding ML capabilities to existing applications. Some examples of popular Cognitive Services are the following:

- *Vision*: Computer Vision and Face API
- *Language*: Text analytics and translator service
- *Speech*: Text analytics, speech-to-text, text-to-speech, and speech translation
- *Decision*: Anomaly detection and content moderation

Most of the Cognitive Services APIs work very similarly. You first deploy a specific Cognitive Service (for example, Computer Vision and text analytics) or a Cognitive Services multi-service account in Azure. Once the service is deployed, you can retrieve the API endpoint and access key from the service and call the Cognitive Service API with your data and API key. This is all you have to do to enrich an existing application with AI capabilities.

To give you a taste of how these services are used, we will walk you through an example of the Cognitive Service for Computer Vision. We will embed the functionality in a simple Python application. The following code is an example for calling the Cognitive Services API for computer vision. We will use the Analyze Image API with the free F0 tier to extract categories, tags, and a description from a sample image. Let's start with some setup code so that we can later use the `requests` library and fetch predictions from the Cognitive Services API:

```python
import requests

region='eastus2'
language='en'
version='v3.1'
key = '<insert access key>'

url = f"https://{region}.api.cognitive.microsoft.com" \
    + f"/vision/{version}/analyze"
```

In the previous code snippet, we defined the region, language, API version, and access key for the Cognitive Services API. You can find these details on the **Service overview** or **Properties** tab in the Azure portal. We will use these components to build the service endpoint. Next, let's define the parameters for the API call, including a URL to an image of the Eiffel Tower:

```python
params = {
    'visualFeatures': 'Categories,Tags,Description',
    'language': language
}
headers = {
    'Content-Type': 'application/json',
    'Ocp-Apim-Subscription-Key': key
}
payload = {
    'url': 'https://../Eiffel_Tower.jpg'
}
```

The only thing that is left is calling requests with all the parameters and the image URL. We get back a JSON response containing the scores of multiple models:

```
response = requests.post(url,
                         json=payload,
                         params=params,
                         headers=headers)
result = response.json()
print(result)
```

As you can see in the preceding code example, using Cognitive Services boils down to sending an HTTP request. In Python, this is straightforward, using the requests library. The response body contains standard JSON and encodes the results of the Cognitive Services API. The resulting JSON output from the API will have the following structure:

```
{
    "categories": [...],
    "tags": [...],
    "description": {...},
    "requestId": "...",
    "metadata": {
        "width": 288,
        "height": 480,
        "format": "Jpeg"
    }
}
```

The categories key contains object categories and derived classifications, such as a landmark detection result, including a confidence score. In the example of the Eiffel Tower image, the Cognitive Service detected a building with a score of almost 95% and identified it as a landmark with almost 100% confidence:

```
"categories": [
    {
        "name": "building_",
        "score": 0.9453125,
        "detail": {
            "landmarks": [
                {
                    "name": "Eiffel Tower",
```

```
                    "confidence":  0.99992179870605469
              }
         ]
     }
 }
]
```

The `tags` key shows you multiple tags that are relevant for the whole image. In addition, each tag comes with a confidence score. As we can see in the response of the API, the model is confident that the picture was taken outdoors:

```
"tags": [
    {
        "name": "outdoor",
        "confidence": 0.99838995933532715
    },
    {
        "name": "tower",
        "confidence": 0.63238395233132431
    }, ...
]
```

Finally, the `description` tag gives you more tags and an auto-generated image caption. This is cool, isn't it? Imagine how fast you could implement a tag-based image search by simply extracting image tags using Azure Cognitive Services and indexing the tags for each image URL:

```
"description": {
    "tags": [
        "outdoor", "building", "tower", ...
    ],
    "captions": [
        {
            "text": "a large clock tower in the background with
Eiffel Tower in the background",
            "confidence": 0.74846089195278742
        }
    ]
}
```

The result of the Cognitive Services computer vision API is just one example of how this service can be used. We requested the image features of categories, tags, and description from the API, which are returned as keys of the JSON object. Each of the category and tag predictions returns the top results in combination with a confidence value. Some categories might trigger other detection models, such as faces, handwritten text recognition, and OCR.

> **Important Note**
>
> You can explore and test many of the other Azure Cognitive Services APIs by visiting the respective service websites. Here are a few examples:
>
> https://azure.microsoft.com/en-us/services/
> cognitive-services/computer-vision/
>
> https://azure.microsoft.com/en-us/services/
> cognitive-services/language-service/
>
> https://azure.microsoft.com/en-us/services/
> cognitive-services/speech-to-text/

Using the preceding example, calling Azure Cognitive Service with `requests`, you can implement a method that automatically adds image captions to your product images in a retail application by wrapping the preceding snippet in an `analyze()` method and applying it to all images in your dataset:

```
for url in product_image_urls:
    res = analyze(url, key, features=['Description'])
    caption = res['description']['captions'][0]['text']
    print(caption)
```

You can see that this is the quickest way to integrate a scalable deep learning-based image analysis service (such as creating a caption for an image) into your custom application. If you find this interesting, it is time to also experiment with the other Cognitive Services APIs.

All Azure Cognitive Services have one thing in common – they use a pre-trained black-box ML model to perform predictions of the individual ML tasks. This is fine when we are dealing with faces or photos but can be problematic when dealing with a specific application domain, such as medical images. In this case, you will be delighted to hear that you can fine-tune some of the Cognitive Services for your custom application domain by providing custom training data. Let's take a closer look at these customizable services in the next section.

Custom Cognitive Services

One major downside with Cognitive Services is that you can only use the functionalities that are provided by the API. This means you can't customize the labels or tags in the image classification API or, for example, use the model to classify different types of materials. To do so, you would need to customize the model in the Cognitive Services API – and this is exactly what some **custom Cognitive Services** allow you to do.

Here is a list of popular customizable Cognitive Service APIs that can be fine-tuned to a specific application domain using your own training data:

- *Vision*: Azure Custom Vision
- *Language*: Language Understanding and QnA Maker
- *Speech*: Custom speech-to-text
- *Speech*: Custom text-to-speech
- *Speech*: Speaker recognition
- *Decision*: Azure Personalizer

Each of the preceding services provides an interface to train or customize a built-in ML model with your own domain-specific training data. We won't go into details for each of these services in this book but rather look at two examples of these customizable Cognitive Services – Azure Personalizer and Custom Vision. Azure Personalizer is an interesting service that lets you optimize an online recommendation engine through reinforcement learning. We will take a closer look at Azure Personalizer in *Chapter 13, Building a Recommendation Engine in Azure*, and compare it to other state-of-the-art recommendation systems.

Let's look into the Azure Custom Vision service as an example of a customizable managed AI service in Azure in this chapter. Azure Custom Vision lets you fine-tune a pre-trained ML model on your own training data. This process is called transfer learning and is often used in ML to transfer previously learned feature extraction capabilities to a new objective or domain.

Azure Custom Vision provides a UI to upload and classify your images (or tag your objects) and subsequently train the model, using a state-of-the-art computer vision model through the press of a button. *Figure 2.3* shows the finished training for an object detection model in the Azure Custom Vision service:

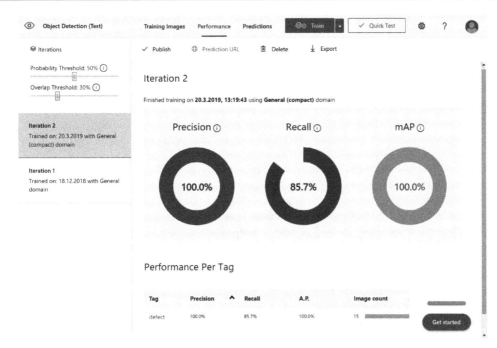

Figure 2.3 – Azure Custom Vision training results

You can see in the preceding figure that training is as easy as clicking the **Train** button with the **Quick Test** option enabled at the top right, or customizing the training process using the advanced option. You don't have to write any code or select an error metric to be optimized; it's all managed for you. In the screenshot, you can see the result of training, with three metrics that are automatically computed on a validation set. By moving the classification probability threshold at the top left, you can even shift the weight toward higher precision or higher recall, depending on whether you want to avoid false positives or maximize true positives.

This gives you the power of a pre-trained managed Cognitive Service with the flexibility of a custom application domain. Once the model is trained and published, it can be consumed using a REST API as we did with Cognitive Services. Click the **Prediction URL** button at the top to retrieve the prediction endpoint and parameters. The following code block is a sample snippet for Python using the `requests` library:

```
import requests

def score(img_url, key, project_id, iteration_name):
    endpoint = 'https://%s.api.cognitive.microsoft.com' \
        + '/customvision/v3.0/Prediction/%s' \
        + '/detect/iterations/%s/url' \
```

```
        % (region, project_id, iteration_name)
    headers = {
        'Content-Type': 'application/json',
        'Prediction-Key': key
    }
    payload = { 'url': img_url }

    r = requests.post(url, json=payload, headers=headers)
    return r.json()
```

In the preceding code, we implement a function that looks very similar to the one we used with Cognitive Services. In fact, only the endpoints and `requests` parameter have changed. We can now call the function as before:

```
url = 'https://../Material_Experiment_1.jpg'
key = '<insert api key>'
project_id = '<insert project key>'
iteration_name = 'Iteration2'
res = score(url, key, project_id, iteration_name)
print(res)
```

The response is also a JSON object and now looks like the following:

```
{
    "Id":"7796df8e-acbc-45fc-90b4-1b0c81b73639",
    "Project":"00ae2d88-a767-4ff6-ba5f-33cdf4817c44",
    "Iteration":"59ec199d-f3fb-443a-b708-4bca79e1b7f7",
    "Created":"2019-03-20T16:47:31.322Z",
    "Predictions":[
        {
            "TagId":"d9cb3fa5-1ff3-4e98-8d47-2ef42d7fb373",
            "TagName":"defect",
            "Probability":1.0
        },
        {
            "TagId":"9a8d63fb-b6ed-4462-bcff-77ff72084d99",
            "TagName":"defect",
            "Probability":0.1087869
```

```
        }
    ]
}
```

The preceding response now contains a `Predictions` key with all the predicted categories and confidence values from Custom Vision. As you can see, the example looks very similar to the Cognitive Services example. However, we need to pass arguments to specify the project and published iteration of the trained model. Using this built-in serving API, we save ourselves a lot of effort in implementing and operating a deployment infrastructure. If we want to use the trained model somewhere else (for example, in an iPhone or Android application, or in a Kubernetes cluster), we can export the model in many different formats, such as TensorFlow, TensorFlow.js, Core ML, and ONNX.

Custom Cognitive Services are a fantastic way to efficiently test or showcase an ML model for a custom application domain when dealing with a well-defined ML problem. You can use either the GUI or API to interact with these services and consume the models through a managed API or export them to any device platform. Another benefit is that you don't need deep ML expertise to apply the transfer learning algorithm and can simply use the predefined models and error metrics.

Azure Applied AI Services

In the previous sections, we saw examples for Azure Cognitive Services for both fully pre-trained models and for customizable models. In this section, we will extend the list of customizable managed AI services to all services grouped under the name **Azure Applied AI Services**. These Applied AI Services are – like custom Cognitive Services – pre-trained customizable AI services loosely grouped under a common name to build specialized services.

These Applied AI Services are all services that have been developed by Microsoft on top of Cognitive Services due to strong demand from large enterprise customers for these exact services. The following services are currently part of Applied AI Services, but unlike Cognitive Services, they don't fit neatly into categories. Here is a list of Applied AI Services that you can use to build your own custom models for specific applications:

- *Conversations*: Azure Bot Service

- *Documents*: Azure Form Recognizer

- *Search*: Azure Cognitive Search

- *Monitoring*: Azure Metrics Advisor

- *Videos*: Azure Video Analyzer

- *Accessibility*: Azure Immersive Reader

We will not go into much detail about every service in this list, but we encourage you to look into them in more detail if some of them made you curious. You can find detailed information and examples in the Azure documentation (`https://docs.microsoft.com/en-us/azure/applied-ai-services/`) or the Azure product page for Applied AI Services (`https://azure.microsoft.com/en-us/product-categories/applied-ai-services`). Both Azure Form Recognizer and Azure Cognitive Search use the Cognitive Service image APIs to extract text and handwritten notes from documents. While the former helps you to parse this data from structured documents, the latter creates a search index on all extracted data and provides a full-text search over unstructured documents, including handwritten documents.

As you can see, if you have these exact same problems, then it is easy to use these Applied AI Services and integrate them into your application. While the application domain is limited, you can greatly accelerate any project that deals with these use cases.

If you require full customization of the algorithms, models, and error metrics, you need to implement the model and ML pipeline on your own. In the following sections, we will discuss how this can be done in Azure using custom ML services.

Custom ML services

Azure provides many PaaS services for different specialized domains. Platform services are built on top of IaaS services and implement useful abstractions and functionalities commonly used for the relevant domain. One such domain is ML, where you will find various services for building custom ML models. In this section, we will take a look at the most popular custom ML PaaS services.

We will start first with the GUI-based solutions Azure Machine Learning Studio (classic) and Azure Machine Learning designer, and then switch to the GUI and API-based Azure Automated Machine Learning. Finally, we will take a look at Azure Machine Learning, the service that provides the workspaces for resources and assets for both previous services.

Azure Machine Learning will help us to create notebook instances for authoring, train clusters for training, upload and register datasets, track experiments and trained models, as well as to track our Conda/PIP environments and Docker images.

Azure Machine Learning Studio (classic)

Azure Machine Learning Studio (classic) is a widely adopted tool in Azure to build, train, optimize, and deploy ML models using a GUI and drag and drop, block-based programming model. It's one of the oldest managed cloud services for ML in Azure and provides a robust and large number of features, algorithms, and extensions through R and Python support. The service provides built-in building blocks for clustering, regression, classification, anomaly detection, and recommendation, as well as data and statistical and text analysis. You can also extend the functionality of Azure Machine Learning Studio by using custom code blocks for Python or R.

> **Important Note**
>
> Azure Machine Learning Studio (classic) will be retired by August 31, 2024, and customers will have to transition to Azure Machine Learning. Therefore, we strongly recommend starting any new projects in Azure Machine Learning.

Figure 2.4 shows an overview of the main drag and drop GUI of Azure Machine Learning Studio (classic):

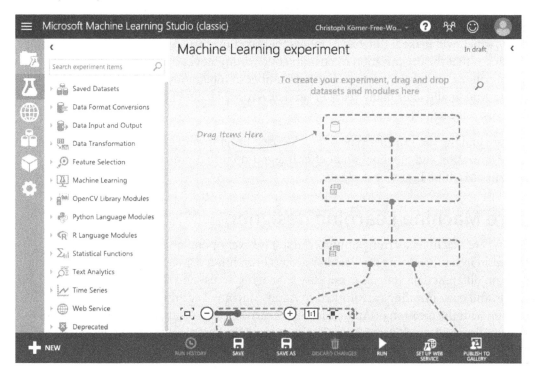

Figure 2.4 – Azure Machine Learning Studio (classic)

Functional blocks can be chosen from the catalog on the left, dropped onto the canvas on the right, and connected to form a complex computational graph. Each block can define input and output data, which is passed along through the connections from other blocks.

Azure Machine Learning Studio (classic) lets you import data from many different sources, such as CSV files from Azure Blob storage or direct imports from SQL Server, Azure Cosmos DB, or Apache Hive. It also provides many built-in blocks for the conversion of common data formats and data types, normalization, and cleaning.

One of the reasons why Azure Machine Learning Studio (classic) was very popular lies in its deployment capabilities. If you have created a data pipeline and trained a model, you can save the trained model within Machine Learning Studio (classic). Now, within a few clicks, you can create a web service using the trained model to deploy a scoring service. The user input is defined through the very same data import block that was used for the training data. It can be connected to pipe user input to the pipeline or return the model predictions to the web service. With another click, you can deploy the pipeline to production using a web service plan.

While Azure Machine Learning Studio was a very popular GUI-based tool for building ML pipelines – and to build simple web-based ML applications – it is not the tool of choice for writing custom ML applications. The workspace can get convoluted very quickly, which will make it difficult to follow the data flow through the pipeline. Another drawback is that the organization of custom code within blocks becomes difficult for larger pipelines, and that there are a limited number of integrations into other Azure services. And finally, after many years in service, Azure Machine Learning (classic) will be discontinued by 2024.

If you are looking for a similar type of block-based programming, with better support for code organization and pipelines and better integration into Azure, then you should look into Azure Machine Learning designer.

Azure Machine Learning designer

While Azure Machine Learning Studio (classic) was very popular and feature-rich, its integration into other Azure services has always been limited. Ingesting and pre processing data from different data sources is not easy, managing access and sharing datasets is difficult, and customizations are limited to Azure Machine Learning Studio (classic). However, with the creation of Azure Machine Learning, Microsoft also revamped the old Studio and created a new version inside Azure Machine Learning called the designer.

Azure Machine Learning designer is fully integrated with Azure Machine Learning and therefore has access to and can share all resources and assets within the workspace. It allows the GUI-based creation of ML pipelines while collaborating with other data engineers and data scientists in the same workspace. They all can share the same compute resources that automatically scale up and down to the needs of the developers.

Figure 2.5 shows the UI of the designer, which is based on the same block-based, drag and drop UI as Azure Machine Learning Studio (classic):

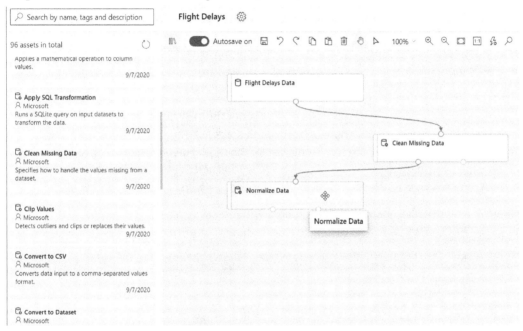

Figure 2.5 – The Azure Machine Learning designer UI

As you can see in the previous figure, creating ML processes through graphical dataflows still has the same disadvantages as discussed previously. However, we can at least share data ingestion, preprocessing, cleaning, and feature extraction stages with other users in the workspace and focus solely on ML tasks in the designer.

GUIs to create block-based ML training pipelines are not for everyone. However, if you prefer a block-based, drag and drop environment, then Azure Machine Learning designer is the right choice for you. On top, all your work is stored in the Azure Machine Learning workspace, which means you can easily extend or migrate parts of your GUI-based pipeline to a code-based version and vice versa. Overall, it's a good choice to start your ML project in Azure Machine Learning using the designer. However, if you want to build a scalable ML project that allows the collaboration of multiple teams, it's recommended to use a non-GUI service such as the Azure Machine Learning workspace, which we will use throughout this book.

Azure Automated Machine Learning

Every user should be given the possibility to create predictive models and turn conforming datasets into ML models. This is the democratization of AI, where every user who can use a spreadsheet application has the possibility to *create* ML models out of data in spreadsheets without any ML expertise.

This is where **Azure Automated Machine Learning** comes into play! Azure Automated Machine Learning is a no-code tool that lets you specify a dataset, a target column, and ML tasks to train an ML model from a spreadsheet. It is a great abstraction for a user who just wants to fit training data to a target variable without the knowledge about feature extraction, modeling, training, and optimization. Similar to Azure Machine Learning designer, Automated ML is a service that can be created from the Azure Machine Learning workspace and, therefore, has access to all resources and assets defined in the workspace.

It's worth noting that the typical spreadsheet user is not the only target group for using Automated ML to automatically train, optimize, and stack ML models. Automated ML is a natural extension of hyperparameter tuning, where the model architecture and preprocessing itself become hyperparameters. We will take a closer look at this field of application and its Python API in *Chapter 11*, *Hyperparameter Tuning and Automated Machine Learning*.

Figure 2.6 shows the last step in the Automated ML interface, where the user needs to choose the ML task to be solved for the specified data:

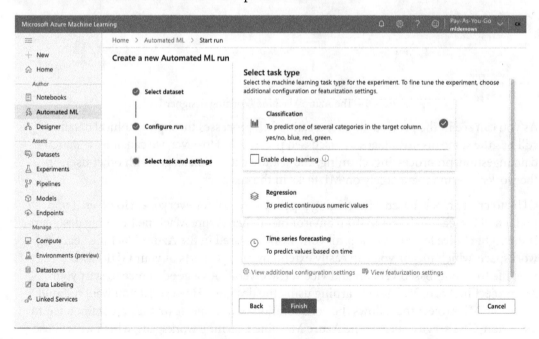

Figure 2.6 – Automated ML

As we can see in the previous figure, Automated Machine Learning currently supports classification, regression, and time-series forecasting tasks. Together with the informative explanations for each task, this is something we can put into the hands of Excel users and can help ML engineers to quickly build and deploy a great baseline model.

In addition, Automated Machine Learning gives you access to all training runs, all trained models, and their training scores, as well as useful built-in metrics, visualization, and insights. In *Figure 2.7*, we can see the ROC curve as one example of many built-in visualizations of the training runs:

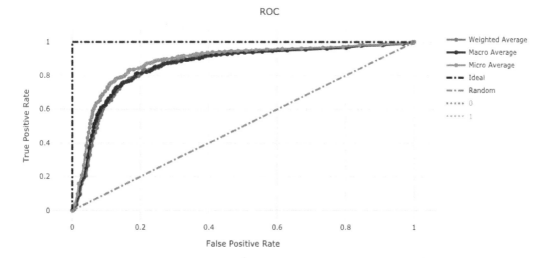

Figure 2.7 – The Receiver Operating Characteristic (ROC) curve for the Automated ML result

> **Important Note**
>
> Automated Machine Learning can also be accessed programmatically directly from your authoring environment through the Azure Machine Learning SDK. You can find more information about the Automated ML feature in the Azure Machine Learning Python SDK in the Microsoft documentation: `https://docs.microsoft.com/en-us/python/api/azureml-automl-core/azureml.automl.core?view=azure-ml-py`.

Automated Machine Learning is a great service, providing a true ML-as-a-service platform with a reasonable abstraction for non-experienced and highly skilled users. This service empowers every developer to take advantage of ML and will power the AI capabilities of future products.

Azure Machine Learning workspace

Azure Machine Learning is Azure's flagship ML service to implement and autornize all steps of the end-to-end ML process for building custom ML applications. It was initially built to combine all other ML services under a single workspace and facilitate the sharing of resources, assets, and permissions – therefore, is also often referred to as the Azure Machine Learning workspace.

Currently, Azure Machine Learning provides, combines, and abstracts many important ML infrastructure services and functionalities, such as tracking experiment runs and training jobs, a model registry, an environment and container registry based on conda/ pip and Docker, a dataset registry, pipelines, and compute and storage infrastructure. It also implements a common set of identities and permissions to facilitate access to these individual components from within the Azure workspace.

Besides all the infrastructure services, it also integrates Azure Automated Machine Learning, Azure Machine Learning designer (the new Azure Machine Learning Studio (classic)), and a data-labeling service in a single workspace. All the services in the workspace can access and share resources and assets. Azure Machine Learning provides many useful abstractions and functionalities to develop custom ML applications and has a great trade-off in flexibility, ease of use, and price. Therefore, it is also our service of choice for building custom ML solutions in Azure, and we will use it throughout this book.

Figure 2.8 shows Azure Machine Learning Studio, the UI of Azure Machine Learning. As mentioned previously, the name is not to be confused with Azure Machine Learning Studio (classic), which is the old GUI- and block-based ML service.

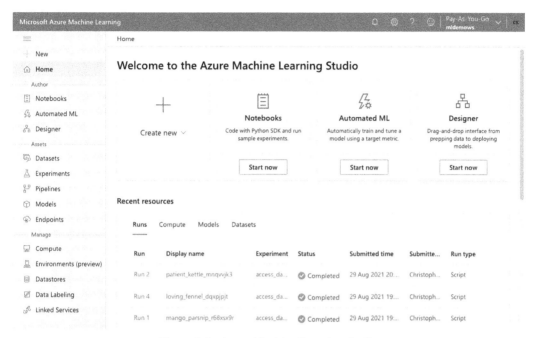

Figure 2.8 – Azure Machine Learning Studio

As you can see in the previous figure, we can manage different resources and assets in the Azure Machine Learning workspace. All these resources can not only be accessed through the UI but also through the SDK and the Azure Machine Learning CLI. Throughout this book, we will mostly use the Python SDK for Azure Machine Learning. You can find more information about the Azure Machine Learning Python SDK in the Microsoft documentation: `https://docs.microsoft.com/en-us/python/api/overview/azure/ml/?view=azure-ml-py`.

Throughout the book, we will use three types of compute resources for the different steps in the ML process. We can create these resources directly from within Azure Machine Learning with a couple of lines of code and the Azure Machine Learning SDK:

- **A compute instance for the authoring runtime and Jupyter**: This is a compute instance with pre-installed and pre-configured ML libraries and the Azure Machine Learning SDK optimized for authoring and experimentation.

- **A training cluster for the ML execution runtime during training**: This is an auto-scalable compute cluster with pre-installed and pre-configured ML libraries and the Azure Machine Learning SDK optimized for large- scale training and optimization.

- **An inferencing cluster for the execution runtime during scoring**: This is a managed Kubernetes cluster using Azure Kubernetes Service.

Besides compute, we will also use Azure Machine Learning to create storage resources that serve as storage for authoring and application code, job logs and output, visualization, trained models, dataset snapshots, and so on. We can use the ML SDK to manage Azure Blob storage containers in the ML workspace and to write the output and assets of jobs directly to the storage.

Besides managing infrastructure, Azure Machine Learning can do a lot more for us. Most importantly, it can track our experiment runs and collect output files, graphs, artifacts, logs, and custom metrics, such as training loss. This is also by far the most powerful gateway to enter the Azure Machine Learning platform.

By simply annotating your existing ML project, you can track all your model scores, stream your log output, collect all your output images, and store the best model for each iteration or run. All you need is a few simple lines of code to never lose track of a model for a particular training run ever again, or to keep track of your training scores, graphs, and artifacts. All this can be done without changing anything about your ML setup; your experiments can run on a local machine and your training runs can be scheduled on AWS.

Besides tracking job artifacts, you can also track dataset versions, environments, and models in Azure Machine Learning using only a few lines of code. This gives you the benefit of being able to keep a predictable history of changes in your workspace. By doing this, you can create repeatable experiments that always read the same data snapshot for a training run, use the same specified Conda or PIP environment, and update the trained model in the model history and artifact store. This brings you on track toward a **Continuous Integration/Continuous Deployment (CI/CD)** approach for your training pipeline. We will discuss this approach in more detail in *Chapter 16, Bringing Models into Production with MLOps*.

Speaking of pipelines, Azure Machine Learning lets you abstract your authoring code into pipelines. A pipeline can trigger or run data preparation jobs in parallel, create and start training clusters, execute a training script on the cluster, or initiate and perform blue/green deployments. You can see how everything guides you toward a repeatable, versioned, end-to-end pipeline for your training process. The greatest part, however, is that you don't have to go all in to benefit from Azure Machine Learning.

Instead, you can start little by little, adding more and more useful functionalities to your existing training process and then gradually move an existing or new ML project to the Azure Machine Learning workspace. You will get your feet wet and set up your Azure Machine Learning workspace in the next chapter. This will show you how easy it is to get started, to integrate with existing ML projects, and how to set up your authoring and training environment for new projects.

Azure Machine Learning is the best PaaS service for building custom ML applications in Azure. However, if you prefer tinkering with VMs, debugging distributed job executions, and setting up MPI for distributed training jobs, you should take a closer look at the next section, where will learn more about custom compute services commonly used for ML.

Custom compute services for ML

So far, we have had a look at services offering managed pre-trained ML models with and without some degree of customization, as well as custom ML services, including Azure Machine Learning. Azure Machine Learning is our service of choice for developing custom ML applications, due to the great trade-off between flexibility, functionality, and comfort.

However, we understand that these trade-offs might not work for everyone and that some people want the highest flexibility for building custom ML applications using only IaaS services. These are the same services that build the foundation for any other PaaS service in Azure, including Azure Machine Learning. Hence, as a final step, we will delve into options where you can use custom compute services in Azure to build flexible ML solutions.

Azure Databricks

Azure Databricks is a managed service on Azure, offering the Databricks platform as a completely integrated solution. Azure Databricks is, therefore, a so-called first-class citizen in Azure. This means, compared to other third-party solutions, a user can deploy from the Azure Marketplace, and it is fully integrated with Azure Active Directory, allowing Azure administrators to treat this service the same way as any other Microsoft managed service on the platform.

The Databricks platform itself is a big data analytics platform utilizing Apache Spark. The company behind this platform is also called Databricks (https://databricks.com/) and was founded by the original creators of Spark to offer this ever-changing open source technology as a ready-made product to customers.

To understand how to perform ML in Azure Databricks, we will first have a look at the underlying technology for distributed computing that powers all computation and processing – Apache Spark.

Distributed computing using Apache Spark

Apache Spark is a distributed in-memory analytical engine, taking its roots from the Apache Hadoop framework. The main idea behind it is to distribute a graph of computations to the cluster's worker nodes. Think of these nodes as different independent servers, possibly even in different physical locations, that all together work on the same job, or – to be more precise – on their own part of the job. They are, in turn, controlled and orchestrated by a primary node that keeps an eye on scheduling, resource availability, and wiring up data streams.

Figure 2.9 shows the most important components of Apache Spark. In the middle, we can see the main compute engine called Spark Core. Spark Core oversees job scheduling and monitoring, interaction with the underlying storage system, memory management on the nodes, and general fault tolerance for the overall cluster. For the scheduling, it either uses its own scheduler called **Spark Scheduler** or can run on other scheduling options, namely **Apache YARN** or **Apache Mesos**. When using Apache Spark in Azure Databricks, the job scheduling engine is part of the managed service and managed by Databricks:

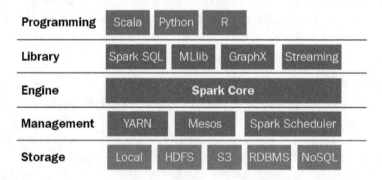

Figure 2.9 – The Apache Spark framework

As a storage system, it supports a myriad of options, from standard local storage and the **Hadoop Distributed File System** (**HDFS**) to Azure Data Lake and Amazon S3 storage, and even has direct access to **Relational Database Management Systems** (**RDBMS**) and documents from NoSQL systems.

Finally, to define and dispatch jobs, the end user can utilize different programming languages, such as Scala, Python and R, to define the computational graphs that will be executed via Apache Spark. In addition to all available libraries and frameworks, Apache Spark provides a few built-in libraries to facilitate both data access and manipulation via Spark SQL, as well as distributed computations via Spark Streaming, MLlib, and GraphX.

ML libraries for Azure Databricks

To train ML models on Spark and consequently on Azure Databricks, we require libraries that, on the one hand, implement the relevant ML algorithms and numerical functions and, on the other hand, understand the Spark framework to take advantage of the distributed computation primitives.

Apache Spark comes with such a built-in ML library called MLlib. This library is designed to implement traditional ML algorithms, such as different clustering and embedding techniques, logistic regression, random forest, gradient boosting, and **Alternating Least Squares (ALS)** matrix factorization for recommendations, while taking advantage of the distributed computation capabilities of Apache Spark.

Thanks to the supported languages, you can also use all other popular ML libraries in Apache Spark on Azure Databricks, such as TensorFlow, XGBoost, scikit-learn, PyTorch, Horovod, and many other well-known libraries (see `https://databricks.com/ product/machine-learning-runtime`).

Azure Databricks also supports MLflow, an open source framework for automating the end-to-end ML process, which we will see in action in *Chapter 16, Bringing Models into Production with MLOps*, as well as their own version of AutoML, and a notebook server.

However, large-scale distributed compute engines usually don't come without any downsides, and the same is true for Apache Spark and Databricks. While Databricks did a great job of hiding most of the complexity and made it easy to get up and running with Spark, the complexity is not gone. Monitoring jobs and utilized cluster resources, debugging, and optimizing jobs, as well as reading and understanding logs becomes very complex without in-depth knowledge about Spark.

Simply put, in addition to understanding machine learning processes and algorithms, the user also has to understand the internals of Spark and its distributed job scheduling and execution model. This adds another layer of complexity for running, debugging, and optimizing ML jobs, which makes the whole experience a lot more difficult.

Moreover, not all ML libraries and algorithms are easily capable of distributing the workload to different nodes, which often leads to suboptimal utilization of the cluster resources. Why use a complex framework for distributed computing and pay a premium for primary orchestration nodes when the underlying algorithms are executed on a single worker node?

Azure Databricks is a good choice when migrating on-premises Spark-based services to Azure, or building big data analytics, transformation, or recommendation services. However, it's complexity and premium price make it most often a poor choice for ML projects.

Azure Batch

Azure Batch is a very mature and flexible batch-processing and scheduling framework for running massive parallel workloads in Azure. It lets you define custom applications and jobs that can be scheduled and executed on a pool of VMs. It processes data stored in Azure Storage and can dynamically scale the compute resources for you to up to tens of thousands of VMs. **Azure Batch** is the foundation for Azure Machine Learning training clusters and, hence, is a great solution if you want to build your own custom ML service.

Azure Batch is usually used for *embarrassing parallel* workloads, namely work that can be easily parallelized across multiple machines without the need for any orchestration. This makes Azure Batch less flexible than Azure Databricks, which provides primitives for distributed coordination, but therefore is also less complicated for end users. Typical applications are computing 3D renderings, video and image processing, compute-intensive simulations, or general batch computations, such as computing recommendation results or batch-scoring ML models.

Batch jobs will be executed on compute pools or custom VMs, which means Azure Batch supports many *exotic* compute instances, including high-performance compute instances, memory-optimized and GPU-enabled VMs, just to name a few. It also supports multi-instance workloads using a **Message Passing Interface** (**MPI**) and **Remote Direct Memory Access** (**RDMA**).

If you are building your custom ML solution and want to avoid the comfort and flexibility of Azure Machine Learning, then Azure Batch is a great choice for you. It gives you all the flexibility to choose custom instances, frameworks, libraries, and data formats. However, Azure Machine Learning is – in almost every aspect – a better, easier, and more integrated solution, specifically for building ML applications.

Data Science Virtual Machines

It doesn't require a separate section to explain that you can use traditional VMs in Azure for building a custom cloud-based ML service on top of IaaS services. This would be as low-level as it gets within a cloud service, where you have full control over every network interface, disk configuration, and user permission on the VM. You can use any instance type available in your region that fits any of your memory, compute, or graphics needs and requirements.

However, if you are looking for a VM to be your cloud-based ML workstation – for example, to take advantage of flexible cloud compute, to run your ML experiments, or to perform on-demand GPU-accelerated training – there is a better choice than using a standard VM, namely **Data Science Virtual Machines** (**DSVMs**).

A DSVM is a pre-built pre-configured VM optimized for data science and ML applications. It comes with many of the popular ML libraries pre-installed and supports Windows and Linux. Pre-installed libraries and services include CUDA and cuDNN, NVIDIA drivers and system management interfaces (`nvidia-smi`), CRAN-R, Julia, Python, Jupyter, TensorFlow, PyTorch, Horovod, XGBoost, LightGBM, OpenCV, and ONNX. You can start a DSVM on many different instance types, including GPU-accelerated instances.

A DSVM is your service of choice whenever you need a carefree VM with your popular ML tools pre-installed and pre-configured. However, it is worth noting that you probably don't need a DSVM when working in an Azure Machine Learning workspace, as you can create compute instances and training clusters to run your ML experiments and training. Nevertheless, it's a great alternative ML experimentation environment.

Summary

In this chapter, you learned how to navigate the Azure AI landscape and choose the right ML service for your application and domain. While IaaS services give you great flexibility, PaaS services often provide useful abstractions and manage complex integrations for you. SaaS applications are great if they are designed for your application domain or can be customized.

We investigated Azure services for building ML applications in each of the preceding categories, such as Azure Cognitive Services (SaaS), Azure Machine Learning (PaaS), and Azure Batch (IaaS). Azure Machine Learning is not only the most comprehensive and integrated ML service in Azure but also provides a good trade-off between flexibility, functionality, and comfort. Therefore, we will use Azure Machine Learning throughout this book to develop an end-to-end custom ML solution.

If you really want to build your own ML infrastructure from scratch and not rely on any managed ML service, you should look into custom compute services that are optimized for large computational workloads, such as Azure Databricks or Azure Batch. If you simply need a VM ready for ML experiments without any pre-built service integrations or model and experiment tracking, you can choose a DSVM.

In the next chapter, we will continue our journey by setting up an Azure Machine Learning workspace. In order to do this, we will first learn how to deploy resources in Azure programmatically; we will then have an in-depth look at the ML workspace itself, at how we can use notebooks and incorporate compute nodes for model training, and finally, we will run our first little experiment.

3

Preparing the Azure Machine Learning Workspace

In the previous chapter, we learned how to navigate different Azure services for implementing ML solutions in the cloud. We realized that the best service for training custom ML models programmatically and automating infrastructure and deployments is the Azure Machine Learning service. In this chapter, we will set up and explore the Azure Machine Learning workspace, create a cloud training cluster, and perform data experimentation locally and on cloud compute, while collecting all the artifacts of the ML runs in Azure Machine Learning.

In the first section, we will learn how to manage Azure resources using different tools such as the Azure **Command-Line Interface (CLI)**, the Azure SDKs, and **Azure Resource Manager (ARM)** templates. We will set up and explore the Azure CLI, as well as Azure Machine Learning extensions, and subsequently deploy an Azure Machine Learning workspace.

We will then look under the hood of Azure Machine Learning by exploring the resources that were deployed as part of Azure Machine Learning, such as the storage account, Azure Key Vault, Azure Application Insights, and Azure Container Registry. Following that, we will dive into Azure Machine Learning and explore the workspace to better understand the individual components.

Finally, in the last section, we will put all this knowledge into practice and run our first experiment with Azure Machine Learning. After setting up our environment, we will enhance a simple ML Keras training script to log metrics, logs, models, and code snapshots into Azure Machine Learning. We will then progress to schedule training runs on our local machine as well as on a training cluster in Azure.

By the end of this chapter, you will see all your successful training runs, metrics, and tracked models in your Azure Machine Learning workspace, and you will have a good understanding of Azure Machine Learning to start your ML journey.

The following are the topics that will be covered in this chapter:

- Deploying an Azure Machine Learning workspace
- Exploring the Azure Machine Learning service
- Running ML experiments with Azure Machine Learning

Technical requirements

In this chapter, we will use the following Python libraries and versions to perform and manage experiment runs on Azure Machine Learning:

- `azureml-core 1.34.0`
- `azureml-sdk 1.34.0`
- `azureml-widgets 1.34.0`
- `tensorflow 2.6.0`

You can run this code using either a local Python interpreter or a notebook environment hosted in Azure Machine Learning. However, some scripts need to be scheduled to execute in Azure.

All code examples in this chapter can be found in the GitHub repository for this book: `https://github.com/PacktPublishing/Mastering-Azure-Machine-Learning-Second-Edition/tree/main/chapter03`.

Deploying an Azure Machine Learning workspace

Before we can start delving deep into ML on Azure itself, we need to understand how to deploy an Azure Machine Learning workspace or Azure services in general, what tooling is supported, and which one of those we will use to work with throughout the book.

As a first step, we will require an Azure subscription.

If you are working in an organization and want to use your work account, you can go to portal.azure.com and log in with your work account. If the login works, you will land on the portal itself, and your work account is shown at the top right. This means that your company already has an **Azure Active Directory** (**AAD**) instance set up. In this case, talk to your Azure Global Administrator, if you haven't already, to discuss which Azure subscription to use for your purpose.

If you are new to Azure and want to use your private account, go to azure.com and click on **Free Account** to create an AAD for yourself with a free trial subscription. This trial gives you a certain amount of money to spend for 30 days on Azure services.

In any case, in the end, you should have the capability to log in to the Azure portal with your identity, and you should know which Azure subscription (name and/or subscription ID) you want to deploy your ML services to.

With this all done, we will now have a look at how to deploy and manage our Azure environment in general and what options and tooling there are to choose from.

Understanding the available tooling for Azure deployments

In Azure, any action that deploys or changes an Azure service goes through the so-called ARM. As shown in *Figure 3.1*, ARM accepts requests from either the **Azure portal**, **Azure PowerShell** (a PowerShell extension), the **Azure CLI**, or the **Azure REST API**:

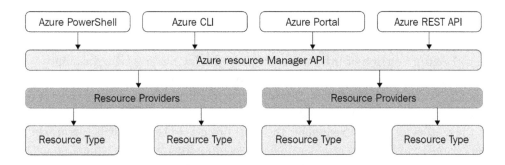

Figure 3.1 – Azure Resource Manager

In the Azure portal, you can select **Create a resource** from the left-hand menu to deploy any service or Marketplace image to your subscription. If you search for `machine learning`, the set of results set will show a service called **Machine Learning** from Microsoft. Clicking on this card and then **Create** will open the deployment wizard for this service. This will give you a sense of what is required to deploy this service.

But we will not go any further on the portal itself, as we want to facilitate a more programmatic approach in this book. Using this approach will greatly enable the reproducibility and automation of all the tasks performed in Azure. Therefore, we will concentrate on the latter solutions – let's take a look at them:

- **Azure CLI**: This is a fully fledged command-line environment that you can install on every major operating system. The latest version can be downloaded from `https://docs.microsoft.com/en-us/cli/azure/install-azure-cli`.

- **Azure Power Shell**: As the name suggests, this is a library of PowerShell modules, which can be added to a PowerShell environment. Previously, PowerShell was only available on Windows, but the new PowerShell Core 7.x now officially supports the major Linux releases and macOS. The following description shows how to install it on your system: `https://docs.microsoft.com/en-us/powershell/azure/install-az-ps`.

- **Azure REST API**: This is available to call ARM through REST, which allows you to manage Azure resources through `curl` or the popular Python `requests` library. The following article describes the given syntax: `https://docs.microsoft.com/en-us/rest/api/resources/`.

All of these options allow the use of so-called **ARM templates** (`https://docs.microsoft.com/en-us/azure/azure-resource-manager/templates/overview`), Azure's version of **Infrastructure as Code (IaC)**. It gives you the ability to save and version-control infrastructure definitions in files. This way is highly recommended when dealing with complex infrastructure deployment, but we will not dive any further into this topic. The only additional point to make here is that there are other tools on the market for IaC management. The most prominent tool is called **Terraform** (`https://www.terraform.io/`), which allows infrastructure management of any cloud vendor or on-premises environment, including Azure. To achieve this, Terraform utilizes the Azure CLI under the hood.

In summary, you can choose any of the aforementioned options for the tasks at hand, especially if you have a strong preference for one of them.

As we will not manage complex infrastructure and want to avoid any unnecessary additional levels of complexity, we will utilize the Azure CLI throughout the rest of the book. Furthermore, the new ML CLI extension offers a couple of neat features for Azure Machine Learning, which we will discover throughout the chapter:

```
PS C:\> az


       /\
      /  \    _____   _ _  ___ _
     / /\ \  |_  / | | | '__/ _ \
    / ____ \  / /| |_| | | |  __/
   /_/    \_\/___|\__,_|_|  \___|


Welcome to the cool new Azure CLI!

Use `az --version` to display the current version.
Here are the base commands:

    account            : Manage Azure subscription information.
    acr                : Manage private registries with Azure Container Registries.
    ad                 : Manage Azure Active Directory Graph entities needed for Role Based Access
                         Control.
    advisor            : Manage Azure Advisor.
    afd                : Manage Azure Front Door.
    aks                : Manage Azure Kubernetes Services.
    ams                : Manage Azure Media Services resources.
    apim               : Manage Azure API Management services.
    appconfig          : Manage App Configurations.
    appservice         : Manage App Service plans.
    aro                : Manage Azure Red Hat OpenShift clusters.
    backup             : Manage Azure Backups.
    batch              : Manage Azure Batch.
```

Figure 3.2 – The Azure CLI

If you haven't already, please feel free to download and install or update the CLI with the latest version. When you are ready, open your favorite command line or terminal and type `az` into the console. You should be greeted by the screen shown in *Figure 3.2*.

Deploying the workspace

After this short introduction to ARM, let's deploy our first ML workspace. We will deploy a workspace using the Azure CLI. If you would like to rather deploy it via the Azure portal, you can follow this tutorial: `https://docs.microsoft.com/en-us/azure/machine-learning/quickstart-create-resources`.

If you had a short look through the list of commands in the CLI, you might have noticed that there seems to be no command referencing ML. Let's rectify this and set up our first Azure Machine Learning workspace via the CLI following these steps:

1. Log in to your Azure environment through the CLI:

    ```
    $ az login
    ```

    This command will open a website with an AAD login screen. After you have done this, return to the console. The screen will now show you some information about your AAD tenant (homeTenantId), your subscriptions (id, name), and your user.

2. If you have more than one subscription shown to you and need to check which subscription is active, use the following command:

    ```
    $ az account show --output table
    ```

    In the output, check whether the IsDefault column shows True for your preferred subscription. If not, use the following command to set it to your chosen one by typing in the name of it – <yoursub> – and checking again:

    ```
    $ az account set --subscription "<yoursub>"
    ```

3. Now that we are deploying to the correct subscription in the correct tenant, let's check the situation with the installed extension. Type in the following command in your terminal:

    ```
    $ az extension list
    ```

    If neither azure-cli-ml nor ml is shown in the list, you are missing an extension for using Azure Machine Learning via the CLI. The first of them denotes Azure ML CLI 1.0, the second one Azure ML CLI 2.0. Version 2 of the ML CLI was announced at Microsoft Build 2021 (https://techcommunity.microsoft.com/t5/azure-ai/announcing-the-new-cli-and-arm-rest-apis-for-azure-machine/ba-p/2393447), offering fine-grained control of the ML workspace. Therefore, we will be using the new version of the CLI extension.

    > **Important Note**
    > Azure ML CLI 2.0 offers new abilities to directly control the jobs, clusters, and pipelines of the ML workspace from the command line. It also offers support for YAML configuration files, which are crucial for MLOps.

4. If you are running the old version, you should remove that version, but be aware that, as some commands are slightly different, you might break a script you are already using. To clean up the namespace and remove the previous version, you can use the following commands:

    ```
    $ az extension remove -n azure-cli-ml
    $ az extension remove -n ml
    ```

5. Let's install the ML extension using the following command:

    ```
    $ az extension add -n ml
    ```

    After that, feel free to check the installed extensions again.

6. Now, we will be able to use it. First off, we will have a look at the help page for the extension:

    ```
    $ az ml -h
    ```

    This will show you the following subgroups:

    ```
    code: Manage Azure ML code assets.
    compute: Manage Azure ML compute resources.
    data: Manage Azure ML data assets.
    datastore: Manage Azure ML datastores.
    endpoint: Manage Azure ML endpoints.
    environment: Manage Azure ML environments.
    job: Manage Azure ML jobs.
    model: Manage Azure ML models.
    workspace: Manage Azure ML workspaces.
    ```

    As you can see, we have a lot of options to control our workspace from the CLI. We will come back to many of them later in the book. For now, we are interested in managing our workspace.

7. If you type the following command, we will have a look to see whether we are still missing requirements for the creation of the ML workspace:

    ```
    $ az ml workspace create -h
    ```

    Going through the arguments, you will see that a **resource group** is required. A resource group in Azure is a logical construct where resources need to be deployed to. It is one vital part of the **Azure management hierarchy**. For further reading, have a look at access management in Azure: https://docs.microsoft.com/en-us/azure/cloud-adoption-framework/ready/azure-setup-guide/organize-resources.

Furthermore, if you scroll down to the examples in the console output, you will also see that the new version of the CLI has a neat property that lets us deploy the workspace from a **Yet Another Markup Language** (**YAML**) file. We will not do this now, but it is something to keep in mind.

> **Important Note**
> The Azure Machine Learning service can be completely operated using the Azure ML CLI 2.0 extension, YAML configuration files, and a training or inference script.

8. A resource group in Azure also requires a location. Therefore, let's have a look at the available data center locations for the Azure cloud by running this command:

```
$ az account list-locations -o table
```

Have a look at the name of your preferred region and use it in the following command to create the resource group. Our example here will create a resource group in West US 2 with the name mldemo:

```
$ az group create -n mldemo -l westus2
```

> **Important Note**
> Even though we define the resource group to be in West US 2, resources inside a resource group can be in different regions. It is just best practice to define a group in a specific region and let the resources inside that group be in the same region.

9. Now, we can create the workspace itself by using the following command:

```
$ az ml workspace create -w mldemows -g mldemo -l westus2
```

This will create a workspace named mldemows in the mldemo resource group. If we remove the location setting, it will take the location of the resource group.

This command can take a bit of time. When it is done, you will see output like this:

```
AppInsights  Done (7s)
StorageAccount ...  Done (31s)
KeyVault  Done (23s)
Workspace ..............  Done (1m 49s)
Total time : 2m 26s
{
```

```
  "application_insights": "/subscriptions/... ",
  "description": "mldemows",
  "discovery_url":"https://westus2.api.azureml.ms/
  discovery",
  "friendly_name": "mldemows",
  "hbi_workspace": false,
  "key_vault": "/subscriptions/... ",
  "location": "westus2",
  "mlflow_tracking_uri": "azureml://westus2.api.azureml.ms/
  mlflow/v1.0/subscriptions/... ",
  "name": "mldemows",
  "storage_account": "/subscriptions/... ",
  "tags": {}
  }
```

As you can see, the preceding command created multiple resources, together with the Azure Machine Learning workspace, that are required for running ML experiments. We will come back to the reasons in the next section.

10. Finally, to have a look at the deployment at any point, you can run the following command:

```
$ az ml workspace show -g mldemo -w mldemows
```

We have created our first Azure Machine Learning workspace. Good work! In the next section, we will have a look at what this entails.

Exploring the Azure Machine Learning service

Before we continue to set up our own development environment and do some ML, we will have a look at what was just deployed besides the main workspace, get a base understanding of all features available in the service, which we will utilize throughout the book, and have a first short look at **Azure Machine Learning Studio**.

Analyzing the deployed services

We will start by navigating to the Azure portal again. There, type the name of the workspace as `mldemows` in the top search bar. You should see something like the result shown in *Figure 3.3*:

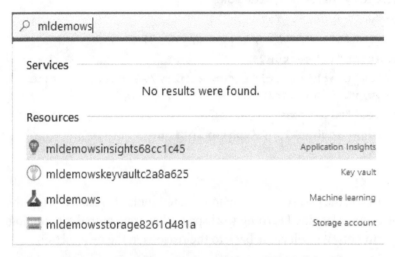

Figure 3.3 – An Azure portal search for an ML workspace

As you can see, besides the main `mldemows` workspace, three other services were deployed, namely **Storage account**, **Key vault**, and **Application Insights**. As most of them require unique names, you will see a random alphanumeric code at the end of each name. For each one of these additional services, we can provide our own already existing service when we deploy the workspace.

In addition, an **Azure container registry** will be required at a later stage but does not need to be there during the initial deployment of the workspace.

Knowing now what additional services were deployed, let's discuss why they are there.

The storage account for an ML workspace

The storage account, typically referred to as the **default storage account**, is the main datastore for the workspace. This storage is vital for the operation of the service. It stores among other things experiment runs, models, snapshots, and even source files, such as Jupyter notebooks. We will have a more in-depth look at default workspace storage, many other datastores in and around Azure, and how they can be integrated in *Chapter 4, Ingesting Data and Managing Datasets*.

> **Important Note**
>
> Be aware that if you would want to use your own storage account as default storage when deploying the workspace, it cannot have a hierarchical namespace (Azure Data Lake) and it cannot be premium storage (high-performant SSDs).

Azure Key Vault for an ML workspace

Key Vault is a cloud-managed service that can store *secrets* such as passwords, API keys, certificates, and cryptographic keys. Secrets in the service are held either in a software vault or a managed **Hardware Security Module** (**HSM**). For the ML workspace, and any other service for that matter, it is crucial to store your access keys in a secure environment.

So far, we have only handled relatively unimportant information such as a subscription ID, but if we want, for example, to pull data from external storage, we will either need a key to access it or call a function to another service, where this information is stored securely. You can be the judge of what is the better choice.

The developers of the ML workspace chose the latter options. Due to that, an Azure key vault is required to store the internal secrets for the workspace and give you the possibility to store any secret necessary to read out datasets, perform ML training on compute targets, and deploy your final models to internal or external targets.

Now, the question might arise of how to get secure access to Key Vault itself. This is done through a so-called **managed identity**, which gives the workspace (the app) itself an identity to assign rights to.

> **Managed Identities on Azure**
>
> A managed identity is an identity given to an application that behaves the same way as a user identity.

As with the other services, you could have linked an already existing key vault during deployment without any restrictions.

Application Insights for an ML workspace

Applications Insights is a module of **Azure Monitor**, which in turn is a suite in Azure to monitor infrastructure and applications, which stores and surfaces infrastructure metrics such as CPU usage and log files of applications.

The Azure Machine Learning workspace uses Application Insights to store compute infrastructure logs, ML script logs, and defined metrics of the ML model runs and is therefore required for the operation of the workspace.

Azure Container Registry for an ML workspace

Azure Container Registry (ACR) is a service based on the **Docker Registry**. It is used to store and manage Docker container images and artifacts. For the workspace, the registry is required at the point when we start running training on or deploying models to a compute that is not our local machine. In this process, a container is packed and registered to ACR, which then can be tracked and utilized in ML scripts or by deployment pipelines.

> **Important Note**
> Please be aware that the ML service by default deploys ACR in the basic service tier. To reduce the time for building and deploying an image to a compute target, you might want to change the Container Registry service level to Standard or Premium.

Understanding the workspace interior

Now that we understand the additional deployed service, we will have a look at the interior of the workspace itself. *Figure 3.4* shows nearly every aspect of note of an Azure Machine Learning workspace:

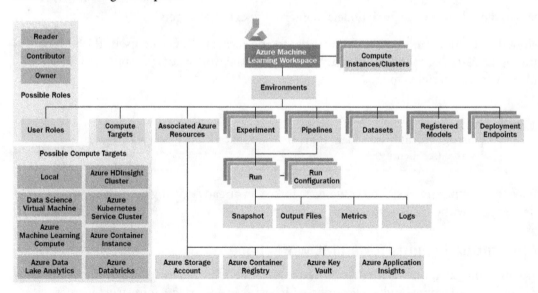

Figure 3.4 – A structural view of an Azure Machine Learning workspace

Let's get an understanding of each of these aspects, except for **Associated Azure resources**, as we already discussed that in the *Analyzing the deployed services* section.

User roles

As with any other service in Azure, user authentication and authorization are performed through AAD and so-called **Azure Role-Based Access Control** (**Azure RBAC**).

Role-based Access Control on Azure

Azure RBAC is used to assign to an identity from AAD (a user, a service principal, or a managed identity) a specific role on a resource, which defines the level of access to the resource and the type of granular action that can be performed.

In the case of the ML workspace, we can assign an identity the Azure predefined base roles (**Owner**, **Contributor**, or **Reader**) and two custom roles named **AzureML Data Scientist** and **AzureML Metrics Writer**. Here are their details:

- **Reader**: This role is allowed to look at everything but cannot change any data or action anything that would change the state of the resource (for example, deploying a compute or changing a network configuration).

- **Contributor**: This role is allowed to look at and change everything but is not allowed to change the user roles and rights on the resource.

- **Owner**: This role is allowed to do any action on a specific resource.

- **AzureML Data Scientist**: This role is not allowed any action in the workspace except creating or deleting compute resources or modifying the workspace settings.

- **AzureML Metrics Writer**: This role is only allowed to write metrics to the workspace.

Besides these, the ML workspace does not offer additional custom roles.

To give you more fine-grained control in this matter, RBAC lets you build your own custom roles, as a lot of actions a user can perform in the ML workspace are defined as so-called **actions** in RBAC. All available actions for the Azure Machine Learning service can be found in this list of resource providers, `https://docs.microsoft.com/en-us/azure/role-based-access-control/resource-provider-operations`, under the operation group named **Microsoft.MachineLearningServices**.

To get some inspiration for different roles, have a look at common scenarios and custom roles suggested by Microsoft: `https://docs.microsoft.com/en-us/azure/machine-learning/how-to-assign-roles#common-scenarios`. We will have a look in the next section where you can define and assign them.

Experiments

The goal of ML – in a nutshell – is to find a mathematical function, which would be hard to find algorithmically, that when given specific input results in as many cases as possible in the expected output. This function is typically referred to as an **ML model**. A model we train might be a function that assigns voices in a sound file to specific speakers or that recommends products for customers on a web shop based on the buying behavior of similar buyers (see *Chapter 13*, *Building a Recommendation Engine in Azure*).

To achieve this, we need to train ML models utilizing already existing ML algorithms, with the goal to lower the output of the so-called **loss function** of said model. This requires tweaking the settings of our models and, mathematically speaking, in the best case, finding the global minimum of the loss function on the n-dimensional room of all possible functions. Depending on the complexity of our model, this requires a lot of reiterations.

Therefore, to keep track of the iterations of our model training, we define them as **runs** and align them to a construct called an **experiment**, which collects all information concerning a specific model we want to train. To do this, we will connect any training script run we perform to a specific experiment.

Datasets and datastores

Any ML model requires data to operate with, either for training or for testing purposes. Instead of linking data sources and different data files directly in our scripts, we can reference **datasets**, which we can define inside the workspace. Datasets, in turn, curate data from **datastores**, which we can define and attach in the workspace. We will go into more detail on how to handle data, datasets, and datastores in *Chapter 4*, *Ingesting Data and Managing Datasets*.

Compute targets

In order to run experiments and, later on, host models for inferencing, we require a **compute target**. The ML service comes with two options in this area, namely the following:

- **Compute instance**: A single virtual machine typically used for development, as a notebook server, or as a target for training and inference
- **Compute cluster**: A multi-node cluster of machines typically used for complex training and production environments for inference

You can find a list of supported compute targets (virtual machines) here: `https://docs.microsoft.com/en-us/azure/machine-learning/concept-compute-target#supported-vm-series-and-sizes`. There are more details concerning their pricing in the following overview: `https://azure.microsoft.com/en-us/pricing/details/virtual-machines/linux/`.

Besides these two options, the workspace offers a bunch of other possible targets for both training and inferencing. Popular compute options are your own local computer, any type of Spark engine (**Apache Spark**, **Azure Databricks**, or **Synapse**) for training, and **Azure Kubernetes Service** (**AKS**) for inferencing. For a full updated list of options, refer to `https://docs.microsoft.com/en-us/azure/machine-learning/concept-compute-target`.

Environments

When you write a simple Python script and run it in the Python interpreter, you run it in a so-called **environment**. In this example, your environment would be defined by the Python version (for example, Python 3.8.10), specific library extensions you might have installed (for example, `numpy`), and certainly the operating system you are running it on. This is also true for any ML script that we run.

For our purpose, we operate in an environment that requires a specific Python version and certain libraries such as the Azure Machine Learning Python SDK and libraries containing ML algorithms and tooling, such as **TensorFlow**. For our own local machine, and especially if we want to run our script on a much faster compute cluster in the workspace, we need a good way to define the environment for the compute target.

To facilitate this, the workspace gives us the ability to define and register ML environments. These are typically **Docker containers** encompassing the OS and every runtime, library, and dependency required. For defining libraries and dependencies for Python inside the container, the package manager **Conda** (`https://conda.io/`) is used in most cases under the hood. Speaking of that, let's classify the types of environments we can work with or create:

- **Curated environments** use predefined environments containing typical runtimes and ML frameworks.

- **System-managed environments** (using default behavior) build environments starting from a base image with dependency management through Conda.

- **User-managed environments** build environments by either starting from a base image but allowing you to handle all libraries and dependencies yourself through Docker steps, or by creating a complete custom Docker image.

When we start our first experiments at the end of this chapter, we will see how to use environments in our ML runs.

> **Azure Machine Learning Environments**
>
> An environment in Azure Machine Learning is a Docker container encompassing an OS and any runtimes, libraries, and additional dependencies required.

We can conclude that we require a defined environment to run experiments on compute clusters in the workspace. For our local computer, on the other hand, we could just run on the *environment* we curated on the machine and ignore the ML workspace environments. But if we were to use the environment methods of the Azure Machine Learning Python SDK in our ML scripts, the run would require some type of defined environment. This can either be the given environment our machine exists in, a local Docker runtime, or a runtime powered by a Conda environment definition.

Runs

A **run** is the actual execution of a model training on a compute target. Before executing a run, it requires (in most cases) a so-called **run configuration**. This configuration is composed of the following:

- **A training script**: The training script that performs the actual ML training (which basically takes your source folder with all source files, zips it, and sends it to the compute target)

- **An environment**: The ML environment described previously

- **A compute target**: The target compute instance or cluster that the run will be executed in

We will see later in the chapter when we do our first experiments that there is a RunConfiguration class in the Azure Machine Learning Python library that needs to be used to execute the run.

> **Azure Machine Learning Experiment Runs**
>
> A run is the execution of a training script in a given environment on a specified compute target.

On top of that, during and after the execution of the run, it tracks and collects the following information:

- **Log files**: Includes the log files generated during the execution and any statement we add to the logging

- **Metrics**: Includes standard run metrics and any type of object (values, images, and tables) that we want to track specifically during the run

- **Snapshots**: Includes a copy of the source directory containing our training scripts (using the ZIP file that we already required for the run configuration)

- **Output files**: Includes the files generated by the algorithm (the model) and any file we additionally want to attach to the run

We will see later that we can utilize the Run class in the Azure Machine Learning Python library to influence what is tracked.

Registered models

As said before, the output of our experiment runs is an ML model. This model is basically a mathematical function or, to be more precise, a piece of code implementing a function. Depending on the ML framework we utilize, the function is stored in binary format in one or multiple output files found in the identically named folder. Popular formats for serialized ML models are **pickle** (Python), **H5** (Keras), **Protobuf** (TensorFlow and Caffe), and other custom formats.

As all models from different runs would *just* be stored in the output files of the run itself, the workspace offers the ability to register a model to the *model registry*. In the registry, the models are stored with a name and a version. Each time you add a model with the same name, the registry adds a new version of the existing model with a new version number. In addition, you can tag each model with metainformation, such as the framework utilized.

> **Azure Machine Learning Model Registry**
> The model registry in Azure Machine Learning stores names and versions of registered models for tracking and deployment.

In the end, the model registry helps you to keep track of the different results you achieved through training and allows you to deploy different versions of the model for production, development, and test environments.

Deployments and deployment endpoints

Once a model is trained and registered, it can be packaged as a service – by defining an entry script and environment – and deployed to a compute target. The entry script's job is to load the model during initialization, as well as parse user inputs, evaluate the model, and return the results for a user request. This process is called **deployment** in Azure Machine Learning. Compute targets for deployments can be either managed services such as **Azure Container Instances** (**ACI**) or **Azure Kubernetes Service** (**AKS**), or a completely custom user-managed AKS cluster. Every deployment typically serves a single model.

If you want to abstract multiple model deployments behind a common endpoint, you can define an **endpoint service**. This is a common requirement for rolling out multiple model versions, performing **blue-green deployments**, or **A/B testing**. An endpoint is a separate service in Azure Machine Learning that provides a common domain for multiple model deployments, performs **Secure Socket Layer (SSL)/Transport Layer Security (TLS)** termination, and allows traffic allocation between deployments. Endpoints can also be deployed to multiple compute targets, including ACI and AKS.

> **Azure Machine Learning Endpoints**
>
> A deployment endpoint in Azure Machine Learning is a service offering a common domain for accessing and testing multiple versions of a model.

For both deployments and endpoints, we differentiate between **online scoring** and **batch scoring**:

- **Online scoring**: A model is evaluated synchronously for a single input record (or small batch of input records) where the input data, as well as the scoring results, are passed directly in the request and response.
- **Batch scoring**: A user typically passes a location to the input data instead of sending input data with the request. In this case, the model is evaluated asynchronously and provides the results in an output location.

We will discuss the deployment of models and endpoints in more detail in *Chapter 14, Model Deployments, Endpoints, and Operations*.

Pipelines

The final part to mention is **ML pipelines**. Everything we have discussed so far might be enough to do some data preparation, model training, model deployment, and inferencing for ourselves. But even that would entail multiple manual steps. Certainly, we can automate most parts of this using the Azure CLI through some scripting and be quite happy with our setup.

Now, imagine that we want to work with a team and build automated retraining and deployment of our model whenever there is new data to train on. We would have to run similar steps again, such as preprocessing, training, and optimization – just this time with new training data. This process is typically repeated whenever there is significant data drift between the training data and the inferencing data. This is the point where we need to think about bringing in ideas and proven solutions from DevOps, as in the end, we will also write code and deploy infrastructure into a production environment.

Therefore, pipelines are used to facilitate workflows and bring automation to every step of the ML chain; we will take a closer look at them in *Chapter 8*, *Azure Machine Learning Pipelines*. Pipelines are also one of the integral parts of MLOps, and we will see them in action in *Chapter 16*, *Bringing Models into Production with MLOps*.

Surveying Azure Machine Learning Studio

Now that we have a good understanding of the features of the workspace, let's continue where we left off before and have a look into the Azure portal and **Azure Machine Learning Studio**, the web service to operate every aspect of the ML process. This time, search again for our workspace name and click on **mldemows**, the ML workspace. You will be shown the typical menu structure for an Azure resource on the left and the **Overview** page of the service on the right, as shown in *Figure 3.5*:

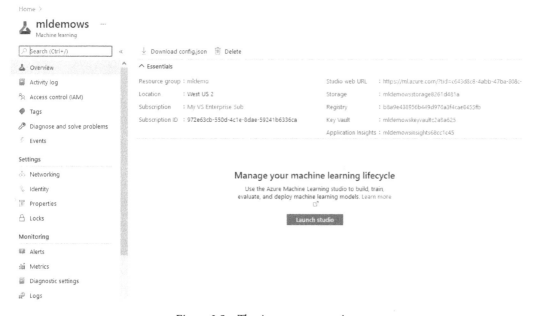

Figure 3.5 – The Azure resource view

This is the administration view from an infrastructure perspective. The major points of interest for you to keep in mind are the following:

- **Overview**: The panel showing the names and attached services of the workspace and the button to launch the ML studio.
- **Access control (IAM)**: The panel to set user access rights on every aspect of the workspace, as discussed in the last section.
- **Networking**: The panel to integrate the service into a private virtual network by activating a **private endpoint** for the workspace.
- **Identity**: The panel showing the already created managed identity of the workspace, which can be used to give the workspace access to external Azure services, such as a storage account using RBAC.
- **Usage + quotas**: The panel to access the available quota on the subscription, which defines how many cores of which type of virtual machine the user is allowed to deploy within the subscription.

By clicking on the **Launch studio** button on the overview page, the actual Azure Machine Learning Studio will open in a new tab, greeting you with the view shown in *Figure 3.6*.

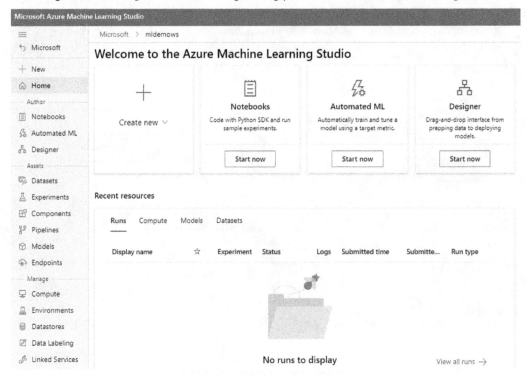

Figure 3.6 – The Azure Machine Learning Studio home page

You can theoretically do everything we will do in this book through this web application, but in certain areas, this can be cumbersome. We will discuss in detail how we set up and operate our development environment in the next section, but it is a good idea to get an understanding of this web service, as we will come back to it throughout the book.

Looking at the menu to the left, there are three major categories, namely **Author**, **Assets**, and **Manage**. Let's match what we already know about the workspace to what is shown to us in the web service.

Author

The first section of the menu shows you the options for authoring your ML experiments. They are as follows:

- **Notebooks**: Create and author Jupyter notebooks utilizing a notebook **virtual machine (VM)** (compute instance) in the cloud.
- **Automated ML**: Create ML models through a wizard, offering insights and suggestions based on your given dataset and problem to solve.
- **Designer**: Build ML models through a GUI interface using logical building blocks.

We have already discussed why we prefer using code and notebooks in *Chapter 2*, *Choosing the Right Machine Learning Service in Azure*. We will come back to automated ML later in this book in *Chapter 11*, *Hyperparameter Tuning and Automated Machine Learning*.

For now, the options to author our notebooks are to either work in the web service environment and utilize a Jupyter server on a compute instance in the cloud, or to work from our local computer with a local Jupyter server.

> **Important Note**
> We will stay in our own local environment for most of the book, but be aware that in a bigger team, it might be of value to have a notebook server in the cloud.

Assets

The second section of the menu shows you the assets available to utilize in your scripts. They are as follows:

- **Datasets**: View and create datasets in the workspace and configure dataset monitoring for understanding data drift between your training data and the inference data from a deployed model (imaging a sensor that is placed differently in production than when gathering test data or that is suddenly broken).

- **Experiments**: View all experiments and all runs that have been tracked, including their detailed run statistics (metrics, snapshots, logs, and outputs) and infrastructure monitoring logs of the compute target.

- **Pipelines**: Create pipelines, view pipeline runs, and define endpoints for pipelines.

- **Models**: Register models and view their properties, including their version, the datasets they are using, the artifacts they are made of, and the endpoints they are actively deployed to.

- **Endpoints**: View and create web service endpoints.

Going through these pages, we can see a lot of the workspace items we already discussed, from datasets to model training through experiments and their runs, registering models, and surfacing service endpoints for our deployments, up to managing all of this through ML pipelines.

You might have seen some other additional features, such as **Dataset Monitoring**, which we will come back to in *Chapter 4, Ingestion Data and Managing Datasets*.

We will have a closer look at the experiment and run statistics at the end of this chapter when we have an experiment and a run has been shown in Azure Machine Learning Studio.

Manage

The final section of the menu shows us the machines and services that we can manage in our workspace. They are as follows:

- **Compute**: Create, view, and manage compute instances, compute clusters, inference clusters, and other attached computes (for example, external VMs or Databricks clusters), including performed runs, distribution of runs on nodes (if existing), and monitoring of the infrastructure itself (for example, CPU usage).

- **Environments**: View available curated environments and create your own custom environments from a Python virtual environment, a Conda YAML configuration, a Docker image stored in the container registry, or from your own Docker file.

- **Datastores**: View, manage, and browse the workspace datastores (`workspacefilestore` and `workspaceblobstore`), the global Azure Machine Learning dataset repository (`azureml_globaldatasets`), and any already attached external storage or attach new ones, including Azure Data Lake, Azure Blob storage, Azure file shares, and Azure SQL, MySQL, and PostgreSQL databases.

- **Data Labeling**: Create labeling projects for image classification and object detection.

- **Linked Services**: Link an Azure Synapse Spark pool to the workspace.

In these views, we find the final missing pieces, the compute targets in the workspace, the environments, and our available datastores, from which we source our datasets for modeling. Furthermore, we find a service to help us with data labeling of source files (typically images) and the possibility to link Azure Synapse to our workspace.

We will go into more detail on the datastores in the next chapter and on data labeling in *Chapter 6*, *Feature Engineering and Labeling*. We will not cover the Azure Synapse integration in detail in this book.

Now that we have a good overview of the features and tooling of the Azure Machine Learning service, we can now return to our local machine and start our first experiments with Azure Machine Learning.

Running ML experiments with Azure Machine Learning

So far, we have installed the Azure CLI locally, deployed our ML workspace to our Azure subscription, and had a look through the features and functionalities of the Azure Machine Learning workspace.

In this final section of the chapter, we will set up our local environment, including Python, the Azure Machine Learning Python SDK, and optionally Visual Studio Code, and embark on our first experiments locally and with compute targets in the cloud.

Setting up a local environment

In the beginning, we discussed briefly the tooling available for deploying Azure resources through Azure Resource Manager. In the same vein, let's have a look at the options for authoring and orchestrating the workspace from our local environment. The options are as follows:

- Using Python 3, the Azure Machine Learning Python SDK, a Jupyter Python extension, and the Azure ML CLI (1.0/2.0) extension (and an editor of choice)

- Using Python3, the Azure Machine Learning Python SDK, an Azure ML CLI (1.0/2.0) extension, **Visual Studio Code (VS Code)**, and VS Code extensions (Azure, Azure Machine Learning, Jupyter, and so on)

- Using Python3, an Azure ML CLI 2.0 extension, YAML, and VS Code (or an editor of choice)

- Using R, an Azure ML CLI 2.0 extension, YAML, and VS Code (or an editor of choice)

The first two options are the de facto standard at the time of writing and the ones we will focus on primarily in this book. We will use the Azure Machine Learning Python SDK with Python 3 and leave it to you if you prefer to work mostly from the console with source files and optionally an editor of choice, or if you want to use an **integrated development environment (IDE)** such as VS Code, which comes with a feature-rich editor and helpful extensions for Azure, Azure Machine Learning, and Jupyter.

In both cases, we will author a Jupyter notebook to orchestrate our ML experiments on the workspace and one or more Python source files to implement the training procedures.

The latter two options were introduced with the more extensive **Azure ML CLI 2.0**. Instead of writing a Jupyter notebook, we completely detach the orchestration of the workspace (run configuration, environments, deployments, and endpoints) from the training and inference source code. This is done through YAML configuration files. An example of an ML experiment run looks like this:

```
$schema: https://.../commandJob.schema.json
code:
  local_path: <path-to-python-scripts>
command: python <script-name> --data {inputs.trainingData1}
environment:
  docker:
    image: docker.io/python
compute:
  target: azureml:goazurego
inputs:
  trainingData1:
    mode: mount
    data:
      local_path: <path-to-training-data>
```

As you can see, this YAML structure references the actual code to be executed (code), the runtime to use (command), and defines every part (environment, compute, and data) necessary for the training run in a descriptive manner.

> **YAML Configurations**
>
> YAML configuration files are a descriptive way to run experiments, create compute services and endpoints, and deploy models in Azure Machine Learning.

This is a more structural way of thinking about the task we will perform and will come in handy when we talk about production systems and MLOps in *Chapter 16, Bringing Models into Production with MLOps*. Finally, this option is the only one allowing source files to be written in **R**, the domain-specific language for data science, and is highly supported in VS Code through the Azure Machine Learning VS Code extension.

Setting up the Python environment

Now that we have a good idea about the possible local development environments we can work with, let's set up our Python environment:

> **Important Note**
>
> The following actions only have to be done if you run your experiments on your own local machine and not if you are using a notebook compute instance in the Azure Machine Learning Studio authoring environment or a **Data Science Virtual Machine (DSVM)** in Azure.

1. First, check whether there is already a Python version installed on your system by running the following command:

```
$ python --version
```

2. Next, please check the metadata of the Azure Machine Learning Python extension on https://pypi.org/project/azureml-sdk/. There are certain times when the extension is behind the most recent Python release. If you already have an unsupported Python version on your system, either uninstall that version or read up on how to operate multiple Python environments on the same machine.

3. After you have verified the supported Python release, either go to https://www.python.org/ and find the supported version for Windows and macOS or use the Terminal and the apt-get command under your Linux distribution. An example for Python 3.8 would look like this:

```
$ sudo apt-get install python3.8
```

4. If you have installed Python for the first time or reinstalled it again, please check that Python is correctly integrated into the path environment variable by checking for the Python version (see *step 1*). If all is good, we can move forward and install the SDK by running the following command:

```
$ python -m pip install azureml-sdk
```

If this command is trying to resolve a lot of dependencies, you might still be operating with an unsupported version of Python or the package installer **PIP**.

5. If you want to work with VS Code, you can jump to the next paragraph now. If you prefer to work primarily with the command line, please install either a local JupyterLab or a local Jupyter notebook server (`https://jupyter.org/index.html`) with one of the following commands:

```
$ python -m pip install jupyterlab
$ python -m pip install notebook
```

After that, you can start either environment from the command line, like this:

```
$ jupyter-lab
$ jupyter notebook
```

With this version of the setup, you can now proceed to the *Running a simple experiment with Azure Machine Learning* section.

Setting up Visual Studio Code

VS Code is a lightweight but very powerful IDE. It is highly integrated with Azure, Azure Machine Learning, and Git, and has a very good editor, an integrated terminal, and a long list of useful extensions to choose from.

Let's have a look at it:

1. Download the tool either from `https://code.visualstudio.com/` or through Azure Marketplace and install it.

2. After you open it, you will be greeted by the view shown in *Figure 3.7* (probably with a darker theme):

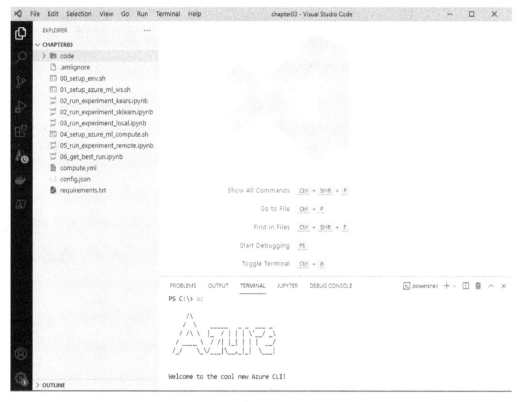

Figure 3.7 – The VS Code interface

3. If you click on the top menu on **View** | **Command Palette** (or hit *Ctrl + Shift + P*), you will see the first highlight of the IDE – you can search for, and issue commands to, the tool itself. Any extension we add will bring its own options to this palette. It helps us to quickly navigate through the environment. For example, if you want to change the theme of the UI, simply type >Theme and look for >Preferences: Color Themes.

    Clicking on it will give you a quick way to set the theme of the UI.

4. Now, to open the terminal, you can click on the top menu on **View** | **Terminal**. You can enter az again to see the same as shown in *Figure 3.7*.

5. Looking at the left menu, you will find an **EXPLORER** tab, where you can add your source folders and files, a **Source Control** tab to connect to Git, a **Run and Debug** tab that lets you handle the debugging of your code, and an **Extensions** tab where you can search for VS Code extensions.

Go to the **Extensions** tab and search and install the following extensions, if they are not already installed: **Azure Tools**, **Azure Machine Learning**, **Python**, **Pylance**, **YAML**, and **Jupyter**.

6. After the installation, you will find a new tab in the left menu called **Azure**. Have a look around here. If you now either click on the option to sign in or if you open the command palette again and search for something such as `sign in azure`, you will find a way to sign in.

    After you are through with signing in to Azure, the **Azure** tab will populate with your subscription names, resource groups, and any resource you might have. If you look under the **MACHINE LEARNING** headline, you will also find your previously deployed workspace, as shown in *Figure 3.8*:

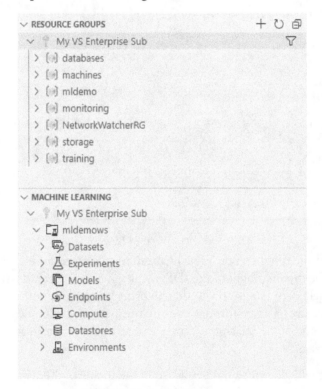

Figure 3.8 – The VS Code Azure Machine Learning extension

7. In the next section, download the files for this chapter to work with. Just open the folder via **File | Open Folder…**, which will add them to the **Explorer** tab, from where you can start the journey.

VS Code has much more to offer, but we will concentrate primarily on understanding ML and the Azure Machine Learning workspace from now on, not on operating every aspect of this editor. If you need more help using VS Code, please feel free to visit `https://code.visualstudio.com/docs/introvideos/basics` or any other resource that can help you with it.

Enhancing a simple experiment

One great use case for starting with Azure Machine Learning is to add advanced logging, tracking, and monitoring capabilities to your existing ML scripts and pipelines. Imagine you have a central place to track all ML experiments from all your data scientists, monitor training, and validation metrics, upload your trained models and other output files, and save a snapshot of the current environment every time a new training run is executed. You can achieve this with Azure Machine Learning by simply adding a few lines of code to your training scripts.

We will start by adding Azure Machine Learning workspace functionality to a **Keras** (`https://keras.io`) ML training script. Keras is one of many ML libraries we can choose from, depending on the ML algorithms we require.

A working directory and preparation

Before we begin, please download the code files for this chapter from the repository and extract them to your preferred working directory. After that, either switch to this directory in the console or open it as a folder in VS Code.

In either case, you will find the following files in the directory:

- `.azureml/config.json`: The Azure Machine Learning workspace configuration file

- `.azureml/requirements.txt`: The Python PIP environment requirements

- `00_setup_env.sh`: A shell script to set up the Azure CLI and Python environment from scratch (as we already did)

- `01_setup_azure_ml_ws.sh`: A shell script to set up the Azure Machine Learning workspace (as we did already)

- `0x_run_experiment_*.ipynb`: Multiple Jupyter notebooks for the upcoming experiments

- `04_setup_azure_ml_compute.sh`: A shell script to create a workspace compute instance from a YAML configuration

- `compute.yml`: A YAML configuration file for a workspace compute instance
- `code/*.py`: A folder containing the Python model training scripts we will use
- `.amlignore`: A file denoting everything that should be ignored by the run snapshot

Let's start with our first experiment:

1. First, we need to install the missing Python package we will need for the following experiments. Run the following command, which will install the packages defined in the PIP requirements file:

    ```
    $ python -m pip install -r .azureml/requirements.txt
    ```

    PIP will point out that the Azure Machine Learning SDK is already installed.

2. Next, open the `config.json` file and enter your subscription ID after the `subscription_id` key. This is necessary, as we will load this configuration in all notebooks using the following code:

    ```
    from azureml.core import Workspace
    ws = Workspace.from_config()
    ```

    The `from_config()` method looks for a file called `config.json` either in the current working directory or in a directory called `.azureml`. We will choose to add it to the folder, as it is part of the `.amlignore` file.

3. Open the `02_run_experiment_keras_base.ipynb` notebook.

In the following, we will have a look through the notebook in order to understand the actual model training script, how we can add snapshots, outputs, and logs to the Azure Machine Learning experiment, and how we can catalog the best model in the model registry.

A training script for Keras

Navigate to the second block in the notebook. Imagine this part to be your original ML training file (plus the `model.fit()` function that you will find in the final block).

Let's understand the actual training code.

First, we import the classes we require for the training from the `tensorflow` library (Keras is a part of TensorFlow):

```
import tensorflow
from tensorflow.keras.datasets import cifar10
...
```

We then proceed to get our training and test data from the CIFAR-10 dataset and change it into a useful format. The `cifar10.load_data()` function will fill the training set with 50,000 datapoints and the test set with 10,000 data points:

```
(x_train, y_train), (x_test, y_test) = cifar10.load_data()
...
y_train = tensorflow.keras.utils.to_categorical
                         (y_train, num_classes)
...
```

> **Test and Training Datasets**
>
> The training dataset is made up of the data points we train our model on; the test dataset is made up of the data points we will evaluate our model against after it has been trained. These should be completely distinct from each other.

After that, we start defining our model – in this case, a `Sequential` model (https://keras.io/guides/sequential_model/) – and we set the name of the model and the location for the output. We will use the **HDF5** file format (or H5 for short) for Keras, as mentioned before:

```
model = Sequential()
...
model_name       = 'keras_cifar10_trained_model.h5'
model_output_dir = os.path.join(os.getcwd(), 'outputs')
```

After that, we define an optimizer (`RMSProp` in this case), a checkpoint **callback**, which we will discuss later; and finally, we *compile* the model by setting a `loss` function, `optimizer`, and additional `metrics` to track during the training run:

```
opt = RMSprop(learning_rate=0.0001, decay=1e-6)
...
checkpoint_cb = ModelCheckpoint(model_path,
                                monitor='val_loss',
                                save_best_only=True)
...
model.compile(loss='categorical_crossentropy',
              optimizer=opt,
              metrics=['accuracy'])
```

The part that would otherwise complete our original script is the one found in the last block of the notebook, which we will discuss in a moment:

```
model.fit(x_train, y_train,
          batch_size=batch_size,
          epochs=epochs,
          validation_data=(x_test, y_test),
          shuffle=True,
          callbacks=[azureml_cb, checkpoint_cb])
```

As you can see, this is most of the notebook code. The rest of the code you can see is what you need to add to your script to enable tracking of your experiment runs, which we will analyze next.

Tracking snapshots, output, and logs

We will now have a look at the code we have ignored so far. First, return to the first block of the notebook we skipped before:

```
from azureml.core import Workspace, Experiment
ws  = Workspace.from_config()
exp = Experiment(workspace=ws, name="cifar10_cnn_local")
```

In this snippet, we define a workspace object called ws using our config file, and as a second step, we define an experiment object, exp, to be tracked in the defined workspace under a chosen name. As you can see, we name it cifar10_cnn_local because we will utilize the CIFAR-10 dataset (https://www.kaggle.com/c/cifar-10), we will run a **Convolutional Neural Network** (**CNN**), and we will do so on a local machine. If an experiment with the same name already exists, this invocation returns the existing experiment as a handle; otherwise, a new experiment will be created. Through the given name, all the runs in this experiment are now grouped together and can be displayed and analyzed on a single dashboard.

> **Important Note**
> Running this code block might open a website to log in to your Azure account. This is called interactive authentication. Please do this to grant your current execution environment access to your Azure Machine Learning workspace. If you run a non-interactive Python script rather than a notebook environment, you can provide the Azure CLI credentials through other means described here: https://docs.microsoft.com/en-us/azure/machine-learning/how-to-setup-authentication#use-interactive-authentication.

Once you have successfully linked the workspace into the ws object, you can continue adding tracking capabilities to your ML experiments. We will use this object to create experiments, runs, and log metrics, and register models in our Azure Machine Learning workspace.

Now, let's jump to the final block, where we will perform a run of the experiment. As described before, a run is a single execution of your experiment (your training script), with different settings, models, code, and data but the same comparable metric. You use runs to test multiple hypotheses for a given experiment and track all the results within the same experiments.

Typically, we can create a run object and start logging this run here by invoking the following function:

```
# Create and start an interactive run
run = exp.start_logging(snapshot_directory='.')
```

The preceding code not only creates and initializes a new run; it also takes a snapshot of the current environment, defined through the snapshot_directory argument, and uploads it to the Azure Machine Learning workspace. To disable this feature, you need to explicitly pass snapshot_directory=None to the start_logging() function.

In this case, the snapshot will take every file and folder existing in the current directory. To restrict this, we can specify the files and folders to ignore using a .amlignore file.

Looking at the code itself in the last notebook block, you can see that this is not the same line of code shown previously.

This is because it is good practice to wrap your training code in a try and except block in order to propagate the status of your run in Azure. If the training run fails, then the run will be reported as a failed run in Azure. You can achieve this by using the following code snippet:

```
run = exp.start_logging(snapshot_directory='.')
try:
    # train your model here
    run.complete()
except:
    run.cancel()
    raise
```

We included the `raise` statement in order to fail the script when an error occurs. This would normally not happen, as all exceptions are caught. You can simplify the preceding code by using the `with` statement in Python. This will yield the same result and is much easier to read:

```
with exp.start_logging(snapshot_directory='.') as run:
    # train your model here
    pass
```

By using only this single line of code, you can track a snapshot for each execution of your experimentation runs automatically and, hence, never lose code or configurations and always come back to specific code, parameters, or models used for one of your ML runs. This is not very impressive yet, but we are just getting started using the features of Azure Machine Learning.

Now, execute every code block in this notebook and wait for completion.

Once executed, go back to Azure Machine Learning Studio and navigate to the **Experiments** view. You should find the name of our experiment, `cifar10_cnn_local`. When you click on it, you will see some metrics in a graph and a list of runs associated with the experiment. Click on the most recent run and then on **Snapshot**. You should now see that the notebook attached everything in our working directory to the snapshot, except for the folders we ignored (for example, `.azureml`).

Figure 3.9 shows the uploaded snapshot files of a run in our experiment:

Figure 3.9 – A snapshot view of an experiment run

Besides the `snapshot` directory, which is uploaded before the run starts, we also end up with two additional directories after the run created by the ML script, namely `outputs` and `logs`.

Once a run is completed using `run.complete()`, all content of the `outputs` directory is automatically uploaded to the Azure Machine Learning workspace. In our simple example using Keras, we can use a checkpoint callback to only store the *best model* of all epochs to the `outputs` directory, which then is tracked with our run. Have a look at this sample code:

```
import os
from keras.calbacks import ModelCheckpoint


model_output_dir = os.path.join(os.getcwd(), 'outputs')
model_name       = 'keras_cifar10_trained_model.h5'
model_path       = os.path.join(model_output_dir, model_name)


# define a checkpoint callback
checkpoint_cb = ModelCheckpoint(model_path,
                                monitor='val_loss',
                                save_best_only=True)


# train the model
model.fit(x_train, y_train,
          batch_size=batch_size,
          epochs=epochs,
          validation_split=0.2,
          shuffle=True,
          callbacks=[checkpoint_cb])
```

In the preceding code, we trained a Keras model for five epochs. The process sets apart 20% (`validation_split`) of the training data as a so-called validation set.

Validation Datasets

The validation set is the third set of datapoints, which the model is evaluated against during model training. It should neither be a subset of the training data nor the test data.

After that, the function runs through every epoch with a shuffled (`shuffle=True`) training dataset. In every epoch, it takes and overwrites the model file in the defined `output` folder if the model of this epoch is performing better on the validation set, which we defined by having a lower validation loss (`monitor='val_loss'`). Therefore, we will only have the best model stored in the `output` folder at the end. Hence, whenever we run the training with the previous experiment tracking, the model gets uploaded automatically once the run is completed.

If you go back to the second code block in the notebook, you will see that we already added the checkpoint callback in our code. Let's check what we got then.

In Azure Machine Learning Studio, navigate to **Outputs + logs** in the run overview. You can see here that the best model, named `keras_cifar10_trained_model.h5`, was uploaded to the Azure Machine Learning workspace.

This is also very convenient, as you won't lose track of your trained models anymore. On top of that, all artifacts you see here are stored in the workspace Blob storage, which is highly scalable and inexpensive.

Figure 3.10 shows the additional output and log information of a run in our experiment:

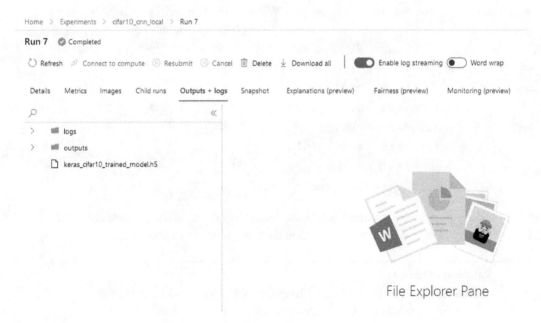

Figure 3.10 – Outputs and logs of an experiment run

The `logs` directory contains the log output from Keras, which you also saw in the Jupyter notebook when executing the last block. In the current run, this was uploaded after the run, together with the `output` folder and the model.

> **Azure Machine Learning Log Streaming**
>
> Log streaming in Azure Machine Learning allows you to see logs in Azure Machine Learning Studio while a run is being executed.

We will see later that if the training script run is invoked through `ScriptRunConfig` rather than being executed directly, the logging will **stream** to the workspace (see also the **Enable log streaming** button). This will allow you to see the logs here while the run is still going on.

Cataloging models to the model registry

As a final step, we want to register our best model, which we have stored in the `output` folder, to the model registry in the Azure Machine Learning workspace.

If we navigate to the final block of the notebook again, we can see that the last lines read like this:

```
# Upload the best model
run.upload_file(model_name, model_path)

# Register the best model
run.register_model(model_name, model_path=model_name,
    model_framework='TfKeras')
```

Here, we first force the upload of the model. This is needed because all output resources are only uploaded when the run is completed and not immediately. Hence, after uploading the model, we can simply register it in the model registry by invoking the `run.register_model()` method.

If you navigate in Azure Machine Learning Studio to **Models**, you should find a model registered under the name `keras_cifar10_trained_model.h5` from the `cifar10_cnn_local` experiment. If you click on it, you will find details about the model under **Details**, including the version number, and you will find the actual model file we created under **Artifacts**.

Figure 3.11 shows the model details of the registered model:

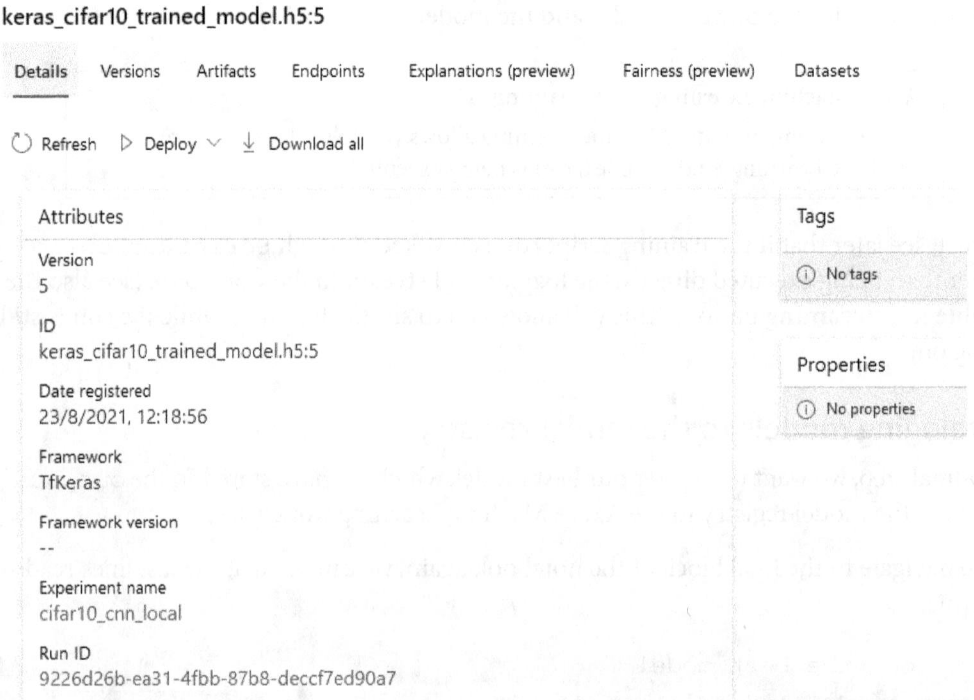

keras_cifar10_trained_model.h5:5

| Details | Versions | Artifacts | Endpoints | Explanations (preview) | Fairness (preview) | Datasets |

◌ Refresh   ▷ Deploy ⌄   ↓ Download all

Attributes	Tags
Version 5	ⓘ No tags
ID keras_cifar10_trained_model.h5:5	
Date registered 23/8/2021, 12:18:56	Properties
Framework TfKeras	ⓘ No properties
Framework version --	
Experiment name cifar10_cnn_local	
Run ID 9226d26b-ea31-4fbb-87b8-deccf7ed90a7	

Figure 3.11 – A registered model in the Azure Machine Learning model registry

The model can then be used for automatic deployments from the Azure Machine Learning service. We will look at this in a lot more detail in *Chapter 14, Model Deployments, Endpoints, and Operations*, and *Chapter 11, Hyperparameter Tuning and Automated Machine Learning*.

Now that we know how to run a simple experiment, let's learn how to log metrics and track results in the next section.

Logging metrics and tracking results

We already saw three useful features to track snapshot code, upload output artifacts, and register trained model files in our Azure Machine Learning workspace. As we saw, these features can be added to any existing experimentation and training Python script or notebook with a few lines of code. In a similar way, we can extend the experimentation script to also track all kinds of variables, such as training accuracy and validation loss per epoch, as well as the test set accuracy of the best model.

Using the `run.log()` method, you can track any parameter during training and experimentation. You simply supply a name and a value, and Azure will do the rest for you. The backend automatically detects whether you send a list of values – hence multiple values with the same key when you log the same value multiple times in the same run – or a single value per run, such as the test performance. In Azure Machine Learning Studio, these values will be used automatically to visualize your overall training performance.

Our Keras model so far is tracking the *loss* as a metric by default and the *accuracy* of the model through our model compilation. We just don't log them to the workspace.

We previously talked about the different datasets we are using in the script, namely the training dataset, the validation dataset, and the test dataset. Remember that the validation dataset is evaluated at the end of each epoch, which also means we can get the **validation loss** and the **validation accuracy** at the end of each epoch. Further, after we have found the best model of all epochs, we want to evaluate this model against the test data, which we have not done yet. This then results in the *test loss* and *test accuracy* of the model.

In the following, we will first add the test metrics to our run, then the validation metrics, and then have a look at them in Azure Machine Learning Studio. Finally, we will enhance the code so that we only register a model if it is better than all of the models from previous runs. Feel free to have the `02_run_experiment_keras_enhanced.ipynb` notebook open to follow along.

Evaluation of the best model

The goal is to evaluate the best training model of all epochs against the test dataset to get the overall test metrics. In order to do this, we need to load it back into our model object. Luckily, we already only stored the best model of the whole run in our `output` folder using the checkpoint callback that we defined before. Let's look at the code:

```
# load the overall best model into the model object
model = load_model(model_path)
# evaluate the best model against the test dataset
scores = model.evaluate(x_test, y_test, verbose=1)
print('Test loss of best model:', scores[0])
run.log('Test loss', scores[0])
print('Test accuracy of best model:', scores[1])
run.log('Test accuracy', scores[1])
```

As you can see, we get back the best model and then evaluate it, extracting the loss (`scores[0]`) and the accuracy (`scores[1]`). Having done this part, let's have a look at the validation metrics.

A Keras callback for validation metrics

The goal is to evaluate the model created in each epoch against the validation dataset to get the validation metrics for each epoch. We already used an existing callback to check for the best model in each epoch, so it might be a good idea to write one ourselves to track the metrics in each epoch.

Open the `keras_azure_ml_cb.py` file in the `code` directory. You will be greeted by the following:

```python
from keras.callbacks import Callback
import numpy as np
class AzureMlKerasCallback(Callback):
    def __init__(self, run):
        super(AzureMlKerasCallback, self).__init__()
        self.run = run
    def on_epoch_end(self, epoch, logs=None):
        # logs is filled by Keras at the end of an epoch
        logs = logs or {}
        for metric_name, metric_val in logs.items():
            if isinstance(metric_val, (np.ndarray, np.generic)):
                self.run.log_list(metric_name, metric_val.tolist())
            else:
                self.run.log(metric_name, metric_val)
```

The preceding code implements a simple Keras callback function. When the callback is executed, Keras passes the current epoch as well as all training and validation metrics as a dictionary (`logs`).

What then happens is that for all dictionary entries, we pull out the name and the value to log them to the experiment run with the `run.log(metric_name, metric_val)` function. We only have to check whether the value is a single value or an array type, as the Azure Machine Learning SDK has a different function called `run.log_list()` for multi-value entries.

We can now use this callback in our model training the same way as we did with the previous callback, by adding it to the `model.fit()` function:

```python
# create an Azure Machine Learning monitor callback
azureml_cb = AzureMlKerasCallback(run)

model.fit(x_train, y_train,
```

```
    batch_size=batch_size,
    epochs=epochs,
    validation_data=(x_test, y_test),
    callbacks=[azureml_cb, checkpoint_cb])
```

This extends Keras naturally using a callback function to track the training and validation loss and accuracy in the Azure Machine Learning service. Any metric defined on the model itself will now be tracked automatically in the experiment run.

Running metric visualization in Azure Machine Learning Studio

After we have added a bunch of metrics to the experiment run, let's run the notebook as is and have a look at the run statistics in Azure Machine Learning Studio.

When you open the run, the **Metrics** list of types, as with both validation metrics, are automatically converted into line charts and plotted, as shown in *Figure 3.12*:

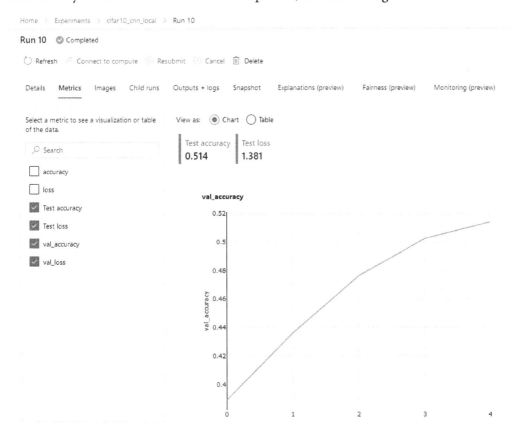

Figure 3.12 – The metrics view of an experiment run

We can see that the test metrics and validation metrics are all accounted for. In addition, we can see **Test loss** and **Test accuracy** as metrics, which are also provided by Keras for each epoch as the evaluation of the model against the training dataset.

Another nifty feature is that the ML workspace experiment gives you an overview of all your runs. It automatically uses both the scalar values and training and validation metrics that were logged per run and displays them on a dashboard. You can modify the displayed values and the aggregation method used to aggregate those values over the individual runs.

Figure 3.13 shows the accuracy and the validation accuracy of all experiment runs:

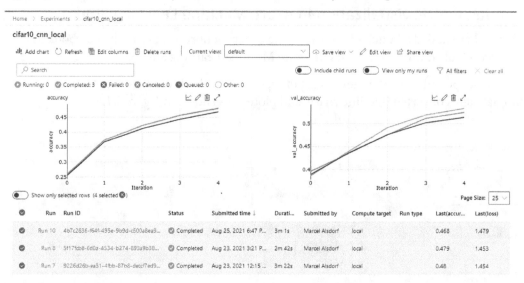

Figure 3.13 – The visualized metrics of all experiment runs

This is the simplest method of tracking values from the runs and displaying them with the corresponding experiments. Adding a few lines of code to your existing ML training scripts – independent of which framework you are using – automatically tracks your model scores and displays all experiments in a dashboard.

Enhancing the registration of models

Now that we have metrics to read out and work with, we can, as a final step, enhance the way we save the best model to the model registry.

So far, we always update the model with a new version as soon as a new model is available. However, this doesn't automatically mean that the new model has a better performance than the last model we registered in the workspace. As we want a new **version** of the model to actually be better than the last version, we need to check for that.

Therefore, a common approach is to register the new model only if the specified metric is better than the highest previously stored metric for the experiment. Let's implement this functionality.

We can define a function that returns a generator of metrics from an experiment, like this:

```
from azureml.core import Run


def get_metrics_from_exp(exp, metric, status='Completed'):
    for run in Run.list(exp, status=status):
        yield run.get_metrics().get(metric)
```

The preceding generator function yields the specified tracked metric for each run that is completed. We can use this function to return the best metric from all previous experiment runs to compare the evaluated score from the current model and decide whether we should register a new version of the model. We should do this only if the current model performs better than the previous recorded model. For that, we need to compare a metric. Using the **test accuracy** is a good idea, as it is the model tested against unknown data:

```
# get the highest test accuracy
best_test_acc = max(get_metrics_from_exp(
                    exp, 'Test accuracy')
                    default = 0)
# upload the model
run.upload_file(model_name, model_path)

if scores[1] > best_test_acc:
    # register the best model as a new version
    run.register_model(model_name, model_path=model_name)
```

As you can see, we get the result for the test accuracy metric of all previously runs tracked in this experiment and select the largest. We then register the model only if the test accuracy of the new model is higher than the previously stored best score. Nevertheless, we still upload and track the model binaries with the experiment run.

We now have an enhanced version of our notebook, including metrics tracking and a better version to register a model in the model registry.

Scheduling the script execution

In the previous section, we saw how you can annotate your existing ML experimentation and training code with a few lines of code in order to track relevant metrics and run artifacts in your workspace. In this section, we move from invoking the training script directly to scheduling the training script on the local machine. You might ask why this extra step is useful because there are not many differences between invoking the training script directly and scheduling the training script to run locally.

The main motivation behind this exercise is that in the subsequent step, we can change the execution target to a remote compute target and run the training code on a compute cluster in the cloud instead of the local machine. This will be a huge benefit, as we can now easily test code locally and later deploy the same code to a highly scalable compute environment in the cloud.

One more thing to note is that when scheduling the training script instead of invoking it, the standard output and error streams, as well as all files in the **logs** directory, will be streamed directly to the Azure Machine Learning workspace run. This has the benefit of tracking the script output in real time in your ML workspace, even if your code is running on the remote compute cluster.

Let's implement this in a so-called **authoring script**. We call it an authoring script (or authoring environment) when the script or environment's job is to schedule another training or experimentation script. In addition, we will now refer to the script that runs and executes the training as the **execution script** (or execution environment).

We need to define two things in the authoring script – an environment we will run on and a run configuration, to which we will hand over the execution script, the environment, and a possible compute target.

Open the `03_run_experiment_local.ipynb` notebook file. Compared to our previous notebooks, you can see that this is a very short file, as the actual Keras training is happening now in the execution script, which you can find in the `cifar10_cnn_remote.py` file in the `code` folder.

First, we need to define an environment. As we are still running locally, we create an environment with **user-managed dependencies** called `user-managed-env`. This will just take our environment as is from our local machine:

```
from azureml.core.environment import Environment
myenv = Environment(name = "user-managed-env")
myenv.python.user_managed_dependencies = True
```

In the next block, we define the location and name of the execution script we want to run locally:

```
import os
script = 'cifar10_cnn_remote.py'
script_folder = os.path.join(os.getcwd(), 'code')
```

Finally, we define a run configuration using a `ScriptRunConfig` object and attach to it the source directory, the script name, and our previously defined local environment:

```
from azureml.core import ScriptRunConfig
runconfig = ScriptRunConfig(source_directory=script_folder,
                            script=script,
                            environment = myenv)
run = exp.submit(runconfig)
run.wait_for_completion(show_output=True)
```

Now, execute the whole notebook, and while doing so, navigate to Azure Machine Learning Studio and look for the current run for our experiment called `cifar10_cnn_remote`. When it is visible, go to the **Outputs + logs** tab of the new run. You will see that the `azureml-logs` and `logs/azureml` folders will now be populated with the logging output during the run.

Figure 3.14 shows an example of the ingested streaming logs:

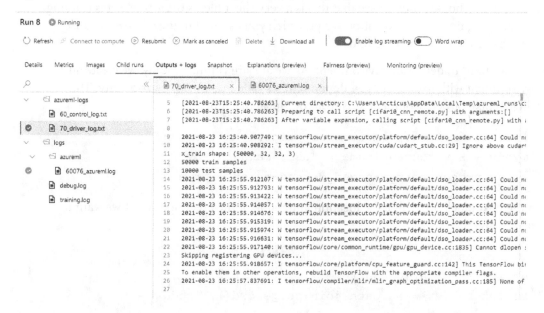

Figure 3.14 – The streaming logs of an Azure Machine Learning experiment run

This is very handy, as now we don't really need to know where the code is ultimately executed. All we care about is seeing the output, the progress of the run while tracking all metrics, generated models, and all other artifacts. The link to the current run can be retrieved by calling the `print(run.get_portal_url())` method.

However, instead of navigating to the Azure portal every time we run a training script, we can embed a widget in our notebook environment to give us the same (and more) functionality, directly within Jupyter, JupyterLab, or VS Code. To do so, we need to replace the `run.wait_for_completion()` line with the following snippet:

```
from azureml.widgets import RunDetails
RunDetails(run).show()
```

Please be aware that you need to add the **Azure Widgets Python extension** to your environment. Please refer to this installation guide for the extension: `https://docs.microsoft.com/en-us/python/api/azureml-widgets/azureml.widgets.rundetails?view=azure-ml-py`.

Finally, let's have a look at the execution script we are using. Open the file named `cifar10_cnn_remote.py` in the code directory. Scanning through this, you should find two additional parts that we added to the original model training code.

The first one is the part where we write debug logs into the `logs` folder:

```
# log output of the script
logging.basicConfig(filename='logs/debug.log',
                    filemode='w',
                    level=logging.DEBUG)
logger_cb = CSVLogger('logs/training.log')
```

The second part looks like this:

```
from azureml.core import Run


# load the current run
run = Run.get_context()
```

The reason for this call is that when we want to move to a remote execution environment, we need to infer the run context. Therefore, we need to load the `run` object from the current execution context instead of creating a new run, as shown in the previous sections, where we used the `exp.start_logging()` call.

The `run` object will be automatically linked with the experiment when it was scheduled through the authoring script. This is handy for remote execution, as we don't need to explicitly specify the `run` object in the execution script anymore. Using this inferred `run` object, we can log values, upload files and folders, and register models exactly as in the previous sections.

Running experiments on a cloud compute

After running our experiments so far on our local machine, let's proceed now as a final step in this chapter to run the same ML model on a compute target in the ML workspace.

The recommended compute target for training ML models in Azure is the managed Azure Machine Learning compute cluster, an auto-scaling compute cluster that is directly managed within your Azure subscription. If you have already used Azure for batch workloads, you will find it similar to Azure Batch and Azure Batch AI, with less configuration and tightly embedded in the Azure Machine Learning service.

There are three options to deploy a cluster, either through the Azure CLI and YAML, through the Python SDK, or through Azure Machine Learning Studio. In the following steps, we will use the first options, as they are becoming more prevalent, especially with MLOps. After that, we will see how with Python code the second option works as well.

Open the `compute.yml` file in the working directory. You will see the following:

compute.yml

```
$schema: https://azuremlschemas.azureedge.net/latest/compute.
schema.json
name: mldemocompute
type: amlcompute
size: STANDARD_D2_V2
location: westus2
min_instances: 0
max_instances: 2
idle_time_before_scale_down: 900
```

This describes a compute cluster named `mldemocompute` that we want to deploy. This configuration defines a compute type (`amlcompute`) in the ML workspace with 0–2 nodes with a VM size of **Standard D2v2** (2 CPUs, 7 GB of RAM, and 100 GB HDD) in the West US 2 Azure region. In addition, we define the idle time before the cluster scales down (shuts off) to be 15 minutes (which equals 900 seconds).

There are many other settings for compute clusters, including diverse network and load balancing settings. You can also define VM types with GPUs as your worker nodes – for example, **Standard_NC6** (6 CPUs, 56 GB of RAM, 340 GB SSD, 1 GPU, and 12 GB GPU memory) – by simply changing the configuration.

In contrast to other managed clusters, such as Azure Databricks, you don't pay for a head or master node, just for worker nodes. We will go into a lot more detail about VM types for deep learning in *Chapter 10, Training Deep Neural Networks on Azure*, and run distributed training on GPU clusters in *Chapter 12, Distributed Machine Learning on Azure*.

If you are working with VS Code, the **Azure ML** extension (reachable in the Azure tab on the left) can show you YAML templates. Just go to your ML workspace, and under **mldemows | Compute | Compute clusters**, click on the + sign on the right. It will generate a template file, which looks like a bare version of the preceding one. In addition, if you have installed the YAML extension, it will understand the schema link in the file and will autocomplete your typing:

1. Open the console and run the following CLI command to create the compute instance from the YAML file:

    ```
    $ az ml compute create -f compute.yml -g mldemo -w
    mldemows
    ```

You can also call the shell script in the working directory called `04_setup_azure_ml_compute.sh`.

After a short while, it will give you an output showing the properties of the created compute cluster.

2. Open the notebook called `05_run_experiment_remote.ipynb`.

The second block in that notebook shows you the following code:

```
from azureml.core.compute import ComputeTarget, AmlCompute
from azureml.core.compute_target import ComputeTargetException
cluster_name = "mldemocompute"
min_nodes = 0
max_nodes = 2
vm_size = "STANDARD_D2_V2"
try:
  aml_cluster = ComputeTarget
                 (workspace=ws, name=cluster_name)
except ComputeTargetException:
  print('Cluster not '%s' not found, creating one now.'
          % cluster_name)
  config = AmlCompute.provisioning_configuration
             (vm_size=vm_size,
              min_nodes=min_nodes,
              max_nodes=max_nodes)
  aml_cluster = ComputeTarget.create
                 (workspace=ws,
                  name=cluster_name,
                  provisioning_configuration=config)
aml_cluster.wait_for_completion(show_output=True)
```

The `except` clause of the `try` construct shows you the way you can create a compute cluster through the Python SDK. As the name of the cluster is the same as the one we already deployed via the CLI, when executing this block, it will just link our compute to the `aml_cluster` object through the `try` clause.

Either way, this `try..except` clause is very handy, as it either gives us back the already existing cluster or creates a new one for us. The final line of code is necessary if the compute target does not already exist, as we need to wait for the compute target to be ready to receive the run configuration in the next steps.

If we now have a look at the environment definition and the run configuration, we will see some minor changes to the code from the `03_run_experiment_local.ipynb` notebook. Our environment definition now looks like this:

```
myenv = Environment.from_pip_requirements
        (name = "remote_env", file_path = pipreq_path)
```

As you can see, we attach to the environment our PIP configuration file we worked with locally. In the backend, the SDK will convert this to a **Conda properties file** and create a container from a Docker base image. If you run the cells up to this one, you will see which base image and configuration Azure Machine Learning builds based on this input. A small excerpt of this is shown here:

```
"docker": {
"baseImage": "mcr.microsoft.com/azureml/openmpi3.1.2-
ubuntu18.04:20210714.v1",
"platform": {
    "architecture": "amd64",
    "os": "Linux"
  }
}
```

Having a look at the final block in the notebook, we can see that the only difference is that we now define the compute target to be our `aml_cluster` in the run configuration and pass the new environment.

Finally, we now run the whole notebook.

The training script is now executed in the remote compute target on Azure. In the experiment run in Azure Machine Learning Studio, the snapshot, outputs, and logs look very similar to the local run. However, we can now also see the logs of the Docker environment build process for the compute target, as shown in *Figure 3.15*:

Figure 3.15 – The Docker build phase for a remote experiment run

As a final exercise, let's understand the steps that are performed when we submit this run to the Azure Machine Learning workspace:

1. The Azure Machine Learning service builds a Docker container from the defined environment if it doesn't exist already.

2. The Azure Machine Learning service registers your environment in the private container registry so that it can be reused for other scripts and deployments.

3. The Azure Machine Learning service queues your script execution.

4. The Azure Machine Learning compute initializes and scales up a compute node using the defined container.

5. The Azure Machine Learning compute executes the script.

6. The Azure Machine Learning compute captures logs, artifacts, and metrics and streams them to the Azure Machine Learning service, and inlines the logs in the Jupyter notebook through the widget.

7. The Azure Machine Learning service stores all artifacts in the workspace storage and your metrics in Application Insights.

8. The Azure Machine Learning service provides you with all the information about the run through Azure Machine Learning Studio or the Python SDK.

9. The Azure Machine Learning compute automatically scales itself down after 15 minutes (in our case) of inactivity.

Congratulations on following along with this exercise. Given that it took us maybe 5 minutes to set up the Azure Machine Learning workspace, we get a fully fledged batch compute scheduling and execution environment for all our ML workloads. Many bits and pieces of this environment can be tuned and configured to our liking, and best of all, everything can be automated through the Azure CLI or the Azure Python SDK. Throughout the book, we will use these tools to configure, start, scale, and delete clusters for training and scoring.

Summary

This concludes the first part of this book. By now, you should have a good idea of what ML in general entails, what services and options are available in Azure, and how to utilize the Azure Machine Learning service to do ML experimentation and enhance your existing ML modeling scripts.

In the next part of the book, we will concentrate on one of the aspects of ML often overlooked, the data itself. It is extremely vital to get this right. You might have heard the phrase *garbage in, garbage out* before, which holds true. Therefore, we will be working on removing as many pitfalls as possible by running automated data ingestion, cleaning and preparing data, extracting features, and performing labeling. In the end, we will bring all our knowledge together to discuss how to set up an ingestion and training ML pipeline.

As the first step of this process, we need to understand different data sources and formats and bring our data to the Azure Machine Learning workspace, which we will discuss in the next chapter.

Section 2: Data Ingestion, Preparation, Feature Engineering, and Pipelining

In this section, we will learn how to load and store data in Azure and how to manage this data from an Azure Machine Learning workspace. We will then investigate techniques to preprocess and visualize our data and how we can get insights from a high-dimensional dataset. From there on, we will concentrate on how to optimize our given dataset through creating and converting features and creating labels for supervised modeling. We will use this knowledge to perform advanced feature extraction for natural-language processing by using complex semantic word embeddings. Finally, we will incorporate what we learned into an automated preprocessing and training pipeline using Azure Machine Learning pipelines.

This section comprises the following chapters:

- *Chapter 4, Ingesting Data and Managing Datasets*
- *Chapter 5, Performing Data Analysis and Visualization*
- *Chapter 6, Feature Engineering and Labeling*
- *Chapter 7, Advanced Feature Extraction with NLP*
- *Chapter 8, Azure Machine Learning Pipelines*

4

Ingesting Data and Managing Datasets

In the previous chapter, we set up and explored the Azure Machine Learning workspace, performed data experimentation, and scheduled scripts to run on remote compute targets in Azure Machine Learning. In this chapter, we will learn how to connect datastores and create, explore, access, and track data in Azure Machine Learning.

First, we will take a look at how data is managed in Azure Machine Learning by understanding the concepts of **datastores and datasets**. We will see different types of datastores and learn best practices for organizing and storing data for **machine learning (ML)** in Azure.

Next, we will create an **Azure Blob storage** account and connect it as a datastore to Azure Machine Learning. We will cover best practices for ingesting data into Azure using popular CLI tools as well as **Azure Data Factory** and **Azure Synapse Spark** services.

In the following section, we will learn how to create datasets from data in Azure, access and explore these datasets, and pass data efficiently to compute environments in your Azure Machine Learning workspace. Finally, we will discuss how to access Azure Open Datasets to improve your model's performance through third-party data sources.

The following are the topics that will be covered in this chapter:

- Choosing data storage solutions for Azure Machine Learning
- Creating a datastore and ingesting data
- Using datasets in Azure Machine Learning

Technical requirements

In this chapter, we will use the following Python libraries and versions to create and manage datastores and datasets:

- `azureml-core 1.34.0`
- `azureml-sdk 1.34.0`

Similar to previous chapters, you can run this code using either a local Python interpreter or a notebook environment hosted in Azure Machine Learning.

All code examples in this chapter can be found in the GitHub repository for this book: `https://github.com/PacktPublishing/Mastering-Azure-Machine-Learning-Second-Edition/tree/main/chapter04`.

Choosing data storage solutions for Azure Machine Learning

When running ML experiments or training scripts on your local development machine, you often don't think about managing your datasets. You probably store your training data on your local hard drive, external storage device, or file share. In such a case, accessing the data for experimentation or training is not a problem, and you don't have to worry about the data location, access permissions, maximal throughput, parallel access, storage and egress cost, data versioning, and such.

However, as soon as you start training an ML model on remote compute targets, such as a VM in the cloud or within Azure Machine Learning, you must make sure that all your executables can access the training data efficiently. This is even more relevant if you collaborate with other people who also need to access the data in parallel for experimentation, labeling, and training from multiple environments and multiple machines. And if you deploy a model that requires access to this data as well – for example, looking up labels for categorical results, scoring recommendations based on a user's history of ratings, and the like – then this environment needs to access the data as well.

In this section, we will learn how to manage data for different use cases in Azure. We will first see the abstractions Azure Machine Learning provides to facilitate data access for ML experimentation, training, and deployment.

Organizing data in Azure Machine Learning

In Azure Machine Learning, data is managed as **datasets** and data storage as **datastores**. This abstraction hides the details of location, data format, data transport protocol, and access permissions behind the dataset and datastore objects and hence lets Azure Machine Learning users focus on exploring, transforming, and managing data without worrying about the underlying storage system.

A **datastore** is an abstraction of a physical data storage system that is used to link the existing storage system to an Azure Machine Learning workspace. In order to connect the existing storage to the workspace – by creating a datastore – you need to provide the connection and authentication details of the storage system. Once created, the data storage can be accessed by users through the datastore object, which will automatically use the provided credentials of the datastore definition. This makes it easy to provide access to data storage to your developers, data engineers, and scientists who are collaborating in an Azure Machine Learning workspace. Currently, the following services can be connected as datastores to a workspace:

- Azure Blob containers
- Azure file share
- Azure Data Lake
- Azure Data Lake Gen2
- Azure SQL Database
- Azure Database for PostgreSQL
- Databricks File System
- Azure Database for MySQL

While datastores are abstractions of data storage systems, a **dataset** is an abstraction of data in general – for example, data in the form of a file on a remote server accessible through a public URL or files and tables within a datastore. Azure Machine Learning supports two types of abstraction on data formats, namely **tabular datasets** and **file datasets**. The former is used to define *tabular* data – for example, from comma- or delimiter-separated files, from Parquet and JSON files, or from SQL queries – whereas the latter is used to specify *any binary* data from files and folders, such as images, audio, and video data.

Tabular datasets can also be defined and used directly from their publicly available URL, which is called a **direct dataset**. This is similar to fetching data through URLs like with other popular libraries such as pandas and requests. Both tabular and file datasets can be registered in your workspace. We will refer to these datasets as **registered datasets**. Registered datasets will show up in your Azure Machine Learning Studio under **Datasets**.

Understanding the default storage accounts of Azure Machine Learning

There exists one special datastore in Azure Machine Learning that is used internally to store all snapshots, logs, figures, models, and more when executing experiment runs. This is called the **default datastore**, is an Azure Blob storage account, and is created automatically with Azure Machine Learning when you set up the initial workspace. You can select your own Blob storage as the default datastore during the workspace creation or connect your storage account and mark it as default in Azure Machine Learning Studio.

Figure 4.1 shows you the list of datastores in Azure Machine Learning Studio. The default datastore is marked as **Default** and generated automatically when setting up an Azure Machine Learning workspace. To go to this view, simply click on **Datastores** under the **Manage** category in the left menu in Azure Machine Learning Studio. To view existing datasets, click on **Datasets** in the **Assets** category:

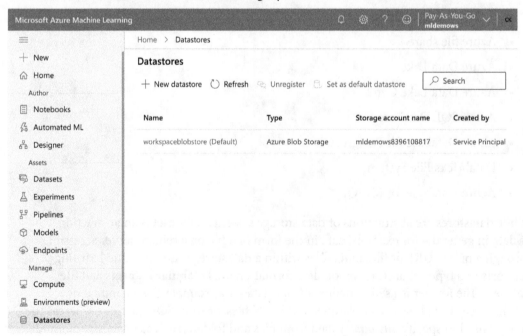

Figure 4.1 – Default datastore in Azure Machine Learning

The default datastore is used by Azure Machine Learning internally to store all assets and artifacts when no other datastore is defined. You can access and use the default datastore in your workspace identically to your custom datastores by creating a datastore reference. The following code snippet shows how to get a reference to the default datastore:

```
from azureml.core import Datastore

default_datastore = Datastore.get_default(ws)
```

The default datastore is used internally by Azure Machine Learning to store all assets and artifacts during the ML life cycle. Using the previous code snippet, you can access the default datastore to store custom datasets and files.

Once we have accessed the default datastore and connected custom datastores, we need to think about a strategy for efficiently storing data for different ML use cases. Let's tackle this in the next section.

Exploring options for storing training data in Azure

Azure supports a myriad of different data storage solutions and technologies to store data in the cloud – and as we saw in the previous section, many of these are supported datastores in Azure Machine Learning. In this section, we will explore some of these services and technologies to understand which ones can be used for machine learning use cases.

Database systems can be broadly categorized by the type of *data* and *data access* into the following two categories:

- **Relational database management systems** (**RDBMSs**) are often used to store normalized transactional data using B-tree-based ordered indices. Typical queries filter, group, and aggregate results by joining multiple rows from multiple tables. Azure supports different RDBMSs, such as Azure SQL Database, as well as Azure Database for PostgreSQL and MySQL.

- **NoSQL**: Key-value-based storage systems are often used to store de-normalized data with hash-based or ordered indices. Typical queries access a single record from a collection distributed based on a partition key. Azure supports different NoSQL-based services such as Azure Cosmos DB and Azure Table storage.

As you can see, depending on your use cases, you can use both database technologies to store data for machine learning. While RDBMSs are great technologies to store training data for machine learning, NoSQL systems are great to store lookup data – such as training labels – or ML results such as recommendations, predictions, or feature vectors.

Instead of choosing a database service, another popular choice for machine learning is to use data storage systems. On disk, most database services persist as data pages on **file** or **blob storage systems**. Blob storage systems are a very popular choice for storing all kinds of data and assets for machine learning due to their scalability, performance, throughput, and cost. Azure Machine Learning makes extensive use of blob storage systems, especially for storing all operational assets and logs.

Popular Azure blob storage services are Azure Blob storage and Azure Data Lake Storage, which provide great flexibility to implement efficient data storage and access solutions through different choices of data formats. While Azure Blob storage supports most common blob-based filesystem operations, Azure Data Lake Storage implements efficient directory services, which makes it a popular general-purpose storage solution for horizontally scalable filesystems. It is a popular choice for storing large machine learning training datasets.

While tabular data can be stored efficiently in RDBMS systems, similar properties can be achieved by choosing the correct data formats and embedded clustered indices while storing data on blob storage systems. Choosing the right data format will allow your filesystem to efficiently store, read, parse, and aggregate information.

Common data format choices can be categorized into textual (CSV, JSON, and more) as well as binary formats (images, audio, video, and more). Binary formats for storing tabular data are broadly categorized into row-compressed (Protobuf, Avro, SequenceFiles, and more) or column-compressed (Parquet, ORC, and more) formats. A popular choice is also to compress the whole file using Gzip, Snappy, or other compression algorithms.

One structure that most data storage systems have in common is a hierarchical path or directory structure to organize data blobs. A popular choice for storing training data for machine learning is to implement a partitioning strategy for your data. This means that data is organized in multiple directories where each directory contains all the data for a specific key, also called the partitioning key.

Cloud providers offer a variety of different storage solutions, which can be customized further by choosing different indexing, partitioning, format, and compression techniques. A common choice for storing tabular training data for machine learning is a column-compressed binary format such as Parquet, partitioned by ingestion date, stored on Azure Data Lake Storage, for efficient management operations and scalable access.

Creating a datastore and ingesting data

After having a look through the options for storing data in Azure for ML processing, we will now create a storage account, which we will use throughout the book for our raw data and ML datasets. In addition, we will have a look at how to transfer some data into our storage account manually and how to perform this task automatically by utilizing integration engines available in Azure.

Creating Blob Storage and connecting it with the Azure Machine Learning workspace

Let's start by creating a storage account. Any storage account will come with a file share, a queue, and table storage for you to utilize in other scenarios. In addition to those three, you can either end up with Blob Storage or a Data Lake, depending on the settings you provide at creation time. By default, a Blob storage account will be created. If we instead want a Data Lake account, we must set the `enable-hierarchical-namespace` setting to `True`, as Data Lake offers an actual hierarchical folder structure and not a flat namespace.

Creating Blob Storage

Keeping that in mind, let's create a Blob Storage account:

1. Navigate to a terminal of your choosing, log in to Azure, and check that you are working in the correct subscription as we learned in *Chapter 3, Preparing the Azure Machine Learning Workspace*.

2. As we want to create a storage account, let's have a look at the options and required settings for doing so by running the following command:

```
$ az storage account create -h
```

Looking through the result, you will see a very long list of possible arguments, but the only required ones are `name` and `resource-group`. Still, we should look further through this, as a lot of the other settings are still set to certain default values, which might be incorrect for our case.

Going through the list, you will find a lot of options concerning network or security settings. The default for most of them is to at least allow access from everywhere. At this moment, we are not too concerned about virtual network integration or handling our own managed keys in Azure Key Vault.

Besides all these options, there are a few that define the type of storage account we set, namely `enable-hierarchical-namespace`, `kind`, `location`, and `sku`.

We already discussed the first option and as the default is `False`, we can ignore it.

Looking at `kind`, you see a list of storage types. You might think we need to choose `BlobStorage`, but unfortunately, that is a legacy setting left there for any storage account still running on the first version, V1. The default (`StorageV2`) is the best option for our scenario.

Looking at `location`, we see that we apparently can set a default location for all deployments, therefore it is not flagged as required. As we did not do that so far, we will just provide it when deploying the storage account.

Finally, looking at `sku`, we see a combined setting of an option concerning the type of disk technology used (`Standard/Premium`), where `Standard` denotes HDD storage and `Premium` denotes SSD storage, and an option defining the data redundancy scheme (LRS/ZRS/GRS/RAGRS/GZRS). If you want to learn more about the redundancy options, follow this link: `https://docs.microsoft. com/en-us/azure/storage/common/storage-redundancy`. As both increase costs, feel free to either stick with the default (`Standard_RAGRS`) or go with local redundancy (`Standard_LRS`).

3. Let's create our storage account. Please be aware that the name you choose must be globally unique, therefore you cannot choose the one you will read in the following command:

```
az storage account create \
    --name mldemoblob8765 \
    --resource-group mldemo \
    --location westus \
    --sku Standard_LRS \
    --kind StorageV2
```

The output this creates will show you the detailed settings for the created storage account.

4. As a final step, let's create a container in our new blob storage. For that, run the following command with the appropriate account name:

```
az storage container create \
    --name mlfiles \
    --account-name mldemoblob8765
```

The result will show `True` at the end, but will give you some warnings beforehand, something like this:

```
There are no credentials provided in your command
and environment, we will query for account key for
your storage account. It is recommended to provide
--connection-string, --account-key or --sas-token in your
command as credentials.
```

The command worked because it automatically pulled the account key of the storage account through our session. Normally, to access a storage account, we either need an AD identity, a key to access the whole account (`account-key`), or a shared-access key (`sas-token`) to access only a specific subset of folders or containers. We will come back to this when connecting from the ML workspace.

To check the result, run this command:

```
az storage container list \
    --account-name mldemoblob8765 \
    --auth-mode login
```

Now that we have our storage, let's connect it to our Azure Machine Learning workspace.

Creating a datastore in Azure Machine Learning

In order to not bother with the storage account itself anymore when working with our ML scripts, we will now create a permanent connection to a container in a storage account and define it as one of our datastores in the Azure Machine Learning workspace.

The following steps will guide you through this process:

1. First, let's understand what is required to create a datastore by running the following command:

    ```
    az ml datastore create -h
    ```

    Looking through the output,, we understand that the name of the resource group, the name of the ML workspace, and a YAML file is needed. We have two of those three things. Therefore, let's understand what the YAML file has to look like.

2. Navigate to `https://docs.microsoft.com/en-us/azure/machine-learning/reference-yaml-datastore-blob`, where you will find the required schema of our file and some examples. Going through the examples, you will see that they mainly differ concerning the way to authenticate to the storage account. The most secure of them is limited access via a SAS token and therefore we will pick that route.

3. Please either download the `blobdatastore.yml` file from the files for *Chapter 4, Ingesting Data and Managing Datasets,* from the GitHub repository or create a file with the same name and the following content:

```
$schema: https://azuremlschemas.azureedge.net/latest/
azureBlob.schema.json
name: mldemoblob
type: azure_blob
description: main ML blob storage
account_name: mldemoblob8765
container_name: mlfiles
credentials:
  sas_token: <your_token>
```

Please enter the appropriate account name for your case. The only thing missing now is the SAS token, which we need to create for our `mlfiles` container.

4. Run the following command to create a SAS token for our container:

```
az storage container generate-sas \
    --account-name mldemoblob8765 \
    --name mlfiles \
    --expiry 2023-01-01 \
    --permissions acdlrw
```

This command generates a SAS token with an expiration date of 01/01/2023 and permissions to **add, create, delete, list, read** and **write** (**acdlrw**) to the `mlfiles` container. Choose an expiration date that is far enough in the future for you to work with this book. In normal circumstances, you would choose a much shorter expiration date and rotate this key accordingly.

The result should be in this kind of format:

```
xx=XXXX-XX-XX&xx=xxxx&xxx=xxx&xx=xxxxxxxxxxx&xx=XXXX-XX-
XXXXX:XX:XXX&xx=XXXX-XX-XXXXX:XX:XXX&xxx=xxxxx&xxx=XXxXXX
xxxxxXXXXXXxXxxxXXXXXxxXXXXXxXXXXxXXXxXXxXX
```

Take this result (without quotations) and enter it in the `sas_token` field in the YAML file.

5. Navigate to the directory the YAML file is in so that we can finally create the datastore in the Azure Machine Learning workspace by running the following command:

```
az ml datastore create \
    --workspace-name mldemows \
    --resource-group mldemo \
    --file ./blobdatastore.yml
```

The result should look like the following:

```
"account_name": "mldemoblob8765",
"container_name": "mlfiles",
"credentials": {},
"description": "main ML blob storage",
"endpoint": "core.windows.net",
"id": <yourid>,
"name": "mldemoblob",
"protocol": "https",
"resourceGroup": "mldemo",
"tags": {},
"type": "azure_blob"
```

With these steps, we have registered a datastore connected to our blob storage using a SAS token.

> **Important Note**
>
> You can follow the same steps when connecting to a Data Lake Storage, but be aware that to access a data lake, you will need to create a **service principal**. A detailed description of this can be found here: https://docs.microsoft.com/en-us/azure/active-directory/develop/howto-create-service-principal-portal.

As discussed before, we could have created a blob storage by navigating to the wizard in the Azure portal, creating a SAS token for the container there, and entering it in the datastore creation wizard in Azure Machine Learning Studio. We used the Azure CLI so that you can get comfortable with this, as this is required to automate such steps in the future, especially when we talk about infrastructure-as-code and DevOps environments.

In any case, feel free to navigate to the **Datastores** tab in Azure Machine Learning Studio. *Figure 4.2* shows our newly created workspace:

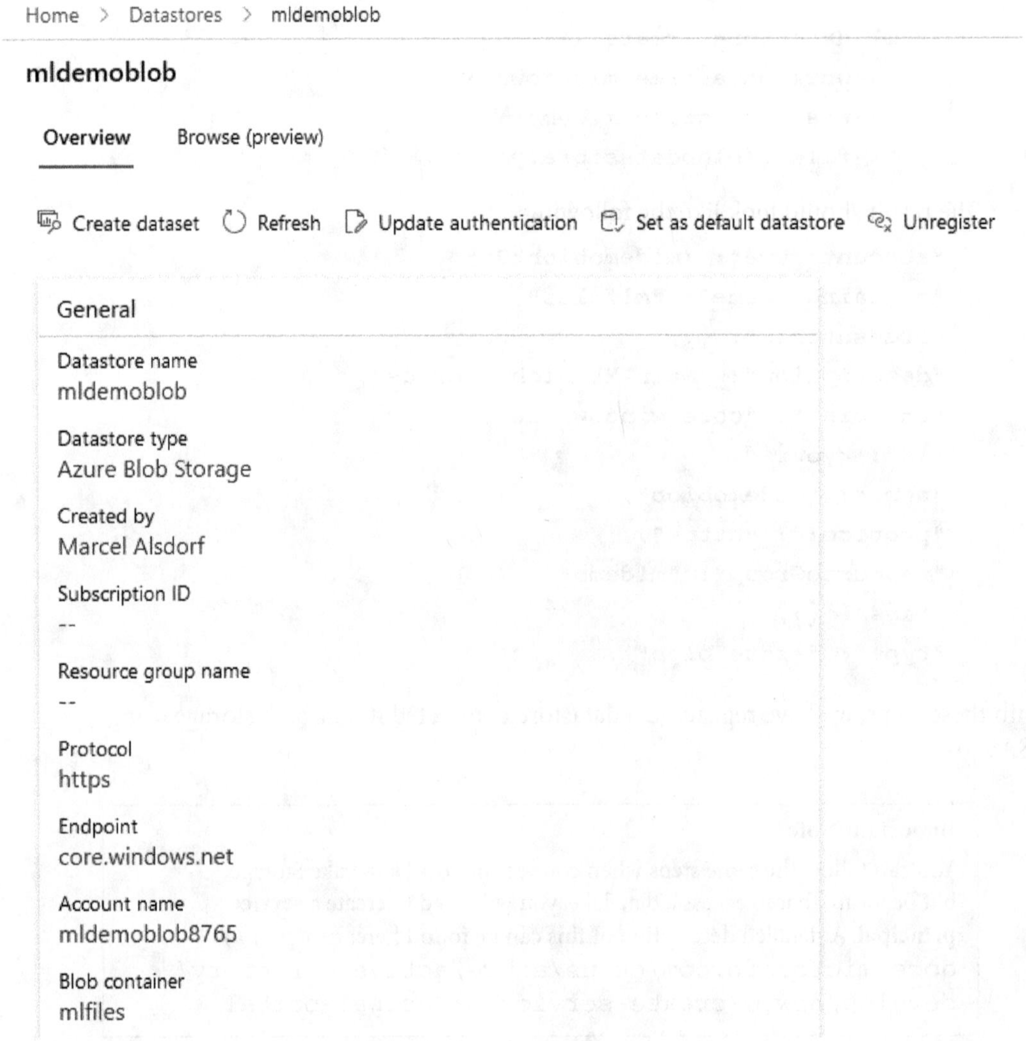

Home > Datastores > mldemoblob

mldemoblob

Overview   Browse (preview)

🖼 Create dataset   ⟳ Refresh   ▷ Update authentication   🖰 Set as default datastore   ⚬ Unregister

General

Datastore name
mldemoblob

Datastore type
Azure Blob Storage

Created by
Marcel Alsdorf

Subscription ID
--

Resource group name
--

Protocol
https

Endpoint
core.windows.net

Account name
mldemoblob8765

Blob container
mlfiles

Figure 4.2 – Created datastore

Keep this tab open, so we can verify later via the **Browse** tab that we copied files to the `mlfiles` container, which we will start doing in the following section.

Ingesting data into Azure

We created an Azure Blob storage account and learned how to organize and format files and tabular data for common ML use cases. However, one often-neglected step is how to efficiently ingest data into these datastores, or into Azure in general. There are different solutions for different datasets and use cases, from ad hoc, automated, parallelized solutions, and more. In this section, we will have a look at methods to upload and transform data either in a manual or an automated fashion to a relational database (SQL, MySQL, or PostgreSQL) or a storage account in Azure. Finally, we will upload a dataset file to the previously created blob storage.

Understanding tooling for the manual ingestion of data

If you work with a small number of datasets and files and you do not need to transfer data from other existing sources, a manual upload of data is the go-to option.

The following list shows possible options to bring data into your datastores or directly into your ML pipelines:

- **Azure Storage Explorer**: Storage Explorer is an interactive application that allows you to upload data to and control datastores, such as storage accounts and managed disks. This is the easiest tool to use for managing storage accounts and can be found here: `https://azure.microsoft.com/en-us/features/storage-explorer/#overview`.

- **Azure CLI**: As we saw before, we basically can do anything with the CLI, including creating and uploading blobs to a storage account. You can find the appropriate commands to upload blobs in the storage extension described here: `https://docs.microsoft.com/en-us/cli/azure/storage/blob`.

- **AzCopy**: This is another command-line tool specifically designed to copy blobs or files to a storage account. Whether you use Azure CLI packages or AzCopy comes down to personal preference, as there are no clear performance differences between these two options. You can find the download link and the description here: `https://docs.microsoft.com/en-us/azure/storage/common/storage-use-azcopy-v10`.

- **The Azure portal**: For any service, you will always find a web interface directly in the Azure portal to upload or change data. If you navigate to a storage account, you can use the inbuilt storage browser to upload blobs and files directly through the web interface. The same is true for any of the database technologies.

- **RDBMS management tooling**: You can use any typical management tool to configure, create, and change tables and schemas in a relational database. For a SQL database and Synapse, this would be **SQL Server Management Studio** (`https://docs.microsoft.com/en-us/sql/ssms/download-sql-server-management-studio-ssms?view=sql-server-ver15`); for PostgreSQL, this would be **pgAdmin** (`https://www.pgadmin.org/`); and for MySQL, this would be **MySQL Workbench** (`https://docs.microsoft.com/en-us/azure/mysql/connect-workbench`).

- **Azure Data Studio**: Data Studio allows you to connect to any Microsoft SQL database, to Synapse, to a PostgreSQL database in Azure, and to Azure Data Explorer. It is a multiplatform tool very similar to the typical management tooling mentioned in the last point but in one platform. You can download this tool here: `https://docs.microsoft.com/en-us/sql/azure-data-studio/download-azure-data-studio?view=sql-server-ver15`.

- **Azure Machine Learning designer (Import Data)**: If you do not want to use an Azure Machine Learning datastore, you can use the **Import Data** component in the Machine Learning designer to add data ad hoc to your pipelines. This is not the cleanest way to operate, but an option nonetheless. You can find all information about this method here: `https://docs.microsoft.com/en-us/azure/machine-learning/component-reference/import-data`.

Before we test out some of these options, let's have a look at the options to create automated data flows and transform data in Azure.

Understanding tooling for automated ingestion and transformation of data

Copying data manually is completely fine for small tests and probably even for most of the tasks we will perform in this book, but in a real-world scenario, we will need to not only integrate with a lot of different sources but will also need a process that does not include a person manually moving data from A to B.

Therefore, we will now have a look at services that allow us to transform and move data in an automated fashion and that integrate very well with pipelines and MLOps in Azure Machine Learning.

Azure Data Factory

Azure Data Factory is the enterprise-ready solution for moving and transforming data in Azure. It offers the ability to connect to hundreds of different sources and to create pipelines to transform the integrated data, calling multiple other services in Azure.

Run the following command to create a data factory:

```
az datafactory create \
    --location "West US 2" \
    --name "mldemoDF8765" \
    --resource-group "mldemo"
```

Please be aware that the name, once again, has to be globally unique. In addition, before deployment, the CLI will ask you to install the datafactory extension.

Once you are done, navigate to the resource in the Azure portal, and on the **Overview** tab, click on **Open Azure Data Factory Studio**, which will lead you to the workbench for your data factory instance. You should see a view as shown in *Figure 4.3*:

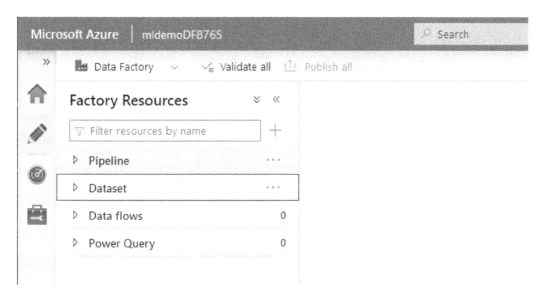

Figure 4.3 – Data Factory resource view

From this view, you can create pipelines, datasets, data flows, and power queries. Let's briefly discuss what they are:

- **Pipelines**: Pipelines are the main star of Azure Data Factory. You can create complex pipelines calling multiple services to pull data from a source, transform it, and store it in a sink.

- **Datasets**: Datasets are used in a pipeline as a source or a sink. Therefore, before building a pipeline, you can define a connection to specific data in a datastore that you want to read from or write to in the end.

- **Data flows**: Data flows allows you to do the actual processing or transformation of data within Data Factory itself, instead of calling a different service to do the heavy lifting.

- **Power Query**: Power Query allows you to do data exploration with DAX inside Data Factory, which is typically only possible with Power BI or Excel otherwise.

If you click on the three dots next to **Pipeline**, you can create a new one, which will result in the following view shown in *Figure 4.4*:

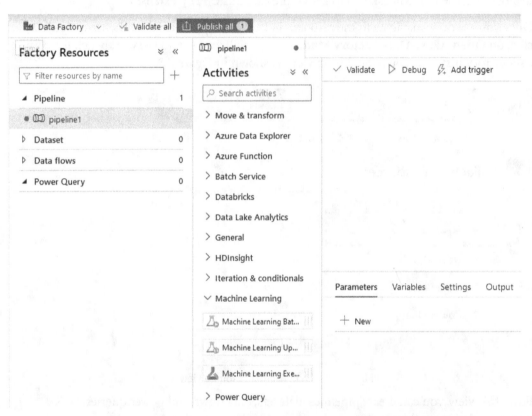

Figure 4.4 – Creating a Data Factory pipeline

Having a look through the possible activities, you will find a way to copy data (**Copy Data**) from A to B, to execute a script in Azure Functions (**Azure Function**), to call a stored procedure in a SQL database (**Stored Procedure**), to execute a notebook in Databricks (**Notebook**), and to execute an ML pipeline (**Machine Learning Execute Pipeline**), among other things. With these activities and the control tools you will find in **General** and **Iteration & conditionals**, you can build very complex data pipelines to move and transform your data.

As you might have noticed, Azure Synapse is missing from the list of activities. The reason for that is that Synapse has its own version of Data Factory integrated into the platform. Therefore, if you are using a SQL pool or a Spark pool in Synapse, you can use the integration tool of Synapse instead, which will give you access to running a notebook in the Synapse Spark pool or a stored procedure on the SQL pool.

If you are looking for an in-depth overview of Azure Data Factory, have a look at Catherine Wilhelmsen's *Beginners Guide to Azure Data Factory*: `https://www.cathrinewilhelmsen.net/series/beginners-guide-azure-data-factory/`.

Now, what we need to understand is that there are two ways to integrate this Data Factory pipeline into Azure Machine Learning:

- **Read results from a storage account**: We can just run the transformation pipeline in Data Factory, transforming our data, and then store the result in a storage account. We then access the data as we learned via an ML datastore. In this scenario, any pipeline we have in Azure Machine Learning is disconnected from the transformation pipelines in Data Factory, which might not be the optimal way for MLOps.

- **Invoke Azure Machine Learning from Data Factory**: We can create a transformation pipeline and invoke the actual Azure Machine Learning pipeline as part of the Data Factory pipeline. This is the preferred way if we are starting to build an end-to-end MLOps workflow.

For further information on this, have a read through the following article: `https://docs.microsoft.com/en-us/azure/machine-learning/how-to-data-ingest-adf`.

Azure Synapse Spark pools

As we discussed in *Chapter 2*, *Choosing the Right Machine Learning Service in Azure*, Azure Databricks and Azure Synapse give you the option to run Spark jobs in a Spark pool. Apache Spark can help you transform and preprocess extremely large datasets by utilizing the distributive nature of the node pool underneath. Therefore, this tool can be helpful to take apart and filter out datasets before starting the actual machine learning process.

We have seen that we can run notebooks from either Azure Data Factory or from the integration engine in Azure Synapse and therefore already have access to these services. On top of that, we have the option to add a Synapse Spark pool as a so-called **linked service** in the Azure Machine Learning workspace (see the **Linked Services** tab in Azure Machine Learning Studio). Doing this step gives us the opportunity to access not only the ML compute targets but also the Spark pool as a target for computations via the Azure Machine Learning SDK.

You can create this link either via Azure Machine Learning Studio or via the Azure Machine Learning Python SDK, both of which are described in the following article: `https://docs.microsoft.com/en-us/azure/machine-learning/how-to-link-synapse-ml-workspaces`.

Through this direct integration, we can run transformation steps in our ML pipelines through a Spark cluster and therefore get another good option for building a clean end-to-end MLOps workflow.

Copying data to Blob storage

Now, that we have a good understanding of most of the options to move and transform data, let's upload a dataset to our storage account.

In *Chapter 5*, *Performing Data Analysis and Visualization*, we will start analyzing and preprocessing data. To prepare for this, let's upload the dataset we will work with in that chapter.

We will work with the **Melbourne Housing dataset**, created by Anthony Pino, which you can find here: `https://www.kaggle.com/anthonypino/melbourne-housing-market`. The reason to work with this dataset is the domain it covers, as everyone understands housing, and the reasonable cleanliness of the data. If you continue your journey through working with data, you will find out that there are a lot of datasets out there, but only a few that are clean and educational.

In addition, to make our lives a bit easier when analyzing the dataset in the next chapter, we will actually work with a subset of this dataset.

Follow the next steps so that we can make this file available in our `mldemoblob` datastore:

1. Download the `melb_data.csv` file from `https://www.kaggle.com/dansbecker/melbourne-housing-snapshot` and store it in a suitable folder on your device.

2. Navigate to that folder and run the following command in the CLI, replacing the storage account name with your own:

```
az storage blob upload \
    --account-name mldemoblob8765 \
    --file ./melb_data.csv \
    --container-name mlfiles \
    --name melb_data.csv
```

3. To verify this, let's have a look at another option to move this file. Install Azure Storage Explorer and log in to your Azure account in that application. Navigate to your storage account and open the `mlfiles` container. It should show you a view as seen in *Figure 4.5*:

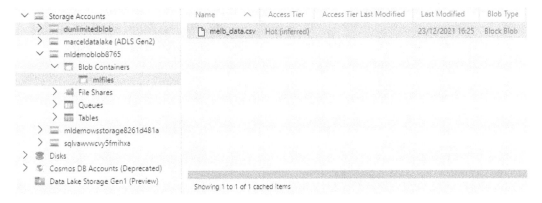

Figure 4.5 – Azure Storage Explorer

As you can see, our file is where it is supposed to be. We could have also just dragged and dropped the file directly here, creating a blob file automatically. From here on out, feel free to use what feels more comfortable to you.

4. To finish this up, have a look at the application itself. For example, if you right-click on the container, you can choose an option called **Get Shared Access Signature**, which opens a wizard allowing you to create a SAS token directly here, instead of as we did via the command line.

With the previous steps, we made our raw dataset file available in our storage account and therefore in our ML datastore. In the next section, we will have a look at how to create an Azure Machine Learning dataset from these raw files and what features they offer to support us in our ongoing ML journey.

Using datasets in Azure Machine Learning

In the previous sections of this chapter, we discussed how to get data into the cloud, store the data in a datastore, and connect the data via a **datastore and dataset** to an Azure Machine Learning workspace. We did all this effort of managing the data and data access centrally in order to use the data across all compute environments, either for experimentation, training, or inferencing. In this section, we will focus on how to create, explore, and access these datasets during training.

Once the data is managed as datasets, we can track the data that was used for each experimentation or training run in Azure Machine Learning. This will give us visibility of the data used for a specific training run and for the trained model – an essential step in creating reproducible end-to-end machine learning workflows.

Another benefit of organizing your data into datasets is that you can easily pass a managed dataset to your experimentation or training scripts via **direct access, download**, or **mount**. The direct access method is useful for publicly available data sources, the *download* method is convenient for small datasets, and the *mount* method is useful for large datasets. In Azure Machine Learning training clusters, this is completely transparent, and the data will be provided automatically. However, we can use the same technique to access the data in any other Python environment, by simply having access to the dataset object.

In the last part of this section, we will explore Azure Open Datasets – a collection of curated Azure Machine Learning datasets you can consume directly from within your Azure Machine Learning workspace.

Creating new datasets

There are multiple ways to create new datasets, but most of them differentiate between tabular and file datasets. You need to use different constructors based on the type of dataset you want to create:

- `Dataset.Tabular.from_*` for tabular datasets
- `Dataset.File.from_*` for file-based datasets (for example, image, audio, and more)

For tabular datasets, we also differentiate between the data being accessed from the original location through a public URL – called a *direct dataset* – or stored on either the default or a custom *datastore*.

A `Dataset` object can be accessed or passed around in the current environment through its object reference. However, a dataset can also be registered (and versioned), and hence accessed through the dataset name (and version) – this is called a *registered dataset*.

Let's see a simple example of a direct dataset, which is defined as a tabular dataset, and a publicly available URL containing a delimiter-separated file with the data:

```
from azureml.core import Dataset


path = 'https://...windows.net/demo/Titanic.csv'
ds = Dataset.Tabular.from_delimited_files(path)
```

As you can see in the code, we can create a *direct dataset* by passing the URL to a publicly accessible delimiter-separated file. When passing this dataset internally, every consumer will attempt to fetch the dataset from its URL.

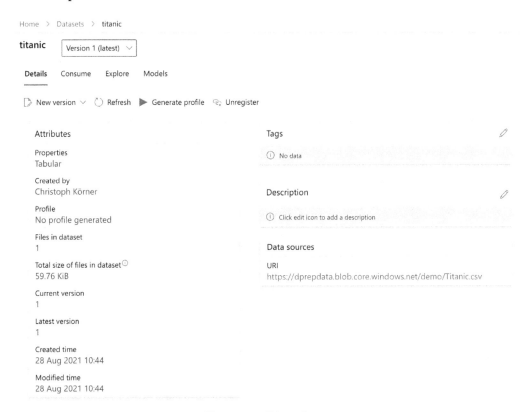

Figure 4.6 – Direct dataset

Once we have a reference to a datastore, we can access data within it. In the following example, we create a file dataset from files stored in a directory of the `mldata` datastore:

```
from azureml.core import Dataset, Datastore

datastore_name = "mldata"
datastore = Datastore.get(ws, datastore_name)
ds = Dataset.File.from_files((datastore, "cifar10/"))
```

As you can see in the example, we can register data from within the datastore as datasets. In this example, we defined all files in a folder as a file dataset, but we could also define a delimiter-separated file in Blob storage as a tabular dataset.

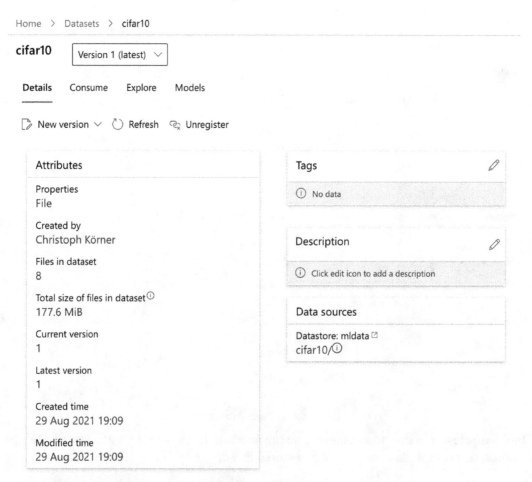

Figure 4.7 – File dataset

In the next step, we register this dataset in the workspace using the following code snippet to create a *registered dataset*:

```
ds = ds.register(ws, name="titanic",
                 create_new_version=True)
```

The previous code will register the direct dataset in your workspace and return a registered dataset. Registered datasets are listed in Azure Machine Learning Studio, and can be accessed via the dataset name instead of the `Dataset` Python object.

The `create_new_version` argument controls whether we want to create a new version of an existing dataset. Once a new dataset version is created, the dataset can be accessed through the dataset name – which will implicitly access the latest version – or through its name and a specific version. Dataset versions are useful to manage different iterations of the dataset within your workspace.

Exploring data in datasets

There are multiple options to explore registered datasets in Azure Machine Learning. For tabular datasets, the most convenient way is to load and analyze a dataset programmatically in an Azure Machine Learning workspace. To do so, you can simply reference a dataset by its name and version as shown in the following snippet:

```
from azureml.core import Dataset

ds = Dataset.get_by_name(ws, name="titanic", version=1)
```

Once you have a reference to the dataset, you can convert a dataset reference to an actual in-memory **pandas** DataFrame or a lazy-loaded **Spark** or **Dask** DataFrame. To do so, you can call one of the following methods:

- `to_pandas_dataframe()` to create an in-memory pandas DataFrame
- `to_spark_dataframe()` to create a lazily loaded Spark DataFrame
- `to_dask_dataframe()` to create a lazily loaded Dask DataFrame

Let's see the three commands in action, starting with the in-memory pandas DataFrame. The following code snippet will load all the data into a pandas DataFrame and then return the first five rows of the DataFrame:

```
panads_df = ds.to_pandas_dataframe()
pandas_df.head()
```

After loading the DataFrame, you can run your favorite pandas methods to explore the datasets. For example, good commands to get started are `info()` to see columns and datatypes and `describe()` to see statistics of the numerical values of the DataFrame.

Lazy datasets are datasets that only load some data to memory when explicitly needed, for example, when a result of a computation is required. Non-lazy datasets load all the data into memory and hence are limited by the available memory.

If you are more familiar with PySpark, you can also transform a dataset into a Spark DataFrame with the following code snippet. In contrast to the previous example, this code won't actually load all data into memory but only fetches the data required for executing the `show()` command – this makes it a great choice for analyzing large datasets:

```
spark_df = ds.to_spark_dataframe()
spark_df.show()
```

Another alternative is to return a Dask DataFrame of the dataset. Dask is a Python library for parallel computing that supports lazy datasets with a pandas- and NumPy-like API. Hence you can run the following code to return the first five rows of the DataFrame lazily:

```
dask_df = ds.to_dask_dataframe()
dask_df.head()
```

Once you have programmatic access to the data in your favorite numeric or statistical libraries, you can slice and dice your dataset as much as needed. While programmatic access is great for reproducibility and customization, users often just want to understand how the data is structured and see a few example records. Azure Machine Learning also offers the possibility to explore the dataset in the Data Studio UI.

To get to this view, go to **Datasets**, select a dataset, and click on the **Explore** tab. The first page shows you a preview of your data, including the first *n* rows as well as some basic information about the data – such as the number of rows and columns. The following screenshot shows an example:

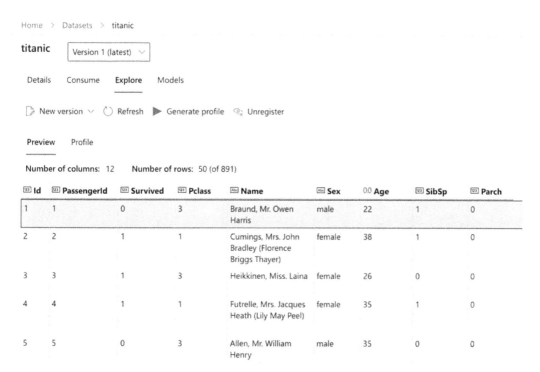

Figure 4.8 – Dataset with data preview

If you click on the second tab, you can generate and view a data profile. This profile is similar to calling `describe()` on the pandas DataFrame – a statistical analysis of each column in the dataset, but with support for categorical data and some more useful information. As you can see in *Figure 4.9*, it also shows a figure with the data distribution for each column:

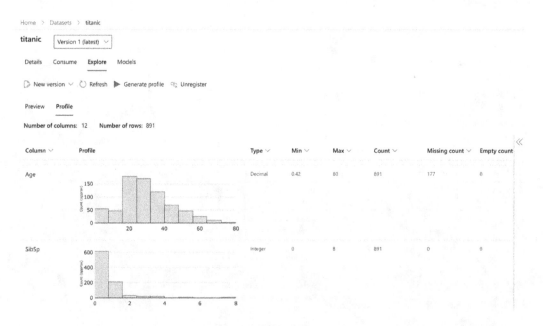

Figure 4.9 – Dataset with data profile

As you can see in the previous figure, this is a very useful summary of the dataset. The insights from this view are important for everyone working with this dataset.

In this section, we saw multiple ways to access and analyze data stored in Azure Machine Learning datasets – programmatically via Python and your favorite numerical libraries or via the UI.

Tracking datasets in Azure Machine Learning

End-to-end tracking of all assets that go into your final production model is essential for reproducibility and interpretability but also auditing and tracking. A machine learning model is a function that minimizes a loss function by iterating and sampling experiments from your training data. Therefore, the training data itself should be treated as being a part of the model itself, and hence should be managed, versioned, and tracked through the end-to-end machine learning process.

We want to take advantage of datasets to add data tracking to our experiments. A good way to understand the differences between data tracking capabilities is to look at two examples: first, loading a CSV dataset from a URL, and then loading the same data from the same URL but through a dataset abstraction in Azure Machine Learning. However, we don't only want to load the data, but also pass it from the authoring script to the training script as an argument.

We will first use `pandas` to load a CSV file directly from the URL and pass it to the training script as a URL. In the next step, we will enhance this method by using a direct dataset instead, allowing us to conveniently pass the dataset configuration to the training script and track the dataset for the experiment run in Azure Machine Learning.

Passing external data as a URL

We start our example using data that is available as a CSV file from a remote URL, a common way to distribute public datasets. In the first example without Azure Machine Learning dataset tracking, we will use the `pandas` library to fetch and parse the CSV file:

1. Let's get started with the first code snippet using pandas' `read_csv()` method as an example to fetch data via a public URL from a remote server. However, this is just an example – you could replace it with any other method to fetch data from a remote location:

```
import pandas as pd
path ='https://...windows.net/demo/Titanic.csv'
df = pd.read_csv(path)
print(df.head())
```

Our goal is to pass the data from the authoring script to the training script, so it can be tracked and updated easily in the future. To achieve this, we can't send the DataFrame directly, but have to pass the URL to the CSV file and use the same method to fetch the data in the training script. Let's write a small training script whose only job is to parse the command-line arguments and fetch the data from the URL:

code/access_data_from_path.py

```
import argparse
import pandas as pd

parser = argparse.ArgumentParser()
parser.add_argument("--input", type=str)
```

```
args = parser.parse_args()


df = pd.read_csv(args.input)
print(df.head())
```

As we see in the preceding code, we pass the data path from the command-line `--input` argument and then load the data from the location using pandas' `read_csv()`.

2. Next, we create a `ScriptRunConfig` constructor to submit an experiment run to Azure Machine Learning that executes the training script from *step 1*. For now, we are not performing any training but only want to understand what data is passed between the authoring and execution runtime:

Access_data_from_path.ipynb

```
src = ScriptRunConfig(
    source_directory="code",
    script='access_data_from_path.py',
    arguments=['--input', path],
    environment=get_current_env())
```

3. Let's execute the run configuration to run the experiment and track the run details in Azure Machine Learning. Once the experiment run has finished, we navigate to Azure Machine Learning and check the details of this run. As we can see in *Figure 4.10*, Azure Machine Learning will track the `script` argument as expected but cannot associate the argument to a dataset:

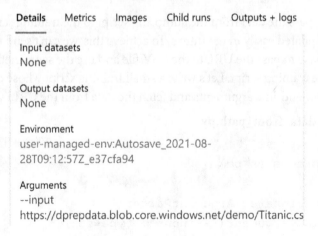

Figure 4.10 – Run details of the experiment

Let's summarize the downsides of this approach:

- We can't pass the pandas DataFrame or a DataFrame identifier to the training script; we have to pass the data through the URL to its location. If the file path changes, we have to update the argument for the training script.

- The training script doesn't know that the input path refers to the input data for the training script, it's simply a string argument to the training script. While we can track the argument in Azure Machine Learning, we can't automatically track the data.

Passing external data as a direct dataset

As promised, we will now enhance the previous example using a dataset in Azure Machine Learning. This will allow us to pass the dataset as a named configuration – abstracting the URL and access to the physical location of the data. It also automatically enables dataset tracking for the experiment:

1. We start in the authoring script, and load the data from the path – only this time, using Azure Machine Learning's `TabularDataset`, created through the `from_delimited_files()` factory method:

```
from azureml.core import Dataset
path ='https://...windows.net/demo/Titanic.csv'
ds = Dataset.Tabular.from_delimited_files(path)
print(ds.to_pandas_dataframe().head())
```

This will output the same set of rows as the previous example in pandas – so there is almost no difference other than using a different method to create the DataFrame. However, now that we have created a *direct dataset*, we can easily pass the dataset to the training script as a named dataset configuration – which will use the dataset ID under the hood.

2. Like the pandas example, we write a simplified training script that will access the dataset and print the first few records by parsing the input dataset from the command-line arguments. In the training script, we can use the `Dataset.get_by_id()` method to fetch the dataset by its ID from a workspace:

code/access_data_from_dataset.py

```
import argparse
from azureml.core import Dataset, Run
```

```
parser = argparse.ArgumentParser()
parser.add_argument("--input", type=str)
args = parser.parse_args()

run = Run.get_context()
ws = run.experiment.workspace

ds = Dataset.get_by_id(ws, id=args.input)
print(ds.to_pandas_dataframe().head())
```

As you can see in the preceding code, we modified the previous code slightly and added code to retrieve the current run context, experiment, and the workspace. This lets us access the direct dataset from the workspace by passing the dataset ID to the `Dataset.get_by_id()` method.

3. Next, we write a run configuration to submit the preceding code as an experiment to Azure Machine Learning. First, we need to convert the dataset into a command-line argument and pass it to the training script so it can be automatically retrieved in the execution runtime. We can achieve this by using the `as_named_input(name)` method on the dataset instance, which will convert the dataset into a named `DatasetConsumptionConfig` argument that allows the dataset to be passed to other environments.

In this case, the dataset will be passed in direct mode and provided as the `name` environment variable in the runtime environment or as the dataset ID in the command-line arguments. The dataset will also get tracked in Azure Machine Learning as an input argument to the training script.

However, as we saw in the previous code snippet, we use the `Dataset.get_by_id()` method to retrieve the dataset in the training script from the dataset ID. We don't need to manually create or access the dataset ID, because the `DatasetConsumptionConfig` argument will be automatically expanded into the dataset ID when the training script is called by Azure Machine Learning with a direct dataset:

Access_data_from_dataset.ipynb

```
src = ScriptRunConfig(
    source_directory="code",
    script='access_data_from_dataset.py',
    arguments=['--input', ds.as_named_input('titanic')],
    environment=get_current_env())
```

As we can see in the preceding code, the dataset is converted to a configuration that can simply be passed to the training script through the `as_named_input(name)` method. If we submit the experiment and check the logs of the run, we can see that Azure Machine Learning passed the dataset ID to the training script:

70_driver_log.txt

```
. . .

After variable expansion, calling script [access_data_from_
dataset.py] with arguments:['--input', '04f8ad60-5a51-4319-
92fe-cdfa7f6c9adc']
```

The run details for this experiment are shown in *Figure 4.11*. If you look at the input arguments, you can see that we passed the `DatasetConsumptionConfig` object to the script, which was then converted automatically to the dataset ID. Not only is the input argument passed without any information about the location of the underlying data, but the input dataset is also recognized as an input to the training data:

Figure 4.11 – Run details of the experiment

By passing a dataset to a training script, Azure Machine Learning automatically tracks the dataset with the experiment run. As you can see in *Figure 4.11*, the dataset ID is a link to the tracked dataset. When clicking on the dataset ID in Azure Machine Learning, it will open a page showing details about the tracked dataset, such as description, URL, size, and type of dataset, as shown in *Figure 4.12*. Like registered datasets, you can also explore the raw data and look at dataset column statistics – called the profile – or see any registered models derived from this data. Tracked datasets can easily be registered – and hence versioned and managed – by clicking on the **Register** action or from code:

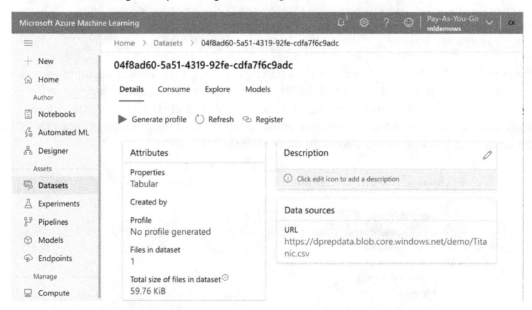

Figure 4.12 – Direct dataset tracked in Azure Machine Learning

As we saw in this section, there are important benefits to passing the input data to your training script as a dataset argument. This will automatically track the dataset in your workspace and connect the dataset with the experimentation run.

In the code snippets of this section, we passed the data as a *direct dataset*, which means that the training script has to fetch the data again from the external URL. This is not always optimal, especially when dealing with large amounts of data or when data should be managed in Azure Machine Learning. In the next section, we will explore different ways to pass data to the training script.

Accessing data during training

In the previous section, we implicitly passed the URL of the original dataset to the training script. While this is a practical and fast solution for small public datasets, it's often not the preferred approach for private or larger datasets. Imagine your data is stored on a SQL server, Blob storage, or file share instead, and password protected. Imagine your dataset contains many gigabytes of files. In this section, we will see techniques that work well for both cases.

While external public data reachable through a URL is created and passed as a *direct dataset*, all other datasets can be accessed either as a **download** or as a **mount**. For big data datasets, Azure Machine Learning also provides an option to mount a dataset as a **Hadoop Distributed File System** (**HDFS**).

In this section, we will see authoring scripts that will pass datasets both as a download and as a mount. Let's first create a reference in the authoring script to the `cifar10` dataset, which we registered in the previous section. The following snippet retrieves a dataset by name from the Azure Machine Learning workspace:

```
from azureml.core import Dataset
dataset = Dataset.get_by_name(ws, "cifar10")
```

Next, we want to pass the dataset to the training script so that we can access the training data from the script. The benefit of using datasets is not only tracking but the fact that we can simply choose the appropriate data consumption configuration that is appropriate for each dataset. It will also help us to separate the training script from the training data, making it easy to pass new, updated, or enriched data to the same training script without needing to update the training script.

Independently of the consumption method, the training script can always load the data from a directory path where it will be either downloaded or mounted. Under the hood, Azure Machine Learning inspects the command-line arguments of `ScriptRunConfig`, detects the dataset reference, delivers the data to the compute environment, and replaces the argument with the path of the dataset in the local filesystem.

Azure Machine Learning uses parameter expansion to replace the dataset reference with the path to the actual data on disk. To make this more obvious, we will write a single training file that will simply list all training files that were passed to it. The following code snippet implements this training script:

code/access_dataset.py

```
import os
import argparse
```

```
parser = argparse.ArgumentParser()
parser.add_argument("--input", type=str)
args = parser.parse_args()

print("Dataset path: {}".format(args.input))
print(os.listdir(args.input))
```

In the previous script, we define a single --input argument that we will use to pass the training data. Then we will output this argument and list all files from the directory. We will use this script to pass data with different mounting techniques and will see that the data will always be available in the folder.

Having the dataset reference and a simple training script, we can now look at a different ScriptRunConfig to pass the cifar10 dataset using the different data consumption configurations. While the code is downloaded or mounted by Azure Machine Learning before the training script is invoked, we will also explore what happens under the hood – so we can apply the same technique to load the training data outside of Azure Machine Learning-managed compute environments.

Accessing data as a download

We will first look at downloading the data to the training instance. To do so, we will first create a ScriptRunConfig constructor in the authoring environment where we pass the data to as_download(). We will schedule a code snippet that will access and output the files passed to the script:

Access_dataset_as_download.ipynb

```
from azureml.core import ScriptRunConfig

src = ScriptRunConfig(
  source_directory="code",
  script='access_dataset.py',
  arguments=['--input',
    dataset.as_named_input('cifar10').as_download()],
  environment=get_current_env())
```

Azure will interpolate the dataset passed by the `input` parameter and replace it with the location of the dataset on disk. The data will be automatically downloaded to the training environment if the dataset is passed with the `Dataset.as_download()` method.

If you run this script configuration, the `access_dataset.py` script will output the temporary location of the dataset, which was automatically downloaded to disk. You can replicate the exact same process in your authoring environment that Azure Machine Learning does under the hood. To do so, you can simply call the following:

```
folder = '/tmp/cifar10-data'
paths = dataset.download(folder)
```

Passing data as a download is convenient for small datasets or when using a large number of consumers that require a high throughput on the data. However, if you are dealing with large datasets, you can also pass them as a *mount* instead.

Accessing data as a mount

In this example, we will mount the data on the training environment. To do so, we will again create a `ScriptRunConfig` constructor in the authoring environment and this time we invoke the `as_mount()`. We will schedule a code snippet that will access and output the files passed to the script:

Access_dataset_as_mount.ipynb

```
from azureml.core import ScriptRunConfig

src = ScriptRunConfig(
  source_directory="code",
  script='access_dataset.py',
  arguments=['--input',
    dataset.as_named_input('cifar10').as_mount()],
  environment=get_current_env())
```

As you can see, the preceding example is very similar to the previous example where data was downloaded to disk. In fact, we are reusing the exact same scheduled script, `access_dataset.py`, which will output the location of the data on disk. However, in this example, the data is not downloaded to this location but mounted to the file path.

Azure Machine Learning will interpolate the dataset passed through the input argument with the mounted path on disk. Similar to the previous example, you can replicate what happens under the hood in Azure Machine Learning and mount the data from within your authoring environment:

```
import os
folder = '/tmp/cifar10-data'


# Or you can also use the start and stop methods
mount_context = dataset.mount(folder)


try:
    mount_context.start()
    print(os.listdir(folder))
finally:
    mount_context.stop()
```

As you can see in the previous snippet, the dataset is mounted and released using the mount context's `start` and `stop` methods. You can also simplify the code snippet using Python's `with` statement to automatically mount and unmount the data as shown in the following snippet:

```
with dataset.mount() as mount_context:
    print(os.listdir(mount_context.mount_point))
```

Hence, depending on the use case, we have different options to pass a dataset reference to a scheduled script. Independent of the data transport, Azure Machine Learning will implement the correct method under the hood and interpolate the input arguments so that the training script doesn't need to know how a dataset was configured. For the executed script, the data is simply made available through a path in the filesystem.

Using external datasets with open datasets

One of the most effective methods to improve the prediction performance of any ML model is to add additional information to your training data. A common way to achieve this is by joining external datasets to the training data. A good indication to join external data is the availability of popular joining keys in your dataset, such as dates, locations, countries, and more.

When you work with transactional data that contains dates, you can easily join external data to create additional features for the training dataset and hence improve prediction performance. Common derived features for dates are weekdays, weekends, time to or since weekends, holidays, time to or since holidays, sports events, concerts, and more. When dealing with country information, you can often join additional country-specific data, such as population data, economic data, sociological data, health data, labor data, and more. When dealing with geolocation, you can join distance to points of interest, weather data, traffic data, and more. Each of these additional datasets gives you additional insights and hence can boost your model's performance significantly.

Open Datasets is a service that provides access to curated datasets for the transportation, health and genomics, labor and economics, population, and safety, categories and common datasets that you can use to boost your model's performance. Let's look into three examples.

> **Important Note**
>
> Before using a specific dataset for a commercial service, please make sure that your application is covered by the license. If in doubt, reach out to Microsoft via aod@microsoft.com.

In the first example, we will investigate the dataset for *worldwide public holidays*. The data covers holidays in almost 40 countries or regions from 1970 to 2099. It is curated from Wikipedia and the holidays Python package. You can import them into your environment and access these holidays using the opendatasets library as shown in the following example:

```
from azureml.opendatasets import PublicHolidays
from dateutil import parser

end_date = parser.parse("Jan 10 2000 12:00AM")
start_date = parser.parse("Jan 10 2010 12:00AM")
ds = PublicHolidays(start_date=start_date,
                    end_date=end_date)
df = ds.to_pandas_dataframe()
```

As we see in the code, we can access the dataset from the azureml-opendatasets package and use it as an Azure Machine Learning dataset. This means we can return the pandas or Spark DataFrame for further processing.

Another popular dataset is the *US population* by county for the years 2000 and 2010. It is broken down by gender and race and sourced from the United States Census Bureau:

```
from azureml.opendatasets import UsPopulationZip

population = UsPopulationZip()
population_df = population.to_pandas_dataframe()
```

Another example open dataset is the *Current Employment Statistics* of the United States, published by the US **Bureau of Labor Statistics** (**BLS**). It contains estimates of employment, hours, and earnings of workers on payrolls in the US:

```
from azureml.opendatasets import UsLaborEHENational

ds = UsLaborEHENational()
df = ds.to_pandas_dataframe()
```

As you saw in this section, Azure Open Datasets gives you a convenient option to access curated datasets in the form of Azure Machine Learning datasets right from within your Azure Machine Learning workspace. While the number of available datasets is still manageable, you can expect the number of available datasets to grow over time.

Summary

In this chapter, we learned how to manage data in Azure Machine Learning using datastores and datasets. We saw how to configure the default datastore that is responsible for storing all assets, logs, models, and more in Azure Machine Learning, as well as other services that can be used as datastores for different types of data.

After creating an Azure Blob storage account and configuring it as a datastore in Azure Machine Learning, we saw different tools to ingest data into Azure, such as Azure Storage Explorer, Azure CLI, and AzCopy, as well as services optimized for data ingestion and transformation, Azure Data Factory and Azure Synapse Spark.

In the subsequent section, we got our hands on datasets. We created file and tabular datasets and learned about direct and registered datasets. Datasets can be passed as a download or a mount to executed scripts, which will automatically track datasets in Azure Machine Learning.

Finally, we learned how to improve predication performance by joining third-party datasets from Azure Open Datasets to our machine learning process. In the next chapter, we will learn how to explore data by performing data analysis and visualization.

5

Performing Data Analysis and Visualization

In the previous chapter, we learned how to bring our datasets to the cloud, define data stores in the Azure Machine Learning workspace to access them, and register datasets in the Azure Machine Learning dataset registry to have a good basis to start data preprocessing from. In this chapter, we will learn how to explore this raw data.

First, you will learn about techniques that can help you explore tabular and file datasets. We will also talk about how to handle missing values, how to cross-correlate features to understand statistical connections between them, and how to bring domain knowledge to this process to improve our understanding of the context and the quality of our data cleansing. In addition, we will learn how to use ML algorithms not for training but for exploring our datasets.

After that, we will apply these methods to a real-life dataset while learning how to work with pandas DataFrames and how to visualize the properties of our dataset.

Finally, we will look at methods that can map high-dimensional data to a low-dimensional plane, which will help us see similarities and relationships between data points. Additionally, these methods can give us clear hints on how clean our data is and how effective the chosen ML algorithms will be on the dataset.

In this chapter, we will cover the following topics:

- Understanding data exploration techniques

- Performing data analysis on a tabular dataset

- Understanding dimensional reduction techniques

Technical requirements

In this chapter, we will use the following Python libraries and versions to perform data pre-processing and high-dimensional visualizations:

- `azureml-sdk 1.34.0`

- `azureml-widgets 1.34.0`

- `azureml-dataprep 2.20.0`

- `pandas 1.3.2`

- `numpy 1.19.5`

- `scikit-learn 0.24.2`

- `seaborn 0.11.2`

- `plotly 5.3.1`

- `umap_learn 0.5.1`

- `statsmodels 0.13.0`

- `missingno 0.5.0`

Similar to previous chapters, you can execute this code using either a local Python interpreter or a notebook environment hosted in Azure Machine Learning.

All code examples in this chapter can be found in the GitHub repository for this book: `https://github.com/PacktPublishing/Mastering-Azure-Machine-Learning-Second-Edition/tree/main/chapter05`.

Understanding data exploration techniques

Descriptive data exploration is, without a doubt, one of the most important steps in an ML project. If you want to clean data and build derived features or select an ML algorithm to predict a target variable in your dataset, then you need to understand your data first. Your data will define many of the necessary cleaning and preprocessing steps; it will define which algorithms you can choose, and it will ultimately define the performance of your predictive model.

Hence, data exploration should be considered an important analytical step to understanding whether your data is informative enough to build an ML model in the first place. By analytical step, we mean that the exploration should be done as a structured analytical process rather than a set of experimental tasks. Therefore, we will go through a checklist of data exploration tasks that you can perform as an initial step in every ML project – before you start any data cleaning, preprocessing, feature engineering, or model selection.

The possible tasks we can perform are tied to the type of dataset we are working with. A lot of datasets will come in the form of tabular data, which means we have either continuous or categorical features defined for each instance of the dataset. These datasets can be visualized as a table, and we can perform basic and complex mathematical operations on them. The other general type of dataset we may encounter will come in the form of media files. This includes images, videos, sound files, documents, and anything else that is not made up of data points that you could fit into a table structure.

To represent these different types of datasets, Azure Machine Learning gives us the option to save our data in one of the following objects:

- **TabularDataset:** This class offers methods for performing basic transformations on tabular data and converting them into known formats such as pandas (`https://docs.microsoft.com/en-us/python/api/azureml-core/azureml.data.tabulardataset`).

- **FileDataset:** This class primarily offers filtering methods on file metadata (`https://docs.microsoft.com/en-us/python/api/azureml-core/azureml.data.filedataset`).

Both types of dataset objects can be registered to the Azure Machine Learning Dataset Registry for further use after preprocessing.

Judging only by the methods that are available in those two classes, it becomes clear that the possible tasks and operations we can perform differ greatly between tabular datasets and file datasets. In the next few sections, we will look at both types and how we can prepare them to influence the result of our ML model.

Exploring and analyzing tabular datasets

A tabular dataset allows us to utilize the full spectrum of mathematical and statistical functions to analyze and transform our dataset, but in most cases, we do not have the time or resources to randomly run every dataset through all the possible techniques in our arsenal.

Choosing the right methods does not only involve having experience in analyzing a lot of different datasets but also subject matter expertise of the domain we are working in. There are areas where everyone has some general expertise (think the influencing factors of house prices, for example), but then there are a lot of areas where specialized knowledge is needed to understand the data at hand. Imagine that you want to increase the yield of a blast furnace creating steel. In such a scenario, to understand the data, you need to have intimate knowledge of the chemical processes in the furnace, or you need a **subject matter expert** to support you. In every step of exploration and analysis, we need to apply domain knowledge to interpret the result and relationships we see.

Besides understanding the domain, we also need to understand the features in the datasets and their targets or labels. Imagine having a dataset made up of features of houses in a certain city but without their market prices. To predict house prices, we would need labels or target values for the price of each house. On the other hand, if we were to predict if an email is spam or not and we have a dataset that contains a bunch of emails containing a lot of metadata, this might be good enough to train a model through unsupervised learning.

Therefore, to get a good understanding of the dataset, we need to thoroughly explore its content and get as many insights as possible on the features and the possible target to make good decisions.

> **Important Note**
> Please keep in mind that not only the feature dimensions but also the target variable needs to be preprocessed and analyzed thoroughly.

To achieve this, we will start by looking at the following aspects of every feature and target vector in the dataset:

- **Data type:** Is the content of the vector continuous, ordinal, nominal, or a text string? Are they stored in the correct programmatic data type (`datetime`, `string`, `int`, `object`)? Do we need to do a data type conversion?
- **Missing data:** Are there any missing entries? How do we handle them?

- **Inconsistent data**: Are date and time stored in different ways? Are the same categories written in different ways? Are there different categories with the same meaning in the given context?

- **Unique values**: How many unique values exist for a categorical feature? Are there too many? Should we create a subset of them?

- **Statistical properties**: What are the mean, median, and variance of a feature? Are there any outliers? What are the minimum and maximum values? What is the most common value (mode)?

- **Statistical distribution**: How are the values distributed? Is there a data skew? Would normalization or scaling be useful?

- **Correlation**: How are different features correlated to each other? Are there features containing similar information that could be omitted? How much are my features correlated with the target?

Analyzing each dimension of a dataset with more than 100 feature dimensions is an extremely time-consuming task. However, instead of randomly exploring feature dimensions, you can analyze the dimensions ordered by feature importance and significantly reduce your time working through the data. Like many other areas of computer science, it is good to use an 80/20 principle for the initial data exploration, which means using only 20% of the features to achieve 80% of the performance. This sets you up for a great start and you can always come back later to add more dimensions if needed.

Therefore, it is wise to understand the importance of the features for your modeling. We can do this by looking at the relationship between features and the target variable. There are many ways to do this, some of which are as follows:

- **Regression coefficient**: Used in regression

- **Feature importance**: Used in classification

- **High error rates for categorical values**: Used in binary classification

By applying these steps, you can understand the data and gain knowledge about the required preprocessing tasks for your data, features, and target variables. Along with that, it will give you a good estimate of what difficulties you can expect in your prediction task, which is essential for judging the required algorithms and validation strategies. You will also gain insight into what possible feature engineering methods could be applied to your dataset and have a better understanding of how to select a good error metric.

> **Important Note**
>
> You can use a representative subset of the data and extrapolate your hypothesis and insights to the whole dataset.

Once the data has been uploaded to a storage service in Azure, we can bring up a notebook environment and start exploring the data. The goal is to thoroughly explore our data in an analytical process to understand the distribution of *each* dimension of our data. We will perform some of these steps on a tabular dataset in the *Performing data analysis on a tabular dataset* section.

But first, we will look at some of the techniques that we've discussed in more detail and take a quick look at file datasets.

Handling missing values and outliers

One of the first things to look for in a new dataset is **missing values** for each feature and target dimension. This will help you gain a deeper understanding of the dataset and what actions could be taken to resolve them. It is not uncommon to remove missing values or impute them with zeros at the beginning of a project – however, this approach bears the risk of not properly analyzing missing values in the first place and losing a lot of data points.

> **Important Note**
>
> Missing values can be disguised as *valid* numeric or categorical values. Typical examples are minimum or maximum values, -1, 0, or NaN. Hence, if you find the values 32,767 (= 2^{15}-1) or 65,535 (= 2^{16}-1) appearing multiple times in an integer data column, they may well be missing values disguised as the maximum signed or unsigned 16-bit integer representation. Always assume that your data contains missing values and outliers in different shapes and representations. Your task is to uncover, find, and clean them.

Any prior knowledge about the data or domain will give you a competitive advantage when you're working with the data. The reason for this is that you will be able to understand **missing values, outliers**, and **extremes** concerning the data and domain, which will help you perform better imputation, cleansing, or transformation. As the next step, you should look for these outliers in your data, specifically for the absolute number or percentages of the following:

- The null values (look for `Null`, `"Null"`, `" "`, `NaN`, and so on)
- The minimum and maximum values
- The most common value (`MODE`)

- The 0 value
- Any unique values

Once you have identified these values, you can use different preprocessing techniques to impute missing values and normalize or exclude dimensions.

The typical options for dealing with missing values are as follows:

- **Deletion**: Delete entire rows or columns from the dataset. This can result in bias or having insufficient data for training.
- **New category**: Add a category called Missing for categorical features.
- **Column average**: Fill in the mean, median, or mode value of the entire data column or a subset of the column based on relationships with other features.
- **Interpolation**: Fill in an interpolated value based on the column's data.
- **Hot-deck imputation**: Fill in the logical previous value from the sorted records of the data column (useful in time series datasets).

The typical options for dealing with outliers are as follows:

- **Erroneous observations**: If the value is wrong, drop either the full column or replace the outlier with the mean of the column.
- **Leave as-is**: If it contains important information and if the model does not get distorted by it.
- **Cap or floor**: Cap or floor the value to a maximum deviation from the mean (for example, three standard deviations).

To get more context when choosing the right way to handle missing values and outliers, it is useful to statistically analyze the column distribution and correlations. We will do this in the following sections.

Calculating statistical properties and visualizing data distributions

Now that you know the outliers, you can start exploring the **value distribution** of your dataset's features. This will help you understand which transformation and normalization techniques should be applied during data preparation. Some common distribution statistics to look for in a continuous variable are as follows:

- The mean or median value
- The minimum and maximum value

- The variance and standard deviation
- The 25th, 50th (median), and 75th percentiles
- The data skew

Common techniques for visualizing these distributions include using **boxplots, density plots**, or **histograms**. The following screenshot shows these different visualization techniques plotted per target class for a multi-class recognition dataset. Each method has advantages and disadvantages – boxplots show all the relevant metrics while being a bit harder to read, density plots show very smooth shapes while hiding some of the outliers, and histograms don't let you spot the median and percentiles easily while giving you a good estimate of the data skew:

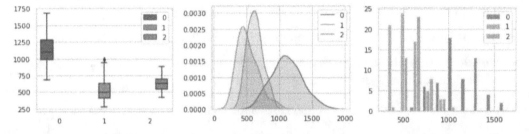

Figure 5.1 – A boxplot (left), a density plot (middle), and a histogram (right)

Here, we can see that only histograms work well for categorical data (both nominal and ordinal). However, you could look at the number of values per category. You can find the code for creating these plots in the `01_data_distribution.ipynb` file in this book's GitHub repository.

Another nice way to display the value distribution versus the target rate is in a binary classification task. The following diagram shows the **version number** of Windows Defender against the malware **detection rate** (for non-touch devices) from the *Microsoft Malware detection dataset* (`https://www.kaggle.com/c/microsoft-malware-prediction/data`):

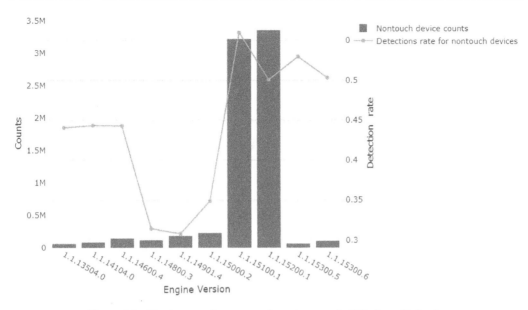

Figure 5.2 – Version number versus detection rate for Windows Defender

Many statistical ML algorithms require the data to be normally distributed, so it needs to be normalized or standardized. Knowing the data distribution helps you decide which transformations need to be applied during data preparation. In practice, data often needs to be transformed, scaled, or normalized.

Finding correlated dimensions

Another common task in data exploration is looking for correlations in the dataset. This will help you dismiss feature dimensions that are highly correlated and thus may influence your ML model. In linear regression models, for example, two highly correlated independent variables will lead to large coefficients with opposite signs that ultimately cancel each other out. A much more stable regression model can be found by removing one of the correlated dimensions. Therefore, it is important not only to look at correlations between features and targets but also among features.

The **Pearson correlation coefficient**, for example, is a popular technique that's used to measure the *linear* relationship between two variables on a scale from -1 (strongly negatively correlated) to 1 (strongly positively correlated). A 0 indicates no linear relationship between two variables.

The following diagram shows an example of a correlation matrix for the *California Housing dataset* (https://www.dcc.fc.up.pt/~ltorgo/Regression/cal_housing.html), consisting of only continuous variables. The correlations range from -1 to 1 and are colored accordingly, where red denotes a negative correlation and blue denotes a positive correlation. The last row shows the linear correlation between each feature dimension and the target variable (MedHouseVal). We can immediately tell that there is a correlation between Longitude and Latitude, between MedHouseVal and MedInc, and between AveRooms and AveBedrms. All of these relationships are relatively unsurprising:

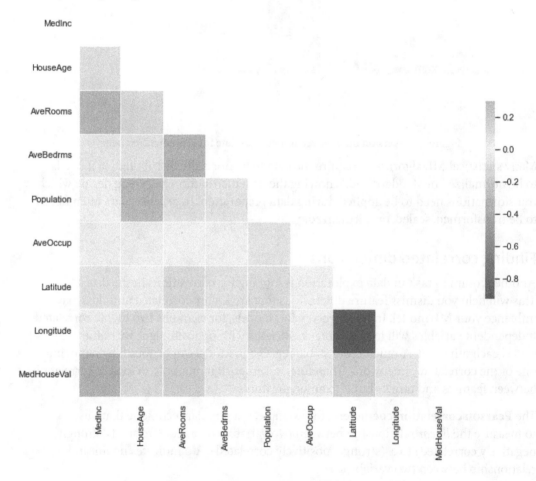

Figure 5.3 – Correlation matrix for the California Housing dataset

You can find the code for creating this correlation matrix in the `02_correlation.ipynb` file in this book's GitHub repository.

It is worth mentioning that many correlation coefficients can only be between numerical values. Ordinal variables can be encoded, for example, using integer encoding and can also compute a meaningful correlation coefficient. For nominal data, you need to fall back on different methods, such as **Cramér's V** to compute the correlation. It is worth noting that the input data doesn't need to be normalized (linearly scaled) before you compute the correlation coefficient.

Measuring feature and target dependencies for regression

Once we have analyzed the missing values, data distribution, and correlations, we can start analyzing the relationship between the features and the target variable. This will give us a good indication of the difficulty of the prediction problem and, hence, the expected baseline performance, which is essential for prioritizing feature engineering efforts and choosing an appropriate ML model. Another great benefit of measuring this dependency is ranking the feature dimensions by their impact on the target variable, which you can use as a priority list for data exploration and preprocessing.

In a regression task, the target variable is numerical or ordinal. Therefore, we can compute the correlation coefficient between the individual features and the target variable to compute the linear dependency between the feature and the target. High correlation – that is, a high absolute correlation coefficient – indicates that a strong linear relationship exists. This gives us a great place to start exploring further. However, in many practical problems, it is rare to see a high (linear) correlation between the feature and target variables.

You can also visualize this dependency between the feature and the target variable using a **scatter plot** or **regression plot**. The following diagram shows a regression plot between the average number of rooms per dwelling (**RM**) and the median value of owner-occupied homes (**MEDV**) from the *Boston Housing dataset*. If the regression line is at 45 degrees, then we have a perfect linear correlation:

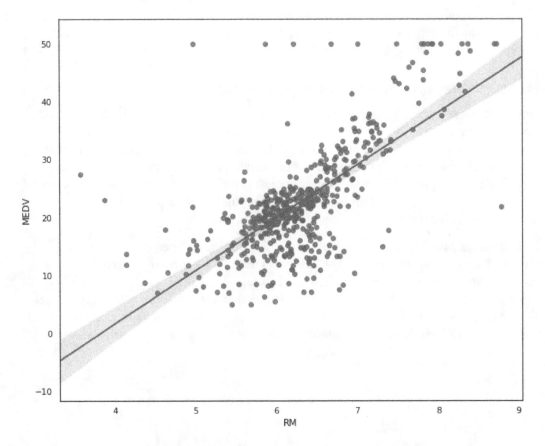

Figure 5.4 – Scatter plot with a regression line between the feature and the target

Another great approach to determining this dependency is to fit a linear or logistic regression model to the training data. The resulting model coefficients should give you a good explanation of the relationship – the higher the coefficient, the larger the linear (for linear regression) or marginal (for logistic regression) dependency on the target variable. Hence, sorting by coefficients results in a list of features ordered by importance. Depending on the regression type, the input data should be normalized or standardized.

The following screenshot shows an example of the correlation coefficients (the first column) of a fitted **Ordinary Least Squares** (**OLS**) regression model:

	coef	std err	t	P>|t|	[0.025	0.975]
CRIM	-0.1214	0.033	-3.678	0.000	-0.186	-0.057
ZN	0.0470	0.014	3.384	0.001	0.020	0.074
INDUS	0.0135	0.062	0.217	0.829	-0.109	0.136
CHAS	2.8400	0.870	3.264	0.001	1.131	4.549
NOX	-18.7580	3.851	-4.870	0.000	-26.325	-11.191
RM	3.6581	0.420	8.705	0.000	2.832	4.484
AGE	0.0036	0.013	0.271	0.787	-0.023	0.030
DIS	-1.4908	0.202	-7.394	0.000	-1.887	-1.095
RAD	0.2894	0.067	4.325	0.000	0.158	0.421
TAX	-0.0127	0.004	-3.337	0.001	-0.020	-0.005
PTRATIO	-0.9375	0.132	-7.091	0.000	-1.197	-0.678
LSTAT	-0.5520	0.051	-10.897	0.000	-0.652	-0.452
intercept	41.6173	4.936	8.431	0.000	31.919	51.316

Omnibus:	171.096	Durbin-Watson:	1.077
Prob(Omnibus):	0.000	Jarque-Bera (JB):	709.937
Skew:	1.477	Prob(JB):	6.90e-155
Kurtosis:	7.995	Cond. No.	1.17e+04

Figure 5.5 – The correlation coefficients of an OLS regression model

You can find the code for creating the plot and coefficients in the `03_regression.ipynb` file in this book's GitHub repository.

While the resulting **R-squared metric** (not shown) may not be good enough for a baseline model, the ordering of the coefficients can help us prioritize further data exploration, preprocessing, and feature engineering.

Visualizing feature and label dependency for classification

In a classification task with a multi-class nominal target variable, we can't use the regression coefficients without preprocessing the data further. Another popular method that works well out of the box is fitting a simple tree-based classifier to the training data. Depending on the size of the training data, we could use a decision tree or a tree-based ensemble classifier, such as **random forest** or **gradient-boosted trees**. Doing so results in a feature importance ranking of the feature dimensions according to the chosen split criterion. In the case of splitting by entropy, the features would be sorted by *information gain*, which would indicate which variables carry the most information about the target.

The following diagram shows the feature importance fitted by a tree-based ensemble classifier using the entropy criterion from the *UCI Wine Recognition dataset* (`https://archive.ics.uci.edu/ml/datasets/wine`):

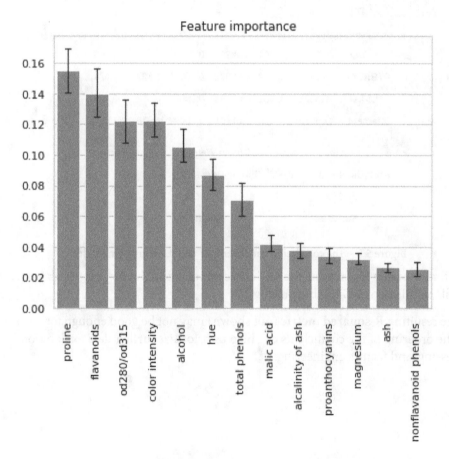

Figure 5.6 – Feature importance of the tree-based ensemble classifier

The lines represent variations in the information gain of features between individual trees. This output is a great first step to further data analysis and exploration in order of feature importance. You can find the code for calculating the feature importance and visualizing it in the `04_feature_importance.ipynb` file in this book's GitHub repository.

Here is another popular approach to discovering the separability of your dataset. The following screenshot shows a dataset with three classes, where one is linearly separable and one isn't:

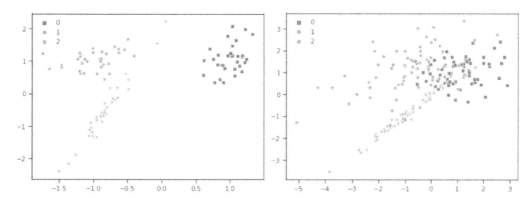

Figure 5.7 – A linearly separable dataset (left) versus a non-linearly separable dataset (right)

You can find the code for creating these separability graphs in the `05_separability.ipynb` file in this book's GitHub repository.

By looking at the three clusters and the overlaps between these clusters, you can see that having separated clusters means that a trained classification model will perform very well on this dataset. On the other hand, when we know that the data is not linearly separable, we know that this task will require advanced feature engineering and modeling to produce good results.

Exploring and analyzing file datasets

A dataset that's made up of media files is a different beast entirely. If we think of images, for example, we could present every pixel as a vector of information and see this as one feature of the image. But what could we do in terms of exploration and data cleaning? Probably not much on single features. Most of the time, what we need to do concerns a large group of pixels or the entire image itself. Broadly speaking, we could think of the following aspects:

- **Uniformity**: All the images in the dataset should be the same size. If not, they need to be rescaled, which may involve centering pixel values per channel, possibly followed by some form of normalization.

- **Augmentation**: This involves diversifying the dataset without taking on new data (new images). This is useful if we have a small dataset and typically involves horizontal and vertical flipping, cropping, and rotating, among other transformations.

Looking at these options, it is clear that we are trying to fix something in an image dataset that could have been resolved already to a great extent when we took the images in the first place. Therefore, the reality is that when we're handling most types of media files, it is paramount to bring higher concentration toward taking good training samples for the dataset than to desperately fix them in the preprocessing stage.

Let's imagine that we are a manufacturer who wants to take pictures of the products they produce passing on a conveyor belt to find defective products and discard them. Let's say that we have production facilities around the globe. What would you do to make sure the pictures are taken as uniformly as possible while covering a lot of different scenarios? Here are some aspects to consider:

- **Camera type**: We probably need the same type of camera to be taking pictures in the same format all around the globe.

- **Environmental conditions**: Is the lighting similar in all places? Are the temperature and humidity similar in all places? This could influence the electronics in the camera.

- **Positioning**: Is the same angle being used to take the pictures? Can we take pictures from vastly different angles to increase variety?

These are only some points to consider when you're taking the images.

Now, let's look at another form of file data – sound files. Let's say that we want to build a speech-to-text model that converts what we say into written text. Such models are, for example, used in voice assistants to map a request to a set of actions to perform.

In this context, we could use **Fourier transformations**, among other methods, to decompose our sound files. However, we may want to think about the samples or training data we want to train on and how we can increase the quality of them while considering the following aspects:

- **Recording hardware:** If we have a voice assistant at home, it is probably the same microphone for everyone. But what if we build a voice assistant for mobile phones? Then, we have vastly different microphones.

- **Environment**: We probably need recordings of voices in different environments. There is certainly a different sound spectrum when we are standing in a tram compared to when we are in a recording booth.

- **Pronunciation**: The *ML algorithm* in your brain may have a hard time deciphering different pronunciations – especially dialects. How can an actual ML model handle this?

These are just some points to consider when you're handling sound files. Regarding pronunciation, if you look at **Azure Speech Services**, you will soon realize that two models are running in the background – one for the acoustic and one for the language. Look at the requirements for samples when building a custom model (`https://docs.microsoft.com/en-us/azure/cognitive-services/speech-service/how-to-custom-speech-test-and-train`) as this can give you a good idea of what is required when you're building such a model from scratch.

In summary, for file datasets, we do not have as many options to statistically eliminate problems, so we should concentrate on taking good and clean samples that simulate the kind of realistic environment we would get when the model is running in production.

Now that we have familiarized ourselves with the methods to explore and analyze different types of datasets, let's try this out on a real tabular dataset.

Performing data analysis on a tabular dataset

If you haven't followed the steps in *Chapter 4, Ingesting Data and Managing Datasets*, to download the snapshot of the *Melbourne Housing dataset* from **Kaggle** (`https://www.kaggle.com/dansbecker/melbourne-housing-snapshot`), please do this before continuing with this section. In the end, you should have the raw dataset file, `melb_data.csv`, in the `mlfiles` container in your storage account and have this connected to a datastore called `mldemoblob` in your Azure Machine Learning workspace.

In the following sections, we will explore the dataset, do some basic statistical analysis, find missing values and outliers, find correlations between features, and take an initial measurement of feature importance while utilizing a random forest model, as we saw in the *Visualizing feature and label dependency for classification* section of this chapter. You can either create a new Jupyter notebook and follow along with this book or open the `06_ dataprep_melbhousing.ipynb` file in the GitHub repository for this chapter.

Note that the steps we will perform now are not exhaustive. As shown on the web page for the dataset, we have 21 features to work with. So, to be thorough, you will have to analyze each.

This section should give you a good understanding of the types of tasks you can perform, but we will leave a lot of questions open for you to find answers for. If you need some inspiration for that, have a look at this dataset on the Kaggle website. You will find notebooks from a lot of users trying to analyze this dataset.

Finally, we will not completely transform the actual data at this point as we will come back to this problem in *Chapter 6, Feature Engineering and Labeling*, where we will learn how to select features and create new ones based on the statistical analysis and knowledge we will gain through the upcoming process.

Initial exploration and cleansing of the Melbourne Housing dataset

In this section, we will load the data from a data store that is registered in Azure Machine Learning and look at its content. After that, we will start doing some basic cleaning regarding the raw data:

1. Download the following packages through Python PIP either separately or using the requirements file you can find in this book's GitHub repository: pandas, seaborn, plotly, scikit-learn, numpy, missingno, umap-learn, and statsmodels.

2. Create a new Jupyter notebook or follow along in the one mentioned previously.

3. Connect to your ML workspace through the configuration file, as we learned previously.

4. Use the following code to pull the dataset to your local computer:

```
from azureml.core import Datastore, Dataset
import pandas as pd
import seaborn as sns
import numpy as np
import plotly.express as px
import matplotlib.pyplot as plt


# retrieve an existing datastore in the workspace by name
datastore_name = 'mldemoblob'
datastore = Datastore.get(ws, datastore_name)
```

```
# create a TabularDataset from the file path in datastore
datastore_path = [(datastore, 'melb_data.csv')]
tabdf = Dataset.Tabular.from_delimited_files
    (path=datastore_path)
```

Here, we're retrieving the data from your defined ML data store, `yourname`, and loading the dataset into a tabular dataset object. Adapt the path and name of the file in the second to last line, depending on your folder structure in your data store.

5. The methods that are available on a tabular dataset object are not as abundant as they are for a pandas DataFrame. So, let's transform it into a pandas DataFrame and have our first look at the data:

```
# increase display of all columns of rows for pandas
datasets
pd.set_option('display.max_columns', None)
pd.set_option('display.max_rows', None)
# create pandas dataframe
raw_df = tabdf.to_pandas_dataframe()
raw_df.head()
```

The `pd.set_option()` method gives you access to the general settings for pandas operations. In this case, we want all the columns and rows to be shown and not truncated in the visualization. You can set this to whatever value works for you.

The `head()` function will give you a first look at the first five rows of the dataset. Have a look at them.

You will see a bunch of features that make a lot of sense, such as `Suburb`, `Address`, and `Bathroom`. But some others might not be so clear, such as `Type`, `Method`, or `Distance`.

Typically, as with any dataset, there is some form of data definition for the fields that are supplied with it. Have a look at the website of the datasets to find them.

6. Now that we've looked at the definition, let's look at the so-called shape of the datasets, which will show us how many columns (features and labels) and how many rows (samples) the dataset contains:

```
raw_df.shape
```

The preceding command shows us a dataset with 13,580 samples and 21 features/labels.

7. Finally, run the following code so that we can look at the number of unique values, the number of missing values, and the data type of each feature:

```
stats = []
for cl in raw_df.columns:
    stats.append((cl,
                  raw_df[cl].nunique(),
                  raw_df[cl].isnull().sum(),
                  raw_df[cl].isnull().sum() * 100 /
                                  raw_df.shape[0],
                  raw_df[cl].value_counts(
                      normalize=True,
                      dropna=False).values[0] * 100,
                  raw_df[cl].dtype))

# create new dataframe from stats
stats_df = pd.DataFrame(stats, columns=[
            'Feature',
            'Unique Values',
            'Missing Values',
            'Missing Values [%]',
            'Values in the biggest category [%]',
            'Datatype'])

stats_df.sort_values('Missing Values [%]',
                  ascending=False)
```

After running the preceding code, you should see something similar to the following:

	Feature	Unique Values	Missing Values	Missing Values [%]	Values in the biggest category [%]	Datatype
14	BuildingArea	602	6450	47.496318	47.496318	float64
15	YearBuilt	144	5375	39.580265	39.580265	float64
16	CouncilArea	33	1369	10.081001	10.081001	object
12	Car	11	62	0.456554	41.170839	float64
0	Suburb	314	0	0.000000	2.643594	object
11	Bathroom	9	0	0.000000	55.316642	float64
19	Regionname	8	0	0.000000	34.572901	object
18	Longtitude	7063	0	0.000000	0.125184	float64
17	Lattitude	6503	0	0.000000	0.154639	float64
13	Landsize	1448	0	0.000000	14.278351	float64
10	Bedroom2	12	0	0.000000	43.416789	float64
1	Address	13378	0	0.000000	0.022091	object
9	Postcode	198	0	0.000000	2.643594	float64
8	Distance	202	0	0.000000	5.441826	float64
7	Date	58	0	0.000000	3.483063	datetime64[ns]
6	SellerG	268	0	0.000000	11.524300	object
5	Method	5	0	0.000000	66.435935	object
4	Price	2204	0	0.000000	0.832106	float64
3	Type	3	0	0.000000	69.580265	object
2	Rooms	9	0	0.000000	43.306333	int64
20	Propertycount	311	0	0.000000	2.643594	float64

Figure 5.8 – Melbourne Housing dataset feature overview

Looking at this table, we can make the following observations:

- Four features seem to have missing values (**BuildingArea**, **YearBuilt**, **CouncilArea**, and **Car**).

- A lot of numeric values (such as **YearBuilt**, **Bathroom2**, **Bedroom**, and **Postcode**) seem to be of the float64 type. This is not necessarily a problem, but it's a waste of space since each probably fits into int8, int16, or int32.

- There are seven features of the object type, all of which are probably string values. We'll look at them in more detail shortly.

- There is a feature called **Price**, which is probably a good label/target for supervised learning, such as classification.

- There is a feature named **Postcode** and a feature named **Suburb**. We may not need both. Judging by the unique values, **Suburb** seems to be more granular.

- There is a feature called **Address** and a feature called **SellerG**. Even though the seller of a property may have some influence on the price, we can drop them for now for simplicity. The same goes for addresses as they are extremely precise. Nearly every sample has a unique address.

By looking at the seven features of the `object` type, we can see the following:

- **Type**: This has **3** distinct values; our data definition shows **6**. We need to check this discrepancy.
- **Method**: This has **5** distinct values; our data definition shows **11**. We need to check this as well.
- **SellerG**: This has **268** distinct seller names.
- **Address**: This has **13378** distinct values, but we have **13580** samples, so there seem to be multiple places with the same address. Still, we have an extreme amount of variety here, which makes this feature quite unimportant.
- **Regionname**: This has **8** distinct values – that is, the regions of Melbourne.
- **Suburb**: This has **314** distinct values – that is, the suburbs of Melbourne.
- **CouncilArea**: This has **33** distinct values and is the only categorical feature with missing values.

At this point, we have found some interesting information and some leads that show us where we need to have a look in the next phase. For now, let's drill down into the content of the features and do some initial dataset cleaning.

8. Let's start by removing some of the not so important features:

```
df = raw_df.drop(['Address', 'SellerG'],axis=1)
```

As you can see, we stick with our original DataFrame, called `raw_df`, and create a new one called `df`. By doing this, we can add removed features at any time. Every row in a DataFrame has an index, so even if we filter out the rows, we can still match the original values.

9. Next, we will rename some columns to increase our understanding of them:

```
df = df.rename(columns={'Bedroom2': 'Bedrooms',
                        'Bathroom': 'Bathrooms',
                        'Regionname': 'Region',
                        'Car': 'Parking',
                        'Propertycount':
                        'SuburbPropCount'})
df.head()
```

10. At this point, it might be a good idea to look for duplicates. Let's run the following code snippet to find duplicates:

```
s = df.duplicated(keep = False)
s = s[s == True]
s
```

Setting `keep` to `False` will show each row that has a duplicate. Here, we can see that two of the rows are the same. We can look at them by using the following command:

```
df.loc[[7769,7770]]
```

As you can see, these denote the same entry. So, let's remove one of them using the following command:

```
df.drop([7769], inplace=True)
```

As this is just one sample, we can drop it by its row index. Normally, operations like these just return a new DataFrame, but in a lot of operations, we can use an attribute called `inplace` to directly overwrite the current DataFrame.

11. Now, let's look at the categorical features that seem to have missing categories, starting with `Method`:

```
df['Method'].unique()
```

The categories in our datasets are S, SP, PI, VB, and SA. Judging from the list in the data definition, we can see that the only entries in the dataset specify where the property was sold and where we know the selling price. Someone has already cleaned this for us.

By looking at `Type`, we can see that single bedrooms, development sites, and other residential areas have been removed as well, leaving houses, units, and townhouses:

```
df['Type'].unique()
```

To make these entries a bit clearer, let's replace the single letters with a full name:

```
df = df.replace({'Type':
                {'h':'house','u':'unit','t':'townhouse'}})
df = df.replace({'Method': {'S':'Property Sold',
                            'SP':'Property Sold Prior',
                            'PI':'Property Passed In',
                            'VB':'Vendor Bid',
                            'SA':'Sold After Auction'}})
df.head()
```

12. Now, let's concentrate on the categorical features that contain a lot of entries. The following code shows the list of unique values in the column:

```
df['CouncilArea'].unique()
```

We will get the following result set:

```
array(['Yarra', 'Moonee Valley', 'Port Phillip',
'Darebin', 'Hobsons Bay', 'Stonnington', 'Boroondara',
'Monash', 'Glen Eira', 'Whitehorse', 'Maribyrnong',
'Bayside', 'Moreland', 'Manningham', 'Banyule',
'Melbourne', 'Kingston', 'Brimbank', 'Hume', None,
'Knox', 'Maroondah', 'Casey', 'Melton', 'Greater
Dandenong', 'Nillumbik', 'Whittlesea', 'Frankston',
'Macedon Ranges', 'Yarra Ranges', 'Wyndham', 'Cardinia',
'Unavailable', 'Moorabool'], dtype=object)
```

Here, we can see that there is a category called None, which contains our missing values, and a category called Unavailable. Otherwise, it seems like every other entry is very well defined, and there seem to be no duplicate entries with the same meaning; they only differ due to typing errors or spaces. Such errors are typically denoted as **structural errors**.

By running the same command for the Suburb feature, we get a much larger result set. At this point, it gets very complicated to see structural errors, so we need to take a programmatic approach to check this category. Something such as pattern matching or fuzzy matching can be used here, but we will leave this out for now. Feel free to look up topics such as **fuzzy matching** and **Levenshtein distance**, which can be used to find groups of similar words in the result set.

13. Finally, we are left with one last question we had concerning the relationship between postcodes and suburbs and if we could get rid of one of them. So, let's see how many postcodes are targeting more than one suburb:

```
postcodes_df = df.groupby(
    'Postcode', as_index=False).Suburb.nunique()
postcodes_df.columns = ['Postcode',
                        '#Assigned Suburbs']
postcodes_df.loc[postcodes_df['#Assigned Suburbs'] > 1]
```

Here, we created a new DataFrame that shows us the postcodes and the number of assigned suburbs. By searching for the ones that have been mapped to multiple suburbs, we can find the respective list. Let's count them:

```
postcodes_df.loc[postcodes_df['#Assigned Suburbs'] >
1].count()
```

Here, we can see that 73 out of 198 postcodes refer to multiple suburbs. Nevertheless, every suburb has a postcode, so let's stick with the suburbs and drop the postcodes from the DataFrame:

```
df = df.drop(['Postcode'],axis=1)
df.head()
```

This already looks quite nice. As a final step, we could change the data type from `float64` to one of the integer types (`int8`, `int16`, `int32`, or `int64`), but we do not know enough about the spread of the data points yet and we cannot do this for columns with missing values. We'll come back to this later.

So far, we have done some basic exploration and base pruning of our dataset. Now, let's learn more about statistics.

Running statistical analysis on the dataset

It's time to look at the statistical properties of our numerical features. To do so, run the following code snippet:

```
dist_df = df.describe().T.apply(lambda s: s.apply(lambda x:
format(x, 'g')))
dist_df
```

Here, the `describe()` method will give you a table of typical statistical properties for the numeric features of the dataset. `T` will pivot the table, while the `apply()` and `lambda()` methods will help format the data points into normal numerical notations. Feel free to remove the `apply` methods and look at the difference.

The result will show you some information, but we would like to add some more statistical values, including the **skew**, the **mode**, and the **number of values** in a feature that are equal to the mode, the maximum, and the minimum. With the following code, we can realize that:

```
from pandas.api.types import is_numeric_dtype
max_count=[]
min_count=[]
mode_count=[]
mode=[]
skew=[]
for cl in df.columns:
    if (is_numeric_dtype(df[cl])):
```

```
        max_count.append(df[cl].value_counts(
                          dropna=False).loc[df[cl].max()])
        min_count.append(df[cl].value_counts(
                          dropna=False).loc[df[cl].min()])
        mode_count.append(df[cl].value_counts(
                      dropna=False).loc[df[cl].mode()[0]])
        skew.append(df[cl].skew())
        mode.append(int(df[cl].mode()[0]))
dist_df['mode'] = mode
dist_df['skew'] = skew
dist_df['#values(min)'] = min_count
dist_df['#values(max)'] = max_count
dist_df['#values(mode)'] = mode_count
dist_df
```

Here, we are creating a bunch of lists and appending the calculated value for each column in our base DataFrame to each list. We are also adding a new column to our distribution DataFrame, dist_df, for each of the property lists that we calculated. To ease your understanding of the code, we used Python list objects here. You could shorten this code by using another pandas DataFrame, which we leave for you as an exercise.

You should see an output similar to the following after running the preceding code:

	count	mean	std	min	25%	50%	75%	max	mode	skew	#values(min)	#values(max)	#values(mode)
Rooms	13580	2.938	0.955748	1	2	3	3	10	3	0.376478	681	1	5881
Price	13580	1.07568e+06	639311	85000	650000	903000	1.33e+06	9e+06	1100000	2.239624	1	1	113
Distance	13580	10.1378	5.86872	0	6.1	9.2	13	48.1	11	1.676937	6	1	739
Bedrooms	13580	2.91473	0.965921	0	2	3	3	20	3	0.774082	16	1	5896
Bathrooms	13580	1.53424	0.691712	0	1	1	2	8	1	1.377406	34	2	7512
Parking	13518	1.61008	0.962634	0	1	2	2	10	2	1.369676	1026	3	5591
Landsize	13580	558.416	3990.67	0	177	440	651	433014	0	95.237400	1939	1	1939
BuildingArea	7130	151.968	541.015	0	93	126	174	44515	120	77.691541	17	1	114
YearBuilt	8205	1964.68	37.2738	1196	1940	1970	1999	2018	1970	-1.541279	1	1	866
Lattitude	13580	-37.8092	0.0792598	-38.1825	-37.8568	-37.8024	-37.7564	-37.4085	-37	-0.426695	1	1	21
Longtitude	13580	144.995	0.103916	144.432	144.93	145	145.058	145.526	144	-0.210991	1	1	17
SuburbPropCount	13580	7454.42	4378.58	249	4380	6555	10331	21650	21650	1.069339	1	359	359

Figure 5.9 – Statistical properties of the Melbourne Housing dataset

Let's see what we can deduct for each feature by looking at this table:

- **Price**: This is skewed to the right. Here, we will probably see a few high prices, which is not surprising. The highest house price is 9 million.

- **Distance**: This is skewed to the right, probably due to one of the samples being 48.1km away from the CBD in Melbourne. Interestingly enough, there are **6** samples with **0** distance. Sometimes, 0 is a dummy value, so we should check those samples. Judging by the fact that mode **11** has been set **739** times, the distance might not be exactly the distance from the city center, but perhaps the mean distance of a suburb from the city center. We should figure that out as well.

- **Bedrooms**: This is skewed to the right due to lots of bedrooms in some places. Curiously, there are **16** samples with **0** bedrooms, which needs to be verified.

- **Bathrooms**: This is similar to the distribution of the **Bedrooms** feature, with **34** samples having **0** bathrooms, which again is curious.

- **Parking**: This is similar to the distribution of the **Bedrooms** feature. There are **1026** samples with no parking spaces, which sounds reasonable.

- **Landsize**: This is extremely skewed (**95.24**) to the right. The maximum value is **433014**. If we presume we're using square meters here, there are about 43 hectares of land. This isn't impossible, but this is clearly an outlier and would probably distort our modeling.

- **BuildingArea**: This is extremely skewed to the right due to the maximum value of **44515** m². This sounds quite improbable, so we may want to remove this one. Also, there are **17** samples with **0** m², which needs to be checked.

- **YearBuilt**: This is skewed to the left due to the one building being built in **1196**. We may want to discard that one.

- **Longitude/Latitude**: These seem to be reasonably well distributed, but curiously with the **17** and **21** values being the same, respectively – specifically **-37** and **144**. This gives us some idea that the coordinates might not be as precise as we may think.

- **SuburbPropCount**: This is slightly skewed to the right. We have to analyze how helpful this value is.

Now, let's think about what relationships we would expect and have a look at these between features:

- **Rooms with Bathrooms/Bedrooms**: If you have a look at the distribution for these, it becomes clear that we are not quite sure what **Rooms** means. The maximum for **Rooms** is **10**, while the maximum for **Bedrooms** is **20**. Looking at the data definition, we can see that **Bedrooms** was taken from a bunch of different sources, so we may have a discrepancy between those data points.

- **BuildingArea with Rooms/Bathrooms/Bedrooms**: We would expect a positive correlation of some sort, but we cannot judge this from the data at hand.

As we can see, we can get some very good insights just from this table alone and have a good idea of what to look at next. We will check the **Price** and **BuildingArea** features for now, but in reality, we would have to follow all these avenues. Feel free to do this on your own and have a look at the supplied notebook to get some more ideas.

First, let's look at the **Price** label. At this point, it is a good idea to visualize our distributions. To do that, you can either use the `seaborn` or `plotly` library. Read up on how they work and differ from each other. For simplicity, we will use `plotly` for now. Use the following code to plot a boxplot with a data points distribution shown next to it:

```
fig = px.box(df, x="Price",points="all")
fig.show()
```

You should see the following graph:

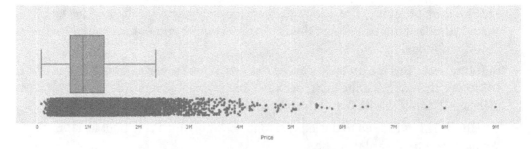

Figure 5.10 – Boxplot for the Price target

Hovering over the box will show you the **upper and lower fence** of the distribution. The upper fence is at 2.35 million. We can still see a lot of points above this. As we can ensure that these are valid prices, we should think of rescaling this target value. Let's calculate the `log` value of the **Price** vector and have a look again.

To do this, let's add a new column to our DataFrame with the `log` value of **Price** and run the visualization again:

```
df["Price_log"] = np.log(df['Price'])
fig = px.box(df, x="Price_log",points="all")
fig.show()
```

This will result in the following graph:

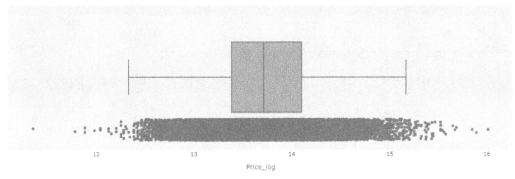

Figure 5.11 – Boxplot for the log (Price) target

Doing this seems to be a good idea as it's distributed better. Feel free to check the skew of this distribution.

Now, let's look at the **BuildingArea** feature. Once again, let's create a boxplot using the following code:

```
fig = px.box(df, y="BuildingArea",points="all")
fig.show()
```

This will result in the following graph:

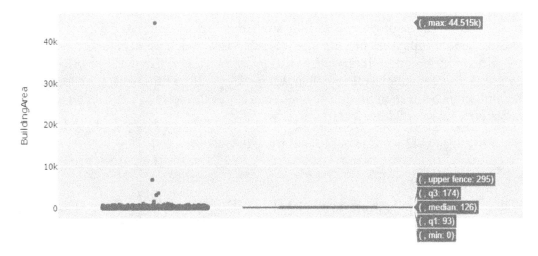

Figure 5.12 – Boxplot of the BuildingArea feature

We are greeted by a very distorted boxplot. Hovering over it, we can see **upper fence** at **295** m², while **maximum** is at **44515** m². There is one major outlier and a bunch of small ones.

Let's look how many samples are above **295** with the following code:

```
df.loc[raw_df['BuildingArea'] > 295]['BuildingArea'].count()
```

The result still shows that there are **353** samples above this threshold. Looking at the boxplot, this may thin out rather quickly toward 2,000 m². So, let's check the result set for above 2,000 m² with the following code:

```
df.loc[raw_df['BuildingArea'] > 2000]
```

This will give us the following output:

Distance	Bedrooms	Bathrooms	Parking	Landsize	BuildingArea	YearBuilt	CouncilArea	Lattitude	Longtitude	Region
11.8	4.0	1.0	2.0	732.0	6791.0	NaN	Manningham	-37.76150	145.08970	Eastern Metropolitan
7.8	5.0	2.0	4.0	730.0	3112.0	1920.0	Boroondara	-37.84240	145.06390	Southern Metropolitan
3.5	2.0	3.0	0.0	2778.0	3558.0	NaN	Yarra	-37.79030	144.98590	Northern Metropolitan
48.1	5.0	3.0	5.0	44500.0	44515.0	NaN	None	-37.45392	144.58864	Northern Victoria

Figure 5.13 – Top four samples by BuildingArea size

As we can see, the largest property is 48.1 km away from the city center, so having a **Landsize** and **BuildingArea** in that range is feasible. However, if we want to understand house prices in Melbourne, this may not be that important. It is also in the Northern Victoria region and not in the metropolitan regions. We could go further here and look at the connection between these specific houses outside of the norm in conjunction with other features, but we will leave it at this for now.

Let's drop the major outlier from our dataset using the following code:

```
df.drop([13245], inplace=True)
```

As it just contains one sample, we can drop it by row ID.

At this point, we could continue doing this kind of analysis with the rest of the features, but we will leave it as an exercise for you to have a deeper look at the rest of the features and their statistical dependencies. Now, let's continue by looking at what we would do after that.

But before we continue, let's save our dataset to Azure Machine Learning using the following function:

```
Dataset.Tabular.register_pandas_dataframe(
        dataframe = df,
        target = datastore,
        name ='Melbourne Housing Dataset',
        description = 'Data Cleansing 1 - removed address,
                        postcode, duplicates and outliers')
```

We will continue to do so during this exercise to have different version at our disposal later.

Finding and handling missing values

Our next order of business is to handle the missing values in the dataset. We can use a very nice extension called `missingno` to get some interesting visualizations of our missing values.

But before that, let's run the following code to see what would happen if we removed all the samples with missing values:

```
df.dropna(how='any').shape
```

As we can see, the resulting DataFrame would contain **6196** samples, which would be less than half of the dataset. So, it might be a good idea to handle missing values.

Now, run the following code:

```
import missingno as msno
msno.matrix(df);
```

This will result in the following output:

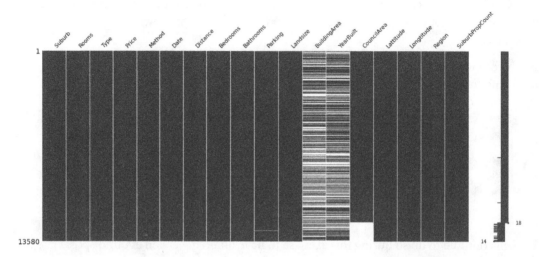

Figure 5.14 – Structural visualization of the DataFrame and its missing values

As we can see, the **CouncilArea** feature is only missing values in the latter samples of the DataFrame, **Parking** is only missing in a very small part in the latter samples, and **BuildingArea** and **YearBuilt** are missing throughout the DataFrame.

As we've already learned, we can perform replacement by either inventing a *new category* for missing categorical data or replacing them with the *mean value* for missing continuous data.

Let's start with the **CouncilArea** feature. As you may recall from our initial data exploration, there is a category called Unavailable, so let's look at the samples with this category by selecting any sample with that characteristic:

```
df.loc[df.CouncilArea.isin(['Unavailable'])]
```

As we can see, there is only one entry with this category. It seems to be a valid entry; it is just missing the name of the council area. So, let's replace this entry and the missing values with a new category called Missing using the following code:

```
df['CouncilArea'].fillna(value = "Missing", inplace = True)
df['CouncilArea'].replace(to_replace="Unavailable",
value="Missing", inplace=True)
```

Checking the unique values in the feature after shows us that there are no values in the `None` or `Unavailable` categories anymore:

```
df['CouncilArea'].unique()
```

This is the simplest way to replace features. Since these are council areas of Melbourne and every house should be assigned to one, a better idea would be to find another dataset that matches suburbs or addresses to council areas and do a cross-reference. Feel free to search for one and do this.

Continuing with the three continuous features, we can use the following code to replace any missing value with the mean of the column and check if there are still missing values left afterward:

```
BA_mean = df['BuildingArea'].mean()
df['BuildingArea'].replace(to_replace=np.nan, value=BA_mean,
inplace=True)
df['BuildingArea'].isnull().sum()
```

The result of the final command shows the mean value we filled, **145.749**. Adapt this code to do the same for **YearBuilt** and **Parking**. However, you may want to use the *median* rather than the *mean* value for these.

For now, this solves the problem with missing values and is, statistically speaking, a reasonable approach. However, as we've discussed, this is one of the simplest ways to do this. A better way would be to find relationships between features and use them to fill in missing values. Instead of just using the mean of the entire dataset, we could concentrate on finding a subset of data that has similar characteristics as the sample with the missing value. For example, we could find a dependency between the number of parking spots on one side and the number of rooms in the house or the size of the house on the other side. Then, we could define a function that gives us a value for **Parking** depending on these other features.

So, to handle missing values better, we need to figure out relationships, which we will have a look at in the next section.

But before that, let's register this dataset again with this description: `Data Cleansing 2 - replaced missing values`.

Calculating correlations and feature importance

So far, we've looked at single features, their content, and their distribution. Now, let's look at the relationships between them.

Use the following code to produce a correlation matrix between our features and targets:

```
# compute the correlation matrix
corr = df.corr()
# define and create seaborn plot
mask = np.triu(np.ones_like(corr, dtype=np.bool))
f, ax = plt.subplots(figsize=(11, 9))
cmap = sns.diverging_palette(220, 10, as_cmap=True)

sns.heatmap(corr, mask=mask, cmap=cmap, vmax=.3,
            center=0, square=True, linewidths=.5,
            cbar_kws={"shrink": .5})
plt.show()
```

The resulting matrix will show you the correlation of 13 of our features, but not all of them. If you check the visible ones, you will see that we are missing everything of the object or datetime type.

So, before we analyze the matrix, let's add the missing features by starting to carve out the left-over columns of the object type from our DataFrame:

```
obj_df = df.select_dtypes(include=['object']).copy()
obj_df.head()
```

Here, we can see that the remaining columns are **Suburb**, **Type**, **Method**, **CouncilArea**, and **Region**. When you read through the list of pandas data types, you will find a type called category, which we will now convert our columns into:

```
for cl in obj_df.columns:
    obj_df[cl] = obj_df[cl].astype('category')
obj_df.dtypes
```

With that, we have created a DataFrame called `obj_df` with five features of the `category` type. Now, let's assign each category a numeric value. For this, we will use the `cat.codes` method and create five new columns in our DataFrame with `_cat` as the name extension:

```
for cl in obj_df.columns:
    obj_df[cl+"_cat"] = obj_df[cl].cat.codes
obj_df.head()
```

Perfect! We have created a DataFrame with encoded categories. We will combine these new features with our original DataFrame, `df`, into a new DataFrame called `cont_df`:

```
column_replacement = {'Type':'Type_cat','Suburb':'Suburb_
cat','Method':'Method_cat','CouncilArea':'CouncilArea_
cat','Region':'Region_cat'}
cont_df = df.copy()
for key in column_replacement:
    cont_df[key] = obj_df[column_replacement[key]]
cont_df.dtypes
```

The output of the preceding code shows the data types of all our columns in the new dataset. We can still see the **Date** column of the `datetime` type and some original columns that should be of the `int` type. Let's rectify this before creating the correlation matrix again.

First, let's create a new column called `Date_Epoch` that consists of an integer that denotes the seconds from the epoch (`https://docs.python.org/3/library/time.html`) and drop the original **Date** column:

```
cont_df['Date_Epoch'] = cont_df['Date'].apply(lambda x:
x.timestamp())
cont_df.drop(['Date'], axis=1, inplace=True)
cont_df.dtypes
```

We could also break **Date** apart into a **Month** column and a **Year** column, as they may have an impact. Feel free to add them as well.

Now, let's convert all the `float64` columns into integers, except for the ones where float is correct:

```
for cl in cont_df.columns:
    if (cont_df[cl].dtype == np.float64 and cl not in
```

```
                                      ['Lattitude', 'Longtitude',
                                       'Price_log', 'Distance']):
        cont_df[cl] = cont_df[cl].astype('int')
cont_df.dtypes
```

The preceding code shows that our DataFrame is now made up of only numerical data types in the most optimal size and format (some features only taking up 8-bits of memory per value).

Now, it's time to run the correlation matrix again. Use the same code that we did previously – just replace df with our new cont_df. The result should look as follows:

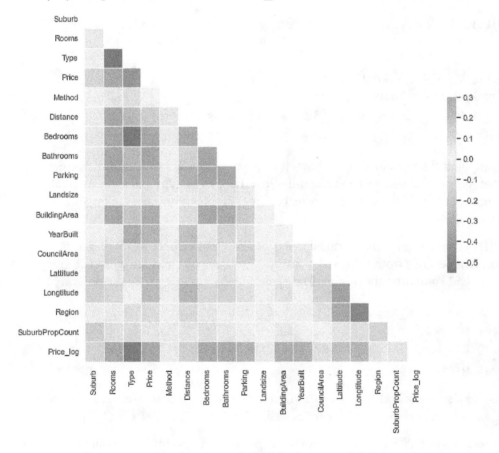

Figure 5.15 – Correlation matrix of all the features and their targets

A strong red color denotes a **positive correlation**, while a strong blue color denotes a **negative correlation**. Based on this, we can conclude the following:

- **Rooms** is strongly correlated with **Price, Price_log, Distance, Bedrooms, Bathrooms, Parking,** and **BuildingArea**.

- **Type** is strongly correlated with **Price, Price_log, Bedrooms, YearBuilt,** and **Rooms**.

- **Price** is strongly correlated with **Rooms, Type, Bedrooms, Bathrooms, Parking,** and **BuildingArea**.

- **Suburb, Method, Landsize,** and **SuburbPropCount** don't seem to have too much influence in their current state on other features or the target.

Looking at these results, they are not surprising. **Suburb** has too many categories to be precise for anything, **Method** shouldn't have too much influence either, **Landsize** is probably not the biggest factor, and **SuburbPropCount** may also have too much variety. Possible transformations could involve either dropping **Suburb** and **SuburbPropCount** or mapping them to a category with much less variety.

Before we continue, let's register `cont_df` as a version of the dataset with the description: `Data Cleansing 3 - all features converted to numerical values`.

As the final task, let's double-check what we've figured out so far by using an **ensemble decision tree model** to calculate the **feature importance** (`https://scikit-learn.org/stable/modules/generated/sklearn.tree.DecisionTreeRegressor.html`). You can find the code for creating the random forest and visualizing the results at the end of the `06_dataprep_melbhousing.ipynb` file. There, you will see that we calculated the feature importance for the **Price** and **Price_log** targets. The results for both are shown here:

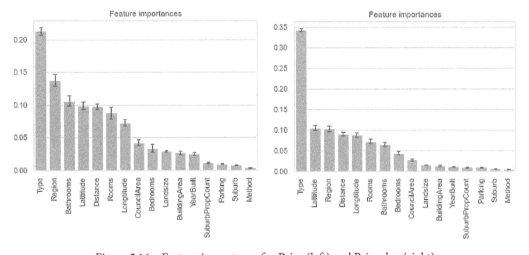

Figure 5.16 – Feature importance for Price (left) and Price_log (right)

As we can see, the type of the property clearly influences its price. This influence might not look that massive, but be aware, we are looking at logarithmical house prices.

What we've learned so far matches these results. Looking at the difference between the graphs, we can see that adding **logarithmic scaling** to our target variable has strengthened the most influential feature. The **Type** feature seems to have a strong influence on our target.

Let's end this exercise by looking at this relationship using the following code:

```
fig = px.box(df, y="Price_log",x='Type', color = 'Type',
                  category_orders={"Type": ["house",
                                   "townhouse", "unit"]})
fig.show()
```

The results of this are as follows:

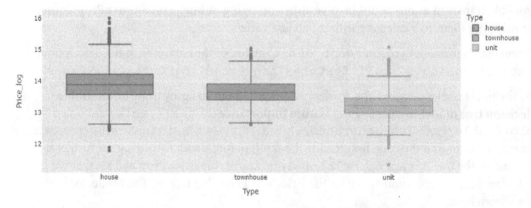

Figure 5.17 – Correlation between Type and Price_log

With that, we've completed this exercise. We were able to clean up our dataset, find some very good initial insights, and find a very strong correlation between our target variable and one of the features.

There are a lot of open questions left and we are still at the beginning of fully understanding this dataset. As an example, besides the **Price** target, we did not look at scaling or normalizing features, another possible requirement for certain algorithms.

We will continue working with this dataset in *Chapter 6*, *Feature Engineering and Labeling*. Until then, feel free to drill down into the secrets of this dataset or try to use your newfound knowledge on a different dataset.

Tracking figures from exploration in Azure Machine Learning

During our data exploration, we created a lot of different plots and visuals. Let's learn how to track them with Azure Machine Learning so that they are not just living in our Jupyter notebook.

In *Chapter 3*, *Preparing the Azure Machine Learning Workspace*, we learned how to track metrics and files for ML experiments using Azure Machine Learning. Other important outputs of your data transformation and ML scripts are visualizations, figures of data distributions, insights about models, and the results. Therefore, Azure Machine Learning provides a similar way to track metrics for images, figures, and `matplotlib` references.

Let's imagine that we created a `pairplot` of the popular *Iris Flower dataset* (https://archive.ics.uci.edu/ml/datasets/iris) using the following code:

```
import seaborn as sns
sns.set(style="ticks")

df = sns.load_dataset("iris")
sns.pairplot(df, hue="species")
```

With a few lines of code, we can track all the `matplotlib` figures and attach them to our experimentation run. To do so, we only have to pass the `matplotlib` reference to the `run.log_image()` method and give it an appropriate name. The following code shows what this would look like in an experiment:

```
with exp.start_logging() as run:
    fig = sns.pairplot(df, hue="species")
    run.log_image("pairplot", plot=fig)
```

Now, this is the amazing part. By calling the function with the `matplotlib` reference, Azure Machine Learning will render the figure, save it, and attach it to the experiment run. The following screenshot shows Azure Machine Learning studio with the **Images** tab open. Here, you can see the `pairplot` image that we just created and registered attached to the run:

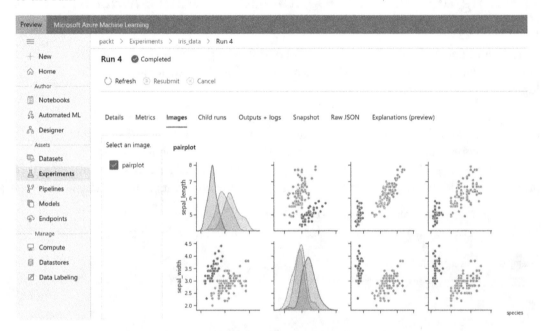

Figure 5.18 – Pairplot tracked and shown in Azure Machine Learning studio

It seems like a tiny feature, but it is insanely useful in real-world experimentation. Get used to automatically generating plots of your data, models, and results and attaching them to your run. Whenever you are going through your experiments later, you'll have all the visualizations already attached to your run, metrics, and configuration.

Think about storing regression plots when you're training regression models, and confusion matrices and ROC curves when training classification models. Store your feature importance when you're training tree-based ensembles and activations for neural networks. You can implement this once and add a ton of useful information to your data and ML pipelines.

> **Important Note**
> When you're using AutoML and HyperDrive to optimize parameters, pre-processing, feature engineering, and model selection, you will get a ton of generated visualizations out of the box to help you understand the data, model, and results.

Now that we know how to store visualizations in the Azure Machine Learning workspace, let's learn how to create visuals denoting high-dimensional data.

Understanding dimensional reduction techniques

We looked at a lot of ways to visualize data in the previous sections, but high-dimensional data cannot be easily and accurately visualized in two dimensions. To achieve this, we need a projection of some sort or an embedding technique to embed the feature space in two dimensions. There are many linear and non-linear embedding techniques that you can use to produce two-dimensional projections of data. The following are the most common ones:

- **Principal Component Analysis (PCA)**
- **Linear Discriminant Analysis (LDA)**
- **t-Distributed Stochastic Neighbor Embedding (t-SNE)**
- **Uniform Manifold Approximation and Projection (UMAP)**

The following diagram shows the **LDA** and **t-SNE** embeddings for the 13-dimensional *UCI Wine Recognition dataset* (`https://archive.ics.uci.edu/ml/datasets/wine`). In the **LDA** embedding, we can see that all the classes should be linearly separable. That's a lot we have learned from using two lines of code to plot the embedding before we have even started the model selection or training process:

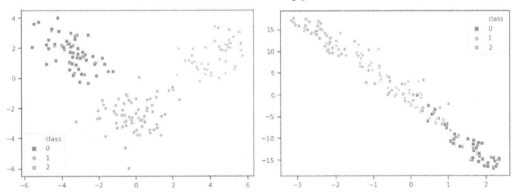

Figure 5.19 – Supervised LDA (left) versus unsupervised t-SNE (right)

Both the **LDA** and **t-SNE** embeddings are extremely helpful for judging the separability of the individual classes and hence the difficulty of your classification task. It's always good to assess how well a particular model will perform on your data before you start selecting and training a specific algorithm.

A great way to get quick insights and a good understanding of your data is to visualize it. This will also help you identify clusters in your data and irregularities and anomalies – all things that need to be considered in all further data processing. But how can you visualize a dataset with 10, 100, or 1,000 feature dimensions? And where should you keep the analysis?

In this section, we will answer all these questions. First, we will look into the *linear* embedding techniques – **PCA**, an *unsupervised* technique, and **LDA**, a *supervised* technique. Then, we will compare both techniques to two popular *unsupervised non-linear* embedding techniques, **t-SNE** and **UMAP**, the latter of which is a generalized and faster version of t-SNE. Having those four techniques in your toolchain will help you understand datasets and create meaningful visualizations. We will run all these techniques against datasets of increasing complexity, namely the following:

- **The Iris Flower dataset**: This dataset contains three classes and four feature dimensions.

- **The UCI Wine Recognition dataset**: This dataset contains three classes and thirteen feature dimensions.

- **The MNIST Handwritten Digits dataset**: This dataset contains 10 classes and 784 feature dimensions (28 x 28-pixel images).

The code to generate the embeddings in this section has been omitted for brevity but can be found in the `07_dimensionality_reduction.ipynb` file in this book's GitHub repository.

Unsupervised dimensional reduction using PCA

The most popular linear dimensionality reduction technique is PCA. This is because, since it is an unsupervised method, it doesn't need any training labels. PCA embedding linearly transforms a dataset so that the resulting projection is uncorrelated. The axes of this project are called **principal components** and are computed in such a way that each has the next highest variance.

The principal components are the directions of the highest variance in the data. This means that the principal components or Eigenvectors describe the strongest direction of the dataset, and the next dimension shows the orthogonal difference from the previous direction. In NLP, the main components correspond with high-level concepts – in recommendation engines, they correspond with user or item traits.

PCA can be computed as the Eigenvalue decomposition of the covariance or correlation matrix, or on a non-square matrix, by using SVD. PCA and Eigenvalue decomposition are often used as data experimentation steps for visualization, whereas SVD is often used as dimensionality reduction for sparse datasets; for example, a Bag-of-Words model for NLP. We will see how SVD is used in practice in *Chapter 7, Advanced Feature Extraction with NLP*.

An embedding technique can be used as a form of dimensionality reduction by simply removing all but the first x components because these first – and largest – components explain a certain percentage of the variance of the dataset. Hence, we must remove data with low variance to receive a lower-dimensional dataset.

To visualize data after performing PCA in two dimensions (or after performing any embedding technique) is to visualize the first two components of the transformed dataset – the two largest principal components. The resulting data is rotated along the axis – the principal components – scaled, and centered at zero. The following diagram shows the results of PCA for the first two datasets. As you can see, all the visualizations have the highest variance projected across the x axis, the second-highest across the y axis, and so on:

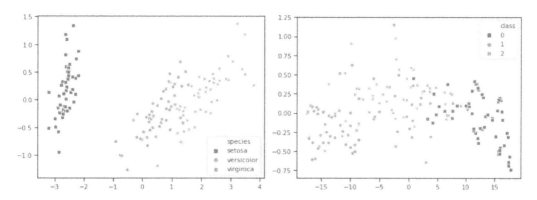

Figure 5.20 – PCA for the Iris Flower dataset (left) and the UCI Wine Recognition dataset (right)

Here, we should acknowledge that it is a great first step that we can show all these three datasets in only two dimensions, and immediately recognize clusters.

By projecting the data across the first two principal components and looking at the Iris Flower dataset on the left, we can see that all the clusters look linearly separable (in two dimensions). However, when we look at the UCI Wine Recognition dataset on the right, we can already tell that the clusters are not extremely obvious anymore. Now, 13 feature dimensions are projected along with the first two principal components, with the highest variance along the x axis and the second-highest variance along the y axis. In PCA, it's typical for the cluster's shape to be aligned with the x axis because this is how the algorithm works.

Now, let's run PCA on the most complex dataset – the MNIST Handwritten Digits dataset. The result of doing so can be seen in the following diagram:

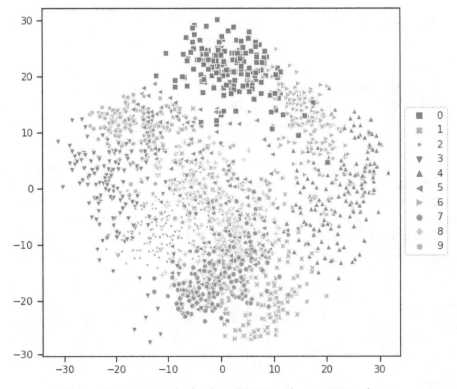

Figure 5.21 – PCA results for the MNIST Handwritten Digits dataset

When we look at the much more complex embedding of the MNIST Handwritten Digits dataset, we cannot see many clusters besides maybe the cluster for **0** at the top. The data is centered across zero and scaled to a range between **-30** and **30**. Hence, we can already tell the downsides of PCA – it doesn't consider any target labels, which means it doesn't optimize for separable classes.

In the next section, we'll look at a technique that takes target labels into account.

Supervised dimensional reduction using LDA

In LDA, we linearly transform the input data – similar to PCA – and optimize the transformation in such a way that the resulting directions have the highest inter-cluster variance and the lowest intra-cluster variance. This means that the optimization tries to keep samples of the same cluster close to the cluster's mean, all while trying to keep the cluster's means as far apart as possible.

In LDA, we also receive a linear weighted set of directions as a resulting transformation. The data is centered around 0 and the directions are ordered by their highest inter-cluster variance. Hence, in that sense, LDA is like PCA in that it takes target labels into account. Both LDA and PCA have no real tuning knobs, besides the number of components we want to keep in the projection and probably a random initialization seed.

The following diagram shows the results of performing LDA on our first two datasets:

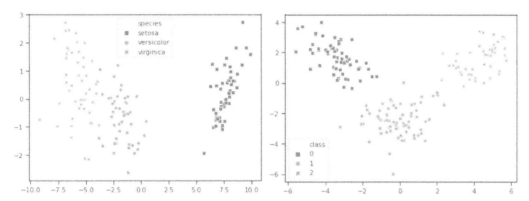

Figure 5.22 – LDA results for the Iris Flower dataset (left) and the UCI Wine Recognition dataset (right)

Here, we can see that the data is transformed into two dimensions in such a way that the cluster's means are the farthest apart from each other across the *x* axis. We can see the same effect for both the Iris Flower and UCI Wine Recognition datasets. Another interesting fact that we can observe in both embeddings is that the data also becomes linearly separable. We can almost put two straight lines in both visualizations to separate the clusters from each other.

The LDA embedding for both datasets looks quite good in terms of how the data is separated by classes. From this, we can be confident that a linear classifier for both datasets should achieve great performance – for example, above 95% accuracy. While this might be just a ballpark estimate, we already know what to expect from a linear classifier with minimal analysis and data preprocessing.

Unfortunately, most real-world embeddings look a lot more like the one shown in the following diagram, where we used LDA on the final dataset. This is because most real-world datasets often have above 10 or even 100 feature dimensions:

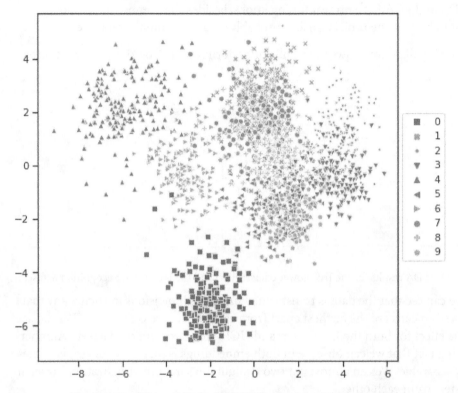

Figure 5.23 – LDA results for MNIST Handwritten Digits dataset

Here, we can also see a good separation of the cluster containing the **0** digits at the bottom and the two clusters of fours and sixes on the left-hand side. All the other clusters are drawn on top of each other and don't look to be linearly separable.

Hence, we can tell that a linear classifier won't perform well and will have maybe only around 30% accuracy – which is still a lot better than if we were to do this randomly. However, we can't tell what performance we would expect from a complex non-linear model – not even a non-parametric model such as a decision tree-based ensemble classifier.

As we can see, LDA performs a lot better than PCA as it takes class labels into account. Therefore, labeling data is something to consider when you're optimizing results. We will learn how to do efficient labeling in *Chapter 6, Feature Engineering and Labeling*.

LDA is a great embedding technique for linearly separable datasets with less than 100 dimensions and categorical target variables. An extension of LDA is **Quadratic Discriminant Analysis (QDA)**, which performs a non-linear projection using combinations of two variables. If you are dealing with continuous target variables, you can use a very similar technique called **analysis of variance (ANOVA)** to model the variance between clusters. The result of ANOVA transformations indicates whether the variance in the dataset is attributed to a combination of the variance of different components.

As we have seen neither PCA nor LDA performed well when separating high-dimensional data such as image data. In the Handwritten Digits dataset, we are dealing with *only* 784 feature dimensions from 28 x 28-pixel images. Imagine that your dataset consists of 1,024 x 1,024-pixel images – your dataset would have more than 1 million dimensions. Hence, we need a better embedding technique for very high-dimensional datasets.

Non-linear dimensional reduction using t-SNE

Projecting high-dimensional datasets into two or three dimensions was extremely difficult and cumbersome a couple of years ago. If you wanted to visualize image data on a two-dimensional graph, you could use any of the previously discussed techniques – if they could compute a result – or try exotic embeddings such as self-organizing maps.

Even though t-SNE was released in a paper in 2008 by Laurence van der Maaten and Geoffrey Hinton (`https://lvdmaaten.github.io/publications/papers/JMLR_2008.pdf`), it took until 2012 for someone to apply it to a major dataset. It was used by the team ranked first in the Merck Viz Kaggle competition – a rather unconventional way to apply a great embedding algorithm for the first time. However, since the end of that competition, t-SNE has been used regularly in other Kaggle competitions and by large companies for embedding high-dimensional datasets with great success.

t-SNE projects high-dimensional features into a two- or three-dimensional space while minimizing the difference of similar points in high-and low-dimensional space. Hence, high-dimensional feature vectors that are close to each other are likely to be close to each other in the two-dimensional embedding.

The following diagram shows t-SNE applied to the Iris Flower and UCI Wine Recognition datasets. As we can see, the complex non-linear embedding doesn't perform a lot better than the simple PCA or LDA techniques. However, its real power is highlighted in very large and high-dimensional datasets that contain up to 30 million observations of thousands of feature dimensions:

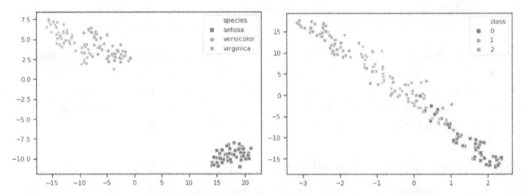

Figure 5.24 – The t-SNE results for the Iris Flower dataset (left) and
the UCI Wine Recognition dataset (right)

In the following diagram, you can see how t-SNE performs against the MNIST dataset:

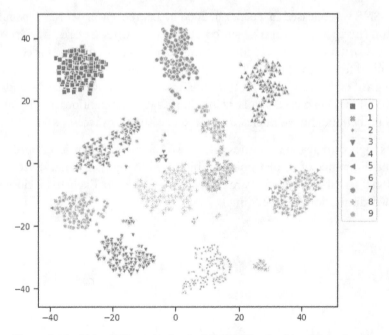

Figure 5.25 – The t-SNE results for the MNIST Handwritten Digits dataset

As we can see, t-SNE performs a lot better on the MNIST dataset and effortlessly separates the clusters of 10 handwritten digits. This suggests that 99% accuracy might be possible.

What is beautiful with this type of visualization is not only that we can see that the data is separable, but we can also imagine what the confusion matrix will look like when a classifier gets trained on the data, simply by looking at the preceding visualization. Here are some observations about the data that we can infer from just looking at the embedding:

Replace this bullet list with the following list:

- There are three clusters containing samples of digit 1, where one cluster is further away from the mean.

- There are three clusters containing samples of digit 9, where in a couple of cases, some of these samples are very close to the clusters for digit 1 and digit 7 samples.

- There is a cluster containing samples of digit 3 in the middle, that are close to the cluster for digit 8 samples.

- There is a small cluster containing samples of digit 2, that are close to the cluster for digit 8 samples.

- The clusters containing samples for digits 3 and 9 are quite close to each other, so they may look similar.

- The clusters containing samples for digits 0, 4 and 6 have a very good distance from other clusters, suggesting that they are quite separable.

These are brilliant insights since you know what to expect and what to look for in your data when you're manually exploring samples. It also helps you tune your feature engineering to, for example, try to differentiate the images for the **1**, **7**, and **9** digits as they will lead to the most misclassifications later in modeling.

Generalizing t-SNE with UMAP

UMAP for dimension reduction is an algorithm for general-purpose manifold learning and dimension reduction. It is a generalization of t-SNE that's based on Riemannian geometry and algebraic topology.

In general, UMAP provides similar results to t-SNE with a topological approach, better scalability of feature dimensions, and faster computation at runtime. Since it is faster and performs slightly better in terms of topological structure, it is quickly gaining popularity.

If we look at the embeddings for the Iris Flower and UCI Wine Recognition datasets again, we will see a similar effect to what we saw with t-SNE. The results are shown in the following diagram:

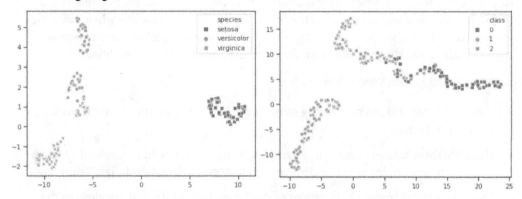

Figure 5.26 – UMAP results for the Iris Flower dataset (left) and
the UCI Wine Recognition dataset (right)

The resulting embeddings look reasonable but they aren't better than the linearly separable results of LDA. However, we can't measure computational performance by only comparing the results, and that's where UMAP shines.

When it comes to higher-dimensional data, such as the MNIST Handwritten Digits dataset, UMAP performs exceptionally well as a two-dimensional embedding technique. We can see the results for UMAP on the MNIST Handwritten Digits dataset in the following diagram:

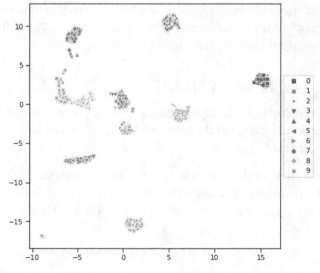

Figure 5.26 – The UMAP results for the MNIST Handwritten Digits dataset

As we can see, UMAP reduces clusters to completely separable entities in the embedding, with minimal overlaps and a great distance between the clusters themselves. Making similar observations to what we made previously, for example, concerning the clusters of the **1** and **9** digits, are still possible, but the clusters look a lot more separable.

From these data experimentation and visualization techniques, we would like you to take away the following key points:

- Perform PCA to try to analyze Eigenvectors

- Perform LDA or ANOVA to understand the variance of your data

- Perform t-SNE or UMAP embedding if you have complex high-dimensional data

Armed with this knowledge, we can dive right into feature engineering as we know which data samples will be easy to handle and which samples will cause high misclassification rates in production.

Summary

In the first two parts of this chapter, you learned what techniques exist for you to explore and statistically analyze raw datasets and how to use them hands-on on a real-life dataset.

After that, you learned about the dimensionality reduction techniques you can use to visualize high-dimensional datasets. There, you learned about techniques that are extremely useful for you to understand your data, its principal components, discriminant directions, and separability.

Furthermore, everything you have learned in this chapter can be performed on a compute cluster in your Azure Machine Learning workspace, through which you can keep track of all the figures and outputs that are generated.

In the next chapter, using all the knowledge you've gained so far, you will dive into the topic of feature engineering, where you learn how to select and transform features in datasets to prepare them for ML training. In addition, you will have a closer look at labeling and how Azure Machine Learning can help with this tedious task.

6
Feature Engineering and Labeling

In the previous chapter, we learned how to clean our data and do basic statistical analysis. In this chapter, we will delve into two more types of actions we must perform before we can start our ML training. These two steps are the most important of all besides efficiently cleaning your dataset, and to be good at them, you will require a high amount of experience. This chapter will give you a basis to build upon.

In the first section, we will learn about feature engineering. We will understand the process, how to select predictive features from our dataset, and what methods exist to transform features from our dataset to make them usable for our ML algorithm.

In the second section, we will look at data labeling. Most ML algorithms fall into the category of supervised learning, which means they require labeled training data. We will look at some typical scenarios that require labels and learn how Azure Machine Learning can help with this tedious task.

In this chapter, we will cover the following topics:

- Understanding and applying feature engineering
- Handling data labeling

Technical requirements

In this chapter, we will use the following Python libraries and versions to perform feature engineering on different datasets.

- `azureml-sdk 1.34.0`
- `azureml-widgets 1.34.0`
- `azureml-dataprep 2.20.0`
- `pandas 1.3.2`
- `numpy 1.19.5`
- `scikit-learn 0.24.2`
- `seaborn 0.11.2`
- `plotly 5.3.1`
- `umap_learn 0.5.1`
- `statsmodels 0.13.0`
- `missingno 0.5.0`

Similar to previous chapters, you can execute this code using either a local Python interpreter or a notebook environment hosted in Azure Machine Learning.

All code examples in this chapter can be found in the GitHub repository for this book: `https://github.com/PacktPublishing/Mastering-Azure-Machine-Learning-Second-Edition/tree/main/chapter06`.

Understanding and applying feature engineering

Feature engineering is the general term that describes the process of transforming existing features in our dataset, creating missing features, and eventually selecting the most predictive features from our dataset to start the ML training process with a given ML algorithm. These cannot just be seen as some mathematical functions we must apply to our data. This is an art form and doing it well makes the difference between a mediocre and highly performing predictive model. If you want to understand where you should invest your time, feature engineering is the step where you can have the most impact on the quality of your final ML model. To create this impact and be efficient, we must consider the following:

- **ML algorithm requirements**: Do the features have to be in a specific format or range? How do I best avoid overfitting and underfitting the model?

- **Domain knowledge**: Are the given features sufficient for our model? Can we create additional features or derive features that contain more predictive information?

In this section, we'll define the different classes of feature engineering techniques and then look at some of the most prominent methods to apply to different types of datasets.

> **Important Note**
> Keep in mind that the usefulness of a specific feature engineering method depends on the utilized type of features (categorical, continuous, text, image, audio) and the chosen ML algorithm.

Classifying feature engineering techniques

Broadly speaking, feature engineering methods can be grouped into the following categories:

- **Feature creation**: Create new features from the given set of features or additional information sources.

- **Feature transformation**: Transform single features to make them useful and stable for the utilized ML algorithm.

- **Feature extraction**: Create derived features from the original data.

- **Feature selection**: Choose the most prominent and predictive features.

Let's look at each of these categories and what they entail.

Feature creation

The first step to take in feature engineering is finding all the features that should be included in the model. To be good at this, you must have an intimate understanding of the relevant domain or know someone who is a **subject matter expert** (**SME**) in the domain. In the end, we want to be sure that we consider any type of data point that is predictive and that is feasible to acquire in a reasonable amount of time.

In turn, we must understand all the methods that can help us create new features in our dataset, either taken from additional sources or the initial dataset. Typically, these methods can be classified as follows:

- **Adding missing predictive features**: We add external information that is missing to achieve a more predictive model.

- **Combining the available features**: We create new features by combining already available features in our dataset.

Why do we have to change already existing features in our dataset?

The reason for this is that a lot of connections between features and labels, that we understand, may not be clear to the utilized ML algorithm. Therefore, it is a good idea to think about what features or representations of the available features we would assume are necessary to make it easier for the ML algorithm to grasp the intrinsic connections.

Let's look at some examples to understand this better.

Imagine that you have a dataset for predicting house prices, like the one we examined in *Chapter 5*, *Performing Data Analysis and Visualization*. Furthermore, imagine that the features we have are the **length** and **width** of the house or apartment. In this case, it is probably useful to combine these two features to create a new one called the **surface area**. In addition, if the **type** of building is missing (house, flat, condo, and so on), we may want to add this from other sources since we know the type has an impact on the price of a property.

> **Important Note**
>
> If you create new features from existing ones, it is typically wise to only stick with the newly created feature by dropping those initial features from the dataset.

Now, imagine the amount of money a person spends throughout their life. Being young, this might be very little. When they grow older, they may have mortgages and children and eventually, their spending may drop when their children move out of the house, and they are nearing retirement. As this would form something of a parabolic relationship between **age** and **cost of living**, it may not be easy for an ML algorithm to grasp this. Therefore, one possible option is to square the values of the **cost of living** feature to emphasize higher costs and deemphasize lower costs.

In the previous two examples, we used our domain knowledge to create new features. But what if we do not have this at our disposal?

There is a way to create new features mathematically using the so-called **polynomial extension**. The idea is to create new features by raising the value of a feature to a certain power and multiplying it by one or multiple other features. Here, we define the **degree** as the maximum power a single feature can be raised to, and we define the **order** as the number of features we allow to be multiplied by each other. The following diagram shows all the possible combinations for a degree of 2 and order of 2 on the left-hand side, and a degree of 3 and order of 3 on the right-hand side:

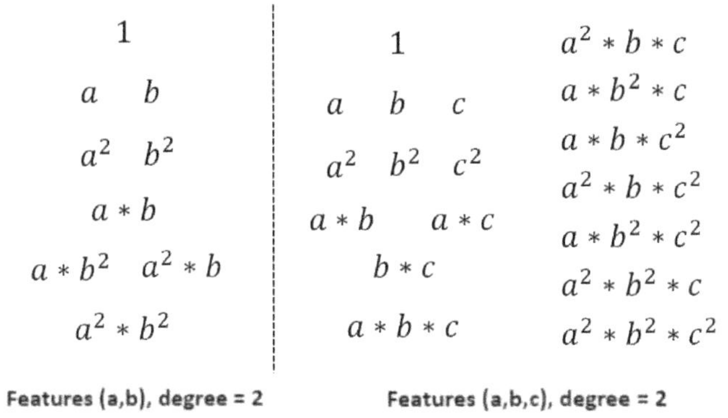

$$1$$

$$a \quad b$$

$$a^2 \quad b^2$$

$$a * b$$

$$a * b^2 \quad a^2 * b$$

$$a^2 * b^2$$

Features (a,b), degree = 2

$$1$$

$$a \quad b \quad c$$

$$a^2 \quad b^2 \quad c^2$$

$$a * b \quad\quad a * c$$

$$b * c$$

$$a * b * c$$

$$a^2 * b * c$$

$$a * b^2 * c$$

$$a * b * c^2$$

$$a^2 * b * c^2$$

$$a * b^2 * c^2$$

$$a^2 * b^2 * c$$

$$a^2 * b^2 * c^2$$

Features (a,b,c), degree = 2

Figure 6.1 – Possible combinations for polynomial extension
(degree=2, order=2 on the left/degree=2, order=3 on the right)

You should only consider a maximum order of 3 because, as shown in the preceding diagram, even with a degree of 2, this operation already creates too many combinations. Still, this automatic process may lead to much better predictive features than the originating ones.

To try this method, you can use the `PolynomialFeatures` class from the `sklearn` library (`https://scikit-learn.org/stable/modules/generated/sklearn.preprocessing.PolynomialFeatures.html`).

With all these methods in mind, we can create new features in our dataset that might be easier for our ML algorithm to handle and contain more precise, predictive information.

Next, let's look at some methods that let us change a single feature by transforming its values or its representation.

Feature transformation

Feature transformation is about manipulating a feature to change its value or create a new representation of the same. The following list covers the types of transformations we can perform on single features:

- **Discretization**: Divide feature values into different groups or intervals to reduce complexity. This can be done on numerical or categorical features.

- **Splitting**: Split a feature into multiple elements. This is typically done on datetime and string values.

- **Categorical encoding**: Represent a categorical feature numerically, by creating new numerical features while following specific methods.

- **Scaling**: Transform a continuous feature so that it fits into a specified range of values.

- **Standardization**: Transform a continuous feature so that it represents a normal distribution with a mean of 0 and a standard deviation of 1.

- **Normalization**: Transform a vector (row) of multiple continuous features individually into a so-called unit norm (unit magnitude).

- **Mathematical transformation**: Transform a continuous feature by applying a specific mathematical function to it (`square`, `square root`, `exp`, `log`, and so on).

In *Chapter 5, Performing Data Analysis and Visualization*, we used the `log` function to calculate the logarithm of all house price values. We did this to reduce the impact that a handful of outliers would have on our ML training. Therefore, the main reason to transform features is to adapt the feature to the possible mathematical requirements of the given ML algorithm. Often, you may run into the following requirements of the ML algorithm:

- **Numerical format**: The algorithm requires all the features to be numerical.

- **Same scale**: The algorithm requires all the predictive features to be on the same scale, maybe even with a mean of 0 and a standard deviation of 1.

- **Mathematical theory**: The domain itself may require certain transformations based on mathematical theory. For example, a price feature for predictions concerning economic theory should nearly always be transformed with the natural logarithm.

- **Computational limits**: The algorithm may require each feature value to have a small scale. Such algorithms often require values to be in an interval of `[-1,1]`.

- **Complexity**: Most algorithms require very precise features. Therefore, reducing the complexity of the possible values a feature can take is often worthwhile.

An example would be discretizing features. One such method is called **binning**, which transforms numerical continuous values into a handful of discrete values. We will see this in action on text data in *Chapter 7, Advanced Feature Extraction with NLP*.

Another example would be splitting datetime features. Imagine that we want to predict the amount of traffic on a certain road at specific times of the day. Let's assume that we got a feature denoting the **date and time** of our recording and the **number of cars** we tracked at that point. To make a better prediction, one idea would be to create three new features, denoting whether it is a *workday*, *weekend*, or *holiday*. There will be less traffic on a Sunday at 7 A.M. compared to a workday morning at 7 A.M.

Let's learn how to perform this transformation. The following screenshot shows our initial small dataset and the first transformation adding day of the week:

	time of measurement	number of cars	day of the week
0	2021-01-01 11:00:00	60	Friday
1	2021-01-02 11:00:00	412	Saturday
2	2021-01-03 11:00:00	230	Sunday
3	2021-01-04 11:00:00	1234	Monday
4	2021-01-05 11:00:00	854	Tuesday
5	2021-01-06 11:00:00	1432	Wednesday
6	2021-01-07 11:00:00	1103	Thursday

Figure 6.2 – Dataset with a new weekday feature

In the next step, we must enrich the data by adding a new categorical feature called daytype, which denotes whether a day is either a weekday, a weekend, or a holiday:

	time of measurement	number of cars	day of the week	daytype
0	2021-01-01 11:00:00	60	Friday	holiday
1	2021-01-02 11:00:00	412	Saturday	weekend
2	2021-01-03 11:00:00	230	Sunday	weekend
3	2021-01-04 11:00:00	1234	Monday	weekday
4	2021-01-05 11:00:00	854	Tuesday	weekday
5	2021-01-06 11:00:00	1432	Wednesday	weekday
6	2021-01-07 11:00:00	1103	Thursday	weekday

Figure 6.3 – Dataset enrichment

Theoretically, we are done. But our ML algorithm may beg to differ here. Our ML model may make up a natural order for our categorical data that does not exist or it simply cannot handle categorical data. In this case, it is prudent to **encode** our categorical data with numerical values. One such method is called **one-hot encoding**, which transforms a categorical feature into multiple numerical features by creating a new feature with two valid values (0 or 1) for every existing category. The following screenshot shows this encoding for our example:

	time of measurement	number of cars	day of the week	daytype	holiday	weekday	weekend
0	2021-01-01 11:00:00	60	Friday	holiday	1	0	0
1	2021-01-02 11:00:00	412	Saturday	weekend	0	0	1
2	2021-01-03 11:00:00	230	Sunday	weekend	0	0	1
3	2021-01-04 11:00:00	1234	Monday	weekday	0	1	0
4	2021-01-05 11:00:00	854	Tuesday	weekday	0	1	0
5	2021-01-06 11:00:00	1432	Wednesday	weekday	0	1	0
6	2021-01-07 11:00:00	1103	Thursday	weekday	0	1	0

Figure 6.4 – One-hot encoding the new feature

Here, we created three new features named `holiday`, `weekday`, and `weekend`, each representing our initial categories. Where a sample had this initial category, the value of that feature is set to `1`; otherwise, it is set to `0`.

What have we done in this example? We transformed a very unintuitive datetime feature into something with more predictive power by splitting the feature into components, adding external knowledge through feature creation, and performing categorical encoding on the created feature.

Now that we have a good grasp of feature transformation, let's look at what falls under feature extraction.

Feature extraction

With **feature extraction**, we group all the methods that do not manipulate features by simple means but extract useful information from a high-dimensional dataset. This is typically done by using complex mathematical algorithms or ML algorithms.

Extraction is often required when the underlying dataset is too complex to be processed, so it needs to be brought into a simplified form while keeping its predictive value.

The following are some typical extraction types for different scenarios:

- **High-dimensional reduction**: Create representative features based on an n-dimensional dataset.

- **Feature detection**: Find points of interest in every image in an image dataset.

- **Word embeddings**: Create numeric encodings for words in a text dataset.

- **Signal processing**: Extract the characteristics of sound waves from an audio dataset.

We discussed high-dimensional reduction methods in *Chapter 5*, *Performing Data Analysis and Visualization*, when we looked at visualizing high-dimensional datasets. In a process like **principal component analysis (PCA)**, the dataset is projected onto a two- or three-dimensional space by creating principal component vectors. Instead of only using this method for visualization, we could use these calculated vectors as derived and less complex features that represent our dataset.

> **Important Note**
>
> High-dimensional reduction techniques can be used for feature extraction, but keep in mind that we lose our intrinsic understanding of the features. Instead of features called suburbs or rooms, we end up with features called Principal Component 1 and Principal Component 2.

Looking at the other scenarios, it seems that extraction typically happens when we are working with complex datasets made up of text, image, or audio data. In all these cases, there are specific methods to consider when extracting information from the raw data.

In the case of an image dataset, we might be interested in key areas or points of interest, including finding edges and objects. In *Chapter 10*, *Training Deep Neural Networks on Azure*, you will see that such image extraction steps are done automatically by **deep neural networks**, removing the need to perform manual feature extraction on images in a lot of cases.

In the case of text data, we can use extraction methods such as **bag of words** and **TF-IDF**, both of which help create numerical representations of text, capturing meaning and semantic relationships. We will have an in-depth look at these methods in *Chapter 7*, *Advanced Feature Extraction with NLP*.

In the case of audio data, we can use signal processing to extract information and new features from the source. In this scenario, there are also two domains – the time domain and the frequency domain – that we can pull information from. From the time domain, we would typically extract something like the **amplitude envelope**, which is the maximum amplitude of the signal per frame, the **root mean square energy**, which hints at the loudness of the signal, and the **zero-crossing rate**, which is the number of times the wave is crossing the horizontal time axis. If you must work with data from this domain, make yourself comfortable with such processing techniques.

> **Important Note**
>
> A lot of feature extraction and feature transformation techniques are already embedded in common ML frameworks and algorithms, removing the need for you to manually touch features. Have a good understanding of what the algorithm does by itself and what you need to do manually when you're preprocessing.

So far, we've learned how to create new features, transform features, and extract features from our dataset. Now, let's look at some methods that can help us select the most predictive feature from our feature set.

Feature selection

With **feature selection**, we define all the methods that help us understand how valuable and predictive a feature is for the target so that we can choose a useful subset of our feature variables for training. The reasons to reduce complexity are two-fold. On the one hand, we want the simplicity to make the model **explainable** while on the other, we want to avoid **overfitting** the model. With too much input information, we will end up with a model that, in most cases, will perfectly fit our training data and nothing else but will perform poorly on unseen data.

Generally, there are three different types of feature selection methods, as follows:

- **Filter-based methods**: These define a derived metric, that is not the target error rate, to measure the quality of a subset of features.

- **Wrapper-based methods**: These use greedy search algorithms to run a prediction model on different combinations of feature subsets.

- **Embedded methods**: These are specific selection methods that are already embedded into our final ML model.

Filter-based methods can be very efficient in terms of computational resources but are only evaluated against a simpler filter. Typically, statistical measures such as correlation, mutual information, and entropy are used as metrics in these approaches.

On the other hand, wrapper-based methods are computationally intense. At the same time, they can find a great performing feature set since the same error function or metric is being used for the selection of the features as the one that's being used in the actual model training. The downside of this approach is that without an independent metric, the selected subset is only useful for the chosen ML training algorithm. Typically, this is done by performing one of the following processes:

- **Step forward feature selection**: Features are added one by one based on the training results of each feature until the model does not improve its performance.

- **Step backward feature selection**: The model is evaluated with the full set of features. These features are subsequently removed until a predefined number of features is reached. This removal is done in a round-robin fashion.

- **Exhaustive feature selection**: All the feature subsets are evaluated, which is the most expensive method.

Finally, a selection method is called an embedded method when the selection step is part of the model learning algorithm itself. Embedded methods often combine the qualities of filter and wrapper methods through the fact that the learning algorithm takes advantage of its selection process and performs selection and training at the same time. Typical examples of embedded methods are ensemble models, **Lasso**, and **Ridge**.

You may have realized this by now, but we used such methods in *Chapter 5*, *Performing Data Analysis and Visualization*. The **Pearson correlation coefficient** we used for generating a correlation matrix is a derived metric, so it falls under the filter-based selection methods. In addition, we used an **ensemble decision tree model** to calculate feature importance for our dataset. This helped us get a clear understanding of which features may have more influence on the target than others. This ensemble method utilizes the **random forest** approach. A random forest not only implements the so-called **bagging** technique to randomly select a subset of samples to train on but also takes a random selection of features rather than using all the features to grow each tree. Therefore, for feature selection, random forests fall into the embedded category.

We will have a more detailed look at the tree-based ensemble classifier, as well as bagging and boosting, in *Chapter 9*, *Building ML Models Using Azure Machine Learning*.

Besides all these mathematical approaches to feature selection, sometimes, a more manual approach might be far superior. For example, when we removed the postal code from our **Melbourne housing dataset** in *Chapter 5, Performing Data Analysis and Visualization*, we did so because we understood that the postal code and the suburbs contain the same information, which made them redundant. We did this because we have domain knowledge and understand the relationship between postal codes and suburbs. Note that this additional knowledge lessens the burden for the model to learn these connections by itself.

> **Important Note**
>
> For feature engineering, the more outside knowledge about the data or the domain, the simpler a lot of these preprocessing steps can get, or they become avoidable altogether.

We will iterate this notion throughout this book as it needs to be ingrained into everything you do so that you get more efficient and better at working with data.

We now have a general understanding of the general types of feature engineering we can perform. In the next section, we will provide an overview of the most prominent methods and drill deeper into some of them.

Discovering feature transformation and extraction methods

Now that we have a good grasp of the types of feature engineering action we can apply to our feature, let's look at some of the most prominent feature engineering techniques and their names. The following table provides a good overview of most of the well-known methods in the different categories we have learned about:

Scaling and Normalization	Mathematical Transformation	Discretization	Categorical Encoding	Text Extraction	Image Extraction
Standard Scaler	Logarithmic Transformer	Binarizer	One-Hot Encoding	Count Embedding	Hog Descriptor
Min-Max Scaler	Square Root Transformer	Equal Width Discretization	Ordinal Encoding	TF-IDF	Speed-Up Robust Features (SURF)
Robust Scaler	Exponential Transformer	Equal Frequency Discretization	Weight of Evidence	Co-Occurrence	Scale-Invariant Feature Transform (SIFT)
Quantile Scaler	Reciprocal Transformer	Binning	Target Encoding	Bag of Words	Local Binary Patterns
L1 Norm	Box-Cox Transformer	K-Means Discretization	Frequency Encoding	N-grams	Haar Wavelet
L2 Norm	Yeo-Johnson Transformer		Count Encoding	Prediction-based Word Embedding	Harris Corner Detector
Max Norm			Rare Label Encoding		Viola Jones Facial Detector

Figure 6.5 – Overview of different feature engineering methods

Keep in mind that this list is far from exhaustive and as we mentioned previously, some of these methods are already implemented as part of specific ML algorithms.

In the following sections, we will look at some of these. Feel free to download the `01_feateng_examples.ipynb` file in the GitHub repository for this chapter, which contains the code for the upcoming examples. If you would like to learn more about some of the feature extraction methods we will cover, we will come back to them in the upcoming chapters. For the methods we won't cover, feel free to research them.

Scaling, standardization, and normalization

Since all the scaling and normalization methods are very similar to each other, we will discuss all of them in detail here.

Let's begin with the so-called **StandardScaler**. This scaling transforms our feature values so that the resulting value distribution has a mean (μ) of 0 and a standard deviation (s) of 1. The formula to apply to each value looks like this:

$$z_i = \frac{x_i - \mu}{\sigma}$$

Here, μ is the mean value of the given distribution and s is the standard deviation of the given distribution. With this, we can convert every value, x_i, into a new scaled value, z_i.

The following diagram shows how this scaler changes the shape of multiple distributions:

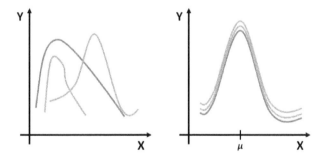

Figure 6.6 – StandardScaler distribution (left: before scaling, right: after scaling)

You should only use this scaler if the underlying distribution is *normally distributed*, as this is the requirement.

Next, we will look at the **MinMaxScaler**. This scaling method is very similar to standardization, except that we are not working with the mean or standard deviation of the value distribution; instead, we are scaling the values to a range of [0,1] or [-1,1] (if negative values exist). Scaling a feature like this will often increase the performance of ML algorithms as they are typically better at handling small-scale values.

Mathematically, this scaling is defined as follows:

$$z_i = \frac{x_i - x_{min}}{x_{max} - x_{min}}$$

Here, x_{min} defines the minimum value and x_{max} defines the maximum value in our initial distribution.

The MinMaxScaler is a good choice if the minimum and maximum values are well-defined – think about the color intensity in an RGB picture. Furthermore, we can change the formula to influence the resulting range of values.

> **Important Note**
>
> The StandardScaler and the MinMaxScaler are both very susceptible to outliers in a distribution, which, in turn, can skew certain ML algorithms.

A lot of ML algorithms pay more attention to large values, so they have a problem with outliers. A scaler fittingly named **RobustScaler** was defined to tackle this behavior. This scaler uses the **interquartile range (IQR)** instead of the standard deviation as a measure of dispersion and uses the **median** value instead of the mean value of the distribution as a measure of central tendency. The interquartile range denotes the middle 50% of the distribution, which means it is the difference between the 75th percentile and the 25th percentile.

Therefore, the mathematical scaling function looks like this:

$$z_i = \frac{x_i - x_{median}}{Q_3(x) - Q_1(x)}$$

Here, x_{median} denotes the median of the distribution, $Q_1(x)$ denotes the value where the first quartile starts, and $Q_3(x)$ denotes the value where the third quartile starts.

Why does this scaler work better with outliers?

In the previous formulas, the biggest outlier would still be falling into the predefined interval because the maximum outlier would be x_{max}. Therefore, the further the outlier is from the bulk of the data points, the more the center values would be scaled toward 0. On the other hand, with the RobustScaler, all the data points in the middle 50% would be scaled into the unit distance, and everything above or below this would be scaled to the appropriate values outside of the main interval while keeping the relative distance between the values in the middle of the distribution intact.

Simply put, the median and the interquartile range are not influenced greatly by outliers, so this scaler is not influenced greatly by outliers.

Let's look at all these scalars on a sample distribution. For this, we will take the `Price` column of the **Melbourne Housing dataset** we used in *Chapter 5, Performing Data Analysis and Visualization.* The following table shows the statistical distribution for the `Price` column and the distribution resulting from applying each scaling method we've discussed:

	count	mean	std	min	25%	50%	75%	max
Price	7130	1.07992e+06	674692	131000	631000	895000	1.335e+06	9e+06
StdSc(Price)	7130	9.96554e-17	1.00007	-1.40655	-0.665421	-0.274104	0.378091	11.7396
MinMaxSc(Price)	7130	0.106993	0.0760731	0	0.0563761	0.0861427	0.135754	1
RobustSc(Price)	7130	0.262674	0.95837	-1.08523	-0.375	0	0.625	11.5128

Figure 6.7 – Distribution scaled using multiple scaling methods

As we can see, **StandardScaler** creates a distribution with a mean of 0 and a standard deviation of 1, **MinMaxScaler** scales the values between 0 and 1, and **RobustScaler** sets the mean to 0. Looking at the box plots in *Figure 6.8* and *Figure 6.9*, we can see the differences in their distributions. Please note the scale of the *y* axis as well:

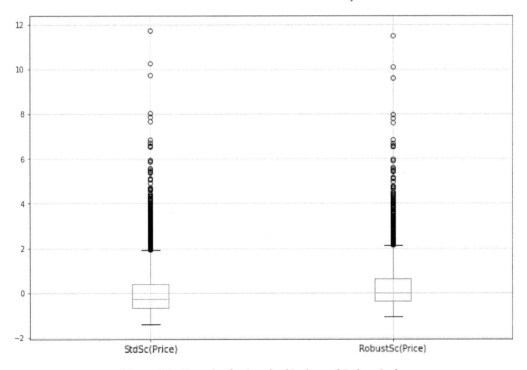

Figure 6.8 – Box plot for StandardScaler and RobustScaler

Comparing the following box plot to *Figure 6.8*, we can see the difference in their distribution:

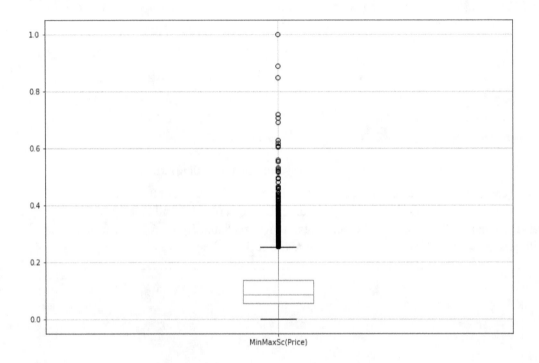

Figure 6.9 – Box plot for MinMaxScaler

Now that we have some idea of how to scale a feature, let's talk about normalization.

Normalization is the process of taking a vector (row) of feature values and scaling them to a **unit magnitude**, typically to simplify mathematical processes such as **cosine similarity**.

Let's start by understanding a process where this normalization step can be of help. The cosine similarity describes how similar two different vectors are to each other. In an n-dimensional room, are they pointing in the same direction, are they perpendicular to each other, or are they facing in the opposite direction?

Such calculations can, for example, help us understand how similar text documents are to each other, by taking a vector of word counts or similar information and comparing them with each other.

Therefore, to understand document similarity, we must calculate a cosine between vectors using the following formula:

$$\cos\theta = \frac{A * B}{\|A\|\,\|B\|}$$

As you can see, to make this calculation, we must calculate the magnitude of each vector – for example, $\|A\|$. This magnitude is defined as follows:

$$\|A\| = \sqrt[2]{a_1^2 + a_2^2 + a_3^2}$$

This single vector magnitude calculation is quite expensive to perform. Now, imagine that we have a dataset that contains hundreds of thousands of documents. We would have to calculate this every time for every combination of vectors (samples) in our dataset. Wouldn't it be easier to have all these vector magnitudes equal to 1? This would greatly simplify the calculation of the cosine.

Therefore, the idea is to normalize all the samples in our dataset to achieve a unit magnitude by scaling them appropriately, as follows:

$$A_{new} = \frac{A_{old}}{\|A\|} = \frac{(a_1, a_2, a_3)}{\sqrt[2]{a_1^2 + a_2^2 + a_3^2}}$$

In this equation, A_{old} denotes our initial vector, $\|A\|$ denotes the magnitude of the initial vector, and A_{new} denotes our scaled vector with the unit magnitude.

This normalization is called **L2 Norm** and is one of three typical normalization methods. Let's look at how the magnitude of a vector is calculated in this and all the other metrics:

- **L1 Norm**: This calculates the magnitude as the sum of the absolute values of the vector components.

- **L2 Norm**: This calculates the traditional vector magnitude (as described).

- **Max Norm**: This calculates the magnitude as the absolute value of the elements of the vector.

The L1 Norm and the Max Norm cannot be used for cosine similarity as they do not calculate the mathematically defined vector magnitude. So, let's look at how those two are calculated.

The L1 Norm is mathematically defined as follows:

$$A_{new} = \frac{A_{old}}{\|A\|} = \frac{(a_1, a_2, a_3)}{|a_1| + |a_2| + |a_3|}$$

The L1 Norm is often used to regularize the values in the dataset when you're fitting an ML algorithm. It keeps the coefficient small, which makes the model training process less complex.

The Max Norm is mathematically defined as follows:

$$A_{new} = \frac{A_{old}}{\|A\|} = \frac{(a_1, a_2, a_3)}{\max\left(|a_1| + |a_2| + |a_3|\right)}$$

The Max Norm is also used for regularization, typically in **neural networks** to keep the weights low at the connections between neurons. It also helps with performing less extreme backpropagation runs to stabilize the ML algorithm's learning.

At this point, you should have a good grasp of the usefulness of scaling and normalization. Next, we'll look at some methods we can use to transform categorical values into numerical representations.

Categorical encoding

When we looked at feature transformation as a concept, we looked at an example where we applied **one-hot encoding**. This method creates new features with two possible values (0,1) for *every* available category in the initial categorical feature. This can be helpful, but a categorical feature of high cardinality would blow up the feature space dramatically. Therefore, when using this method, we must figure out if every single category is predictive or not.

In our previous example, instead of using a category with the days of the week (Monday through Saturday), we opted for only three categories, namely weekday, weekend, and holiday. In such a scenario, one-hot encoding is quite helpful.

Besides this method, there are other ways to encode categorical features. The most basic of them would be **label encoding**. In label encoding, we replace every category with a numeric label $(0,..,n)$, thus making it a numeric feature. Through this, we did not add any additional information to this feature.

The next idea would be to add some intrinsic information from the whole dataset and ingrain it into the values we must encode. Some options for this idea are as follows:

- **Count encoding**: Replace each category with the absolute number of observations of this category in the whole dataset.
- **Frequency encoding**: Replace each category with the relative number (the percentage) of observations of this category in the whole dataset.
- **Target encoding**: Replace each category with the mean value of the target that's been calculated from each entry of this category throughout the whole dataset.

To understand these methods, let's assume that we have a dataset that contains the favorite snack item of 25 people as one of the features and their likelihood of buying a new snack product a company produces as the target. The following table shows the original values and all three encodings we have discussed:

Questionaire ID	Favorite Snack	Likelihood to Buy	CntEnc(FavSnack)	FreqEnc(FavSnack)	TargetEnc(FavSnack)
1	Caramels	0.20	2	0.08	0.217773
2	Chocolate	0.70	8	0.32	0.699729
3	Chewing Gum	0.15	2	0.08	0.181220
4	Gummies	0.05	6	0.24	0.085466
5	Cake	0.50	6	0.24	0.466234
6	Cake	0.40	6	0.24	0.466234
7	Cake	0.60	6	0.24	0.466234
8	Sours	0.65	1	0.04	0.402000
9	Gummies	0.15	6	0.24	0.085466
10	Gummies	0.10	6	0.24	0.085466
11	Chewing Gum	0.05	2	0.08	0.181220
12	Chocolate	0.80	8	0.32	0.699729
13	Chocolate	0.75	8	0.32	0.699729
14	Caramels	0.10	2	0.08	0.217773
15	Chocolate	0.60	8	0.32	0.699729
16	Gummies	0.05	6	0.24	0.085466
17	Gummies	0.10	6	0.24	0.085466
18	Cake	0.50	6	0.24	0.466234
19	Chocolate	0.85	8	0.32	0.699729
20	Chocolate	0.65	8	0.32	0.699729
21	Chocolate	0.65	8	0.32	0.699729
22	Gummies	0.05	6	0.24	0.085466
23	Cake	0.40	6	0.24	0.466234
24	Cake	0.40	6	0.24	0.466234
25	Chocolate	0.60	8	0.32	0.699729

Figure 6.10 – Count, frequency, and target encoding example

With these methods, we can ingrain additional information into the feature, making it easier for an ML algorithm to understand relationships.

Finally, let's talk about **rare label encoding**. This technique is used to replace every rare category in a categorical feature with a single label called `Rare`, thus grouping them into one category. This helps reduce the overall complexity and should especially be done if the `Rare` category will still be a small part of the overall category distribution. You can compare this to grouping small parties under the *Others* label in an election graph, while primarily showing the major parties.

At this point, you should have a good understanding of different encoding techniques. In the next section, we will discuss how we can try out these techniques on a real dataset.

Testing feature engineering techniques on a tabular dataset

In *Chapter 5*, *Performing Data Analysis and Visualization*, we did some cleaning and statistical analysis on the **Melbourne Housing dataset**. After looking through a set of possible feature engineering methods in the previous section, you may have realized that we used some of these methods when we were working with our dataset.

As an exercise, think about where we left off and, keeping the feature engineering options in mind, what we could do now to create new useful features, transform the given features, and eventually select the most prominent and predictive features in our dataset.

For inspiration, have a look at the `02_fe_melbhousing.ipynb` file in the GitHub repository for this chapter.

In the final section of this chapter, we will leave the feature space behind and concentrate on the target or label for our ML training – to be more precise, on the cases where we are missing the labels.

Handling data labeling

In this section, we will look at one of the most time-consuming and important tasks when it comes to preprocessing our dataset for ML training: **data labeling**. As we learned while looking at high-dimensional reduction and other ML techniques in *Chapter 5*, *Performing Data Analysis and Visualization*, for most scenarios, it is vitally important to have labels attached to our samples. As we discussed in *Chapter 1*, *Understanding the End-to-End Machine Learning Process*, there are only a few scenarios where unsupervised learning models are sufficient, such as a model that clusters emails as spam or not spam. In most cases, we want to use a supervised model, which means we will require labels.

In the following sections, we will discuss what scenarios require us to do manual labeling and how Azure Machine Learning can help us be as efficient as possible to perform this monotonous task.

Analyzing scenarios that require labels

We will start by looking at the types of datasets we have discussed so far and in which scenarios we will need to perform manual labeling.

Numerical and categorical data

As we saw when we worked with the **Melbourne Housing dataset**, for tabular datasets, we may often have a column that can be used as the label. In our case, it was the price column that we could use as a label since our goal for ML was to predict house prices based on specific feature inputs.

But even if this column was missing, we could have incorporated other datasets, such as one that shows the mean price for houses in different suburbs of Melbourne, to calculate a reasonable value for each of our dataset samples.

Therefore, the main advantage over any of the other scenarios we will discuss next is that in a dataset made up of numerical and categorical features with clear meaning (not the pixel values of an image), we can use logic and mathematical functions to create a numerical label, or we can classify samples into a categorical label in an automated fashion. This means we do not have to look at every sample manually to define its label.

Natural language processing

Let's start by looking at text data. You may think that a categorical entry would also be text in a sense, but typically, categorical data can also be exchanged with mathematical values without you losing much.

Text data, on the other hand, denote blocks of words, such as those in this book, so they are much more complicated. Look at the following two sentences or utterances:

I would like to book a plane ticket for December 23rd, 2020 from Dubai to Paris.

The room wasn't cleaned, and the heating wouldn't work.

How would we label these utterances? Once again, this very much depends on our goal for training. Maybe we just want to put these utterances into groups, such as order, greeting, or statement. In that scenario, every utterance would receive one label. On the other hand, we may want to drill down into the meaning of the words in the sentence. For our first utterance, we may want to understand the meaning of the order to offer an answer by showing possible flight options. For the second utterance, we may want to understand the sentiment since it is a statement about the quality of a hotel room.

Therefore, we need to start labeling single words or phrases in the utterance itself, while looking for the semantic meaning.

We will come back to this topic in *Chapter 7, Advanced Feature Extraction with NLP*.

Computer vision

When we talk about ML modeling for images, we are typically trying to understand and learn about one of the following:

- **Image classification**: Classify an image into one or more classes. Typical use cases include image searches, library management, and sentiment analysis of a person.

- **Object detection**: Localize specific objects in an image. Typical use cases include pedestrian detection, traffic flow analysis, and object counting.

- **Image segmentation**: Assign each pixel of an image to a specific segment. Typical use cases include precise environment analysis for self-driving cars and pixel-precise anomaly detection in an X-ray or MRI picture.

The following figure shows an example of these three types:

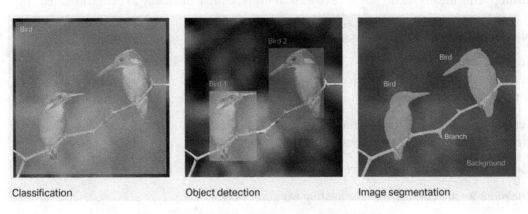

Figure 6.11 – Different image processing methods

For these methods, the process of labeling them becomes more complicated, the further we go down the list. For classification, we can just put one or more labels on an image. For object detection, we start drawing so-called bounding boxes or polygons on the image. Finally, image segmentation becomes very complicated as we must assign labels for each pixel of the image. For this, highly specialized tooling is required.

As we will see shortly, we can use the data labeling tool from Azure Machine Learning Studio to do classification, object detection, and, to some degree, segmentation for image labeling tasks.

Audio annotation

Finally, let's talk about annotating audio data. When it comes to ML modeling for audio data, the following scenarios are possible:

- **Speech-to-text**: Run real-time transcription, voice assistants, pronunciation assessments, and similar solutions.

- **Speech translation**: Translate speech to trigger actions in an application or device.

- **Speaker recognition**: Verify and identify speakers by their voice characteristics.

Therefore, annotating audio data means that we must take out snippets from an audio file and label these snippets accordingly. The following diagram shows a simple example of this:

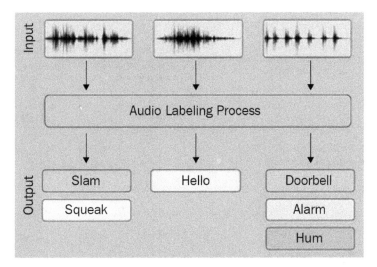

Figure 6.12 – Audio labeling process

As you can imagine, this labeling task is also not very straightforward and requires specialized tooling.

We have seen a lot of scenarios so far, where labeling is of utmost importance. Now, let's try to label some images ourselves.

Performing data labeling for image classification using the Azure Machine Learning labeling service

In this section, we will be using the data labeling service in Azure Machine Learning Studio to label some assets. As we learned in *Chapter 3, Preparing the Azure Machine Learning Workspace*, navigate to the Azure Machine Learning Studio and click on **Data Labeling** at the lower end of the menu, as shown in the following screenshot:

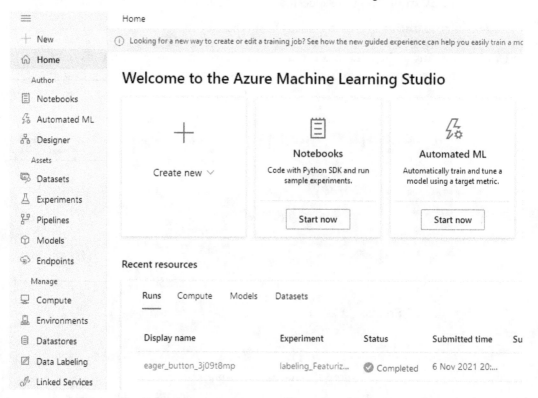

Figure 6.13 – Azure Machine Learning Studio

On the following screen, click **Add Project**, which will take you to the following view:

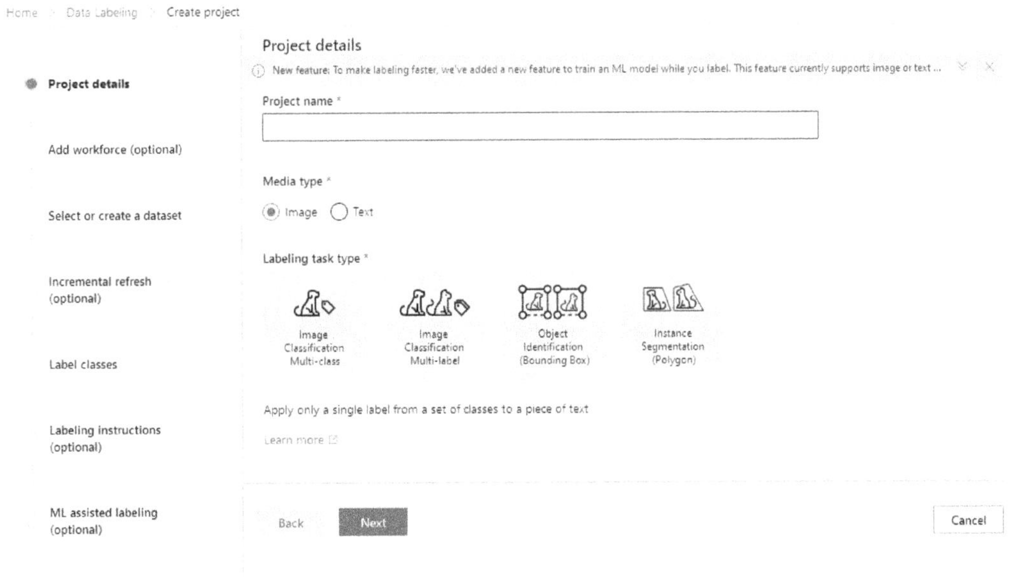

Figure 6.14 – Creation wizard for a labeling project

Before we start the exercise, let's look at what kind of labeling tasks we can perform with the service. As shown in the preceding screenshot, we can work with image and text data as our data source. Switching between the **Image** and **Text** options on-screen, we have the following choices:

- **Image Classification Multi-class**: Attach a single label to each image.

- **Image Classification Multi-label**: Attach multiple labels to each image.

- **Object Detection (Bounding Box)**: Draw one or multiple boxes around an object on an image.

- **Instance Segmentation (Polygon)**: Draw complex polygons around an object on an image.

- **Text Classification Multi-class**: Attach a single label to a piece of text.

- **Text Classification Multi-label**: Attach one or multiple labels to a piece of text.

As we can see, there are a lot of helpful options when it comes to image data. We can even highlight and tag very specific pieces in an image by using a **bounding box** or a **polygon**. Using polygons, you are technically able to do a complete **image segmentation**, but it is quite hard to assign each pixel to a class with this tool.

For text data, however, there are some limitations. We do not have the option to label specific words or phrases in a piece of text, as we discussed in the previous section. At the time of writing, the only option is to single- or multi-label a text block.

Therefore, we will be working with images. To not make using this tool for the first time too complex, we will start by attaching a single label to images in an image dataset. In the following steps, we will create an image dataset and a corresponding labeling project:

1. Before going through the wizard, let's look for a suitable image dataset to use. We will be using the **STL-10 dataset** (`https://cs.stanford.edu/~acoates/stl10/`). This dataset contains a huge amount of small 96x96 images that can be divided into 10 classes (**airplane, bird, car, cat, deer, dog, horse, monkey, ship**, and **truck**). These 10 classes will be our labels. As the original page only offers us the images in binary format, we need to find a different source. On **Kaggle**, you often find these types of datasets prepared in different formats.

2. Go to `https://www.kaggle.com/jessicali9530/stl10` and download `test_images`, which is a set of 8,000 files in png format. Normally, we would use the `unlabeled_images` set, but since there are 100,000 of them, we will leave them be for now.

3. If you haven't done so already, download the files for this chapter to your device and create a new folder called `images` under the `chapter06` folder.

4. Extract all 8,000 images to the `images` folder. After that, open the `03_reg_unlabeled_data.ipynb` file. In this file, you will find the code we have been using so far to connect to our workspace and datastore. Please replace `datastore_name` with the one you have been given in your ML workspace. The last code snippet of the first cell reads as follows:

```
file_ds = Dataset.File.upload_directory(
                    src_dir='./images',
                    target=DataPath
(datastore,
                            'mldata/STL10_
unlabelled'),
                    show_progress=True)
```

The `upload_directory` method will, with one call, upload all the files from the `images` folder to the datastore location you defined in the target and will create a file dataset object called `file_ds`. Once the upload is complete, we can register our new dataset with the following code:

```
file_ds = file_ds.register(workspace=ws,
                            name='STL10_unlabeled',
                            description='
8000 unlabeled
                            STL-10 images')
```

If you navigate to the **Datasets** tab in Azure Machine Learning Studio, you will see our newly registered dataset. Under the **Explore** tab, you will see a subset of the images, including image metadata and a preview of the images.

5. Now that we have registered our dataset, we can set up our labeling project. Go back to the wizard, as shown in *Figure 6.14*, enter `STL10_Labeling` as the project name, and choose **Image Classification Multi-class** as the type. Click **Next**.

6. On the next screen, Microsoft will give you the option to hire a workforce from the **Azure Marketplace** to perform your labeling work. This can be a helpful tool, as you will soon learn how tedious this task can be. For now, we do not require additional help. Click **Next**.

7. Now, we can choose the dataset to work on. Select our newly create dataset, named `STL10_unlabeled`, and click **Next**.

8. We will see an option called **Incremental Refresh**. This feature updates the project once a day if new images have been added to the underlying dataset. We are not planning on doing this here, so leave it as-is and click **Next**.

9. The following screen asks us to define our labels. **STL10 dataset** contains 10 classes of images, which we will now define as labels. Enter `airplane`, `bird`, `car`, `cat`, `deer`, `dog`, `horse`, `monkey`, `ship`, and `truck` as labels. Then, click **Next**.

10. The second to last screen allows us to enter **Labeling instructions**. These are useful if we are not working alone on the project or we have ordered a workforce to do the job. Here, we can give them instructions. For us, as we are working alone, this is unnecessary. So, click **Next**.

11. Finally, we have the option to use **ML-assisted labeling**. If we do not activate this option, we would have to label all 8,000 images by ourselves without help. Please be aware that activating this option requires a GPU compute cluster that runs for a couple of minutes every time the assisting ML model is retrained. We will choose the **Use default** option, which will create an appropriate cluster for us. Click **Create project**. This will bring us back to the overview. When the cluster has been created, click on the project's name to get to the overview page.

You will see a dashboard similar to the following:

Figure 6.15 – The dashboard for the labeling project

The dashboard is divided into the following views:

- **Progress**: This shows the number of assets being labeled. In our case, we are working with 8,000 images. It also shows the status for each asset (**Completed**, **Skipped**, **Needs review**, and **Incomplete**).

- **Label class distribution**: This view will show a bar chart of which label has been used and how many times to classify an image.

- **Labeler performance**: This view shows how many assets each labeler has processed. In our case, only our name will be shown there.

- **Task queue**: This view shows what tasks are in the pipeline. At the moment, we need to label 150 images manually before the next training phase or the next check occurs.

- **ML-assisted labeling experiment**: This view shows the running or already run training experiments for the assisting ML model.

If you switch the view to the **Data** tab, you will see some previews for images and you can review the already labeled images. This is helpful when you're working in a team, where a couple of people are working on labeling the images and some are reviewing their labeling efforts.

Finally, if you look at the **Details** tab, you will find the settings for this project. Here, we can see and change certain settings we chose during creation. If you click on **ML-0assisted labeling**, you can see the name of the training and inference cluster that was created for us. Let's look at that cluster. Switch the main menu of Azure Machine Learning Studio to **Compute and Compute Cluster** and click on the cluster you saw previously, probably named DefLabelNC6.

The following screenshot shows the overview page of this cluster:

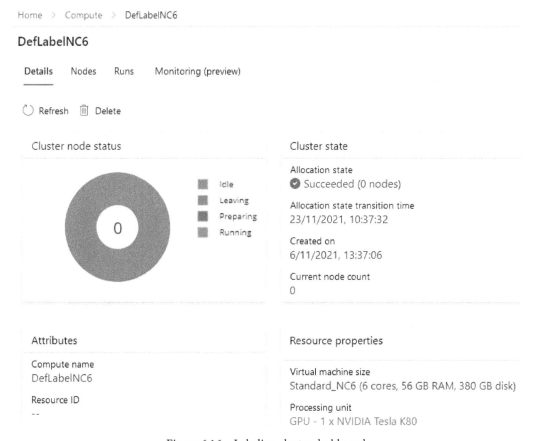

Figure 6.16 – Labeling cluster dashboard

As you can see, the machines that are being used for the nodes sport 6 cores, 56 GB of RAM, and a Tesla K80 GPU. Always check the pricing page (`https://azure.microsoft.com/en-us/pricing/details/virtual-machines/ml-server-ubuntu/`) when you're creating any type of compute instance on Azure. As shown on that page, the node we are using is called **NC6** and costs around $3 per hour. The cluster node shows that the cluster is **Idle**, so there are no costs. Later, you can check the **Runs** tabs for the duration of the training runs to understand the pricing implications. At the moment, a good, educated guess would be that we will need 2 to 4 hours for the ML-assisted support in our labeling project.

So, before we start labeling the images, let's understand what ML-assisted labeling does. When you switch back to the dashboard of our labeling project, you will see three options under **Task queue**, as follows:

- **Manual**: This denotes the assets we must handle without support at any given point.

- **Clustered**: This denotes the assets where a clustering model was being used on the already labeled assets. When you work on these assets, they will be shown to you in groups of images that the model thinks belong to the same class.

- **Prelabeled**: This denotes the assets where a classification model was trained on the already labeled assets. In this case, it predicted labels for unlabeled assets. When you're working on those images, you will be shown the suggested labels and have to check if the model was correct.

Now, let's start labeling. When you click **Label data**, you will see the following view:

STL10_Labeling

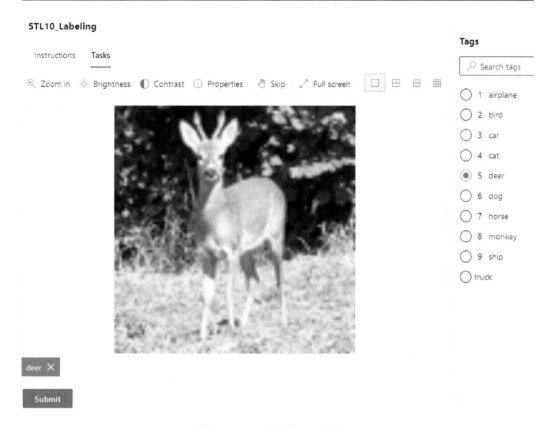

Figure 6.17 – Labeling task view

From this view, you can see the asset in the middle. With the controls up top, you can **Zoom in** and change the **Brightness** and **Contrast** properties of the image. If you are unsure about these options, you can select **Skip** for now. On the right, you can choose the appropriate label. If you are happy with your choice, you can click **Submit**.

Do this for a couple of images to get a grip on things. After that, look at the controls at the top right. Here, we can change how many assets are shown to us at the same time (1, 4, 6, or 9). I would suggest displaying 6 assets at the same time. In addition, to label pictures, you can multi-select them and use the keyboard numbers 1 to 9 (as shown on the right of the preceding screenshot) to label faster.

Now, to see the ML-assisted labeling being triggered, you will need to manually label around 400 to 600 images. You can decide if this is a good use of your time, but it is a good exercise to do as it gives you a perspective of how tedious this task is.

Eventually, the training will be triggered, as shown in the following screenshot:

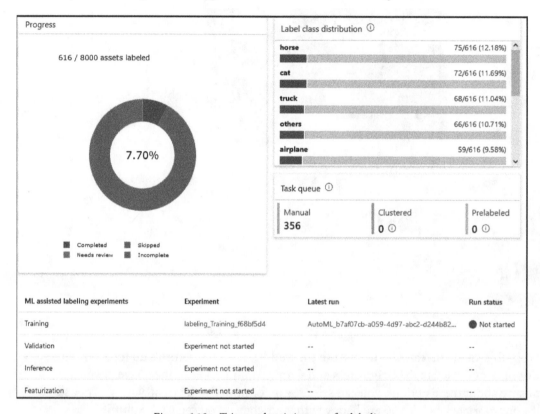

Figure 6.18 – Triggered training run for labeling

I had to label 616 assets manually before the first labeling training would be triggered. As we can see, the tool shows the distribution of label classes that were encountered during the labeling process at that point. As with any other training, this creates an experiment with runs. You can find these under Experiments in the ML workspace, as shown in the following screenshot:

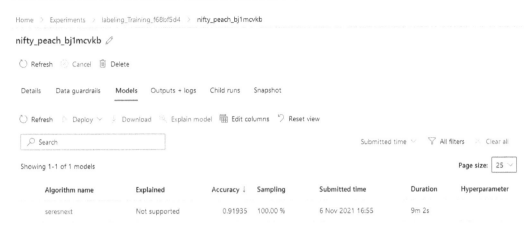

Figure 6.19 – Experiment run for ML-assisted labeling

At this point, just continue to label assets. Eventually, you will either be shown clustered images, defined by **Tasks clustered** at the top of the page (see *Figure 6.20*):

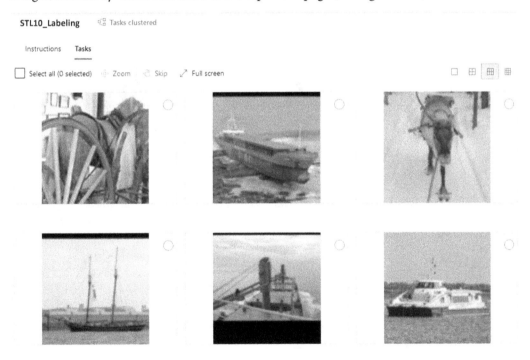

Figure 6.20 – Data labeling showing clustered images

Or you'll be shown prelabeled images, defined by **Tasks prelabeled** at the top of the page (see *Figure 6.21*):

Figure 6.21 – Data labeling showing prelabeled images

With that, you've seen how you can utilize ML modeling to label your assets and how Azure Machine Learning Studio makes this process easier. As you should understand by now, this is a time-consuming task, but it needs to be done if you wish to achieve much better results in your ML training down the line.

Summary

In this chapter, we looked at how to prepare our features through feature engineering and how to prepare our labels through labeling.

In the first section, we learned that feature engineering includes creating new and missing features, transforming existing features, extracting features from a high-dimensional dataset, and using methods to select the most predictive feature for ML training.

In the second section, we learned that labeling is essential and tedious. Therefore, tooling such as Azure Machine Learning data labeling can be a blessing to alleviate this time-consuming task.

The key takeaway from this chapter is that creating, transforming, and selecting predictive features has the biggest impact on the quality of the ML model. No other step in the ML pipeline will have more influence on its outcome.

To pull off quality feature engineering, you must have intimate knowledge of the domain (or you must know someone with that knowledge) and a clear grasp of how the chosen ML algorithm works internally. This includes understanding the mathematical theory, the required data structure the algorithm expects as input, and the feature engineering methods that are applied automatically when you're fitting the model.

In the next chapter, we will see feature engineering in action. We will look at how to perform feature extraction on text data for natural language processing.

7
Advanced Feature Extraction with NLP

In the previous chapters, we learned about many standard transformation and preprocessing approaches within the Azure Machine Learning service as well as typical labeling techniques using the Azure Machine Learning Data Labeling service. In this chapter, we want to go one step further to extract semantic features from textual and categorical data—a problem that users often face when training ML models. This chapter will describe the foundations of feature extraction with **Natural Language Processing (NLP)**. This will help you to practically implement semantic embeddings using NLP for your ML pipelines.

First, we will take a look at the differences between *textual*, *categorical*, *nominal*, and *ordinal* data. This classification will help you to decide the best feature extraction and transformation technique per feature type. Later, we will look at the most common transformations for categorical values, namely **label encoding** and **one-hot encoding**. Both techniques will be compared and tested to understand the different use cases and applications for both techniques.

Next, we will tackle the numerical embedding of textual data. To achieve this, we will build a simple **bag-of-words** model, using a **count vectorizer**. To sanitize the input, we will build an NLP pipeline consisting of a **tokenizer**, stop word removal, **stemming**, and **lemmatization**. We will learn how these different techniques affect a sample dataset step by step.

Following this, we will replace the word count method with a much better word frequency weighting approach—the **Term Frequency-Inverse Document Frequency (TF-IDF)** algorithm. This will help you to compute the importance of words when given a whole corpus of documents by weighting the occurrence of a term in one document over the frequency in the corpus. Additionally, we will look at **Singular Value Decomposition (SVD)** for reducing the size of the term dictionary. As a next step, we will improve the term embedding quality by leveraging word semantics, and we will look under the hood of semantic embeddings such as **Global Vectors (GloVe)** and **Word2Vec**.

In the last section, we will take a look at current state-of-the-art language models that are based on sequence-to-sequence deep neural networks with over 100 million parameters. We will train a small end-to-end model using **Long Short-Term Memory (LSTM)**, perform word embedding and sentiment analysis using **Bidirectional Encoder Representations from Transformers (BERT)**, and compare both custom solutions to Azure's text analytics capabilities in Cognitive Services.

In this chapter, the following topics will be covered:

- Understanding categorical data
- Building a simple bag-of-words model
- Leveraging term importance and semantics
- Implementing end-to-end language models

Technical requirements

In this chapter, we will use the following Python libraries and versions to create categorical encodings, create semantic embeddings, train an end-to-end model, and perform classic NLP preprocessing steps:

- `azureml-sdk 1.34.0`
- `azureml-widgets 1.34.0`
- `tensorflow 2.6.0`
- `numpy 1.19.5`
- `pandas 1.3.2`
- `scikit-learn 0.24.2`
- `nltk 3.6.2`
- `genism 3.8.3`

Similar to previous chapters, you can execute this code using either a local Python interpreter or a notebook environment hosted in Azure Machine Learning.

All code examples in this chapter can be found in the GitHub repository for this book:
`https://github.com/PacktPublishing/Mastering-Azure-Machine-Learning-Second-Edition/tree/main/chapter07`.

Understanding categorical data

Categorical data comes in many forms, shapes, and meanings. It is extremely important to understand what type of data you are dealing with—is it a string, text, or numeric value disguised as a categorical value? This information is essential for data preprocessing, feature extraction, and model selection.

In this section, first, we will take a look at the different types of categorical data—namely *ordinal*, *nominal*, and *text*. Depending on the type, you can use different methods to extract information or other valuable data from it. Please bear in mind that categorical data is ubiquitous, whether it is in an ID column, a nominal category, an ordinal category, or a free-text field. It's worth mentioning that the more information you have on the data, the easier the preprocessing is.

Next, we will actually preprocess the ordinal and nominal categorical data by transforming it into numerical values. This is a required step when you want to use an ML algorithm later on that can't interpret categorical data, which is true for most algorithms except, for example, decision tree-based approaches. Most other algorithms can only operate (for example, compute a loss function) on a numeric value and so a transformation is required.

Comparing textual, categorical, and ordinal data

Many ML algorithms, such as support vector machines, neural networks, linear regression, and more, can only be applied to numeric data. However, in real-world datasets, we often find non-numeric columns, such as columns that contain textual data. The goal of this chapter is to transform textual data into numeric data as an advanced feature extraction step, which allows us to plug the processed data into any ML algorithm.

When working with real-world data, you will be confronted with many different types of textual and/or categorical data. To optimize ML algorithms, you need to understand the differences in order to apply different preprocessing techniques to the different types. But first, let's define the three different textual data types:

- *Textual data*: Free text
- *Categorical nominal data*: Non-orderable categories
- *Categorical ordinal data*: Orderable categories

The difference between textual data and categorical data is that, in textual data, we want to capture semantic similarities (that is, the similarity in the meaning of the words), whereas, in categorical data, we want to differentiate between a small number of variables.

The difference between categorical nominal data and categorical ordinal data is that nominal data cannot be ordered (all categories have the same weight), whereas ordinal categories can be logically ordered on an ordinal scale.

Figure 7.1 shows an example dataset of comments on news articles, where the first column, named `statement`, is a textual field, the column named `topic` is a nominal category, and `rating` is an ordinal category:

statement	topic	rating
Great article!	international	good
Very interesting.	sports	very good
I don't like this.	sports	bad
Not accurate.	international	average
Good read.	politics	good

Figure 7.1 – Comparing different textual data types

Understanding the differences between these data representations is essential to find the proper embedding technique afterward. It seems quite natural to replace ordinal categories with an ordinal numeric scale and to embed nominal categories in an orthogonal space. On the contrary, it's not obvious how to embed textual data into a numerical space where the semantics are preserved—this will be covered in the later sections of this chapter that deal with NLP.

Please note that instead of categorical values, you will also see continuous numeric variables representing categorical information, for example, IDs from a dimension or lookup table. Although these are numeric values, you should consider treating them as categorical nominal values, if possible. Here is an example dataset:

timestamp	sensorId	value
2019-01-01 00:01:00.000	1	18.5
2019-01-01 00:02:00.000	1	18.6
2019-01-01 00:03:00.000	1	18.4
2019-01-01 00:04:00.000	2	18.5
2019-01-01 00:05:00.000	2	18.6

Figure 7.2 – Comparing numerical categorical values

In this example, we can see that the `sensorId` value is a numeric value that should be interpreted as a categorical nominal value instead of a numeric value by default because it doesn't have a numeric meaning. What do you get when you subtract `sensorId` 2 from `sensorId` 1? Is `sensorId` 10 10 times larger than `sensorId` 1? These are the typical questions to ask to discover and encode these categorical values. We will discover, in *Chapter 9*, *Building ML Models Using Azure Machine Learning*, that by specifying that these values are categorical, a gradient-boosted tree model can optimize these features instead of treating them as continuous variables.

Transforming categories into numeric values

Let's start by converting categorical variables (both ordinal and nominal) into numeric values. In this section, we will look at two common techniques for categorical encoding: **label encoding** and **one-hot encoding** (also called *dummy coding*). While **label encoding** replaces a categorical feature column with a numerical feature column, **one-hot encoding** uses multiple columns (where the number of columns equals the number of unique values) to encode a single feature.

Both techniques are applied in the same way. During the training iteration, these techniques find all of the unique values in a feature column and assign them a specific numeric value (multidimensional value for one-hot encoding). As a result, a lookup dictionary defining this replacement is stored in the encoder. When the encoder is applied, the values in the applied column are transformed (replaced) using the lookup dictionary. If the list of possible values is known beforehand, most implementations allow the encoder to initialize the lookup dictionary directly from the list of known values, rather than finding the unique values in the training set. This has the benefit of specifying the order of the values in the dictionary, so orders the encoded values.

Important Note

Please note that it's often possible that certain categorical feature values in the test set don't appear in the training set and, hence, are not stored in the lookup dictionary. So, you should add a default category to your encoder that can also transform unseen values into numeric values.

Now, we will use two different categorical data columns, one ordinal and one nominal category, to showcase the different encodings. *Figure 7.3* shows a nominal feature, `topic`, which could represent a list of articles by a news agency:

id	topic	content
1	international	...
2	sports	...
3	sports	...
4	international	...
5	politics	...

Figure 7.3 – Nominal categorical data

Figure 7.4 contains the ordinal category of `rating`; it could represent a feedback form for purchased articles on a website:

id	rating	comment
1	good	...
2	very good	...
3	bad	...
4	average	...
5	good	...

Figure 7.4 – Ordinal categorical data

To preserve the meaning of the categories, we require different preprocessing techniques for the different categorical data types. First, we take a look at the *label encoder*. The label encoder assigns an incrementing value to each unique categorical value in a feature column. So, it transforms categories into a numeric value between 0 and N-1, where N represents the number of unique values.

Let's test the label encoder in the `topic` column within the first table. We train the encoder on the data and replace the `topic` column with a numeric topic ID. Here is an example snippet to train the label encoder and transform the dataset:

```
from sklearn import preprocessing
data = load_articles()
enc = preprocessing.LabelEncoder()
```

```
enc.fit(data)
enc.transform(data)
```

Figure 7.5 shows the results of the preceding transformation. Each topic was encoded as a numerical increment, `topicId`:

id	topicId	content
1	0	. . .
2	1	. . .
3	1	. . .
4	0	. . .
5	2	. . .

Figure 7.5 – Label-encoded topics

The generated lookup table for `topicId` is shown in *Figure 7.6*. This lookup dictionary was learned by the encoder during the `fit()` method and can be applied to categorical data using the `transform()` method:

topicId	topic
0	international
1	sports
2	politics

Figure 7.6 – A lookup dictionary for topics

As you can see in the previous screenshots, encoding nominal data with labels is easy and straightforward. However, the resulting numerical data has different mathematical properties from the distinct nominal categories. So, let's find out how this method works for ordinal data.

In the next example, we naïvely apply the label encoder to the ratings dataset. The encoder is trained by iterating the training data in order to create the lookup dictionary:

```
from sklearn import preprocessing
data = load_ratings()
enc = preprocessing.LabelEncoder()
enc.fit(data)
enc.transform(data)
```

Figure 7.7 shows the result of the encoded ratings as `ratingId`, which is very similar to the previous example. However, in the case of ratings, the numerical properties of the ratings data are similar to the ordinal properties of the categorical ratings:

id	ratingId	comment
1	0	. . .
2	1	. . .
3	2	. . .
4	3	. . .
5	0	. . .

Figure 7.7 – Label-encoded ratings

Additionally, let's look at the lookup dictionary, in *Figure 7.8*, that the encoder learned from the input data:

ratingId	rating
0	good
1	very good
2	bad
3	average

Figure 7.8 – The lookup dictionary for ratings

Do you see something odd in the autogenerated lookup dictionary? Due to the order of the categorical values in the training data, we created a numeric list with the following order:

```
good < very good < bad < average
```

This is probably not what we anticipated when applying a label encoder to an ordinal categorical value. The ordering we would be looking for is similar to the following:

```
very bad < bad < average < good < very good
```

In order to create a label encoder with the right order, we can pass the ordered list of categorical values to the encoder. This would create a more meaningful encoding, as shown in *Figure 7.9*:

id	rating	comment
1	3	. . .
2	4	. . .
3	1	. . .
4	2	. . .
5	3	. . .

Figure 7.9 – Label-encoded ratings with custom order

To achieve this in Python, we have to use pandas' categorical ordinal variable, which is a special kind of label encoder that requires a list of ordered categories as input:

```python
import pandas as pd
data = load_ratings()
categories = [
    'very bad', 'bad', 'average', 'good', 'very good']
data = pd.Categorical(data,
                      categories=categories,
                      ordered=True)
print(data.codes)
```

Under the hood, we implicitly created the following lookup dictionary for the encoder by passing the categories directly to it in order:

ratingId	rating
0	very bad
1	bad
2	average
3	good
4	very good

Figure 7.10 – A lookup dictionary for ratings with custom orders

As you can see in the preceding example, a label encoder can be quickly applied to any categorical data without much afterthought. The result of the label encoder is a single numerical feature and a categorical lookup table. Additionally, we can see, in the examples with topics and ratings, that label encoding is more suitable for ordinal data.

> **Important Note**
>
> The key takeaway is that the label encoder is great for encoding ordinal categorical data. You also learned that the order of elements matters, and so it is good practice to manually pass the categories to the encoder in the correct order.

Orthogonal embedding using one-hot encoding

In the second part of this section, we will take a look at the **one-hot encoder**. This will help us to create an equal-length encoding for nominal categorical values. The one-hot encoder replaces each unique categorical value in a feature column with a vector of size N, where N represents the number of unique values. This vector contains only zeros, except for one column that contains 1 and represents the column for this specific value. Here is a code snippet showing you how to apply the one-hot encoder to the articles dataset:

```
from sklearn import preprocessing
data = [load_articles()]
enc = preprocessing.OneHotEncoder()
enc.fit(data)
enc.transform(data)
```

The output of the preceding code is shown in *Figure 7.11*:

id	topic_international	topic_sports	topic_politics
1	1	0	0
2	0	1	0
3	0	1	0
4	1	0	0
5	0	0	1

Figure 7.11 – One-hot-encoded articles

The lookup dictionary for one-hot encoding has N+1 columns, where N is the number of unique values in the encoded column. As we can see in the lookup dictionary in *Figure 7.12*, all N-dimensional vectors in the dictionary are orthogonal and of an equal length, 1:

topic_internationa l	topic_sports	topic_politics	topic
1	0	0	international
0	1	0	sports
0	0	1	politics

Figure 7.12 – The lookup dictionary for articles

Now, let's compare this technique with ordinal data and apply one-hot encoding to the ratings table. The result is shown in *Figure 7.13*:

id	rating_good	rating_very_good	rating_bad	rating_averag e
1	1	0	0	0
2	0	1	0	0
3	0	0	1	0
4	0	0	0	1
5	1	0	0	0

Figure 7.13 – One-hot-encoded ratings

In the preceding figure, we can see that even if the original category values are ordinal, the encoded values can no longer be sorted, and so, this property is lost after the numeric encoding. Therefore, we can conclude that one-hot encoding is great for nominal categorical values where the number of unique values is small.

So far, we've learned how to embed nominal and ordinal categorical values into numeric values by using a lookup dictionary and one-dimensional or N-dimensional numeric embedding. However, we discovered that it is somewhat limited in many aspects, such as the number of unique categories and capabilities to embed free text. In the following sections, we will learn how to extract words using a simple NLP pipeline.

Semantics and textual values

It's worth taking the time to understand that a categorical value and a textual value are not the same. Although they might both be stored as a string and could have the same data type in your dataset, usually, a categorical value represents a finite set of categories, whereas a text value can hold any textual information.

So, why is this distinction important? Once you preprocess your categorical data and embed it into a numerical space, nominal categories will often be implemented as orthogonal vectors. You will not automatically be able to compute a distance from category A to category B or create a semantic meaning between the categories.

However, with textual data, usually, you start feature extraction with a different approach that assumes that you will find similar terms in the same text feature of your dataset samples. You can use this information to compute meaningful similarity scores between two textual columns; for example, to measure the number of words that are in common.

Therefore, we recommend that you thoroughly check what kind of categorical values you have and how you are aiming to preprocess them. Also, a great exercise is to compute the similarity between two rows and see whether it matches your prediction. Let's take a look at a simple textual preprocessing approach using a dictionary-based bag-of-words embedding.

Building a simple bag-of-words model

In this section, we will look at a surprisingly simple concept to tackle the shortcomings of label encoding for textual data using a technique called bag-of-words, which will build a foundation for a simple NLP pipeline. Don't worry if these techniques look too simple when you read through them; we will gradually build on top of them with tweaks, optimizations, and improvements to build a modern NLP pipeline.

A naïve bag-of-words model using counting

In this section, the main concept that we will build is the bag-of-words model. It is a very simple concept; that is, it involves modeling any document as a collection of words that appear in a given document with the frequency of each word. Hence, we throw away sentence structure, word order, punctuation marks, and more and reduce the documents to a raw count of words. Following this, we can vectorize this word count into a numeric vector representation, which can then be used for ML, analysis, document comparisons, and much more. While this word count model sounds very simple, we will encounter quite a few language-specific obstacles along the way that we will need to resolve.

Let's get started and define a sample document that we will transform throughout this section:

```
Almost before we knew it, we had left the ground. The unknown
holds its grounds.
```

Applying a naïve word count to the document gives us our first (too simple) bag-of-words model:

word	count
we	2
.	2
Almost	1
before	1
knew	1
it	1
,	1
had	1
left	1
the	1
ground	1
The	1
unknown	1
holds	1
its	1
grounds	1

Figure 7.14 – A naïve bag-of-words model

However, there are many problems with a naïve approach such as the preceding one. We have mixed different punctuation marks, notations, nouns, verbs, adverbs, and adjectives in different declinations, conjugations, tenses, and cases. Therefore, we have to build a pipeline to clean and normalize the data using NLP. In this section, we will build a pipeline with the following cleaning steps before feeding the data into a **count vectorizer** that, ultimately, counts the word occurrences and collects them in a feature vector.

Tokenization – turning a string into a list of words

The first step in building the pipeline is to separate a corpus into documents and a document into words. This process is called **tokenization** because the resulting tokens contain words and punctuation marks. While splitting a corpus into documents, documents into sentences, and sentences into words sounds trivial, with a bit of **Regular Expression** (**RegEx**), there are many non-trivial language-specific issues. Think about the different uses of periods, commas, and quotes, and think about whether you would have thought about the following words in English: *don't, Mr. Smith, Johann S. Bach*, and more. The **Natural Language Toolkit** (**NLTK**) Python package provides implementations and pretrained transformers for many NLP algorithms, as well as for word tokenization. Let's split our document into tokens using `nltk`:

```
from nltk.tokenize import word_tokenize
nltk.download('punkt')
tokens = word_tokenize(document)
print(tokens)
```

The preceding code will output a list of tokens that contains words and punctuation marks:

```
['Almost', 'before', 'we', 'knew', 'it', ',', 'we', 'had',
'left', 'the', 'ground', '.', 'The', 'unknown', 'holds', 'its',
'grounds', '.']
```

When you execute the preceding code snippet, nltk will download the pretrained punctuation model in order to run the word tokenizer. The output of the tokenizer is the words and punctuation marks.

In the next step, we will remove the punctuation marks as they are not relevant for the subsequent *stemming* process. However, we will bring them back for *lemmatization* later in this section:

```
words = [word.lower() for word in tokens if word.isalnum()]
print(words)
```

The result will only contain the words of the original document without any punctuation marks:

```
['almost', 'before', 'we', 'knew', 'it', 'we', 'had', 'left',
'the', 'ground', 'the', 'unknown', 'holds', 'its', 'grounds']
```

In the preceding code, we used the word.islanum() function to only extract alphanumeric tokens and make them all lowercase. The preceding list of words already looks much better than the initial naïve model. However, it still contains a lot of unnecessary words, such as *the*, *we*, *had*, and more, which don't convey any information.

In order to filter out the noise for a specific language, it makes sense to remove these words that often appear in texts and don't add any semantic meaning to the text. It is common practice to remove these so-called **stop words** using a pretrained lookup dictionary. You can load and use such a dictionary by using the pretrained nltk library in Python:

```
from nltk.corpus import stopwords
stopword_set = set(stopwords.words('english'))
words = [word for word in words if word not in stopword_set]
print(words)
```

Now the resulting list only contains words that are not stop words:

```
['almost', 'knew', 'left', 'ground', 'unknown', 'holds',
'grounds']
```

The preceding code gives us a nice pipeline where we end up with only the semantically meaningful words. We can take this list of words to the next step and apply a more sophisticated transformation/normalization to each word. If we applied the count vectorizer at this stage, we would end up with the simple bag-of-words model, as shown in *Figure 7.15*:

word	count
almost	1
knew	1
left	1
ground	1
unknown	1
holds	1
grounds	1

Figure 7.15 – A simple bag-of-words model

As you can see in the previous figure, the list of terms that are included in the bag-of-words model is already far cleaner than the naïve example. This is because it doesn't contain any punctuation marks or stop words.

You might ask what qualifies a word as a stop word other than it occurring relatively often in a piece of text? Well, that's an excellent question! We can measure the importance of each word in the current context compared to its occurrences across the text using the **TF-IDF** method, which will be discussed in the *Measuring the importance of words using TF-IDF* section.

Stemming – the rule-based removal of affixes

In the next step, we want to normalize affixes—word endings to create plurals and conjugations. You can see that with each step, we are diving deeper into the concept of a single language—in this case, English. However, when applying these steps to a different language, it's likely that completely different transformations will need to be used. This is what makes NLP such a difficult field.

Removing the affixes of words to obtain the stem of a word is also called **stemming**. Stemming refers to a rule-based (heuristic) approach to transform each occurrence of a word into its word stem. Here is a simple example of some expected transformations:

```
cars    -> car
saying -> say
flies   -> fli
```

As you can see in the preceding example, such a heuristic approach for stemming has to be built specifically for each language. This is generally true for all other NLP algorithms as well. For the sake of brevity, in this book, we will only discuss English examples.

A popular algorithm for stemming in English is Porter's algorithm, which defines five sequential reduction rules, such as removing *-ed, -ing, -ate, -tion, -ence, -ance,* and more, from the end of words. The nltk library comes with an implementation of Porter's stemming algorithm:

```
from nltk.stem import PorterStemmer
stemmer = PorterStemmer()
words = [stemmer.stem(word) for word in words]
print(words)
```

The resulting list of words after stemming looks like this:

```
['almost', 'knew', 'left', 'ground', 'unknown', 'hold',
 'ground']
```

In the preceding code, we simply apply stemmer to each word in the tokenized document. The bag-of-words model after this step is shown in *Figure 7.16*:

word	count
ground	2
almost	1
knew	1
left	1
unknown	1
hold	1

Figure 7.16 – The bag-of-words model after stemming

While this algorithm works well with affixes, it can't avoid normalizing conjugations and tenses. This will be our next problem to tackle using lemmatization.

Lemmatization – dictionary-based word normalization

When looking at the stemming examples, we can already see the limitations of that approach. For example, what would happen with irregular verb conjugations—such as *are*, *am*, or *is*—that should all be normalized to the same word, *be*? This is exactly what lemmatization tries to solve using a pretrained set of vocabulary and conversion rules, called lemmas. The **lemmas** are stored in a lookup dictionary and look similar to the following transformations:

```
are     -> be
is      -> be
taught -> teach
better -> good
```

There is one very important point to make when discussing lemmatization. Each lemma needs to be applied to the correct word type, hence a lemma for nouns, verbs, adjectives, and more. The reason for this is that a word can be either a noun or a verb in the past tense. In our example, `ground` could come from the noun *ground* or the verb *grind*; `left` could be an adjective or the past tense of *leave*. So, we also need to extract the word type from the word in a sentence—this process is called **Point of Speech** (**POS**) tagging. Luckily, the `nltk` library has us covered once again. To estimate the correct POS tag, we also need to provide the punctuation mark:

```
import nltk
nltk.download('averaged_perceptron_tagger')
tags = nltk.pos_tag(tokens)
print(tags)
```

Here are the resulting POS tags:

```
[('Almost', 'RB'), ('before', 'IN'), ('we', 'PRP'), ('knew',
'VBD'), ('it', 'PRP'), (',', ','), ('we', 'PRP'), ('had',
'VBD'), ('left', 'VBN'), ('the', 'DT'), ('ground', 'NN'), ('.',
'.'), ('The', 'DT'), ('unknown', 'JJ'), ('holds', 'VBZ'),
('its', 'PRP$'), ('grounds', 'NNS'), ('.', '.')]
```

The POS tags describe the word type of each token in the document. You can find a complete list of tags using the `nltk.help.upenn_tagset()` command. Here is an example of how to do so from the command line:

```
import nltk
nltk.download('tagsets')
nltk.help.upenn_tagset()
```

The preceding command will print the list of POS tags:

```
CC: conjunction, coordinating
    & 'n and both but either et for less minus neither nor or
    plus so therefore times v. versus vs. whether yet
CD: numeral, cardinal
    mid-1890 nine-thirty forty-two one-tenth ten million 0.5
    one forty- seven 1987 twenty '79 zero two 78-degrees
    eighty-four IX '60s .025 fifteen 271,124 dozen quintillion
    DM2,000 ...
DT: determiner
    all an another any both del each either every half la many
    much nary neither no some such that the them these this
    those
EX: existential there
    there
FW: foreign word
    gemeinschaft hund ich jeux habeas Haementeria Herr K'ang-si
    vous lutihaw alai je jour objets salutaris fille quibusdam
    pas
...
```

The POS tags also include tenses for verbs and other very useful information. However, for the lemmatization in this section, we only need to know the word type—*noun*, *verb*, *adjective*, or *adverb*. One possible choice of lemmatizer is the WordNet lemmatizer in nltk. WordNet is a lexical database of English words that groups them into groups of concepts and word types.

To apply the lemmatizer to the output of the stemming, we need to filter the POS tags by punctuation marks and stop words, similar to the previous preprocessing step. Then, we can use the word tags for the resulting words. Let's apply the lemmatizer using nltk:

```
from nltk.corpus import wordnet
from nltk.stem import WordNetLemmatizer
nltk.download('wordnet')
lemmatizer = WordNetLemmatizer()
tag_dict = {
    "J": wordnet.ADJ,
```

```
      "N": wordnet.NOUN,
      "V": wordnet.VERB,
      "R": wordnet.ADV
}
pos = [tag_dict.get(t[0].upper(), wordnet.NOUN) \
        for t in zip(*tags)[1]]
words = [lemmatizer.lemmatize(w, pos=p) \
        for w, p in zip(words, pos)]
print(words)
```

The code outputs the lemmatized words:

```
['almost', 'know', 'leave', 'ground', 'unknown', 'hold',
 'ground']
```

The preceding list of words looks a lot cleaner than what we found in previous models. This is because we normalized the tenses of the verbs and transformed them into their infinitive form. The resulting bag-of-words model is shown in *Figure 7.17*:

word	count
ground	2
almost	1
know	1
leave	1
unknown	1
hold	1

Figure 7.17 – The bag-of-words model after lemmatization

This technique is extremely helpful for cleaning up irregular forms of words in your dataset. However, it works based on rules—called lemmas—and, hence, it can only be used for languages and words where such lemmas are available.

A bag-of-words model in scikit-learn

Finally, we can put all our previous steps together to create a state-of-the-art NLP preprocessing pipeline to normalize the input documents and run them through a count vectorizer so that we can transform them into a numeric feature vector. Doing so for multiple documents allows us to easily compare the semantics of the document in a numerical space. We could compute cosine similarities on the document's feature vectors to compute their similarity, plug them into a supervised classification method, or perform clustering on the resulting document concepts.

To recap, let's take a look at the final pipeline for the simple bag-of-words model. I want to emphasize that this model is only the start of our journey in feature extraction using NLP. We performed the following steps for normalization:

1. Tokenization
2. Removing punctuation marks
3. Removing stop words
4. Stemming
5. Lemmatization with POS tagging

In the last step, we applied `CountVectorizer` in scikit-learn. This will count the occurrences of each word, create a global corpus of words, and output a sparse feature vector of word frequencies. Here is the sample code to pass the preprocessed data from nltk to `CountVectorizer`:

```python
from sklearn.feature_extraction.text import CountVectorizer
count_vect = CountVectorizer()
data = [" ".join(words)]
X_train_counts = count_vect.fit_transform(data)
print(X_train_counts)
```

The transformed bag-of-words model contains coordinates and counts:

(0, 0)	1
(0, 3)	1
(0, 4)	1
(0, 1)	2
(0, 5)	1
(0, 2)	1

The coordinates refer to the (`document id, term id`) pair, whereas the count refers to the term frequency. To better understand this output, we can also look at the internal vocabulary of the model. The `vocabulary_` parameter contains a lookup dictionary for the term ids:

```
print(count_vect.vocabulary_)
```

The code outputs the model's word dictionary:

```
{'almost': 0, 'know': 3, 'leave': 4, 'ground': 1, 'unknown': 5,
'hold': 2}
```

In the preceding example, we transform the preprocessed document back into a string before passing it to `CountVectorizer`. The reason for this is that `CountVectorizer` comes with some configurable preprocessing techniques out of the box, such as tokenization, stop word removal, and more. For this demonstration, we want to apply it to the preprocessed data. The output of the transformation is a sparse feature vector containing the term frequencies.

Let's find out how we can combine multiple terms with semantic concepts.

Leveraging term importance and semantics

Everything we have done up to now has been relatively simple and based on word stems or so-called tokens. The bag-of-words model was nothing but a dictionary of tokens counting the occurrence of tokens per field. In this section, we will take a look at a common technique to further improve matching between documents using n-gram and skip-gram combinations of terms.

Combining terms in multiple ways will explode your dictionary. This will turn into a problem if you have a large corpus; for instance, 10 million words. Hence, we will look at a common preprocessing technique to reduce the dimensionality of a large dictionary through SVD.

While, now, this approach is a lot more complicated, it is still based on a bag-of-words model that already works well on a large corpus, in practice. However, of course, we can do better and try to understand the importance of words. Therefore, we will tackle another popular technique in NLP to compute the importance of terms.

Generalizing words using n-grams and skip-grams

In the previous pipeline, we considered each word on its own without any context. However, as we all know, context matters a lot in language. Sometimes, words belong together and only make sense in context rather than on their own. To introduce this context into the same type of algorithm, we will introduce **n-grams** and **skip-grams**. Both techniques are heavily used in NLP for preprocessing datasets and extracting relevant features from text data.

Let's start with n-grams. An **n-gram** is a concatenation for N consecutive entities (that is, characters, words, or tokens) of an input dataset. Here are some examples for computing the n-grams in a list of characters:

```
A, B, C, D -> 1-Gram: A, B, C, D
A, B, C, D -> 2-Gram: AB, BC, CD
A, B, C, D -> 3-Gram: ABC, BCD
```

Here is an example using the built-in ngram_range parameter in scikit-learn's CountVectorizer to generate multiple n-grams for the input data:

```
from sklearn.feature_extraction.text import CountVectorizer
count_vect = CountVectorizer(ngram_range=(1,2))
X_train_counts = count_vect.fit_transform(data)
print(count_vect.vocabulary_)
```

As you can see, the vocabulary now contains both the 1-gram and 2-gram representations of each term:

```
{'almost': 0, 'before': 2, 'we': 24, 'knew': 15, 'it': 11,
'had': 7, 'left': 17, 'the': 19, 'ground': 4, 'unknown': 22,
'holds': 9, 'its': 13, 'grounds': 6, 'almost before': 1,
'before we': 3, 'we knew': 26, 'knew it': 16, 'it we': 12, 'we
had': 25, 'had left': 8, 'left the': 18, 'the ground': 20,
'ground the': 5, 'the unknown': 21, 'unknown holds': 23, 'holds
its': 10, 'its grounds': 14}
```

In the preceding code, we can see that instead of the original words, we now have a combination of two consecutive words in our trained vocabulary.

We can extend the concept of n-grams to also allow the model to skip words. This a great option, if we for example want to perform a 2-gram, but in one of our samples there is an adjective in-between two words and in the other those words are directly next to each other. To achieve this, we need a method that allows us to define how many words it is allowed to skip to find matching words. Here is an example using the same characters as before:

```
A, B, C, D -> 2-Gram (1 skip): AB, AC, BC, BD, CD
A, B, C, D -> 2-Gram (2 skip): AB, AC, AD, BC, BD, CD
```

Luckily, we find the generalized version of n-grams implemented in `nltk` as the `nltk.skipgrams` method. Setting the skip distance to `0` results in the traditional n-gram algorithm. We can apply it to our original dataset:

```
terms = list(nltk.skipgrams(document.split(' '), 2, 1))
print(terms)
```

Similar to the 2-gram example, the method produces a list of combinations of paired terms. However, in this case, we allowed one skip word to be present between those pairs:

```
[('Almost', 'before'), ('Almost', 'we'), ('before', 'we'),
('before', 'knew'), ('we', 'knew'), ('we', 'it,'), ('knew',
'it,'), ('knew', 'we'), ('it,', 'we'), ('it,', 'had'), ('we',
'had'), ('we', 'left'), ('had', 'left'), ('had', 'the'),
('left', 'the'), ('left', 'ground.'), ('the', 'ground.'),
('the', 'The'), ('ground.', 'The'), ('ground.', 'unknown'),
('The', 'unknown'), ('The', 'holds'), ('unknown', 'holds'),
('unknown', 'its'), ('holds', 'its'), ('holds', 'grounds.'),
('its', 'grounds.')]
```

In the preceding code, we can observe that skip-grams can generate a lot of additional useful feature dimensions for the NLP model. In real-world scenarios, both techniques are often used because the individual word order plays a big role in the semantics.

However, the explosion of new feature dimensions could be devastating if the input documents are, for example, all websites from the web or large documents. Therefore, we also need a way to avoid an explosion of the dimensions while capturing all of the semantics from the input data. We will tackle this challenge in the next section.

Reducing word dictionary size using SVD

A common problem with NLP is the vast number of words in a corpus and, hence, exploding dictionary sizes. In the previous example, we saw that the size of the dictionary defines the size of the orthogonal term vector. Therefore, a dictionary size of 20,000 terms would result in 20,000-dimensional feature vectors. Even without any n-gram enrichment, this feature vector dimension is too large to be processed on standard PCs.

Therefore, we need an algorithm to reduce the dimensions of the generated `CountVectorizer` while preserving the present information. Optimally, we would only remove redundant information from the input data and project it onto a lower-dimensional space while preserving all of the original information.

The PCA transformation would be a great fit for our solution and help us to transform the input data into lower linearly unrelated dimensions. However, computing the eigenvalues requires a symmetric matrix (the same number of rows and columns), which, in our case, we don't have. Hence, we can use the SVD algorithm, which generalizes the eigenvector computation to non-symmetric matrices. Due to its numeric stability, it is often used in NLP and information retrieval systems.

The usage of SVD in NLP applications is also called **Latent Semantic Analysis (LSA)**, as the principal components can be interpreted as concepts in a latent feature space. The SVD embedding transforms the high-dimensional feature vector into a lower-dimensional concept space. Each dimension in the concept space is constructed by a linear combination of term vectors. By dropping the concepts with the smallest variance, we also reduce the dimensions of the resulting concept space to something that is a lot smaller and easier to handle. Typical concept spaces have 10s to 100s of dimensions, while word dictionaries usually have over 100,000.

Let's look at an example using the `TruncatedSVD` implementation from `sklearn`. The SVD is implemented as a transformer class, and so, we need to call `fit_transform()` to fit a dictionary and transform it using the same step. The SVD is configured to only keep the components with the highest variance using the `n_components` argument:

```
from sklearn.decomposition import TruncatedSVD
svd = TruncatedSVD(n_components=5)
X_lsa = svd.fit_transform(X_train_counts)
```

In the preceding code, we perform the LSA on the `X_train_counts` data and the output of `CountVectorizer` using SVD. We configure the SVD to only keep the first five components with the highest variance.

By reducing the dimensionality of your dataset, you lose information. Thankfully, we can compute the amount of variance in the remaining dataset using the trained SVD object, as shown in the following example:

```
Print(svd.explained_variance_ratio_.sum())
```

The preceding command outputs the variance as a number between 0 and 1, where 1 means that the SVD transformation is an exact lossless mapping of the original data into the latent space:

```
0.19693920498587408
```

In this case, with only five components, the SVD retained 20% of the variance of the original dataset.

> **Important Note**
>
> Depending on the task, we usually aim to preserve more than 80–90% of the original variance after the latent transformation.

In the previous code example, we computed the variance of the data that is preserved after the transformation to the configured number of components. Hence, we can now increase or reduce the number of components in order to keep a specific percentage of the information in the transformed data. This is a very helpful operation and is used in many practical NLP implementations.

Note that we are still using the original word dictionary from the bag-of-words model. One particular downside of this model is that the more often a term occurs, the higher its count (and, therefore, weight) will get. This is a problem because, now, any term that is not a stop word and appears often in the text will receive a high weight—independent of the importance of the term within a certain document. Therefore, we introduce another extremely popular preprocessing technique—**TF-IDF**.

Measuring the importance of words using TF-IDF

One particular downside of the bag-of-words approach is that we simply count the absolute number of words in a context without checking whether the word generally appears frequently across all documents. A term that appears in every document might not be relevant for our model, as it contains less information and more often it appears across other documents. Hence, an important technique in text mining is to compute the importance of a certain word in a given context.

Therefore, instead of an absolute count of terms in a context, we want to compute the number of terms in the context relative to a corpus of documents. By doing so, we will give higher weight to terms that appear only in a certain context, and reduce the amount of weight given to terms that appear in many different documents. This is exactly what the TF-IDF algorithm does. It is easy to compute a weight (w) for a term (t) in a document (d) according to the following equation:

$$w(t, d) = f_t(t, d) \times \log \frac{N}{f_d(t)}$$

While the term frequency (f_t) counts all of the terms in a document, the inverse document frequency is computed by dividing the total number of documents (N) by the counts of a term in all documents (f_d). The *IDF* term is usually log-transformed, as the total count of a term across all documents can get quite large.

In the following example, we will not use the TF-IDF function directly. Instead, we will use `TfidfVectorizer`, which does the counting and then applies the TF-IDF function to the result in one step. Again, the function is implemented as a `sklearn` transformer, and hence, we call `fit_transform()` to train and transform the dataset:

```
from sklearn.feature_extraction.text import TfidfVectorizer
vect = TfidfVectorizer()
data = [" ".join(words)]
X_train_counts = vect.fit_transform(data)
print(X_train_counts)
```

The result is formatted in a similar manner to the earlier example containing (`document id, term id`) pairs and their TF-IDF values:

```
(0, 2)          0.3333333333333333
(0, 5)          0.3333333333333333
(0, 1)          0.6666666666666666
(0, 4)          0.3333333333333333
(0, 3)          0.3333333333333333
(0, 0)          0.3333333333333333
```

In the preceding code, we apply `TfidfVectorizer` directly, which returns the same result as using `CountVectorizer` and `TfidfTransformer` combined. We transform a dataset containing the words of the bag-of-words model and return the TF-IDF values. We can also return the terms for each TF-IDF value:

```
print(vect.get_feature_names())
```

The preceding code returns the vocabulary of the model:

```
['almost', 'ground', 'hold', 'know', 'leave', 'unknown']
```

In this example, we can see that `ground` gets a TF-IDF value of `0.667`, whereas all the other terms receive a value of `0.333`. This count will now scale relatively when more documents are added to the corpus—hence, if the word `hold` were to be included again, the TF-IDF value would decrease.

In any real-world pipeline, we would always use all the techniques presented in this chapter—tokenization, stop word removal, stemming, lemmatization, n-grams/skip-grams, TF-IDF, and SVD—combined in a single pipeline. The result would be a numeric representation of n-grams/skip-grams of tokens weighted by importance and transformed into a latent semantic space. Using these techniques for your first NLP pipeline will get you quite far, as you can now capture a lot of information from your textual data.

So far, we have learned how to numerically encode many kinds of categorical and textual values by using either one-dimensional or N-dimensional labels or counting and weighting word stems and character combinations. While many of these methods work well in many situations where you require simple numeric embedding, they all have a serious limitation—they don't encode semantics. Let's take a look at how we can extract the semantic meaning of text in the same pipeline.

Extracting semantics using word embeddings

When computing the similarity of news, you would imagine that topics such as tennis, *Formula 1*, or *soccer* would be semantically more similar to each other than topics such as politics, economics, or science. Yet, in terms of the previously discussed techniques, all encoded categories are seen as semantically the same. In this section, we will discuss a simple method of semantic embedding, which is also called **word embedding**.

The previously discussed pipeline using LSA transforms multiple documents into terms and then transforms those terms into semantic concepts that can be compared with other documents. However, the semantic meaning is based on the term occurrences and importance—there is no measurement of semantics between individual terms.

Hence, what we are looking for is an embedding of terms into numerical multidimensional space such that each word represents one point in this space. This allows us to compute a numerical distance between multiple words in this space in order to compare the semantic meaning of two words. The most interesting benefit of word embeddings is that algebra on the word embeddings is not only numerically possible but also makes sense. Consider the following example:

```
King - Man + Woman = Queen
```

We can create such an embedding by mapping a corpus of words on an N-dimensional numeric space and optimizing the numeric distance based on the word semantics—for example, based on the distance between words in a corpus. The resulting optimization outputs a dictionary of words in the corpus and their numeric N-dimensional representation. In this numeric space, words have the same, or at least similar, properties as in the semantic space. A great benefit is that these embeddings can be trained unsupervised, so no training data has to be labeled.

One of the first embeddings is called **Word2Vec** and is based on a continuous bag-of-words model or a continuous skip-gram model to count and measure the words in a window. Let's try this functionality and perform a semantic word embedding using Word2Vec:

1. The best Python implementation for word embeddings is **Gensim**, which we will also use here. We need to feed our tokens into the model in order to train it:

    ```
    from gensim.models import Word2Vec
    ```

    ```
    model = Word2Vec(words, size=100, window=5)
    vector = model.wv['ground']
    ```

    In the preceding code, we load the `Word2Vec` model and initialize it with the list of tokens from the previous sections, which is stored in the `words` variable. The `size` attribute defines the dimension of the resulting vectors, and the `window` parameter decides how many words we should consider per window. Once the model has been trained, we can simply look up the word embedding in the model's dictionary.

    The code will automatically train the embedding on the set of tokens we provided. The resulting model stores the word-to-vector mapping in the `wv` property. Optimally, we also use a large corpus or pretrained model that is either provided by `gensim` or another NLP library, such as `NLTK`, to train the embedding and fine-tune it with a smaller dataset.

2. Next, we can use the trained model to embed all the terms from our document using the Word2Vec embedding. However, this will result in multiple vectors as each word returns its own embedding. Therefore, you need to combine all the vectors into a single vector using the mathematical mean of all the embeddings. This procedure is quite similar to the one used to generate a concept in LSA. Also, other reduction techniques are possible; for example, weighing the individual embedding vectors using their TF-IDF values:

    ```
    dim = len(model.wv.vectors[0])
    X = np.mean([model.wv[w] for w in words if w in model.wv] \
            or [np.zeros(dim)], axis=0)
    ```

    In the preceding function, we compute the mean from all the word embedding vectors of the terms—this is called a **mean embedding**, and it represents the concept of this document in the embedding space. If a word is not found in the embedding, we need to replace it with zeros in the computation.

You can use such a semantic embedding for your application by downloading a pretrained embedding, for example, on the Wikipedia corpus. Then, you can loop through your sanitized input tokens and look up the words in the dictionary of the numeric embedding.

GloVe is another popular technique for encoding words as numerical vectors, developed by Stanford University. In contrast to the continuous window-based approach, it uses global word-to-word co-occurrence statistics to determine the linear relationships between words:

1. Let's take a look at the pretrained 6 B tokens embedding trained on Wikipedia and the Gigaword news archive:

    ```
    # download pre-trained dictionary from
    # http://nlp.stanford.edu/data/glove.6B.zip
    glove = {}
    with open('glove.6B.100d.txt') as f:
      for line in f:
        word, coefs = line.split(maxsplit=1)
        coefs = np.fromstring(coefs, 'f', sep=' ')
        glove[word] = coefs
    ```

    In the preceding code, we only open and parse the pretrained word embedding in order to store the word and vectors in a lookup dictionary.

2. Then, we use the dictionary to look up tokens in our training data and merge them by computing the mean of all GloVe vectors:

    ```
    X = np.mean([glove[w] for w in words if w in glove] \
          or [np.zeros(dim)], axis=0)
    ```

    The preceding code works very similar to before and returns one vector per word, which is aggregated by taking their mean at the end. Again, this corresponds with a semantic concept using all the tokens of the training data.

Gensim provides other popular models for semantic embeddings, such as *doc2word*, *fastText*, and *GloVe*. The gensim Python library is a great place for utilizing these pretrained embeddings or for training your own models. Now you can replace your bag-of-words model with a mean embedding of the word vectors to also capture word semantics. However, your pipeline will still be built out of many tunable components.

In the next section, we will take a look at building end-to-end state-of-the-art language models and reusing some of the language features from Azure Cognitive Services.

Implementing end-to-end language models

In the previous sections, we trained and concatenated multiple pieces to implement a final algorithm where most of the individual steps need to be trained as well. Lemmatization contains a dictionary of conversion rules. Stop words are stored in the dictionary. Stemming needs rules for each language and word that the embedding needs to train—TF-IDF and SVD are only computed on your training data but are independent of each other.

This is a similar problem to the traditional computer vision approach, which we will discuss in more depth in *Chapter 10, Training Deep Neural Networks on Azure*, where many classic algorithms are combined into a pipeline of feature extractors and classifiers. Similar to breakthroughs of end-to-end models trained via gradient descent and backpropagation in computer vision, deep neural networks—especially sequence-to-sequence models—have replaced the classical approach of performing each step of the transformation and training process manually.

In this section, first, we will take a look at improving our previous model using custom embedding and an LSTM implementation to model a token sequence. This will give you a good understanding of how we are moving from an individual preprocessor-based pipeline to a full end-to-end approach using deep learning.

Sequence-to-sequence models are models based on encoders and decoders that are trained on a variable set of inputs. This encoder/decoder architecture is used for a variety of tasks, such as machine translation, image captioning, and summarization. A nice benefit of these models is that you can reuse the encoder part of this network to convert a set of inputs into a fixed-set numerical representation of the encoder.

Next, we will look at the state-of-the-art language representation models and discuss how they can be used for feature engineering and the preprocessing of your text data. We will use BERT to perform sentiment analysis and numeric embedding.

Finally, we will also look at reusing the Azure Cognitive Services APIs for text analytics to carry out advanced modeling and feature extraction, such as text or sentence sentiment, keywords, or entity recognition. This is a nice approach because you can leverage the know-how and amount of training data from Microsoft to perform complex text analytics using a simple HTTP request.

The end-to-end learning of token sequences

Instead of concatenating different pieces of algorithms into a single pipeline, we want to build and train an end-to-end model that can train the word embedding, pre-form latent semantic transformation, and capture sequential information in the text in a single model.

The benefit of such a model is that each processing step can be fine-tuned for the user's prediction task in a single combined optimization process:

1. The first part of the pipeline will look extremely similar to the previous sections. We will build a tokenizer that converts documents into sequences of tokens that are then transformed into a numerical model based on the token sequence. Then, we will use pad_sequences to align all of the documents to the same length:

```python
from tensorflow.keras.preprocessing.text import Tokenizer
from tensorflow.keras.preprocessing.sequence import \
        pad_sequences

num_words = 1000
tokenizer = Tokenizer(num_words=num_words)
tokenizer.fit_on_texts(X_words)
X = tokenizer.texts_to_sequences(X_words)
X = pad_sequences(X, maxlen=2000)
```

2. In the next step, we will build a simple model using Keras, an embedding layer, and an LSTM layer to capture token sequences. The embedding layer will perform a similar operation to GloVe, where the words will be embedded into a semantic space. The LSTM cell will ensure that we are comparing sequences of words instead of single words at a time. Then, we will use a dense layer with a *softmax* activation to implement a classifier head:

```python
from tensorflow.keras.layers import Embedding, LSTM,
Dense
from tensorflow.keras.models import Sequential

embed_dim = 128
lstm_out = 196

model = Sequential()
model.add(Embedding(
    num_words, embed_dim, input_length=X.shape[1]))
model.add(LSTM(
    lstm_out, recurrent_dropout=0.2, dropout=0.2))
model.add(Dense(
    len(labels), activation='softmax'))
```

```
model.compile(loss='categorical_crossentropy',
              optimizer='adam',
              metrics=['categorical_crossentropy'])
```

As you can see in the preceding function, we build a simple neural network using three layers (that is, `Embedding`, `LSTM`, and `Dense`) and a `softmax` activation for classification. This means that in order to train this model, we would also need a classification problem to be solved at the same time. Hence, we do need labeled training data to perform analysis using this approach. In the next section, we will examine how sequence-to-sequence models are used in input-output text sequences to learn an implicit text representation.

State-of-the-art sequence-to-sequence models

In recent years, another type of model has replaced the traditional NLP pipelines—transformer-based models. These types of models are fully end-to-end and use sequence-to-sequence mapping, positional encoding, and multi-head attention layers. This allows the models to look forward and backward in a text, pay attention to specific patterns, and learn tasks fully end to end. As you might be able to tell, these models have complex architectures and usually have well over 100 million or over 1 billion parameters.

Sequence-to-sequence models are now state of the art for many complex end-to-end NLP problems such as classification (for example, sentiment or text analysis), language understanding (for example, entity recognition), translation, text generation, summarization, and more.

One popular sequence-to-sequence model is BERT, which, today, exists in many different variations and configurations. Models based on the BERT architecture seem to perform particularly well but have already been outperformed by newer updated architectures, tuned parameters, or models with more training data.

The easiest way to get started using these new NLP models is with the *Hugging Face* `transformers` library, which provides end-to-end models (or pipelines) along with pretrained tokenizers and models. The `transformers` library implements all model architectures for both *TensorFlow* and *PyTorch*. The models can be easily consumed and used in an application, trained from scratch, or fine-tuned using domain-specific custom training data.

The following example shows how to implement sentiment analysis using the default `sentiment-analysis` pipeline, which, at the time of writing, uses the `TFDistilBertForSequenceClassification` model:

```
from transformers import pipeline
classifier = pipeline("sentiment-analysis")
```

```
result = classifier("Azure ML is quite good.")[0]
print("Label: %s, with score: %.2f" %
            (result['label'], result['score']))
```

As you can see in the previous example, it's very simple to use a pretrained model for an end-to-end prediction task. These three lines of code can easily be integrated into your feature extraction pipeline to enrich your training data with sentiments.

Besides end-to-end models, another popular application of NLP is to provide semantic embeddings for textual data during preprocessing. This can also be implemented using the transformers library and any of the many supported models.

To do this, first, we initialize a pretrained tokenizer for BERT. This will help us to split the input data into the correct format for the BERT model:

```
from transformers import BertTokenizer
tokenizer = BertTokenizer.from_pretrained('bert-base-cased')
inputs = tokenizer("Azure ML is quite good.",
                    return_tensors="tf")
```

Once we have transformed the input into a token sequence, we can evaluate the BERT model. To retrieve the numerical embedding, we need to understand the latent state of the encoder, which we can retrieve using the last_hidden_state property:

```
from transformers import TFBertModel
model = TFBertModel.from_pretrained('bert-base-uncased')
outputs = model(**inputs)
print(outputs.last_hidden_state)
```

The last hidden layer contains the latent representation of the model, which we can now use as a semantic numerical representation in our model:

```
<tf.Tensor: shape=(1, 10, 768), dtype=float32, numpy=
array([[[-0.30760652,  0.19552925,  0.1440584 , ...,
0.08283961,
            0.16151786,  0.23049755],...
```

The key takeaway from these models is that they use an encoder/decoder-based architecture, which allows us to simply borrow the encoder to embed text into a semantic numerical feature space. Hence, a common approach is to download the pretrained model and perform a forward pass through the encoder part of the network. The fixed-sized numerical output can now be used as a feature vector for any other model. This is a common preprocessing step and a good trade-off for using a state-of-the-art language model for numerical embedding.

Text analytics using Azure Cognitive Services

A good approach in many engineering disciplines is to not reinvent the wheel when many other companies have already solved the same problem far better than you will ever be able to solve it. This might be the case for basic text analytics and text understanding tasks that Microsoft has developed, implemented, and trained and now offers as a service.

What if I told you that when working with Azure, text understanding features such as sentiment analysis, key phrase extraction, language detection, named entity recognition, and the extraction of **Personally Identifiable Information** (**PII**) is just one request away? Azure provides the Text Analytics API as part of Cognitive Services, which will solve all of these problems for you.

This won't solve the need to transform a piece of text into numerical values, but it will make it easier to extract semantics from your text. One example would be to perform a key phrase extraction or sentiment analysis using Cognitive Services as an additional feature engineering step, instead of implementing your own NLP pipeline.

Let's implement a function that returns the sentiment for a given document using the Text Analytics API of Cognitive Services. This is great when you want to enrich your data with additional attributes, such as overall sentiment, in the text. Let's start by setting up all the parameters we will need to call the Cognitive Services API:

```
import requests


region='westeurope'
language='en'
version='v3.1'


key = '<insert access key>'


url = "https://{region}.api.cognitive.microsoft.com" + \
    + "/text/analytics/{version}/sentiment".format(
        region=region, version=version)
```

Next, we define the content and metadata of the request. We create a `payload` object that contains a single document and the text we want to analyze:

```
params = {
    'showStats': False
}
headers = {
    'Content-Type': 'application/json',
    'Ocp-Apim-Subscription-Key': key
}
payload = {
    'documents': [{
        'id': '1',
        'text': 'This is some input text that I love.',
        'language': language
    }]
}
```

Finally, we need to send the payload, heads, and parameters to the Cognitive Services API:

```
response = requests.post(url,
                         json=payload,
                         params=params,
                         headers=headers)
result = response.json()
print(result)
```

The preceding code looks very similar to the computer vision example that we saw in *Chapter 2, Choosing the Right Machine Learning Service in Azure*. In fact, it uses the same API but just a different endpoint for Text Analytics and, in this case, sentiment analysis functionality. Let's run this code and look at the output, which looks very similar to the following snippet:

```
{
    'documents': [{
        'id': '1',
        'sentiment': 'positive',
        'confidenceScores': {
            'positive': 1.0,
```

```
        'neutral': 0.0,
        'negative': 0.0},
    ...}],
    ...
}
```

We can observe that the JSON response contains a sentiment classification for each document (`positive`, `neutral`, and `negative`) as well as numeric confidence scores for each class. Also, you can see that the resulting documents are stored in an array and marked with an `id` value. Hence, you can send multiple documents to this API using an ID to identify each document.

Using custom pretrained language models is great, but for standardized text analytics, we can simply reuse Cognitive Services. Microsoft has invested tons of resources into the research and production of these language models, which you can use for your own data pipelines for a relatively small amount of money. Therefore, if you prefer using a managed service instead of running your customer transformer model, you should try this Text Analytics API.

Summary

In this chapter, you learned how to preprocess textual and categorical nominal and ordinal data using state-of-the-art NLP techniques.

You can now build a classical NLP pipeline with stop word removal, *lemmatization* and *stemming*, *n-grams*, and count term occurrences using a *bag-of-words* model. We used *SVD* to reduce the dimensionality of the resulting feature vector and to generate lower-dimensional topic encoding. One important tweak to the count-based bag-of-words model is to compare the relative term frequencies of a document. You learned about the *TF-IDF* function and can use it to compute the importance of a word in a document compared to the corpus.

In the following section, we looked at *Word2Vec* and *GloVe*, which are pretrained dictionaries of numeric word embeddings. Now you can easily reuse a pretrained word embedding for commercial NLP applications with great improvements and accuracy due to the semantic embedding of words.

Finally, we finished the chapter by looking at a state-of-the-art approach to language modeling, using end-to-end language representations, such as *BERT* and BERT-based architectures, which are trained as sequence-to-sequence models. The benefit of these models is that you can reuse the encoder to transform a sequence of text into a numerical representation, which is a very common task during feature extraction.

In the next chapter, we will look at how to train an ML model using Azure Machine Learning, applying everything we have learned so far.

8
Azure Machine Learning Pipelines

In the previous chapter, we learned about advanced preprocessing techniques, such as category embeddings and NLP, to extract semantic meaning from text features. In this chapter, you will learn how to use these preprocessing and transformation techniques to build reusable ML pipelines.

First, you will understand the benefits of splitting your code into individual steps and wrapping those into a pipeline. Not only can you make your code blocks reusable through modularization and parameters, but you can also control the compute targets for individual steps. This helps to optimally scale your computations, save costs, and improve performance at the same time. Lastly, you can parameterize and trigger your pipelines through an HTTP endpoint or through a recurring or reactive schedule.

Then, we will build a complex Azure Machine Learning pipeline in a couple of steps. We will start with a simple pipeline, add data inputs, outputs, and connections between the steps, and deploy the pipeline as a web service. You will also learn about advanced scheduling, based on the frequency and changing data, as well as how to parallelize pipeline steps for large data.

In the last part, you will learn how to integrate Azure Machine Learning pipelines into other Azure services such as Azure Machine Learning designer, Azure Data Factory, and Azure DevOps. This will help you to understand the commonalities and differences between the different pipeline and workflow services and how you can trigger ML pipelines.

In this chapter, we will cover the following topics:

- Using pipelines in ML workflows
- Building and publishing an ML pipeline
- Integrating pipelines with other Azure services

Technical requirements

In this chapter, we will use the following Python libraries and versions to create pipelines and pipeline steps:

- `azureml-core 1.34.0`
- `azureml-sdk 1.34.0`

Similar to previous chapters, you can run this code using either a local Python interpreter or a notebook environment hosted in Azure Machine Learning. However, all scripts need to be scheduled to execute in Azure.

All code examples in this chapter can be found in the GitHub repository for this book: `https://github.com/PacktPublishing/Mastering-Azure-Machine-Learning-Second-Edition/tree/main/chapter08`.

Using pipelines in ML workflows

Separating your workflow into reusable configurable steps and combining these steps into an end-to-end pipeline provides many benefits for implementing end-to-end ML processes. Multiple teams can own and iterate on individual steps to improve the pipeline over time, while others can easily integrate each version of the pipeline into their current setup.

The pipeline itself doesn't only split code from execution; it also splits the execution from orchestration. Hence, you can configure individual compute targets that can be used to optimize your execution and provide parallel execution while you don't have to touch the ML code.

We will take a quick look at Azure Machine Learning pipelines and why they are your tool of choice when implementing ML workflows in Azure. In the following section, *Building and publishing an ML pipeline*, we will dive a lot deeper and explore the individual features by building such a pipeline.

Why build pipelines?

As a single developer doing mostly experimentation and working simultaneously on data, infrastructure, and modeling, pipelines don't add a ton of benefits to the developer's workflow. However, as soon as you perform enterprise-grade development across multiple teams that iterate on different parts of the ML system, then you will greatly benefit from splitting your code into a pipeline of individual execution steps.

This modularization will give you great flexibility, and multiple teams will be able to collaborate efficiently. Teams can integrate your models and pipelines while you are iterating and building new versions of your pipeline at the same time. By using versioned pipelines and pipeline parameters, you can control how your data or model service pipeline should be called and ensure auditing and reproducibility.

Another important benefit of using workflows instead of running everything inside a single file is execution speed and cost improvements. Instead of running a single script on the same compute instance, you can run and scale the steps individually on different compute targets. This gives you greater control over potential cost savings and better optimization for performance, and you only ever have to retry the parts of the pipeline that failed and never the whole pipeline.

Through scheduling pipelines, you can make sure that all your pipeline runs are executed without your manual intervention. You simply define triggers, such as the existence of new training data, that should execute your pipeline. Decoupling your code execution from triggering the execution gives you a ton of benefits, such as easy integration into many other services.

Finally, the modularity of your code allows for great reusability. By splitting your script into functional steps such as cleaning, preprocessing, feature engineering, training, and hyperparameter tuning, you can version and reuse these steps for other projects as well.

Therefore, as soon as you want to benefit from one of these advantages, you can start organizing your code in pipelines, which can be deployed, scheduled, versioned, scaled, and reused. Let's find out how you can achieve this in Azure Machine Learning.

What are Azure Machine Learning pipelines?

Azure Machine Learning pipelines are workflows of executable steps in Azure Machine Learning that compose a complete ML workflow. Hence, you can combine data import, data transformations, feature engineering, model training, optimization, and also deployment as your pipeline steps.

Pipelines are resources in your Azure Machine Learning workspace that you can create, manage, version, trigger, and deploy. They integrate with all other Azure Machine Learning workspace resources such as datasets and datastores for loading data, compute instances, models, and endpoints. Each pipeline run is executed as an experiment on your Azure Machine Learning workspace and gives you the same benefits that we covered in the previous chapters, such as tracking files, logs, models, artifacts, and images while running on flexible compute clusters.

Azure Machine Learning pipelines should be your first choice when implementing flexible and reusable ML workflows. By using pipelines, you can modularize your code into blocks of functionality and versions and share those blocks with other projects. This makes it easy to collaborate with other teams on complex end-to-end ML workflows.

Another great integration of Azure Machine Learning pipelines is the integration with endpoints and triggers in your workspace. With a single line of code, you can publish a pipeline as a web service or web service endpoint and use this endpoint to configure and trigger the pipeline from anywhere. This opens the door for integrating Azure Machine Learning pipelines with many other Azure and third-party services.

However, if you need a more complex trigger, such as continuous scheduling or reactive triggering based on changes in the source data, you can easily configure this as well. The added benefit of using pipelines is that all orchestration functionality is completely decoupled from your training code.

As you can see, you get a lot of benefits by using Azure Machine Learning pipelines for your ML workflows. However, it's worth noting that this functionality does come with some extra overhead, namely wrapping each computation in a pipeline step, adding pipeline triggers, configuring environments and compute targets for each step, and exposing parameters as pipeline options. Let's start by building our first pipeline.

Building and publishing an ML pipeline

Let's go ahead and use all we have learned from the previous chapters and build a pipeline for data processing. We will use the Azure Machine Learning SDK for Python to define all the pipeline steps as Python code so that it can be easily managed, reviewed, and checked into version control as an authoring script.

We will define a pipeline as a linear sequence of pipeline steps. Each step will have an input and output defined as pipeline data sinks and sources. Each step will be associated with a compute target that defines both the execution environment as well as the compute resource for execution. We will set up an execution environment as a Docker container with all the required Python libraries and run the pipeline steps on a training cluster in Azure Machine Learning.

A pipeline runs as an experiment in your Azure Machine Learning workspace. We can either submit the pipeline as part of the authoring script, deploy it as a web service and hence trigger it through a webhook, schedule it as a published pipeline similar to cron jobs, or trigger it from a third-party service such as Logic Apps.

In many cases, running a linear sequential pipeline is good enough. However, when the amount of data increases and pipeline steps become slower and slower, we need to find a way to speed up these large computations. A common solution for speeding up data transformations, model training, and scoring is through parallelization. Hence, we will add a parallel execution step to our data transformation pipeline.

As we learned in the first section of this chapter, one of the main reasons for decoupling ML workflows into pipelines is modularity and reusability. By splitting a workflow into individual steps, we build the foundation for reusable computational blocks for common ML tasks, be it data analysis through visualizations and feature importance, feature engineering through NLP and third-party data, or simply the scoring of common ML tasks such as automatic image tagging through object detection.

In Azure Machine Learning pipelines, we can use modules to create reusable computational steps from a pipeline. A module is a management layer on top of a pipeline step that allows you to version, deploy, load, and reuse pipeline steps with ease. The concept is very similar to to versioning source code or versioning datasets in ML projects.

For any enterprise-grade ML workflow, the usage of pipelines is essential. Not only does it help you decouple, scale, trigger, and reuse individual computational steps, but it also provides auditability and monitorability to your end-to-end workflow. On top, splitting computational blocks into pipeline steps will set you up for a successful transition to MLOps – a **Continuous Integration and Continuous Deployment (CI/CD)** process for ML projects.

Let's get started and implement our first Azure Machine Learning pipeline.

Creating a simple pipeline

An Azure Machine Learning pipeline is a sequence of individual computational steps that can be executed in parallel or a series. Azure Machine Learning provides additional features on top of the pipeline, such as visualization of the computational graph, data transfer between steps, and publishing pipelines either as an endpoint or published pipeline. In this section, we will create a simple pipeline step and execute the pipeline to explore the Azure Machine Learning pipeline capabilities.

Depending on the type of computation, you can schedule jobs on different compute targets such as Azure Machine Learning, Azure Batch, Databricks, Azure Synapse, and more, or run *automated ML* or *HyperDrive* experiments. Depending on the execution type, you need to provide additional configuration to each step.

Let's start with a simple pipeline that consists only of a single step. We will incrementally add more functionality and steps in the subsequent sections. First, we need to define the type of execution for our pipeline step. While `PipelineStep` is the base class for any execution we can run in the pipeline, we need to choose one of the step implementations. The following steps are available at the time of writing:

- `AutoMLStep`: Runs an automated ML experiment
- `AzureBatchStep`: Runs a script on Azure Batch
- `DatabricksStep`: Runs a Databricks notebook
- `DataTransferStep`: Transfers data between Azure storage accounts
- `HyperDriveStep`: Runs a HyperDrive experiment
- `ModuleStep`: Runs a module
- `MpiStep`: Runs an **Message Passing Interface (MPI)** job
- `ParallelRunStep`: Runs a script in parallel
- `PythonScriptStep`: Runs a Python script
- `RScriptStep`: Runs an R script
- `SynapseSparkStep`: Runs a Spark script on Synapse
- `CommandStep`: Runs a script or command
- `KustoStep`: Runs a Kusto query on Azure Data Explorer

For our simple example, we want to run a single Python data preprocessing script in our pipeline, so we'll choose `PythonScriptStep` from the preceding list. We are building on the same examples and code samples that we saw in the previous chapters. In this first pipeline, we will execute a single step that will load the data directly from the script – and hence doesn't require any input or output to the pipeline step. We will add these separately in the following steps:

1. The pipeline steps are all attached to an Azure Machine Learning workspace. Hence, we start by loading the workspace configuration:

    ```
    from azureml.core import Workspace


    ws = Workspace.from_config()
    ```

2. Next, we need a compute target that we can execute our pipeline step on. Let's create an auto-scaling Azure Machine Learning training cluster as a compute target, similar to what we have created in previous chapters:

    ```
    # Create or get training cluster
    aml_cluster = get_aml_cluster(
       ws, cluster_name="cpu-cluster")
    aml_cluster.wait_for_completion(show_output=True)
    ```

3. In addition, we will need a run configuration that defines our training environment and Python libraries:

    ```
    run_conf = get_run_config(['numpy', 'pandas',
       'scikit-learn', 'tensorflow'])
    ```

4. We can now define `PythonScriptStep`, which provides all the required configuration and entry points for a target ML training script:

    ```
    from azureml.pipeline.steps import PythonScriptStep


    step = PythonScriptStep(name='Preprocessing',
                            script_name="preprocess.py",
                            source_directory="code",
                            runconfig=run_conf,
                            compute_target=aml_cluster)
    ```

As you can see in the preceding code, we are configuring `script_name` and the `source_directory` parameter, which contain the preprocessing script. We also pass the `runconfig` runtime configuration and the `compute_target` compute target to `PythonScriptStep`.

5. If you recall from previous chapters, we previously submitted the `ScriptRunConfig` objects as an experiment to the Azure Machine Learning workspace. In the case of pipelines, we first need to wrap the pipeline step in `Pipeline` and instead submit the pipeline as an experiment. While this seems counterintuitive at first, we will see how we can then parametrize the pipeline and add more computational steps to it. In the next code snippet, we define the pipeline:

```
from azureml.pipeline.core import Pipeline


pipeline = Pipeline(ws, steps=[step])
```

As you can see, the pipeline is defined simply through a series of pipeline steps and linked to a workspace. In our example, we only define a single execution step. Let's also check that we didn't make any mistakes configuring our pipeline through the built-in pipeline validation:

```
pipeline.validate()
```

6. Once the pipeline is validated successfully, we are ready for execution. The pipeline can be executed by submitting it as an experiment to the Azure Machine Learning workspace:

```
from azureml.core import Experiment


exp = Experiment(ws, "azureml-pipeline")
run = exp.submit(pipeline)
```

Congratulations! You just ran your first very simple Azure Machine Learning pipeline.

Important Note

You can find many complete and up-to-date examples for using Azure Machine Learning pipelines in the official Azure repository: `https://github.com/Azure/MachineLearningNotebooks/blob/master/how-to-use-azureml/machine-learning-pipelines`.

Once a pipeline is submitted, it is shown under the **Pipelines** section as well as under the **Experiments** section, as shown in *Figure 8.1*. A pipeline is treated as an experiment, where each pipeline run is like an experiment run. Each step of a pipeline, as well as its logs, figures, and metrics, can be accessed as a child run of the experiment:

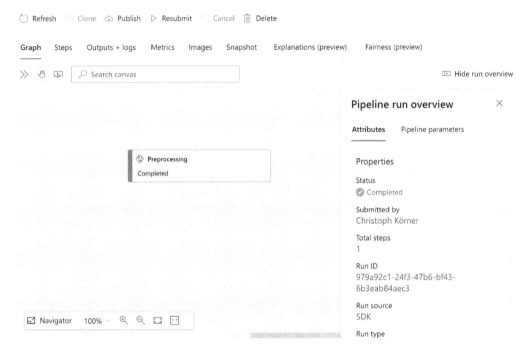

Figure 8.1 – A pipeline run as an experiment in Azure Machine Learning

While this simple pipeline doesn't add a ton of benefits to directly submitting the script as an experiment, we can now add additional steps to the pipeline and configure data input and output. Let's take a look!

Connecting data inputs and outputs between steps

Pipeline steps are computational blocks, whereas the pipeline defines the sequence of step executions. In order to control the data flow, we need to define input and output for the pipeline as well as wire up data input and output for individual steps. The data flow between the computational blocks will ultimately define the execution order for the blocks, and hence turns a sequence of steps into a directed acyclic execution graph. This is exactly what we are going to explore in this section.

In most cases, a pipeline needs external input, connections between the individual blocks, as well as persisted output. In Azure Machine Learning pipelines, we will use the following building blocks to configure this data flow:

- Pre-persisted pipeline input: `Dataset`
- Data between pipeline steps: `PipelineData`
- Persisting pipeline output: `PipelineData.as_dataset()`

In this section, we will look at all three types of data input and output. First, we will look at how we pass data as input into a pipeline.

Input data to pipeline steps

Let's start with adding a data input to the first step in a pipeline. To do so – or to pass any pre-persisted data to a pipeline step – we will use a **dataset**, which we saw previously in *Chapter 4*, *Ingesting Data and Managing Datasets*. In Azure Machine Learning, a dataset is an abstract reference for data stored in a specified path with specified encoding on a specified data storage system. The storage system itself is abstracted as a **datastore** object, a reference to the physical system with information about location, protocol, and access permissions.

If you recall from the previous chapters, we can access a dataset that was previously registered in our Azure Machine Learning workspace by simply referencing it by name:

```
from azureml.core.dataset import Dataset


dataset = Dataset.get_by_name(ws, 'titanic')
```

The preceding code is very convenient when your data was initially organized and registered as a dataset. As pipeline developers, we don't need to know the underlying data format (for example, CSV, ZIP, Parquet, and JSON) and on which Azure Blob storage or Azure SQL database the data is stored. Pipeline developers can consume the specified data and instead focus on pre-processing, feature engineering, and model training.

However, when passing new data into an Azure Machine Learning pipeline, we often don't have the data registered as datasets. In these cases, we can create a new dataset reference. Here is an example of how to create `Dataset` from publicly available data:

```
path ='https://...windows.net/demo/Titanic.csv'
dataset = Dataset.Tabular.from_delimited_files(path)
```

There are multiple ways to transform files and tabular data into `Dataset`. While this seems like a bit of complicated extra work instead of passing absolute paths to your pipelines directly, you will gain many benefits from following this convention. Most importantly, all compute instances in your Azure Machine Learning workspace will be able to access, read, and parse the data without any additional configuration. In addition, Azure Machine Learning will reference and track the dataset used for each experiment run.

Once we have obtained a reference to `Dataset`, we can pass the dataset to the pipeline step as input. When passing a dataset to the computational step, we can configure additional configurations such as the following:

- A name for the dataset reference in the script – `as_named_input()`

- An access type for `FileDataset` – `as_download()` or `as_mount()`

First, we configure the tabular dataset as the named input:

```
from azureml.core.dataset import Dataset


dataset = Dataset.get_by_name(ws, 'titanic')
data_in = dataset.as_named_input('titanic')
```

Next, we will use `PythonScriptStep`, which will allow us to pass arguments to the pipeline step. We need to pass the dataset to two parameters – as an argument to the pipeline script and as an input dependency for the step. The former will allow us to pass the dataset to the Python script, whereas the latter will track the dataset as a dependency of this pipeline step:

```
from azureml.pipeline.steps import PythonScriptStep


step = PythonScriptStep(name='Preprocessing',
                        script_name="preprocess_input.py",
                        source_directory="code",
                        arguments=["--input", data_in],
                        inputs=[data_in],
                        runconfig=run_conf,
                        compute_target=aml_cluster)
```

As you can see in the preceding example, we can pass one (or multiple) datasets to the pipeline step as the `inputs` parameter, as well as an argument to the script. Using a specific name for this dataset will help us to differentiate between multiple inputs in the pipeline. We will update the preprocessing script to parse the dataset from the command-line arguments, as shown in the following snippet:

preprocess_input.py

```
import argparse
from azureml.core import Run, Dataset

run = Run.get_context()
ws = run.experiment.workspace

parser = argparse.ArgumentParser()
parser.add_argument("--input", type=str)
args = parser.parse_args()

dataset = Dataset.get_by_id(ws, id=args.input)
df = dataset.to_pandas_dataframe()
```

As you can see in the preceding code, the dataset gets passed as a dataset name to the Python script. We can use the `Dataset` API to retrieve the data at runtime.

Once we submit the pipeline for execution, we can see the pipeline visualized in the Azure Machine Learning Studio interface, as shown in *Figure 8.2*. We can see that the dataset is passed as the **titanic** named input to the **Preprocessing** step:

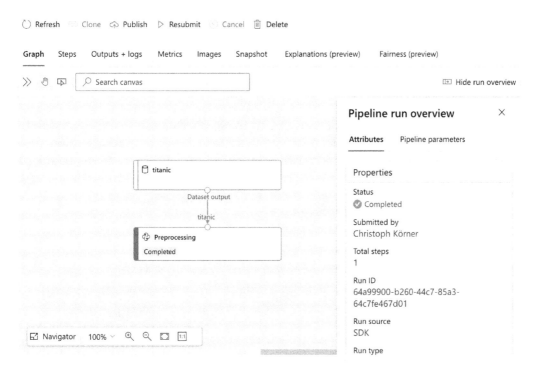

Figure 8.2 – The dataset as a pipeline step input

This is a great way to decouple a block of functionality from its input and helps you to build reusable blocks. We will see in the subsequent section, *Reusing pipeline steps through modularization*, how we can turn these reusable blocks into shared modules.

> **Important Note**
>
> Instead of passing datasets as input arguments to the pipeline step, we can also access named inputs from the run context using the following property on the run context object – `Run.get_context().input_datasets['titanic']`. However, setting up datasets as input and output arguments makes it easier to reuse pipeline steps and code snippets across pipelines and other experiments.

Next, let's find out how to set up a data flow between individual pipeline steps.

Passing data between steps

When we define input to a pipeline step, we often want to configure the output for the computations. By passing in input and output definitions, we separate the pipeline step from predefined data storage and avoid having to move data around as part of the computation step.

While pre-persisted inputs were defined as `Dataset` objects, data connections (input and output) between pipeline steps are defined through `PipelineData` objects. Let's look at an example of a `PipelineData` object used as output for one pipeline step and input for another step:

```
from azureml.core import Datastore
from azureml.pipeline.core import PipelineData


datastore = Datastore.get(ws, datastore_name="mldata")
data_train = PipelineData('train', datastore=datastore)
data_test = PipelineData('test', datastore=datastore)
```

Similar to the previous example, we pass the dataset as arguments and reference them as `outputs`. The former will allow us to retrieve the dataset in the script, whereas the latter defines the step dependencies:

```
from azureml.pipeline.steps import PythonScriptStep


step_1 = PythonScriptStep(name='Preprocessing',
                          script_name= \
                              "preprocess_output.py",
                          source_directory="code",
                          arguments=[
                              "--input", data_in,
                              "--out-train", data_train,
                              "--out-test", data_test],
                          inputs=[data_in],
                          outputs=[data_train, data_test],
                          runconfig=run_conf,
                          compute_target=aml_cluster)
```

Once we pass the expected output path to the scoring file, we need to parse the command-line arguments to retrieve the path. The scoring file looks like the following snippet in order to read the output path and output a pandas DataFrame to the desired output location. We first need to parse the command-line arguments in the training script:

preprocess_output.py

```
import argparse

parser = argparse.ArgumentParser()
parser.add_argument("--input", type=str)
parser.add_argument("--out-train", type=str)
parser.add_argument("--out-test", type=str)
args = parser.parse_args()
```

The `PipelineData` arguments get interpolated at runtime and replaced with the local path for the mounted dataset directory. Therefore, we can simply write the data to this local directory, and it will be automatically registered in the dataset:

preprocess_output.py

```
import os

out_train = args.out_train
os.makedirs(os.path.dirname(out_train), exist_ok=True)
out_test = args.out_test
os.makedirs(os.path.dirname(out_test), exist_ok=True)

df_train, df_test = preprocess(...)
df_train.to_csv(out_train)
df_test.to_csv(out_test)
```

Once we output data to a `PipelineData` dataset, we can pass these datasets to the next pipeline step. Passing the datasets works exactly the same as we saw in the previous section – we pass them as arguments and register them as `inputs`:

```
from azureml.pipeline.steps import PythonScriptStep

step_2 = PythonScriptStep(name='Training',
```

```
                    script_name="train.py",
                    source_directory="code",
                    arguments=[
                        "--in-train", data_train,
                        "--in-test", data_test],
                    inputs=[data_train, data_test],
                    runconfig=run_conf,
                    compute_target=aml_cluster)
```

Now, we can load the data in the training script. If you remember from the previous step, `PipelineData` is interpolated as paths on the local execution environment. Hence, we can read the data from the path that got interpolated in the command-line arguments:

train.py

```
import argparse

parser = argparse.ArgumentParser()
parser.add_argument("--in-train", type=str)
parser.add_argument("--in-test", type=str)
args = parser.parse_args()
...
df_train = pd.read_csv(args.in_train)
df_test = pd.read_csv(args.in_test)
```

Finally, we can wrap both steps as a `Pipeline` object by passing the steps using the pipeline `steps` keyword. The `pipeline` object can be passed as an experiment to Azure Machine Learning:

```
from azureml.pipeline.core import Pipeline

pipeline = Pipeline(ws, steps=[step_1, step_2])
```

As we can see in the previous example, we can read the output path from the command-line arguments and use it in the Python script as a standard file path. Hence, we need to make sure that the file path exists and output some tabular data into the location. Next, we define the input for the second validation step that reads the newly created data:

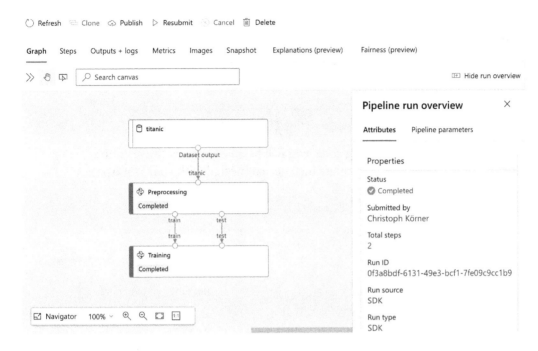

Figure 8.3 – Passing data between pipeline steps

Finally, we will take a look at how to persist the output of a pipeline step for usage outside of the pipeline.

Persisting data outputs

In this last section, we will learn how to persist the output data of a pipeline. A common task for pipelines is building data transformations – and hence we often expect pipelines to output data.

In the previous section, we learned about creating outputs from pipeline steps with `PipelineData`, mainly to connect these outputs to inputs of subsequent steps. We can use the same method to define a final persisted output of a pipeline.

Doing so is very simple once you understood how to create, persist, and version datasets. The reason for this is that we can convert a `PipelineData` object into a dataset using the `as_dataset()` method. Once we have a reference to the `Dataset` object, we can go ahead and either export it to a specific datastore or register it as a dataset in the workspace.

Here is a snippet of how to convert a `PipelineData` object defined as output in a pipeline step to a dataset and register it in the Azure Machine Learning workspace:

```
from azureml.data import OutputFileDatasetConfig

data_out = OutputFileDatasetConfig(name="predictions",
    destination=(datastore, 'titanic/predictions'))
```

By calling the preceding authoring code, you will be able to access the resulting predictions as a dataset in any compute instance connected with your workspace:

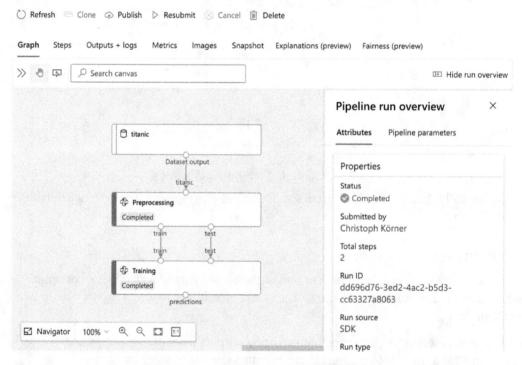

Figure 8.4 – A dataset as a pipeline step output

Next, we will take a look at the different ways to trigger a pipeline execution.

Publishing, triggering, and scheduling a pipeline

After you have created your first simple pipeline, you have multiple ways of running the pipeline. One example that we already saw was submitting the pipeline as an experiment to Azure Machine Learning. This would simply execute the pipeline from the same authoring script where the pipeline was configured. While this is a good start at first to execute a pipeline, there are other ways to trigger, parametrize, and execute it.

Common ways to execute a pipeline are the following:

- Publish the pipeline as a web service.
- Trigger the published pipeline using a webhook.
- Schedule the pipeline to run periodically.

In this section, we will look at all three methods to help you trigger and execute your pipelines with ease. Let's first start by publishing and versioning your pipeline as a web service.

Publishing a pipeline as a web service

A common reason to split an ML workflow into a reusable pipeline is that you can parametrize and trigger it for various tasks whenever needed. Good examples are common pre-processing tasks, feature engineering steps, and batch scoring.

Hence, turning a pipeline into a parametrizable web service that we can trigger from any other application is a great way of deploying our ML workflow. Let's get started and wrap and deploy the previously built pipeline as a web service.

As we want our published pipeline to be configurable through HTTP parameters, we need to first create these parameter references. Let's create a parameter to control the learning rate of our training pipeline:

```
from azureml.pipeline.core.graph import PipelineParameter


lr_param = PipelineParameter(name="lr_arg",
                             default_value=0.01)
```

Next, we link the pipeline parameter with the pipeline step by passing it as an argument to the training script. We extend the step from the previous section:

```
data = mnist_dataset.as_named_input('mnist').as_mount()
args = ["--in-train", data, "--learning-rate", lr_param]


step = PythonScriptStep(name='Training',
    script_name="train.py",
    source_directory="code",
    arguments=args,
    inputs=[data_train],
    runconfig=run_conf,
```

```
                compute_target=aml_cluster)
                        arguments=args ,
                        estimator=estimator,
                        compute_target=cpu_cluster)
```

In the preceding example, we added the learning rate as a parameter to the list of command-line arguments. In the training script, we can parse the command-line arguments and read the parameter:

score.py

```
parser = argparse.ArgumentParser()
parser.add_argument('--learning-rate', type=float,
    dest='lr')
args = parser.parse_args()

# print learning rate
print(args.lr)
```

Now, the only step left is to publish the pipeline. To do so, we create a pipeline and call the publish() method. We need to pass a name and version to the pipeline, which will now be a versioned published pipeline:

```
pipeline = Pipeline(ws, steps=[step])
service = pipeline.publish(name="CNN_Train_Service",
                            version="1.0")

service_id = service.id
service_endpoint = service.endpoint
```

That's all the code you need to expose a pipeline as a parametrized web service with authentication. If you want to abstract your published pipeline from a specific endpoint – for example, to iterate on the development process of your pipeline while letting other teams integrate the web service into their application – you can also deploy pipeline webhooks as endpoints.

Let's look at an example where we take the previously created pipeline service and expose it through a separate endpoint:

```
from azureml.pipeline.core import PipelineEndpoint

application = PipelineEndpoint.publish(ws,
   pipeline=service,
   name="CNN_Train_Endpoint")

service_id = application.id
service_endpoint = application.endpoint
```

We have deployed and decoupled the pipeline and the pipeline endpoint. We can finally call and trigger the endpoint through the service endpoint. Let's look at this in the next section.

Triggering a published pipeline with a webhook

The published pipeline web service requires authentication. Hence, let's first retrieve an Azure Active Directory token before we call the web service:

```
from azureml.core.authentication import AzureCliAuthentication

cli_auth = AzureCliAuthentication()
aad_token = cli_auth.get_authentication_header()
```

Using the authentication token, we can now trigger and parametrize the pipeline by calling the service endpoint. Let's look at an example using the `requests` library. We can configure the learning rate through the `lr_arg` parameter defined in the previous section as well as the experiment name by sending a custom JSON body. If you recall, the pipeline will still run as an experiment in your Azure Machine Learning workspace:

```
import requests

response = requests.post(service_endpoint,
   headers=aad_token,
   json={"ExperimentName": "mnist-train",
         "ParameterAssignments": {"lr_arg": 0.05}})
```

We can see in the preceding code snippet that we call the pipeline webhook using a POST request and configure the pipeline run by sending a custom JSON body. For authentication, we also need to pass the authentication as an HTTP header.

In this example, we used a Python script to trigger the web service endpoint. However, you can use any other Azure service for triggering this pipeline now through the webhook, such as Azure Logic Apps, CI/CD pipelines in Azure DevOps, or any other custom application. If you'd prefer your pipeline to run periodically instead of triggering it manually, you can set up a pipeline schedule. Let's take a look at this in the next section.

Scheduling a published pipeline

Setting up continuous triggers for workflows is a common use case when building pipelines. These triggers can run a pipeline and retrain a model every week or every day if new data is available. Azure Machine Learning pipelines support two types of scheduling techniques – continuous scheduling through a pre-defined frequency, and reactive scheduling and data change detection through a polling interval. In this section, we will take a look at both approaches.

Before we start scheduling a pipeline, we will first explore a way to list all the previously defined pipelines of a workspace. To do so, we can use the `PublishedPipeline.list()` method, similar to the `list()` method from our Azure Machine Learning workspace resources. Let's print the name and ID of every published pipeline in the workspace:

```
from azureml.pipeline.core import PublishedPipeline


for pipeline in PublishedPipeline.list(ws):
    print("name: %s, id: %s" % (pipeline.name, pipeline.id))
```

To set up a schedule for a published pipeline, we need to pass the pipeline ID as an argument. We can retrieve the desired pipeline ID from the preceding code snippet and plug it into the schedule declaration.

First, we will look at continuous schedules that re-trigger a pipeline with a predefined frequency, similar to cron jobs. To define the scheduling frequency, we need to create a `ScheduleRecurrence` object. Here is an example snippet to create a recurring schedule:

```
from azureml.pipeline.core.schedule import \
    ScheduleRecurrence, Schedule

recurrence = ScheduleRecurrence(frequency="Minute",
```

```
                              interval=15)

schedule = Schedule.create(ws,
                           name="CNN_Train_Schedule",
                           pipeline_id=pipeline_id,
                           experiment_name="mnist-train",
                           recurrence=recurrence,
                           pipeline_parameters={})
```

The preceding code is all you need to set up a recurring schedule that continuously triggers your pipeline. The pipeline will run as the defined experiment in your Azure Machine Learning workspace. Using the `pipeline_parameters` argument, you can pass additional parameters to the pipeline runs.

Azure Machine Learning pipelines also support another type of recurring scheduling, namely polling for changes in a datastore. This type of schedule is referred to as a reactive schedule and requires a connection to a datastore. It will trigger your pipeline whenever data changes in your datastore. Here is an example of setting up a reactive schedule:

```
from azureml.core.datastore import Datastore

# use default datastore 'ws.get_default_datastore()'
# or load a custom registered datastore
datastore = Datastore.get(workspace, 'mldemodatastore')

# 5 min polling interval
polling_interval = 5

schedule = Schedule.create(
    ws, name="CNN_Train_OnChange",
    pipeline_id=pipeline_id,
    experiment_name="mnist-train",
    datastore=datastore,
    data_path_parameter_name="mnist"
    polling_interval=polling_interval,
    pipeline_parameters={})
```

As you can see in this example, we set up the reactive schedule using a datastore reference and a polling interval in minutes. Hence, the schedule will check each polling interval to see which blobs have changed, if any and use those to trigger the pipeline. The blob names will be passed to the pipeline using the `data_path_parameter_name` parameter. Similar to the previous schedule, you can also send additional parameters to the pipeline using the `pipeline_parameters` argument.

Finally, let's take a look at how to programmatically stop a schedule once it is enabled. To do so, we need a reference to the schedule object. We can get this, similar to any other resource in Azure Machine Learning, by fetching the schedules for a specific workplace:

```
for schedule in Schedule.list(ws):
  print(schedule.id)
```

We can filter this list using all the available attributes on the schedule object. Once we have found the desired schedule, we can simply disable it:

```
schedule.disable(wait_for_provisioning=True)
```

Using the additional `wait_for_provisioning` argument, we ensure that we block code execution until the schedule is really disabled. You can easily re-enable the schedule using the `Schedule.enable` method. Now, you can create recurring and reactive schedules, continuously run your Azure Machine Learning pipelines, and disable them if not needed anymore. Next, we will take a look at parallelizing execution steps.

Parallelizing steps to speed up large pipelines

It's inevitable in many cases that the pipeline will process more and more data over time. In order to parallelize a pipeline, you can run pipeline steps in parallel or sequence, or parallelize a single pipeline step computation by using `ParallelRunConfig` and `ParallelRunStep`.

Before we jump into parallelizing a single step execution, let's first discuss the control flow of a simple pipeline. We will start with a simple pipeline that is constructed using multiple steps, as shown in the following example:

```
pipeline = Pipeline(ws, steps=[step1, step2, step3, step4])
```

When we submit this pipeline, how will these four steps be executed – in series, in parallel, or even in an undefined order? In order to answer the question, we need to look at the definitions of the individual steps. If all steps are independent and the compute target for each step is large enough, all steps are executed in parallel. However, if we define `PipelineData` as the output of `step1` and input it into the other steps, these steps will only be executed after `step1` has finished:

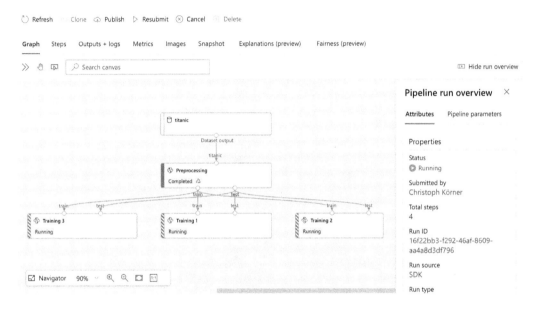

Figure 8.5 – A pipeline with parallel steps

The data connections between the pipeline steps implicitly define the execution order of the steps. If no dependencies exist between the steps, all steps are scheduled in parallel.

There is one exception to the preceding statement, which is enforcing a specific execution order of pipeline steps without a dedicated data object as a dependency. In order to do this, you can define these dependencies manually, as shown in the next code snippet:

```
step3.run_after(step2)
step4.run_after(step3)
```

The preceding configuration will first execute step1 and step2 in parallel before scheduling step3, thanks to your explicitly configured dependencies. This can be useful when you are accessing state or data in resources outside of the Azure Machine Learning workspace; hence, the pipeline cannot implicitly create a dependency:

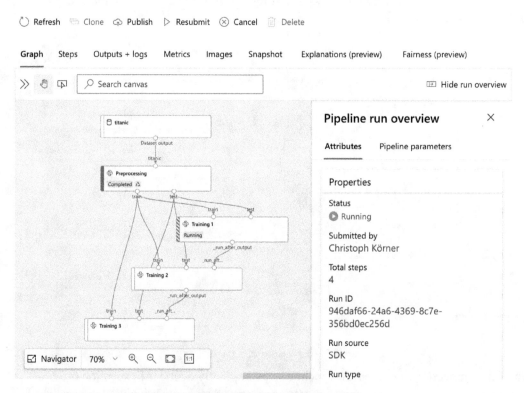

Figure 8.6 – A pipeline with a custom step order

Once we have answered the question of step execution order, we want to learn how we can execute a single step in parallel rather than multiple steps. A great use case for this is batch scoring a large amount of data. Rather than partitioning your input data as input for multiple steps, you want the data as input for a single step. However, to speed up the scoring process, you want a parallel execution of the scoring for the single step.

In Azure Machine Learning pipelines, you can use a `ParallelRunStep` step to configure a parallel execution for a single step. To configure the data partitions and parallelization of the computation, you need to create a `ParallelRunConfig` object. The parallel run step is a great choice for any type of parallelized computation that helps us to split the input data into smaller partitions (also called batches or mini-batches) of data. Let's walk through an example for setting up parallel execution for a single pipeline step. We will configure both batch sizes as a pipeline parameter that can be set when calling the pipeline step:

```
from azureml.pipeline.core import PipelineParameter
from azureml.pipeline.steps import ParallelRunConfig


parallel_run_config = ParallelRunConfig(
  entry_script='score.py',
  mini_batch_size=PipelineParameter(
    name="batch_size",
    default_value="10"),
  output_action="append_row",
  append_row_file_name="parallel_run_step.txt",
  environment=batch_env,
  compute_target=cpu_cluster,
  process_count_per_node=2,
  node_count=2)
```

The preceding snippet defines the run configuration for parallelizing the computation by splitting the input into mini-batches. We configure the batch size as a pipeline parameter, `batch_size`. We also configure the compute target and parallelism by the `node_count` and `process_count_per_node` parameters. Using these settings, we can score four mini-batches in parallel.

The `score.py` script is a deployment file that needs to contain an `init()` and `run(batch)` method. The `batch` argument contains a list of filenames that will get extracted from the input argument of the step configuration. We will learn more about this file structure in *Chapter 11, Hyperparameter Tuning and Automated Machine Learning*.

The run method in the score.py script should return the scoring results or write the data to an external datastore. Depending on this, the output_action argument needs to be set to either append_row, which means that all values will be collected as run in a result file, or summary_only, which means that the user will deal with storing the results. You can define the result file in which all the rows will get appended using the append_row_file_name argument.

As you can see, setting up the run configuration for a parallel batch execution is not very simple and requires a bit of fiddling. However, once set up and configured properly, it can be used to scale out a computational step and run many tasks in parallel. Hence, we can now define ParallelRunStep with all required input and output:

```python
from azureml.pipeline.steps import ParallelRunStep
from azureml.core.dataset import Dataset


parallelrun_step = ParallelRunStep(
  name="ScoreParallel",
  parallel_run_config=parallel_run_config,
  inputs=[Dataset.get_by_name(ws, 'mnist')],
  output=PipelineData('mnist_results',
                       datastore=datastore),
  allow_reuse=True)
```

As you can see, we read from the input dataset that references all files on the datastore. We write the results to the mnist_results folder in our custom datastore. Finally, we can start the run and look at the results. To do so, we submit the pipeline as an experiment run to Azure Machine Learning:

```python
from azureml.pipeline.core import Pipeline


pipeline = Pipeline(workspace=ws, steps=[parallelrun_step])
run = exp.submit(pipeline)
```

Splitting a step execution into multiple partitions will help you to speed up the computation of large amounts of data. It pays off as soon as the time of computation is significantly longer than the overhead of scheduling a step execution on a compute target. Therefore, ParallelRunStep is a great choice for speeding up your pipeline, with only a few changes in your pipeline configuration required. Next, we will take a look into better modularization and the reusability of pipeline steps.

Reusing pipeline steps through modularization

By splitting your workflow into pipeline steps, you are laying the foundation for reusable ML and data processing building blocks. However, instead of copying and pasting your pipelines, pipeline steps, and code into other projects, you might want to abstract your functionality into functional high-level modules.

Let's look at an example. Suppose you are building a pipeline step that takes in a dataset of user and item ratings and outputs a recommendation of the top five items for each user. However, while you are fine-tuning the recommendation engine, you want to enable your colleagues to integrate the functionality into their pipeline. A great way would be to separate the implementation and usage of the code, define the input and output data formats, and modularize and version it. That's exactly what modules do in the scope of the Azure Machine Learning pipeline steps.

Let's create a module, the container that will hold a reference to the computational step:

```
from azureml.pipeline.core.module import Module


module = Module.create(ws,
                       name="TopItemRecommender",
                       description="Recommend top 5 items")
```

Next, we define input and output for the module using the InputPortDef and OutputPortDef bindings. These are input and output references that later need to be bound to data references. We use these bindings to abstract all of our input and output:

```
from azureml.pipeline.core.graph import \
   InputPortDef, OutputPortDef


in1 = InputPortDef(name="in1",
                   default_datastore_mode="mount",
                   default_data_reference_name = \
                      datastore.name,
                   label="Ratings")


out1 = OutputPortDef(name="out1",
                     default_datastore_mode="mount",
                     default_datastore_name=datastore.name,
                     label="Recommendation")
```

Finally, we can define the module functionality by publishing a Python script for this module:

```
module.publish_python_script("train.py",
                             source_directory="./rec",
                             params={"numTraits": 5},
                             inputs=[in1],
                             outputs=[out1],
                             version="1",
                             is_default=True)
```

That's all you need to do to enable others to reuse your recommendation block in their Azure Machine Learning pipelines. By using versioning and default versions, you can ensure exactly which code is pulled by your users. As we can see, you can define multiple inputs and outputs for each module and define configurable parameters for this module. In addition to publishing functionality as Python code, we can also publish an Azure Data Lake Analytics or Azure batch step.

Next, we will take a look at how the module can be integrated into an Azure Machine Learning pipeline and executed together with custom steps. To do so, we will first load the module that was previously created using the following command:

```
from azureml.pipeline.core.module import Module

module = Module.get(ws, name="TopItemRecommender")
```

Now, the great thing about this is that the preceding code will work in any Python interpreter or execution engine that has access to your Azure Machine Learning workspace. This is huge – no copying of code, no need for checking out dependencies, and no need for defining any additional access permissions for your application – everything is integrated with your workspace.

First, we need to write up the input and output for this pipeline step. Let's pass the input from the pipeline directly to the recommendation module and output everything to the pipeline output:

```
from azureml.pipeline.core import PipelineData

in1 = PipelineData("in1",
                   datastore=datastore,
                   output_mode="mount",
```

```
                        is_directory=False)

out1 = PipelineData("out1",
                    datastore=datastore,
                    output_mode="mount",
                    is_directory=False)

input_wiring = {"in1": in1}
output_wiring = {"out1": out1}
```

Now, we parametrize the module with the use of pipeline parameters. This lets us configure a parameter in the pipeline that we can pass through to the recommendation module. In addition, we can define a default parameter for the parameter when used in this pipeline:

```
from azureml.pipeline.core import PipelineParameter

num_traits = PipelineParameter(name="numTraits",
                               default_value=5)
```

We already defined the input and output for this pipeline as well as the input parameters for the pipeline step. The only thing we are missing is bringing everything together and defining a pipeline step. Similar to the previous section, we can define a pipeline step that will execute the modularized recommendation block. To do so, instead of PythonScriptStep, we now use ModuleStep:

```
from azureml.core import RunConfiguration
from azureml.pipeline.steps import ModuleStep

step = ModuleStep(module= module,
                  version="1",
                  runconfig=RunConfiguration(),
                  compute_target=aml_compute,
                  inputs_map=input_wiring,
                  outputs_map=output_wiring,
                  arguments=[
                    "--output_sum", first_sum,
                    "--output_product", first_prod,
                    "--num-traits", num_traits])
```

Finally, we can execute the pipeline by submitting it as an experiment to our Azure Machine Learning workspace. This code is very similar to what we saw already in the previous section:

```
from azureml.core import Experiment
from azureml.pipeline.core import Pipeline


pipeline = Pipeline(ws, steps=[step])
exp = Experiment(ws, "item-recommendation")
run = exp.submit(pipeline)
```

The preceding step executes the modularized pipeline as an experiment in your Azure Machine Learning workspace. However, you can also choose any of the other publishing methods that we discussed in the previous sections, such as publishing as a web service or scheduling the pipeline.

Splitting pipeline steps into reusable modules is extremely helpful when working with multiple teams on the same ML projects. All teams can work in parallel, and the results can be easily integrated with a single Azure Machine Learning workspace. Let's take a look at how Azure Machine Learning pipelines integrate with other Azure services.

Integrating pipelines with other Azure services

It's rare that users only use a single service to manage data flows, experimentation, training, deployment, and CI/CD in the cloud. Other services provide specific features that make them a better fit for a task, such as Azure Data Factory for loading data into Azure and Azure Pipelines for CI/CD for running automated tasks in Azure DevOps.

The strongest argument for choosing a cloud provider is the strong integration of its individual services. In this section, we will see how Azure Machine Learning pipelines integrate with other Azure services. The list for this section would be a lot longer if we were to cover every possible service for integration. As we learned in this chapter, you can trigger a published pipeline by calling a REST endpoint and submitting a pipeline using standard Python code. This means that you can integrate pipelines anywhere where you can call HTTP endpoints or run Python code.

We will first look into integration with Azure Machine Learning designer. The designer lets you build pipelines using graphical blocks, and these pipelines, published pipelines, and pipeline runs will show up in the workspace just like any other pipeline that we built in this chapter. Therefore, it is practical to take a quick look at the commonalities and differences.

Next, we will take a quick look at integrating Azure Machine Learning pipelines with Azure Data Factory, arguably an integration that is used the most. It's a very natural instinct to include ML pipelines with ETL pipelines for scoring, enriching, or enhancing data during the ETL process.

Finally, we will compare Azure Machine Learning pipelines with Azure Pipelines for CI/CD in Azure DevOps. While Azure DevOps was used mainly for application code and app orchestration, it is now transitioning to provide fully end-to-end MLOps workflows. Let's start with the designer and jump right in.

Building pipelines with Azure Machine Learning designer

Azure Machine Learning designer is a graphical interface for creating complex ML pipelines through a drag and drop interface. You can choose a functionality represented as blocks for importing data, which will use a datastore and a dataset under the hood.

The following figure shows a simple pipeline to train and score a Boosted Decision Tree Regression model. As you can see, the block-based programming style requires less knowledge about the individual blocks, and it allows you to build complex pipelines without writing any code:

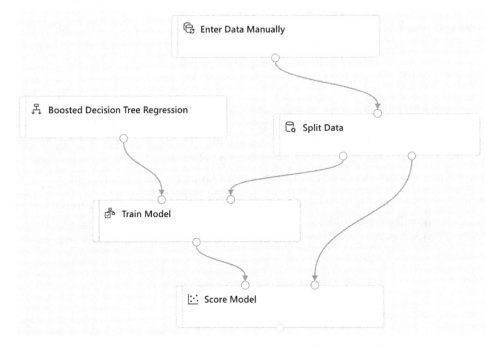

Figure 8.7 – The Azure Machine Learning designer pipeline

Some actions, such as connecting the output of one computation to the input of the next, are arguably more convenient to create in the visual UI than with code. It's also easier to understand the data flow by visualizing the pipeline. Other actions, such as creating parallel executions of large data batches, are a bit easier to handle and maintain in code. However, due to our code-first approach for reproducibility, testability, and version control, we usually prefer code for authoring and execution.

It's worth noting that the functionality of pipelines in the designer and pipelines using code are not the same. While you have a broad set of preconfigured abstract functional blocks, such as the **Boosted Decision Tree Regression** block in the previous *Figure 8.7*, you can't access these functionalities in code. However, you can use scikit-learn, PyTorch, TensorFlow, and so on to reuse an existing functionality or build your own in code.

Thanks to the first-class integration of the designer into the workspace, you can access all of the files, models, and datasets of the workspace from within the designer. An important takeaway is that all the resources that are created in the workspace such as pipelines, published pipelines, real-time endpoints, models, datasets, and so on are stored in a common system – independently of where they were created.

Azure Machine Learning pipelines in Azure Data Factory

When moving data, ETL, and trigger computations in various Azure services, you will most likely come across **Azure Data Factory**. It is a very popular service to move large amounts of data into Azure, perform processing and transformations, build workflows, and trigger many other Azure or third-party services.

Azure Machine Learning pipelines integrate very well with Azure Data Factory, and you can easily configure and trigger the execution of a published pipeline through Data Factory. To do so, you need to drag the **ML Execute Pipeline** activity to your Data Factory canvas and specify the pipeline ID of the published pipeline. In addition, you can also specify pipeline parameters as well as the experiment name for the pipeline run.

The following figure shows how the **ML Execute Pipeline** step can be configured in Azure Data Factory. It uses a linked service to connect to your Azure Machine Learning workspace, which allows you to select the desired pipeline from a drop-down box:

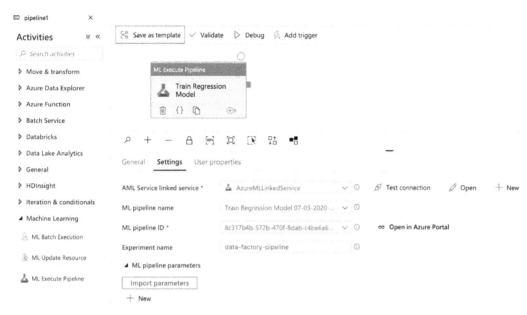

Figure 8.6 – Azure Data Factory with Azure Machine Learning activity

If you are configuring the computational steps using JSON, you can use the following snippet to create an **ML Execute Pipeline** activity with Azure Machine Learning as a linked service. Again, you must specify the pipeline ID and can pass an experiment name, as well as pipeline parameters:

```
{
    "name": "Machine Learning Execute Pipeline",
    "type": "AzureMLExecutePipeline",
    "linkedServiceName": {
        "referenceName": "AzureMLService",
        "type": "LinkedServiceReference"
    },
    "typeProperties": {
        "mlPipelineId": "<insert pipeline id>",
        "experimentName": "data-factory-pipeline",
        "mlPipelineParameters": {
            "batch_size": "10"
        }
    }
}
```

Finally, you can trigger the step by adding triggers or output into the **ML Execute Pipeline** activity. This will finally trigger your published Azure Machine Learning pipeline and start the execution in your workspace. This is a great addition and makes it easy for other teams to re-use your ML pipelines during classical ETL and data transformation processes.

Azure Pipelines for CI/CD

Azure Pipelines is a feature of Azure DevOps that lets you run, build, test, and deploy code as a **Continuous Integration** (**CI**) and **Continuous Deployment** (**CD**) process. Hence, they are flexible pipelines for code and app orchestration with many advanced features, such as approval queues and gated phases.

By allowing you to run multiple blocks of code, the best way to integrate Azure Machine Learning into Azure DevOps is by using Python script blocks. If you have followed this book and used a code-first approach to author your experiments and pipelines, then this integration is very easy. Let's take a look at a small example.

First, let's write a utility function that returns a published pipeline, given a workspace and pipeline ID as parameters. We will need this function in this example:

```
def get_pipeline(workspace, pipeline_id):
  for pipeline in PublishedPipeline.list(workspace):
    if pipeline.id == pipeline_id:
      return pipeline
  return None
```

Next, we can go ahead and implement a very simple Python script that allows us to configure and trigger a pipeline run in Azure. We will initialize the workspace, retrieve the published pipeline, and submit the pipeline as an experiment to the Azure Machine Learning workspace. It's all configurable and all with only a few lines of code:

```
ws = Workspace.get(
  name=os.environ.get("WORKSPACE_NAME"),
  subscription_id=os.environ.get("SUBSCRIPTION_ID"),
  resource_group=os.environ.get("RESOURCE_GROUP"))

pipeline = get_pipeline(args.pipeline_id)
pipeline_parameters = args.pipeline_parameters
```

```
exp = Experiment(ws, name=args.experiment_name)
run = exp.submit(pipeline,
                 pipeline_parameters=pipeline_parameters)

print("Pipeline run initiated %s" % run.id)
```

The preceding code shows us how we can integrate a pipeline trigger into an Azure pipeline for CI/CD. We can see that once the workspace is initialized, the code follows the exact same pattern as if we had submitted the published pipeline from our local development environment. In addition, we can configure the pipeline run through environment variables and command-line parameters. We will see this functionality in action in *Chapter 16, Bringing Models into Production with MLOps*.

Summary

In this chapter, you learned how to use and configure Azure Machine Learning pipelines for splitting an ML workflow into multiple steps using pipeline and pipeline steps for estimators, Python execution, and parallel execution. You configured pipeline input and output using `Dataset` and `PipelineData` and managed to control the execution flow of the pipeline.

As another milestone, you deployed the pipeline as `PublishedPipeline` to an HTTP endpoint. This lets you configure and trigger the pipeline execution with a simple HTTP call. Next, you implemented automatic scheduling based on a time frequency, as well as a reactive schedule based on changes in the underlying dataset. Now, the pipeline can rerun your workflow when the input data changes without any manual interaction.

Finally, we also modularized and versioned a pipeline step so that it can be reused in other projects. We used `InputPortDef` and `OutputPortDef` to create virtual bindings for data sources and sinks. In the last step, we looked into the integration of pipelines into other Azure services, such as Azure Machine Learning designer, Azure Data Factory, and Azure DevOps.

In the next chapter, we will look into building ML models in Azure using decision tree-based ensemble models.

Section 3: The Training and Optimization of Machine Learning Models

In this section, we will learn all about training and optimizing traditional **Machine Learning (ML)** models as well as deep learning models on Azure. First, we will investigate the benefits and downsides of traditional ensemble techniques and their differences from newer neural network-based models. We will then implement and train **Convolutional Neural Networks (CNNs)** on Azure using the capabilities of Azure Machine Learning services. Following this, we will look at ways to optimize model training through hyperparameter tuning and automated ML. Furthermore, we will have a look at how to run ML training not on a single compute instance, but on a distributed cluster. With the knowledge obtained, we'll wrap this section up by building a recommendation engine in the cloud.

This section comprises the following chapters:

- *Chapter 9, Building ML Models Using Azure Machine Learning*
- *Chapter 10, Training Deep Neural Networks on Azure*
- *Chapter 11, Hyperparameter Tuning and Automated Machine Learning*
- *Chapter 12, Distributed Machine Learning on Azure*
- *Chapter 13, Building a Recommendation Engine in Azure*

9
Building ML Models Using Azure Machine Learning

In the previous chapters, we learned about datasets, preprocessing, feature extraction, and pipelines in Azure Machine Learning. In this chapter, we will use the knowledge we have gained so far to create and train a powerful tree-based ensemble classifier.

First, we will look behind the scenes of popular ensemble classifiers such as **random forest**, **XGBoost**, and **LightGBM**. These classifiers perform extremely well in practical real-world scenarios, and all are based on decision trees under the hood. By understanding their main benefits, you will be able to spot problems that can be solved with ensemble decision tree classifiers easily.

We will also learn the difference between **gradient boosting** and **random forest** and what makes these tree ensembles useful for practical applications. Both techniques help to overcome the main weaknesses of decision trees and can be applied to many different classification and regression problems.

Finally, we will train a LightGBM classifier on a sample dataset using all the techniques we have learned so far. We will write a training script that automatically logs all parameters, evaluation metrics, and figures, and is configurable with command-line arguments. We will schedule the training script on an Azure Machine Learning training cluster.

In this chapter, we will cover the following topics:

- Working with tree-based ensemble classifiers
- Training an ensemble classifier model using LightGBM

Technical requirements

In this chapter, we will use the following Python libraries and versions to create decision tree-based ensemble classifiers:

- `azureml-core 1.34.0`
- `azureml-sdk 1.34.0`
- `lightgbm 3.2.1`
- `numpy 1.19.5`
- `pandas 1.3.2`
- `scikit-learn 0.24.2`
- `seaborn 0.11.2`
- `matplotlib 3.4.3`

Similar to previous chapters, you can execute this code using either a local Python interpreter or a notebook environment hosted in Azure Machine Learning.

All code examples in this chapter can be found in the GitHub repository for this book: `https://github.com/PacktPublishing/Mastering-Azure-Machine-Learning-Second-Edition/tree/main/chapter09`.

Working with tree-based ensemble classifiers

Supervised tree-based ensemble classification and regression techniques have proven very successful in many practical real-world applications in recent years. Hence, they are widely used today in various applications, including fraud detection, recommendation engines, tagging engines, and many more. All your favorite mobile and desktop operating systems, Office programs, and audio or video streaming services make heavy use of them every day.

Therefore, in this section, we will dive into the main reasons for their popularity and performance, both for training and scoring. If you are an expert on traditional ML algorithms and know the difference between boosting and bagging, you might as well jump right to the next section, *Training an ensemble classifier model using LightGBM*, where we put the theory into practice.

We will first look at decision trees, a very simple technique that is decades old. We encourage you to follow along even with the simple methods as they build the foundation of today's state-of-the-art classical supervised ML approaches. We will also explore the advantages of tree-based classifiers in detail to help you understand the differences between a classical approach and a deep learning-based ML model.

A single decision tree also has a lot of disadvantages associated with it and is therefore used only in ensemble models and never as an individual model. We will take a closer look at the disadvantages of individual decision trees later in this section. Afterwards, we will discover methods for combining multiple weak individual trees into a single strong ensemble classifier that builds upon the strengths of tree-based approaches and transforms them into what they are today—powerful multi-purpose supervised ML models that are integrated into almost every off-the-shelf ML platform.

Understanding a simple decision tree

Let's first discuss what a **decision tree** is and how it works. A decision tree estimator is a supervised ML approach that learns to approximate a function with multiple nested if/else statements. This function can be a continuous regressor function or a decision boundary function. Hence, like many other ML approaches, decision trees can be used for learning both regression and classification problems.

From the preceding description, we can immediately spot a few important advantages of decision trees:

- One is the flexibility to work on different data distributions, data types (for example, numerical and categorical data), and ML problems (such as classification or regression).

- Another advantage and one of the reasons they compete with more complicated models is their interpretability. Tree-based models and ensembles can be visualized and even printed out on paper to explain the decision (output) from a prediction.

- The third advantage lies in their practical use for training performance, model size, and validity. Integrating a pre-trained decision tree into a desktop, web, or mobile application is a lot less complex and a lot faster than a deep learning approach.

> **Important Note**
>
> Please note that we don't intend to sell tree-based ensembles as the solution to
> every ML problem and to downplay the importance of deep learning approaches.
> We rather want to make you aware of the strengths of traditional approaches in
> this chapter so you can evaluate the right approach for your problem.

The following figure shows an example of a decision tree used to decide whether a person
is fit or not:

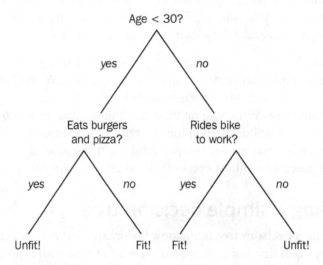

Figure 9.1 – A simple decision tree

Figure 9.1 is an example of a trained decision tree, where we can score the model by simply
walking through each node and arriving at a class label at the leaf of the tree.

Advantages of a decision tree

Decision tree-based ML models are extremely popular due to their strengths when
working on real-world applications where data comes in all forms and shapes and is
messy, biased, and incomplete. These are the key advantages of decision trees:

- They support a wide range of applications.
- They require little data preparation.
- The enable interpretability of the model.
- They provide fast training and fast scoring.

First, let's focus on the *flexibility* of decision trees, which is one of their major strengths as opposed to many other classical/statistical ML approaches. While the general framework is very flexible and supports *classification* and *regression*, as well as *multi-output problems*, it gained a lot of popularity because it can handle both numerical and categorical data out of the box. Thanks to nested `if-else` trees, it can also handle nominal categories as well as NULL or missing values in data. Decision trees are popular because they don't require massive preprocessing and data cleansing beforehand.

While data preparation and cleaning are important steps in every ML pipeline, it's still nice to have a framework that naturally supports categorical input data out of the box. Some ensemble tree-based classifiers are built on top of this advantage, for example, **CatBoost**—a gradient boosted trees implementation from Yandex Research with native support for categorical data.

Another important advantage of tree-based models, especially from a business perspective, is the *interpretability* of the model. Unlike other ML approaches, the output of a decision tree classifier model is not a huge parametric decision boundary function. Trained deep learning models often generate a model with more than 100 million parameters and hence behave like a black box—especially for business decision makers. While it is possible to gain insights and reason about the activations in deep learning models, it's usually very hard to reason about the effect of an input parameter on the output variable.

Interpretability is where tree-based approaches shine. In contrast to many other traditional ML approaches (such as SVM, logistic regression, or deep learning), a decision tree is a non-parametric model and therefore, doesn't use parameters to describe the function to be learned. It uses a nested decision tree that can be plotted, visualized, and printed out on paper. This allows decision makers to understand every decision (output) of a tree-based classification model—it may require a lot of paper, but it is always possible.

While speaking about interpretability, we need to mention another important aspect of decision trees: the decision tree model implicitly develops a notion of *feature importance* during the training process. This is a very useful output of a trained decision tree model that we can use to rank features for preprocessing, without requiring to first clean the data.

> **Important Note**
> While feature importance can also be measured with other ML approaches, for example, linear regression, they usually require a cleaned and normalized dataset as input. Many other ML approaches, such as SVM or deep learning, don't develop a measure of feature importance for the individual input dimensions.

Decision tree-based approaches excel at this as they internally create each individual split (decision) based on an importance criterion. This results in an inherent understanding of how and which feature dimensions are important to the final model.

Let's look at another great advantage of decision trees. Decision trees have many practical benefits over traditional statistical models derived from the non-parametric approach. Tree-based models generally yield good results on a wide variety of input distributions and even work well when the model assumptions are violated. On top of that, the size of the trained tree is small compared to deep learning approaches, and inference/scoring is fast.

Disadvantages of a decision tree

As everything in life comes with advantages and disadvantages, the same is true for decision trees. There are quite a few severe disadvantages associated with individual decision trees that should make you avoid a single decision tree classifier in your ML pipeline. The main weakness of a single decision tree is that the tree is fitted on all training samples and, hence, is very likely to *overfit*. The reason for this is that the model itself tends to build complex `if-else` trees to model a continuous function.

Another important point is that finding the optimal decision tree even for simple concepts is an **NP-hard problem** (also known as a **nondeterministic polynomial time-hard problem**). Therefore, it is solved through heuristics and the resulting single decision is usually not the optimal one.

Overfitting is bad – very bad – and leads to a serious complication in ML. Once a model overfits, it doesn't generalize well and hence has very poor performance on unseen data. Therefore, predictions for new inputs will yield results that are worse than those measured during training. Another related problem is that tiny changes in the training data or the order of training samples can lead to very different nested trees and hence, the training convergence is unstable. Single decision trees are extremely prone to overfitting. On top of that, a single decision tree is very likely to be biased toward the class with the largest number of samples in your training data.

You can overcome the disadvantages of single trees, such as overfitting, instability, and non-optimal trees, by combining multiple decision trees through bagging and boosting to an **ensemble model**. There are also many tree-based optimizations, including **tree pruning**, to improve generalization. Popular models that use these techniques include **random forests** and **gradient boosted trees**, which overcome most of the problems of a single decision tree while keeping most of their benefits. We will look at these two methods in the next section.

> **Important Note**
>
> Some more fundamental disadvantages sometimes crop up even with tree-based ensemble methods that are worth mentioning. Due to the nature of decision trees, tree-based models have difficulties learning complicated functions, such as the XOR problem. For these problems, it's better to use non-linear parametric models, such as neural networks and deep learning approaches.

Combining classifiers with bagging

One key disadvantage of a single decision tree is overfitting to training data and, hence, poor generalization performance and instability from small changes in the training data. A **bagging** (also called *bootstrap aggregation*) classifier uses the simple concept of combining multiple independent models into an **ensemble model** trained on a subset of the training data to overcome this exact problem. The subsets are built by randomly picking samples from the training dataset with replacements. The output of the individual models is either selected through a majority vote for classification or mean aggregation for regression problems.

By combining independent models, we can reduce the variance of the combined model without increasing the bias and thereby greatly improve generalization. However, there is another benefit to training multiple individual models: parallelization. Since each individual model uses a random subset of the training data, the training process can easily be parallelized and trained on multiple compute nodes. Therefore, bagging is a popular technique when training a large number of tree-based classifiers on a large dataset.

The following *Figure 9.2* shows how each classifier is trained independently on the same training data—each model uses a random subset with replacements. The combination of all individual models makes up the ensemble model.

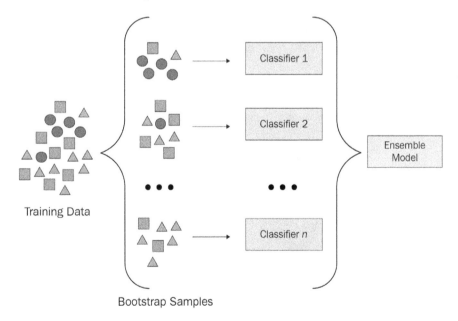

Figure 9.2 – Bagging

Bagging can be used to combine any ML model; however, it is often used with tree-based classifiers as they suffer most from overfitting. The idea of **random forest** builds on top of the bagging method combined with a random subset of features for each split (decision). When a feature is selected at random, the optimal threshold for the split is computed such that a certain *information criterion* is optimized (usually **GINI** or **information gain**). Hence, the random forest uses a random subset of the training data, random feature selection, and an optimal threshold for the split.

Random forests are widely used for their simple decision tree-based model combined with much better generalization and easy parallelization. Another benefit of taking a random subset of features is that this technique also works well with very high-dimensional inputs. Hence, when dealing with classical ML approaches, random forests are often used for large-scale tree ensembles.

Another popular tree-based bagging technique is the **extra-trees** (short for **extremely randomized trees**) algorithm, which adds another randomization step on the dimension split. For each split, thresholds are drawn at random and the best one is selected for that decision. Hence, in addition to random features, the extra-trees algorithm also uses random split thresholds to further improve generalization.

The following *Figure 9.3* shows how all tree ensemble techniques are used for inferencing. Each tree computes an individual score while the result of each tree is aggregated to yield the result:

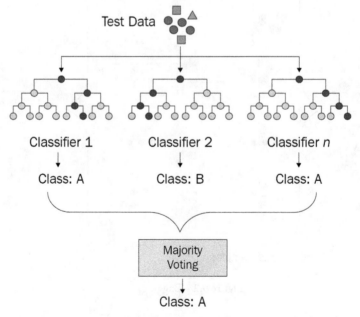

Figure 9.3 – Majority voting

You can find tree-based bagging ensembles such as random forest, and sometimes also extra-trees, in many popular ML libraries, such as scikit-learn, Spark MLlib, ML.NET, and many others.

Optimizing classifiers with boosting rounds

In many problems in computer science, we can replace a random greedy approach with a more complex but more optimal approach. The same holds true for tree ensembles and builds the foundation for **boosted tree ensembles**.

The basic idea behind boosting is the following:

1. We start to train an individual model on the whole training dataset.
2. Then we compute the predictions of the model on the training dataset and start weighting training samples that yield a wrong result higher.
3. Next, we train another decision tree using the weighted training set. We then combine both decision trees into an ensemble and predict the output classes for the weighted training set. We then further increase the weights on the wrongly classified training samples of the combined model for the next boosting round.
4. We continue this algorithm until a stopping criterion is reached.

The following *Figure 9.4* shows how the training error using boosting optimization decreases each iteration (boosting round) with the addition of a new tree:

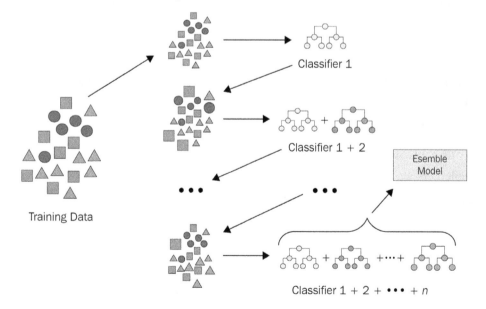

Figure 9.4 – Boosting

The first boosting algorithm was **AdaBoost**, which combined multiple weak models into an ensemble by fitting it on a weighted training set that adapts each iteration through a learning rate. The notion of this approach was to add individual trees that focus on predicting something the previous trees couldn't predict.

One particular successful technique of boosting is **gradient boosted trees** (or **gradient boosting**). In gradient boosting, you combine the gradient descent optimization technique with boosting in order to generalize boosting to an arbitrary loss function. Now, instead of tuning the dataset samples using weights, we can compute the gradient of the loss function and select the optimal weights—the ones that minimize the loss function—during each iteration. Thanks to the usage of optimization, this technique yields very good results, adding to the existing advantages of decision trees.

Gradient boosted tree-based ensembles are included in many popular ML libraries such as scikit-learn, Spark MLlib, and others. However, some individual implementations, such as XGBoost and LightGBM, have gained quite a lot of popularity and are available as standalone libraries and as plugins for scikit-learn and Spark.

Training an ensemble classifier model using LightGBM

Both random forest and gradient boosted trees are powerful ML techniques due to the simplicity of decision trees and the benefits of combining multiple classifiers. In this example, we will use the popular LightGBM library from Microsoft to implement both techniques on a test dataset. LightGBM is a framework for gradient boosting that incorporates multiple tree-based learning algorithms.

For this section, we will follow a typical best-practice approach using Azure Machine Learning and perform the following steps:

1. Register the dataset in Azure.
2. Create a remote compute cluster.
3. Implement a configurable training script.
4. Run the training script on the compute cluster.
5. Log and collect the dataset, parameters, and performance.
6. Register the trained model.

Before we start with this exciting approach, we'll take a quick look at why we chose LightGBM as a tool for training bagged and boosted tree ensembles.

LightGBM in a nutshell

LightGBM uses many optimizations of classical tree-based ensemble techniques to provide excellent performance on both categorical and continuous features. The latter is profiled using a histogram-based approach and converted into discrete bins of optimal splits, which reduces memory consumption and speeds up training. This makes LightGBM faster and more memory efficient than other boosting libraries that use pre-sorted algorithms for computing splits, and hence is a great choice for large datasets.

Another optimization in LightGBM is that trees are grown vertically, leaf after leaf, whereas other similar libraries grow trees horizontally, layer after layer. In a leaf-wise algorithm, the newly added leaf always has the largest decrease in loss. This means that these algorithms tend to achieve less loss compared to level-wise algorithms. However, greater depth also results in overfitting, and therefore you must carefully tune the maximum depth of each tree. Overall, LightGBM produces great results using default parameters on a large set of applications.

In *Chapter 7, Advanced Feature Extraction with NLP*, we learned a lot about categorical feature embedding and extracting semantic meanings from textual features. We looked at common techniques for embedding nominal categorical variables, such as label encoding and one-hot encoding, and others. However, to optimize the split criterion in tree-based learners for categorical variables, there are better encodings to produce optimal splits. Therefore, we don't encode categorical variables at all in this section, but simply tell LightGBM which of the variables used are categorical.

One last thing to mention is that LightGBM can take advantage of GPU acceleration, and training can be parallelized both in a data-parallel or model-parallel way. We will learn more about distributed training in *Chapter 12, Distributed Machine Learning on Azure*.

> **Important Note**
> LightGBM is a great choice for a tree-based ensemble model, especially for very large datasets.

We will use LightGBM with the `lgbm` namespace throughout this book. We can then call different methods from the namespace directly by typing four characters less—a best-practice approach among data scientists in Python. Let's see a simple example:

```
import lightgbm as lgbm
# Construct a LGBM dataset
lgbm.Dataset(..)
# Train a LGBM predictor
clf = lgbm.train(..)
```

What is interesting to note is that all algorithms are trained via the `lgbm.train()` method and we use different parameters to specify the algorithm, application type, and loss function, as well as additional hyperparameters for each algorithm. LightGBM supports multiple decision tree-based ensemble models for bagging and boosting. These are the algorithm options that you can choose from, along with their names, to identify them for the boosting parameter:

- `gbdt`: Traditional gradient boosting decision tree
- `rf`: Random forest
- `dart`: Dropouts meet multiple additive regression trees
- `goss`: Gradient-based one-side sampling

The first two options, namely, *gradient boosting decision tree* (`gbdt`), which is the default choice of LightGBM, and *random forest* (`rf`), are classical implementations of the boosting and bagging techniques, explained in the first section of this chapter, with LightGBM-specific optimizations. The other two techniques, *dropouts meet multiple additive regression trees* (`dart`) and *gradient-based one-side sampling* (`goss`), are specific to LightGBM and provide more optimizations for better results in a trade-off for training speed.

The objective parameter—which is one of the most important parameters—specifies the application type of the model, and hence the ML problem you're trying to solve. In LightGBM, you have the following standard options, which are similar to most other decision tree-based ensemble algorithms:

- `regression`: For predicting continuous target variables
- `binary`: For binary classification tasks
- `multiclass`: For multiclass classification problems

Besides the standard choices, you can also choose between the following more specific objectives: `regression_l1`, `huber`, `fair`, `poisson`, `quantile`, `mape`, `gamma`, `cross_entropy`, and many others.

Directly related to the objective parameter of the model is the choice of loss function to measure and optimize the training performance. Here, too, LightGBM gives us the default options that are also available in most other boosting libraries, which we can specify via the metric parameter:

- `mae`: Mean absolute error
- `mse`: Mean squared error
- `binary_logloss`: Loss for binary classification
- `multi_logloss`: Loss for multi-classification

Apart from these loss metrics, other metrics are supported as well, such as `rmse`, `quantile`, `mape`, `huber`, `fair`, `poisson`, and many others. In our classification scenario, we will choose the `dart` algorithm with the `binary` objective and `binary_logloss` metric.

> **Important Note**
>
> You can also use LightGBM as a scikit-learn estimator. To do so, call the `LGBMModel`, `LGBMClassifier`, or `LGBMRegressor` model from the `lightgbm` namespace. However, the latest features are typically only available through the LightGBM interface.

Now, knowing how to use LightGBM, we can start with the implementation of the data preparation and authoring script.

Preparing the data

In this section, we will read and prepare the data and register the cleaned data as a new dataset in Azure Machine Learning. This will allow us to access the data from any compute target connected with the workspace without the need to manually copy data around, mount disks, or set up connections to datastores. This was discussed in detail in *Chapter 4*, *Ingesting Data and Managing Datasets*. All the setup, scheduling, and operations will be done from an authoring environment—a *Jupyter notebook*.

For the classification example, we will use the *Titanic dataset*, a popular dataset for ML practitioners to predict the binary survival probability (*survived* or *not survived*) for each passenger on the Titanic. The features of this dataset describe the passengers and contain the following attributes: passenger ID, class, name, sex, age, number of siblings or spouse on the ship, number of children or parents on the ship, ticket identification number, fare, cabin number, and embarked port.

> **Important Note**
>
> The details about this dataset, as well as the complete preprocessing pipeline, can be found in the source code that comes with this book.

Without knowing any more details, we'll roll up our sleeves and set up the workspace and start experimentation:

1. We import `Workspace` and `Experiment` from `azureml.core` and specify the name `titanic-lgbm` for this experiment:

```
from azureml.core import Workspace, Experiment
ws = Workspace.from_config()
exp = Experiment(workspace=ws, name="titanic-lgbm")
```

2. Next, we load the dataset using pandas, and start cleaning and preprocessing the data:

```python
import pandas as pd
# Read the data
df = pd.read_csv('data/titanic.csv')

# Prepare the data
df.drop(['PassengerId'], axis=1, inplace=True)

df.loc[df['Sex'] == 'female', 'Sex'] = 0
df.loc[df['Sex'] == 'male', 'Sex'] = 1
df['Sex'] = df['Sex'].astype('int8')

embarked_encoder = LabelEncoder()
embarked_encoder.fit(df['Embarked'].fillna('Null'))
df['Embarked'].fillna('Null', inplace=True)
df['Embarked'] = embarked_encoder.transform(
    df['Embarked'])

df.drop(['Name', 'Ticket', 'Cabin'],
    axis=1,
    inplace=True)
```

In the preceding example, we load the data from a CSV file, remove unused columns, replaced the values of the Sex feature with labels 0 and 1, and encode the categorical values of the Embarked features with labels.

3. Next, we write a small utility function, df_to_dataset(), which will help us to store pandas DataFrames and register and persist them as Azure datasets, in order to reuse them with ease anywhere in the Azure Machine Learning environment:

```python
def df_to_dataset(ws, df, name):
    datastore = ws.get_default_datastore()
    dataset = Dataset.Tabular.register_pandas_dataframe(
        df, datastore, name)
    return dataset
```

First, we retrieve a reference to the default datastore of our ML workspace—this is the Azure Blob storage that was created when we first set up the workspace. Then, we use a helper function to upload the dataset to this default datastore and reference it as a tabular dataset.

4. Next, we use the newly created helper function to register the pandas DataFrame as a dataset with the name `titanic_cleaned`:

```
# Register the data
df_to_dataset(ws, df, 'titanic_cleaned')
```

5. Once the dataset is registered in Azure, it can be accessed anywhere in the Azure Machine Learning workspace. If we now go to the UI and click on the **Datasets** menu, we will find the `titanic_cleaned` dataset. In the UI, we can also easily inspect and preview the data, as shown in the following screenshot:

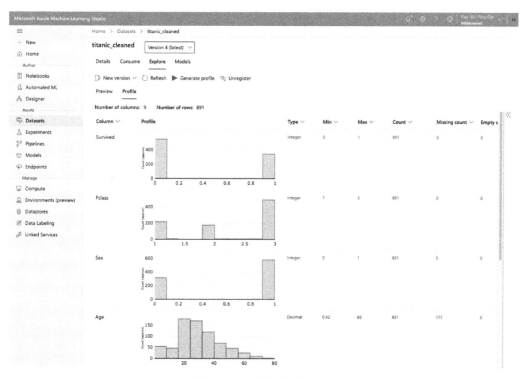

Figure 9.5 – Titanic dataset

One thing worth mentioning is that we will first encode categorical variables to integers using label encoding, but later tell LightGBM which variables contain categorical information in the numeric columns. This will help LightGBM to treat these columns differently when computing the histogram and optimal parameter splits.

The benefit of having the dataset registered is that we can now simply pass the data to a training script or access it from any Python interpreter from within Azure Machine Learning Let's continue with the training example and create a training and execution environment for LightGBM.

Setting up the compute cluster and execution environment

Before we can start training the LightGBM classifier, we need to set up our training cluster and a training environment with all the required Python libraries. For this chapter, we choose a CPU cluster with up to four nodes of the type STANDARD_D2_V2:

1. Let's write a small helper function that lets us retrieve or create a training cluster with a specified name and configuration. We take advantage of ComputeTargetException, which is thrown if a cluster with a specified name was not found:

```
def get_aml_cluster(ws, cluster_name,
                    vm_size='STANDARD_D2_V2',
                    max_nodes=4):
    try:
        cluster = ComputeTarget(
            workspace=ws, name=cluster_name)
    except ComputeTargetException:
        config = AmlCompute.provisioning_configuration(
            vm_size=vm_size, max_nodes=max_nodes)
        cluster = ComputeTarget.create(
            ws, cluster_name, config)
    return cluster
```

We have already seen the ingredients of this script in the previous chapters, where we called AmlCompute.provisioning_configuration() to provision a new cluster. It is extremely helpful that you can define all your infrastructure within your authoring environment.

2. Let's retrieve or create a new training cluster:

```
# Create or get training cluster
aml_cluster = get_aml_cluster(ws,
                              cluster_name="cpu-cluster")
aml_cluster.wait_for_completion(show_output=True)
```

3. Next, we want to do the same for our training environment and Python configuration. We implement a small get_run_config() function to return a remote execution environment with a Python configuration. This will be used to configure all the required Python packages for the training script:

```
def get_run_config(target, packages=None):
    packages = packages or []
    packages += ['azureml-defaults']
    config = RunConfiguration()
    config.target = target
    config.environment.python.conda_dependencies = \
        CondaDependencies.create(pip_packages=packages)
    return config
```

In the preceding script, we define RunConfiguration with the required packages for Azure Machine Learning such as azureml-defaults, and custom Python packages.

4. Next, we use this function to configure a Python image with all the required pip packages, including lightgbm:

```
# Create a remote run configuration
lgbm_config = get_run_config(aml_cluster, [
    'numpy', 'pandas', 'matplotlib', 'seaborn',
    'scikit-learn', 'joblib', 'lightgbm'
])
```

The two functions used in the preceding snippets are very useful. The longer you work with Azure Machine Learning, the more abstractions you will build to easily interact with the Azure Machine Learning service.

Using the custom run configuration and custom Python packages, Azure Machine Learning will set up a Docker image and automatically register it in the *container registry*, as soon as we schedule a job using this run configuration. Let's first construct the training script and then schedule it on the cluster.

Building a LightGBM classifier

Now that we have the dataset ready, and we've set up the environment and cluster for the training of the LightGBM classification model, we can set up the training script. The code from the preceding section was written in a Jupyter notebook. The following code in this section will now be written and stored in a Python file called `train_lgbm.py`. We will start building the classifier using the following steps:

1. First, we configure the run and extract the workspace configuration from the run. This should already look familiar as we have done this for almost every script that we have been scheduling on Azure Machine Learning so far:

```
from azureml.core import Dataset, Run
run = Run.get_context()
ws = run.experiment.workspace
```

2. Next, we set up an argument parser to parse command-line parameters into LightGBM parameters. We start with a handful of parameters but could easily add all available parameters and default values:

```
parser.add_argument('--data', type=str)
parser.add_argument('--boosting', type=str)
parser.add_argument('--learning-rate', type=float)
parser.add_argument('--drop-rate', type=float)
args = parser.parse_args()
```

> **Important Note**
>
> We recommend making your training scripts configurable. Use `argparse` to define datasets, input parameters, and default values. If you stick to this convention, all your model parameters will automatically be tracked in your Azure Machine Learning experiment. Another benefit is that you will later be able to tune the hyperparameters without changing a line of code in your training script.

3. Then, we can reference the cleaned dataset from the input argument and load it to memory using the `to_pandas_dataframe()` method:

```
# Get a dataset by id
dataset = Dataset.get_by_id(ws, id=args.data)
# Load a TabularDataset into pandas DataFrame
df = dataset.to_pandas_dataframe()
```

4. Having loaded the dataset as a pandas DataFrame, we can now start splitting the training data into training and validation sets. We will also split the target variable, Survived, from the training dataset into its own variable:

```
y = df.pop('Survived')
# Split into training and testing set
X_train, X_test, y_train, y_test = train_test_split(
    df, y, test_size=0.2, random_state=42)
```

5. Next, we tell LightGBM about categorical features, which are already transformed into numeric variables, but need special treatment to compute the optimal split values:

```
categories = ['Alone', 'Sex', 'Pclass', 'Embarked']
```

6. Next, we create the actual LightGBM training and test sets from the pandas DataFrames:

```
# Create training set
train_data = lgbm.Dataset(data=X_train, label=y_train,
    categorical_feature=categories, free_raw_data=False)
# Create testing set
test_data = lgbm.Dataset(data=X_test, label=y_test,
    categorical_feature=categories, free_raw_data=False)
```

In contrast to scikit-learn, we cannot work directly with pandas DataFrames in LightGBM but need to use a wrapper class, lgbm.Dataset. This will give us access to all required optimizations and features, such as distributed training, optimization for sparse data, and meta-information about categorical features.

7. Having parsed the command-line arguments, we pass them into a parameter dictionary, which will then be passed to the LightGBM training method:

```
lgbm_params = {
    'application': 'binary',
    'metric': 'binary_logloss',
    'learning_rate': args.learning_rate,
    'boosting': args.boosting,
    'drop_rate': args.drop_rate,
}
```

8. All parameters that are passed through command-line arguments are automatically logged in Azure Machine Learning. However, if you want programmatic access to the model parameters or to display them in the experiment overview in Azure Machine Learning, we can log them in the experiment. This will attach all the parameters to each run and make them available as parameter values in Azure Machine Learning. This means that we can later sort and filter the experiment runs by model parameters:

```
for k, v in params.items():
    run.log(k, v)
```

Gradient boosting is an iterative optimization approach with a variable number of iterations and an optional early stopping criterion. Therefore, we also want to log all metrics for each iteration of the training script. Throughout this book, we will use a similar technique for all ML frameworks—namely, using a callback function that logs all available metrics to your Azure Machine Learning workspace. Let's write such a function using LightGBM's specification for custom callbacks.

9. Here, we create a callback object, which iterates over all the evaluation results and logs them for the run:

```
def azure_ml_callback(run):
    def callback(env):
        if env.evaluation_result_list:
            for data_name, eval_name, result, _ in \
                env.evaluation_result_list:
                run.log("%s (%s)" % (eval_name,
                                    data_name), result)
    callback.order = 10
    return callback
```

10. After we have set the parameters for the LightGBM predictor, we can configure the training and validation procedure using the lgbm.train() method. We need to supply all arguments, parameters, and callbacks:

```
clf = lgbm.train(train_set=train_data,
                 params=lgbm_params,
                 valid_sets=[train_data, test_data],
                 valid_names=['train', 'val'],
                 num_boost_round=args.num_boost_round,
                 callbacks = [azure_ml_callback(run)])
```

What's great about the preceding code is that by supplying the generic callback function, all training and validation scores will be logged to Azure automatically. Hence, we can follow the training iterations in real time, either in the UI or via the API—for example, inside a Jupyter widget that automatically collects all run information.

11. In order to evaluate the final training score, we use the trained classifier to predict a couple of default classification scores, such as `accuracy`, `precision`, and `recall`, as well as the combined `f1` score:

```
y_pred = clf.predict(X_test)
run.log("accuracy (test)", accuracy_score(y_test,
                                          y_pred))
run.log("precision (test)", precision_score(y_test,
                                            y_pred))
run.log("recall (test)", recall_score(y_test, y_pred))
run.log("f1 (test)", f1_score(y_test, y_pred))
```

We could already run the script and see all the metrics and the performance of the model in Azure. But this was just the start – we want more!

12. Let's compute feature importance and track a plot of it and run it in Azure Machine Learning. We can do this in a few lines of code:

```
fig = plt.figure()
ax = plt.subplot(111)
lgbm.plot_importance(clf, ax=ax)
run.log_image("feature importance", plot=fig)
```

Once this snippet is added to the training script, each training run will also store a feature importance plot. This is helpful to see how different metrics influence feature importance.

13. There is one more step we would like to add. Whenever the training script runs, we want to upload the trained model and register it in the model registry. By doing so, we can later take any training run and manually or automatically deploy the model to a container service. However, this can only be done by saving the training artifacts of each run:

```
import joblib
joblib.dump(clf, 'outputs/lgbm.pkl')
run.upload_file('lgbm.pkl', 'outputs/lgbm.pkl')
```

```
run.register_model(model_name='lgbm_titanic',
    model_path='lgbm.pkl')
```

In the preceding snippet, we use the joblib package that originally was part of scikit-learn to save the classifier to disk. We then register the exported model as a LightGBM model in Azure Machine Learning.

That's it – we have written the whole training script. It's not extremely long, it's not super-complicated. The trickiest part is understanding how to pick some of the parameters of LightGBM and understanding gradient boosting in general—and that's why we dedicated the first half of the chapter to that topic. Let's now fire up the cluster and submit the training script.

Scheduling the training script on the Azure Machine Learning cluster

We are logically jumping back to the authoring environment – the Jupyter notebook. The code from the previous section is stored as a train_lgbm.py file, and we'll now get ready to submit it to the cluster. One great thing is that we made the training script configurable via command-line arguments, so we can tune the base parameters of the LightGBM model using CLI arguments. In the following steps, we will configure the authoring script to execute the training process:

1. Let's define the parameters for this model—we will use dart, with a standard learning rate of 0.01 and a dropout rate of 0.15. We also pass the dataset as a named parameter to the training script:

```
script_params = [
  '--data', ds.as_named_input('titanic'),
  '--boosting', 'dart',
  '--learning-rate', '0.01',
  '--drop-rate', '0.15',
]
```

We specified the boosting method, dart. As we learned in the previous section, this technique performs very well but is not extremely performant and is a bit slower than the other options—gbdt, rf, and goss.

> **Important Note**
>
> This is also the same way that hyperparameters are passed by HyperOpt—the hyperparameter tuning tool in Azure Machine Learning—to the training script. We will learn a lot more about this in *Chapter 11, Hyperparameter Tuning and Automated Machine Learning.*

2. Next, we can pass the parameters to `ScriptRunConfig` and kick off the training script:

```
from azureml.core import ScriptRunConfig
src = ScriptRunConfig(
    source_directory=os.getcwd(),
    script='train_lightgbm.py',
    run_config= lgbm_config
    arguments=script_params)
```

In the preceding code, we specify the file of our classifier, which is stored relative to the current authoring script. Azure Machine Learning will upload the training script to the default datastore and make it available on all cluster nodes that run the script.

3. Finally, let's submit the run configuration and execute the training script:

```
from azureml.widgets import RunDetails
run = exp.submit(src)
RunDetails(run).show()
```

The `RunDetails` method gives us an interactive widget with real-time logs of the remote computing service. We can see the cluster getting initialized and scaled up, the Docker images getting built and registered, and ultimately, also the training script logs.

> **Tip**
>
> If you prefer other methods over an interactive Jupyter widget, you can also trail the logs using `run.wait_for_completion(show_output=True)` or `print(run.get_portal_url())` to get the URL to the experiment to run in Azure.

4. Let's now switch over to the Azure Machine Learning UI and look for the run in the experiment. Once we click on it, we can navigate to the **Metrics** section and find an overview of all our logged metrics. You can see in the following *Figure 9.6* how metrics that are logged multiple times with the same name get converted into vectors and displayed as line charts:

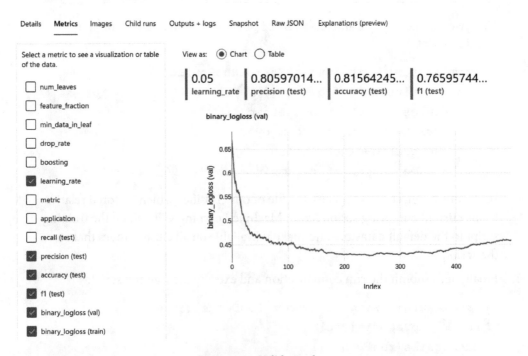

Figure 9.6 – Validation loss

Then, click on the **Images** section. When we do so, we are presented with the feature importance figure that we created in the training script. The following *Figure 9.7* shows how this looks in the Azure Machine Learning UI:

Details   Metrics   **Images**   Child runs   Outputs + logs   Snapshot   Raw JSON   Explanations (preview)

feature importance

Select an image.

☑ feature importance

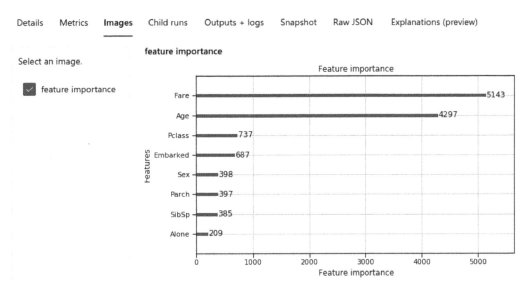

Figure 9.7 – Feature importance

We saw how you can train a LightGBM classifier in Azure Machine Learning, taking advantage of an autoscaling Azure Machine Learning compute cluster. Logging metrics, figures, and parameters keeps all information about the training run in a single place. Together with saving snapshots of the training script, outputs, logs, and the trained model, this is invaluable for any professional, large-scale ML project.

What you should remember from this chapter is that gradient boosted trees are a very performant and scalable classical ML approach, with many great libraries, and support for distributed learning and GPU acceleration. LightGBM is one alternative offered by Microsoft that is well embedded in both the Microsoft and open source ecosystem. If you are looking for a classical, fast, and understandable ML model, our advice is to go with LightGBM.

Summary

In this chapter, you learned how to build a classical ML model in Azure Machine Learning.

You learned about decision trees, a popular technique for various classification and regression problems. The main strengths of decision trees are that they require little data preparation as they work well on categorical data and different data distributions. Another important benefit is their interpretability, which is especially important for business decisions and users. This helps you to understand when a decision tree-based ensemble predictor is appropriate to use.

However, we also learned about a set of weaknesses, especially regarding overfitting and poor generalization. Luckily, tree-based ensemble techniques such as bagging (bootstrap aggregation) and boosting help to overcome these problems. While bagging has popular methods such as random forests that parallelize very well, boosting, especially gradient boosting, has efficient implementations, including XGBoost and LightGBM.

You implemented and trained a decision tree-based classifier in Azure Machine Learning using the LightGBM library. LightGBM is developed at Microsoft and delivers great performance and training time through a couple of optimizations. These optimizations help LightGBM to keep a small memory footprint, even for larger datasets, and yield better losses with fewer iterations. You used Azure Machine Learning not only to execute your training script but also to track your model's training performance and the final classifier.

In the following chapter, we will take a look at some popular deep learning techniques and how to train them using Azure Machine Learning.

10
Training Deep Neural Networks on Azure

In the previous chapter, we learned how to train and score classical ML models using non-parametric tree-based ensemble methods. While these methods work well on many small- and medium-sized datasets that contain categorical variables, they don't generalize well on large datasets.

In this chapter, we will train complex parametric models using **deep learning** (**DL**) for even better generalization with very large datasets. This will help you understand **deep neural networks** (**DNNs**), how to train and use them, and when they perform better than traditional models.

First, we will provide a short and practical overview of why and when DL works well and focus on understanding the general principles and rationale rather than the theoretical approach. This will help you to assess which use cases and datasets need DL and how it works in general.

Then, we will look at one of the popular application domains for DL – computer vision. We will train a simple **convolutional neural network (CNN)** model for image classification using the Azure Machine Learning service and additional Azure infrastructure. We will compare the performance to a model that has been fine-tuned on a pre-trained **residual neural network (ResNet)** model. This will set you up to train your models from scratch, fine-tune existing models for your application domain, and overcome situations where not enough training data is available.

In this chapter, we will cover the following topics:

- Introduction to Deep Learning
- Training a CNN for image classification

Technical requirements

In this chapter, we will use the following Python libraries and versions to create decision tree-based ensemble classifiers:

- `azureml-core 1.34.0`
- `azureml-sdk 1.34.0`
- `numpy 1.19.5`
- `pandas 1.3.2`
- `scikit-learn 0.24.2`

Similar to the previous chapters, you can execute this code using either a local Python interpreter or a notebook environment hosted in Azure Machine Learning.

All the code examples in this chapter can be found in this book's GitHub repository: `https://github.com/PacktPublishing/Mastering-Azure-Machine-Learning-Second-Edition/tree/main/chapter10`.

Introduction to Deep Learning

Deep learning has revolutionized the ML domain recently and is constantly outperforming classical statistical approaches, and even humans, in various tasks such as image classification, object detection, segmentation, speech transcription, text translation, text understanding, sales forecasting, and much more. In contrast to classical models, DL models use many millions of parameters, parameter sharing, optimization techniques, and implicit feature extraction to outperform all previously hand-crafted feature detectors and ML models when trained with enough data.

In this section, we will help you understand the basics of neural networks and the path to training deeper models with more parameters, better generalization, and hence better performance. This will help you understand how DL-based approaches work, as well as why and when they make sense for certain domains and datasets. If you are already an expert in DL, feel free to skip this section and go directly to the practical examples in the *Training a CNN for image classification* section.

Why Deep Learning?

Many traditional optimization, classification, and forecasting processes have worked well over the past decades using classical ML approaches, such as k-nearest neighbor, linear and logistic regression, naïve Bayes, **support vector machines** (**SVMs**), tree-based ensemble models, and others. They worked well on various types of data (transactional, time series, operational, and so on) and data types (binary, numerical, and categorical) for small- to mid-sized datasets.

However, in some domains, data generation has exploded, and classical ML models couldn't achieve better performance even with an increasing amount of training data. This especially affected the domains of computer vision and NLP around late 2010. That's when researchers had a breakthrough with neural networks – also called **multilayer perceptrons** (**MLPs**) – a technique that was used in the late 80s to capture the vast number of features in a large image dataset by using multiple nested layers.

The following chart captures this idea very well. While traditional ML approaches work very well on small- and medium-sized datasets, their performance usually does not improve with more training data. However, DL models are massive parametric models that can capture a vast number of details from training data. Hence, we can see that their prediction performance increases as the amount of data increases:

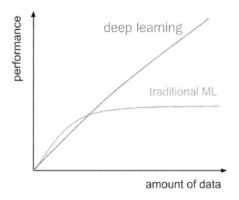

Figure 10.1 – The effectiveness of DL versus traditional ML

Traditional models often use pre-engineered features and are optimized for datasets of various data types and ranges. In the previous chapter, we saw that gradient-boosted trees perform extremely well on categorical data. However, in domains that contain highly structured data or data of variable lengths, many traditional models reach their limits. This is especially true for pixel information in two- and three-dimensional images and videos, as well as waveforms in audio data and characters and character sequences in free-text data. ML models used to process such data using complex manually tuned feature extractors, such as **histogram of oriented gradients** (**HoG**) filters, **scale-invariant feature transform** (**SIFT**) features, or **local binary patterns** (**LBPs**) – just to name a few filters in the computer vision domain.

What makes this data so complicated is that no obvious linear relationship between the input data (for example, a single pixel) and the output exists – in most cases, seeing a single pixel of an image won't help determine the brand of a car in that image. Therefore, there was an increasing need to train larger and more capable parametric models that used raw, unprocessed data as input to capture these relationships from the input pixel to make a final prediction.

It's important to understand that the need for deeper models with many more parameters comes from the vastly increasing amount of highly structured training data in specific domains, such as vision, audio, and language. These new models often have millions of parameters to capture the massive amounts of raw and augmented training data, as well as developing an internal generalized conceptual representation of the training data. Keep this in mind when choosing an ML approach for your use case.

A quick look at your training data often helps to determine whether a DL-based model is suitable for the task – given that DL models have millions of parameters to train. If your data is stored in a SQL database or CSV or Excel files, then you should probably look into classical ML approaches, such as parametric statistical (linear regression, SVM, and so on) or non-parametric (decision tree-based ensembles) approaches. If your data is so big that it doesn't fit into memory or is stored in a **Hadoop Distributed File System** (**HDFS**), blob storage, or a file storage server, then you could use a DL-based approach.

From neural networks to deep learning

The foundation of neural networks and hence today's DL-based approaches – the **perceptron** – is a concept that is over half a century old and was developed in the 1950s. In this section, we will take a look at the basics, and work our way back to **MLPs** – also called **artificial neural networks** (**ANNs**) – and **CNNs** in the 1980s, and then to **DNNs** and DL in the last decade. This will help you understand the foundational concepts of neural networks and hence DL, as well as how model architectures and training techniques have evolved over the last century into the state-of-the-art techniques we are using today.

The perceptron – a classifier from the 50s

Perceptrons are the foundational building blocks of today's neural networks and are modeled on cells in the human brain (so-called **neurons**). They are simple non-linear functions consisting of two components: a weighted sum of all the inputs and an activation function that fires if the output is larger than the specified threshold. While this analogy of a neuron is a great way to model how a brain works, it is a poor model to understand how the input signal is transformed into its output.

Rather than neurons in the brain, we prefer a much simpler, non-biological approach to explain the perceptron, MLPs, and CNNs – namely, a simple geometric approach. When simplified, this method requires you to only understand the two-dimensional line equation. Once you understand the basics in two dimensions, the concept can be extended to multiple dimensions, where the line becomes a plane or hyperplane in a higher-dimensional feature space.

If we look at a single perceptron, it describes a **weighted sum** of its inputs plus constant bias with an **activation function**. Let's break down the two components of the perceptron. Do you know what is also described as a weighted sum of its inputs plus bias? Right, the line equation:

$$y = k \cdot x + b$$

In the preceding equation, x is the input, k is the weight, and b is the bias term. You have probably seen this equation at some point in your math curriculum. A property of this equation is that when you're inserting a point's x and y coordinates into the line equation, it yields $0 = 0$ for all the points that lie on the line. We can use this information to derive the vector form of the line equation, as follows:

$$0 = k' \cdot \begin{pmatrix} x \\ y \end{pmatrix} + \vec{b}' = f(x, y)$$

Hence, $f(x, y)$ is 0 when the point lies on the line. What happens if we insert the coordinates of a point that does not lie on the line? A good guess is that the result will be either positive or negative but certainly not 0. A property of the vector line equation is that the sign of this result describes which side of the line the point lies on. Hence, the point lies either on the left or the right-hand side of the line when $f(x, y)$ is positive or negative but not null.

To determine the side of the line, we can apply the sign function to $f(x,y)$. The sign function is often also referred to as the step function, as its output is either *1* or *-1*, hence positive or negative. The sign or step function here is our activation function and hence the second component of the perceptron. The output of the perceptron, f_p, can be written as follows:

$$f_p(x,y) = sign(k' \cdot \begin{pmatrix} x \\ y \end{pmatrix} + \vec{b'})$$

In the following chart, we can see two points, a line, and their shortest distance to the line. Both points are not lying on the line, so the line separates both points from each other. If we insert both points' coordinates into the vector line equation, then one point would result in a positive value $f(x,y)$, whereas the other point would result in a negative value $f(x,y)$:

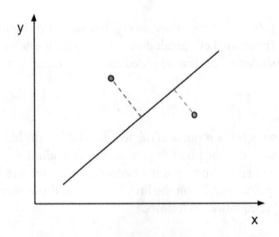

Figure 10.2 – A simple binary classifier

The result would tell us which side of the line the point lies on. This line is a geometric description of the perceptron, which is a very simple classifier. The trained perceptron is defined through the line equation (or a hyperplane in multiple dimensions), which separates a space into left and right. This line is the decision boundary for a classification, and a point is an observation. By inserting a point into the line equation and applying the step function, we return the resulting class of the observation, which is left or right, -1 or +1, or class A or B. This describes a binary classifier.

And how do we find the decision boundary? To find the optimal decision boundary, we can follow an iterative training process while using labeled training samples. First, we must initialize a random decision boundary, then compute the distance from each sample to the decision boundary and move the decision boundary into the direction that minimizes the total sum of distances. The optimal vector to move the decision boundary is if we move it along the negative gradient, such that the distance between the point and the line reaches a minimum. By using a learning rate factor, we iterate this process a few times and end up with a perfectly aligned decision boundary, if the training samples are linearly separable. This process is called **gradient descent**, where we iteratively modify the classifier weights (decision boundaries, in this example) to find the optimal boundary with minimal error.

The multilayer perceptron

A perceptron describes a simple classifier whose decision boundary is a line (or hyperplane) that's been defined through the weighted inputs. However, instead of using a single classifier, we can simply increase the number of neurons, which will result in multiple decision boundaries, as shown in the following chart:

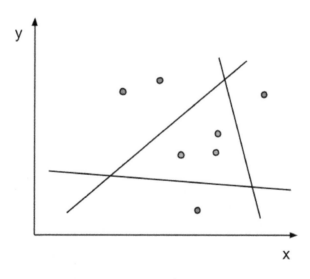

Figure 10.3 – Combining multiple perceptrons

Each neuron describes a decision boundary and hence will have separate weights and a separate output – left or right of the decision boundary. By stacking multiple neurons in layers, we can create classifiers whose inputs are the output of the previous ones. This allows us to combine the results from multiple decision boundaries into a single output – for example, finding all the samples that are enclosed by the decision boundaries of three neurons, as shown in the preceding chart.

While a single layer of perceptrons describes a linear combination of inputs and outputs, researchers began to stack these perceptrons into multiple sequential layers, where each layer was followed by an activation function. This is called MLP, or an ANN. Using the geometric model as an analogy, you could simply stack multiple decision boundaries on complex geometric objects to create more complex decision boundaries.

> **Important Note**
> Another analogy is that the classifier's decision boundary is always a straight hyperplane, but the input samples are transformed to be linearly separated through the decision boundary.

The same geometric analogy helps us understand the layers in DL models. While the first layers of a network describe very low-level geometric features, such as straight edges and lines, the higher levels describe complicated nested combinations of these low-level features; for example, four lines build a square, five squares build a more complex shape, and a combination of those shapes looks like a human face. We just built a face detector using a three-layer neural network.

The Google DeepDream experiment is a fantastic example of this analogy. In the following figure, we can visualize how three layers of different depths in a pre-trained DNN represent features in an image of a cloudy sky. The layers are extracted from the beginning, middle, and end of a DNN and transform the input image to minimize the loss of each layer. Here, we can see how the earlier layer focuses mostly on lines and edges (left), whereas the middle layer sees abstract shapes (middle), and the last layer activates on very specific high-level features in the image (right):

Figure 10.4 – DeepDream – minimizing loss for the layers of a DNN

Next, let's look at CNNs.

CNNs

Using multiple high-dimensional hyperplane equations, where each output feeds into each input of the following layer, requires a very large number of parameters. While a high number of parameters is required to model a massive amount of complex training data, a so-called fully connected neural network is not the best way to describe these connections. So, what's the problem?

In a fully connected network, each output is fed to each neuron of the consecutive layer as input. In each neuron, we require a weight for each input, so we need as many weights as there are input dimensions. This number quickly explodes when we start stacking multiple layers of perceptrons. Another problem is that the network cannot generalize because it learns all the individual weights separately for each dimension.

In the 1980s, CNNs were invented to solve these problems. Their purpose was to reduce the number of connections and parameters on a single layer to a fixed set of parameters, independent of the number of input dimensions. The parameters of a layer are now shared within all the inputs. The idea of this approach comes from signal processing, where filters are applied to a signal through a convolution operation. Convolution means applying a single set of weights, such as a window function, to multiple regions of the input and later summing up all the signal responses of the filter for each location.

This was the same idea for the convolution layers of CNNs. By using a fixed-sized filter that is convolved with the input, we can greatly reduce the number of parameters for each layer and add more nested layers to the network. By using a so-called pooling layer, we can also reduce the image size and apply filters to a downscaled version of the input. Let's take a look at the popular layers that are used for building CNNs:

- **Fully connected (FC)**: The FC layer is a layer of fully connected neurons, as described in the previous section about perceptrons – it connects every output from the previous layer with a neuron. In DNN, FC layers are often used at the end of the network to combine all the spatially distributed activations of the previous convolution layers. The FC layers also have the largest number of parameters in a model (usually around 90%).

- **Convolution**: A convolution layer consists of spatial (often two-dimensional) filters that are convolved along the spatial dimensions and summed up along the depth dimension of the input. Due to weight sharing, they are much more efficient than fully connected layers and have a lot fewer parameters.

- **Pooling**: Convolution layers are often followed by a pooling layer to reduce the spatial dimension of the volume for the next filter – this is the equivalent of a subsampling operation. The pooling operation itself has no learnable parameters. Most of the time, **max pooling** layers are used in DL models due to their simple gradient computation. Another popular choice is **avg pooling**, which is mostly used as a classifier at the end of a network.

- **Normalization**: In modern DNNs, normalization layers are often used to stabilize gradients throughout the network. Due to the unbounded behavior of some activation functions, filter responses have to be normalized. A commonly used normalization technique is **batch normalization**.

Now that we understand the main components of CNNs, we can look into how these models were stacked even deeper to improve generalization and hence improve the prediction's performance.

From CNNs to DL

The perceptron from the 50s, as well as ANNs and CNNs from the 80s, build the foundation for all the DL models that are used today. By stabilizing the gradients during the training process, researchers could overcome the exploding and vanishing gradients problem and build deeper models. This was achieved by using additional normalization layers, rectified linear activation, auxiliary losses, and residual connections.

Deeper models have more learnable parameters – often well over 100 million parameters – so they can find higher-level patterns and learn more complex transformations. However, to train deeper models, you must also use more training data. Therefore, companies and researchers built massive labeled datasets (such as ImageNet) to feed these models with training data.

This development process was facilitated by the availability of cheap parallelizable compute in the form of GPUs and cloud computing. Training these deep models quickly went from months to days to hours within a couple of years. Today, we can train a typical DNN in under an hour with a highly parallelized compute infrastructure.

A lot of research also went into new techniques for stacking layers, from very deep networks with skip connections, as in ResNet152, to networks with parallel layer groups, as in GoogLeNet. A combination of both layer types led to extremely efficient network architectures such as SqueezeNet and Inception. New layer types such as LSTM, GRU, and attention enabled significantly better prediction performance, while the GAN and transform models created entirely new ways to train and optimize models.

All these advances helped make DL what it has become today – a ubiquitous ML technique that, given enough training data, can outperform traditional ML models and often even humans in most prediction tasks. Today, DL is applied to almost any domain where there is sufficient data at hand.

DL versus traditional ML

Let's look at the main differences between classical ML- and DL-based approaches and find out what DL models can do with so many more parameters and how they benefit from them.

If we look at the image or audio processing domain before 2012, we will see that ML models were not usually trained on the raw data itself. Instead, the raw data went through a manually crafted feature extractor and converted into a lower-dimensional feature space. When dealing with images of 256 x 256 x 3 dimensions (RGB) – which corresponds to a 196,608-dimensional feature space – and converting these into, say, a 2,048-dimensional feature embedding as input for the ML models, we greatly reduce the computational requirements for these models. The feature extractors for image and audio features often use a convolution operator and a specific filter (such as an edge detector, blob detector, spike/dip detector, and so on). However, the filter is usually constructed manually.

The classical ML models that have been developed in the past 50+ years are still the ones we are successfully using today. Among those are tree-based ensemble techniques, linear and logistic regression, SVMs, and MLPs. The MLP model is also known as a fully connected neural network with hidden layers and still serves as a classification or regression head in some of the early DL architectures.

The following diagram shows the typical pipeline of a classical ML approach in the computer vision domain:

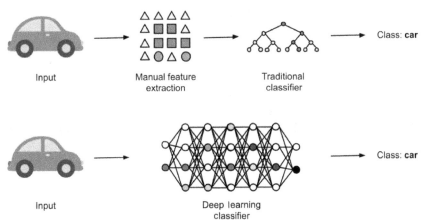

Figure 10.5 – Traditional ML classifier

First, the raw data is converted into a lower-dimensional feature embedding using hand-crafted image filters (SIFT, SURF, HoG, LBPs, Haar filters, and so on). Then, feature embedding is used to train an ML model; for example, a multi-layer, fully connected neural network or decision-tree classifier, as shown in the preceding diagram.

When it is difficult for a human being to express a relationship between an input image and an output label in simple rules, then it is most likely also difficult for a classical computer vision and ML approach to find such rules. DL-based approaches perform a lot better in these cases. The reason for this is that DL models are trained on raw input data instead of manually extracted features. Since convolution layers are the same as randomized and trained image filters, these filters for feature extraction are implicitly learned by the network.

The following diagram shows a DL approach to image classification, which is similar to the previous diagram for the classical ML approach:

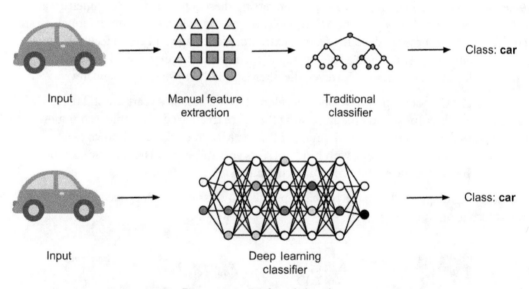

Figure 10.6 – DL-based classifier

As we can see, the raw input data of the image is fed directly to the network, which outputs the final image label. This is why we often refer to a DL model as an end-to-end model – because it creates an end-to-end transformation between the input data (literally, the raw pixel values) and the model's output.

As shown in the preceding diagram, the DL-based model is an end-to-end model that learns both the feature extractor and the classifier in a single model. However, we often refer to the last fully connected layer.

> **Important Note**
>
> Look at the type of data before choosing your ML model. If you are dealing with images, video, audio, time series, language, or text, you may wish to use a DL model or feature extractor for embedding, clustering, classification, or regression. If you are working with operational or business data, then a classic ML approach would be a better fit.

Using traditional ML with DL-based feature extractors

In many cases, especially when you have small datasets, not enough compute resources, or knowledge to train end-to-end DL models, you can also reuse a pre-trained DL model as a feature extractor. This can be done by loading a pre-trained model and performing a forward pass until the classification/regression head. It returns a multi-dimensional embedding (a so-called latent space representation) that you can directly plug into a classical ML model.

Here is an example of such a hybrid approach. We are using the `IncpetionV3` model as a feature extractor, pre-trained on the `imagenet` data. The DL model is only used to transform the raw input image data into a lower-dimensional feature representation. Then, an SVM model is trained on top of the image features. Let's look at the source code for this example:

```
import numpy as np
from tensorflow.keras.applications import InceptionV3


def extract_features(img_data, IMG_SIZE):
    IMG_SHAPE = (IMG_SIZE, IMG_SIZE, 3)
    model = InceptionV3(input_shape=IMG_SHAPE,
                        include_top=False,
                        weights='imagenet',
                        pooling='avg')
    predictions = model.predict(img_data)
    return np.squeeze(predictions)
```

```
labels = [] # loaded previously
features = extract_features(image_data)


X_train, X_test, y_train, y_test = train_test_split(
    features, labels)


from sklearn.svm import SVC
clf = SVC(kernel='linear', C=1)
clf.fit(X_train, y_train)
```

In the preceding code, we used TensorFlow to load the `InceptionV3` model with the ImageNet-based weights but without any classification or regression head. This is achieved by setting the `include_top` property to `False`. Then, we squeezed the output of the prediction – the image's latent representation – into a single vector. Finally, we trained an SVM on the image features using scikit-learn and a default train/test split.

We started with the classical approach, where feature extraction and ML were separated into two steps. However, the filters in the classical approach were hand-crafted and applied directly to the raw input data. In a DL approach, we implicitly learn the feature extraction.

Training a CNN for image classification

Now that we have a good understanding of why and when to use DL models, we can start to implement one and run it using Azure Machine Learning. We will start with a task that DL performed very well with over the past years – computer vision, or more precisely, image classification. If you feel that this is too easy for you, you can replace the actual training script with any other computer vision technique and follow along with the steps in this section:

1. First, we will power up an Azure Machine Learning compute instance, which will serve as our Jupyter Notebook authoring environment. First, we will write a training script and execute it in the authoring environment to verify that it works properly, checkpoints the model, and logs the training and validation metrics. We will train the model for a few epochs to validate the setup, the code, and the resulting model.

2. Next, we will try to improve the algorithm by adding data augmentation to the training script. While this seems like an easy task, I want to reiterate that this is necessary and strongly recommended for any DL-based ML approach. Image data can easily be augmented to improve generalization and therefore model scoring performance. However, through this technique, training the model will take even longer than before because more training data is being used for each epoch.

3. Now, we must move the training script from the authoring environment to a GPU cluster – a remote compute environment. We will do all this – upload the data, generate the training scripts, create the cluster, execute the training script on the cluster, and retrieve the trained model – from within the authoring environment in the Azure Machine Learning service. If you are already training ML models yourself on your server, then this section will show you how to move your training scripts to a remote execution environment and how to benefit from dynamically scalable compute (both vertically and horizontally, hence larger and more machines), auto-scaling, cheap data storage, and much more.

4. Once you have successfully trained a CNN from scratch, you will want to move on to the next level in terms of model performance and complexity. A good and recommended approach is to fine-tune pre-trained DL models rather than train them from scratch. Using this approach, we can often also use a pre-trained model from a specific task, drop the classification head (usually the last one or two layers) from the model, and reuse the feature extractor for another task by training our classification head on top of it. This is called transfer learning and is widely used for training state-of-the-art models for various domains.

Now, let's open a Jupyter notebook and start training a CNN image classifier.

Training a CNN from scratch in your notebook

Let's train a CNN on Jupyter on the Azure Machine Learning service. First, we want to simply train a model in the current authoring environment, which means we must use the compute (CPU and memory) from the compute instance. This is a standard Python/Jupyter environment, so it is no different from training an ML model on your local machine. So, let's go ahead and create a new compute instance in our Azure Machine Learning service workspace, and then open the Jupyter environment:

1. Before we begin creating our CNN model, we need some training data. As we train the ML model on the authoring computer, the data needs to be on the same machine. For this example, we will use the MNIST image dataset:

```python
import os
import urllib

os.makedirs('./data/mnist', exist_ok=True)
BASE_URL = 'http://yann.lecun.com/exdb/mnist/'

urllib.request.urlretrieve(
    BASE_URL + 'train-images-idx3-ubyte.gz',
```

```
        filename='./data/mnist/train-images.gz')
urllib.request.urlretrieve(
    BASE_URL + 'train-labels-idx1-ubyte.gz',
        filename='./data/mnist/train-labels.gz')
urllib.request.urlretrieve(
    BASE_URL + 't10k-images-idx3-ubyte.gz',
        filename='./data/mnist/test-images.gz')
urllib.request.urlretrieve(
    BASE_URL + t10k-labels-idx1-ubyte.gz',
        filename='./data/mnist/test-labels.gz')
```

In the preceding code, we loaded the training and testing data and put it in the data directory of the current environment where the code executes. In the next section, we will learn how to make the data available on any compute instance in the ML workspace.

2. Next, we must load the data, parse it, and store it in multi-dimensional NumPy arrays. We will use a helper function, load, which is defined in the accompanying source code for this chapter. After that, we must preprocess the training data by normalizing the pixel values to a range between 0 and 1:

```
DIR = './data/mnist/'
X_train = load(DIR + 'train-images.gz', False) / 255.0
X_test = load(DIR + 'test-images.gz', False) / 255.0

y_train = load(DIR + 'train-labels.gz', True) \
            .reshape(-1)
y_test = load(DIR + 'test-labels.gz', True) \
            .reshape(-1)
```

Using the reshape method, we checked that the training and testing labels are one-dimensional vectors with a single label per training and testing sample.

Once we have the training data, it is time to decide which Python framework to use to train the neural network models. While you are not limited to any specific framework in Azure Machine Learning, it is recommended you use either TensorFlow (with Keras) or PyTorch to train neural networks and DL models. TensorFlow and Keras are great choices when you're training and deploying standard production models.

> **Important Note**
>
> PyTorch is a great choice for tinkering with exotic models and custom layers
> and debugging customized models. In my opinion, PyTorch is a bit easier to get
> started with, whereas TensorFlow is more complex and mature and has a bigger
> ecosystem. In this chapter, we will use TensorFlow due to its large ecosystem,
> Keras integration, great documentation, and good support in the Azure
> Machine Learning service.

3. Having chosen an ML framework, we can start to construct a simple CNN. Let's use
   `keras` to construct a sequential model:

```
from tensorflow.keras.models import Sequential
from tensorflow.keras.layers import Conv2D, \
    MaxPooling2D, Flatten, Dense

model = Sequential()
model.add(Conv2D(filters=16,
                 kernel_size=3,
                 padding='same',
                 activation='relu',
                 input_shape=(28,28,1)))
model.add(MaxPooling2D(pool_size=2))
model.add(Conv2D(filters=32,
                 kernel_size=3,
                 padding='same',
                 activation='relu'))
model.add(MaxPooling2D(pool_size=2))
model.add(Flatten())
model.add(Dense(256, activation='relu'))
model.add(Dense(10, activation='softmax'))
```

In the preceding code, we took advantage of the `keras.Sequential` model
API to construct a simple CNN model. We went with the default initialization
of the weights and solely specified the model structure here. You can also see the
typical combination of a feature extractor until the `Flatten` layer, and the MLP
classification head outputting 10 probabilities using the `softmax` activation
function at the end.

Let's take a quick look at the model, which has, in total, `409034` parameters, as shown in the following diagram. Please note that we specifically constructed a simple CNN from a tiny image size of `28x28` grayscale images. The following diagram shows the compact structure of the model defined. Here, we can observe that the largest number of parameters is the fully connected layer after the feature extractor, which contains 98% of the parameters of the total model:

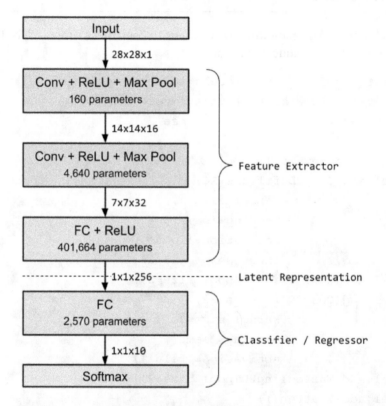

Figure 10.7 – DL model architecture

4. After defining the model structure, we need to define the `loss` metric that we are trying to optimize and specify an optimizer. The optimizer is responsible for computing the changes for all the weights per training iteration, given the total and backpropagated loss. With Keras and TensorFlow, we can easily choose a state-of-the-art optimizer and use a default metric for classification:

```
model.compile(loss='categorical_crossentropy',
              optimizer='adam',
              metrics=['accuracy'])
```

In the preceding code, we defined a `categorical_crossentropy` loss and the `adam` optimizer to train the CNN. We also tracked another metric besides the loss – `accuracy`. This makes it easier to estimate and measure the performance of the CNN during training.

5. Before we start training, we must define a model checkpoint. This is important as it allows us to pause and resume training at any given time after an epoch. Using Keras, it is quite simple to implement this, as follows:

```
from tensorflow.keras.callbacks import ModelCheckpoint

checkpoint_path = "./mnist_cnn.bin"
checkpoint_cb = ModelCheckpoint(checkpoint_path)
```

6. Finally, we can start the training locally by invoking the `fit` method on the Keras model. We must supply the training data as well as the batch size and the number of epochs (iterations) for training. We must also pass the previously created `callback` model checkpoint so that we can save the model after each epoch:

```
model.fit(X_train,
          y_train,
          batch_size=16,
          epochs=10,
          callbacks=[checkpoint_cb])
```

7. Finally, we can use the trained model of the last epoch to compute the final score on the test set:

```
from tensorflow.keras.models import load_model

model = load_model(checkpoint_path)
scores = model.evaluate(X_test, y_test, verbose=1)

print('Test loss:', scores[0])
print('Test accuracy:', scores[1])
```

In the preceding code, we can see that training a CNN on a compute instance in Azure Machine Learning is straightforward and similar to training a model on the local machine. The only difference is that we have to be sure that all the required libraries (and required versions) have been installed and that the data is available.

Generating more input data using augmentation

DL models usually have many millions of parameters to represent the model with the training set distribution. Hence, when dealing with DL, be it in custom vision using Cognitive Services, Azure Machine Learning Studio, or custom models in ML service workspaces, you should always implement data augmentation.

Data augmentation is a way of creating more training data by slightly modifying the available data and providing the modified data to the ML algorithm. Depending on the use case, this could include mirroring, translating, scaling, or skewing images, as well as changing the brightness, luminosity, or color information of images. These modifications strongly improve the generalization of the model, such as enabling better scale, translation, rotation, and transformation invariance.

The benefit of using TensorFlow and Keras is that data augmentation is a built-in capability. First, we can create an `ImageDataGenerator` object, which stores all our modifications and can generate iterators through the augmented dataset. The data augmentation techniques for this generator can be configured when the generator is being initialized. However, we want to use the generator to simply iterate through the training images without augmentation and add augmentation once we have connected all the pieces. Let's take a look:

1. Let's implement an image data generator in Keras using the `ImageDataGenerator` object:

    ```
    from tensorflow.keras.preprocessing.image import \
        ImageDataGenerator
    datagen = ImageDataGenerator()
    ```

2. Now, we can return a data iterator from the image data generator by passing the original training image data and labels to the generator. Before we sample images from the generator, we need to compute the training set statistics that will be required for further augmentations. Similar to the scikit-learn `BaseTransformer` interface, we need to call the `fit` method on the generator:

    ```
    datagen.fit(x_train)
    ```

3. Next, we must create an iterator by using the `flow` method:

    ```
    it = datagen.flow(X_train, y_train, batch_size=16)
    ```

4. If instead of loading the images into NumPy arrays beforehand, we wanted to read individual images from a folder, we could use a different generator function to do so, as shown in the following snippet:

```
it = datagen.flow_from_directory(
        directory='./data/mnist',
        target_size=(28, 28),
        batch_size=16,
        class_mode='categorical')
```

However, in our example, the training images have been combined into a single file, so we don't need to load the image data ourselves.

5. The iterator can now be used to loop through the data generator and yield new training samples with each iteration. To do so, we need to replace the `fit` function with the `fit_generator` function, which expects an iterator instead of a training dataset:

```
model.fit_generator(it,
                steps_per_epoch=256,
                epochs=10,
                callbacks=[checkpoint_cb])
```

As we can see, we can pass the same arguments for `epoch` and `callback` to the `fit_generator` function as we did to the `fit` function. The only difference is that now, we need to fix several steps per epoch so that the iterator yields new images. Once we have added augmentation methods to the generator, we could theoretically generate unlimited modifications of each training image per epoch. Hence, with this argument, we can define how many batches of data we wish to train each epoch with, which should roughly correspond to the number of training samples divided by the batch size.

Finally, we can configure the data augmentation techniques. The default image data generator supports a variety of augmentations through different arguments:

- Translation or shifts
- Horizontal or vertical flips
- Rotations
- Brightness
- Zoom

Let's go back to the image data generator and activate data augmentation techniques. Here is an example generator that is often used for data augmentation in image processing:

```
datagen = ImageDataGenerator(
            featurewise_center=True,
            featurewise_std_normalization=True,
            rotation_range=20,
            width_shift_range=0.2,
            height_shift_range=0.2,
            horizontal_flip=True)
```

By using this data generator, we can train the model with augmented image data and further improve the performance of the CNN. As we saw previously, this is a crucial and strongly recommended step in any DL training pipeline.

Let's move all the code that we have developed so far into a file called `scripts/train.py`. We will use this file in the next section to schedule and run it on a GPU cluster.

Training on a GPU cluster using Azure Machine Learning

Now that we have a training script ready, verified that the script works, and added data augmentation, we can move this training script to a more performant execution environment. In DL, many operations, such as convolutions, pooling, and general tensor operators, can benefit from parallel execution. Therefore, we will execute the training script on a GPU cluster and track its status in the authoring environment.

One benefit of using Azure Machine Learning is that we can set up and run everything in Python from the authoring environment – that is, the Jupyter notebook running on the Azure Machine Learning compute instance:

1. First, we must configure our Azure Machine Learning workspace, which is a single statement without arguments on the compute instance:

    ```
    from azureml.core.workspace import Workspace

    ws = Workspace.from_config()
    ```

2. Next, we must load or create a GPU cluster with autoscaling for the training process:

```
from azureml.core.compute import ComputeTarget, \
    AmlCompute
from azureml.core.compute_target import \
    ComputeTargetException

cluster_name = "gpu-cluster"
vm_size = "STANDARD_NC6"
max_nodes = 3

try:
    compute_target = ComputeTarget(ws,
        name=cluster_name)
    print('Found existing compute target.')
except ComputeTargetException:
    print('Creating a new compute target...')
    compute_config = \
        AmlCompute.provisioning_configuration(
            vm_size=vm_size, max_nodes=max_nodes)

    # create the cluster and wait for completion
    compute_target = ComputeTarget.create(ws,
        cluster_name, compute_config)

compute_target.wait_for_completion(show_output=True)
```

As shown in the preceding code snippet, creating a GPU cluster with autoscaling only requires a couple of lines of code within Jupyter with Azure Machine Learning. But how did we choose the VM size and the number of nodes for the GPU cluster?

In general, you can decide between the NC, ND, and NV types from the N-series VMs in Azure. A later version number (for example, v2 or v3) usually means updated hardware, hence a newer CPU and GPU, and better memory. You can think of the different N-series versions in terms of applications (*NC*, where *C* means compute; *ND*, where *D* means deep learning; and *NV*, where *V* means video). The following table will help you compare the different N-series VM types and their GPU configurations. Most machines can be scaled up to four GPUs per VM.

The following table shows an Azure VM N-series comparison:

VM type	GPU	GPU memory	TFlops (FP32)	Cost (per hour)
NC	½ Tesla K80	12 GB	2	$0.90
NCv2	1 Tesla P100	16 GB	10.6	$2.07
NCv3	1 Tesla V100	16 GB	15	$3.06
NCas_T4_v3	1 Tesla T4	16 GB	8.1	$0.526
ND	1 Tesla P40	24 GB	11.8	$2.07
NDv2	8 Tesla V100 (NVLINK)	256 GB	100	$22.032
NV	½ Tesla M60 (GRID)	8 GB	4	$1.092
NVv3	½ Tesla M60 (GRID)	8 GB	4	$1.14

Figure 10.8 – Azure VM N-series costs

The prices in the preceding table represent pay-as-you-go prices for Linux VMs in the West US 2 region for December 2021. Please note that these prices may have changed by the time you are reading this, but it should give you an indication of the different options and configurations to choose from.

To get a better understanding of the costs and performance, we can look at a typical workload for training a ResNet50 model on the ImageNet dataset. The following table, provided by Nvidia, shows that it makes sense to choose the latest GPU models as their performance increase is much better and the costs are more efficient than the older GPU models:

GPU	Training time	VM type	Cost/instance	Total cost (USD)
8X V100	6h	2 x Standard_NC24s_v3	$13.712/hour	$164.54
8X P100	18h	2 x Standard_NC24s_v2	$9.972/hour	$358.99
8X K80	38h	4 x Standard_NC24	$4.336/hour	$659.07

Figure 10.9 – GPU costs

As shown in the preceding table, the performance increase that's visible in the lower training duration for the same task pays off and results in a much lower cost for the overall task.

Hence, the STANDARD_NC6 model is a great starting point, from a pricing perspective, for experimenting with GPUs, CNNs, and DNNs in Azure. The only thing that we have to make sure of is that our model can fit into the available GPU memory of the VM. A common way to calculate this is to compute the number of parameters for the model, times 2 for storing gradients (times 1 when performing only inferencing), times the batch size, and times 4 for the single-precision size in bytes (or times 2 for half-precision).

In our example, the CNN architecture requires 1.6 MB to store the trainable parameters (weights and biases). To also store backpropagated losses for a batch size of 16, we would require around 51.2 MB (1.6 MB x 16 x 2) of GPU memory to perform the whole end-to-end training on a single GPU. This also fits easily in our 12 GB of GPU memory in the smallest NC instance.

Important Note

While these numbers seem small for our test case, you will often deal with larger models (with up to 100 million parameters) and larger image sizes. To put that into perspective, ResNet152, when trained on image dimensions of 224 x 224 x 3, has approximately 60 million parameters and a size of 240 MB. On the STANDARD_NC6 instance, we could train, at most, at a batch size of 24, according to our equation.

By adding more GPUs or nodes to the cluster, we must introduce a different framework to take advantage of the distributed setup. We will discuss this in more detail in *Chapter 12, Distributed Machine Learning on Azure*. However, we can add more nodes with autoscaling to the cluster so that multiple people can submit multiple jobs simultaneously. The number of maximum nodes can be computed as *simultaneous models/node * number of peak models to be trained simultaneously*. In our test scenario, we will go with a cluster size of 3 so that we can schedule a few models at the same time.

3.   Now that we have decided on a VM size and GPU configuration, we can continue with the training process. Next, we need to make sure that the cluster can access the training data. To do so, we will use the default datastore on the Azure Machine Learning workspace:

```
ds = ws.get_default_datastore()
ds.upload(src_dir='./data/mnist',
          target_path='mnist',
          show_progress=True)
```

In the preceding code, we copied the training data from the local machine to the default datastore – the blob storage account. As we discussed in *Chapter 4, Ingesting Data and Managing Datasets*, there are also other ways to upload your data to blob storage or another storage system.

Mounting blob storage to a machine, or even a cluster, is usually not a straightforward task. Yes, you could have a NAS and mount it as a network drive on every node in the cluster, but this is tedious to set up and scale. Using the Azure Machine Learning datastore API, we can simply request a reference to the datastore, which can be used to mount the correct folder on every machine that needs to access the data:

```
ds_data = ds.as_mount()
```

The preceding command returns a `Datastore Mount` object, which doesn't look particularly powerful. However, if we pass this reference as a parameter to the training script, it can automatically mount the datastore and read the content from the datastore on each training compute in Azure Machine Learning. If you have ever played with mount points or `fstab`, you will understand that this one-liner can speed up your daily workflow.

4. Now, we can create an Azure Machine Learning configuration. Let's create `ScriptRunConfiguration` so that we can schedule the training script on the cluster:

```
from azureml.core import ScriptRunConfig

script_params={
    '--data-dir': ds_data
}

src = src = ScriptRunConfig(
    source_directory='./scripts',
    script='train.py',
    compute_target=compute_target,
    environment=tf_env)
```

5. To read the data from the specified default datastore, we need to parse the argument in the `train.py` script. Let's go back to the script and replace the file-loading code with the following code block:

```
import argparse

parser = argparse.ArgumentParser()
parser.add_argument('--data-dir', type=str)
args = parser.parse_args()
```

```
DIR = args.data_dir


X_train = load(DIR + 'train-images.gz', False) / 255.0
X_test = load(DIR + 'test-images.gz', False) / 255.0


y_train = load(DIR + 'train-labels.gz', True) \
                .reshape(-1)
y_test = load(DIR + 'test-labels.gz', True) \
                .reshape(-1)
```

6. This leaves us with scheduling and running the script on the GPU cluster. However, before doing so, we want to make sure that all the runs are tracked in the Azure Machine Learning service. Therefore, we must also add `Run` to the `train.py` file and reuse the Keras callback for Azure Machine Learning from *Chapter 3, Preparing the Azure Machine Learning Workspace*. Here is what the training script will look like:

```
from azureml.core import Run


# Get the run configuration
run = Run.get_context()


# Create an Azure Machine Learning monitor callback
azureml_cb = AzureMlKerasCallback(run)
callbacks = [azureml_cb, checkpoint_cb]


model.fit_generator(it,
                    steps_per_epoch=256,
                    epochs=10,
                    callbacks=callbacks)


# Load the best model
model = load_model(checkpoint_path)


# Score trained model
scores = model.evaluate(X_test, y_test, verbose=1)
print('Test loss:', scores[0])
```

```
run.log('Test loss', scores[0])
print('Test accuracy:', scores[1])
run.log('Test accuracy', scores[1])
```

As we can see, we added the `Run` configuration and the Keras callback to track all the metrics during the epochs. We also collected the final test set metric and reported it to the Azure Machine Learning service. You can find the complete runnable example in the code provided with this book.

Improving your performance through transfer learning

In many cases, you won't have a dataset containing hundreds of millions of labeled training samples, and that's completely understandable. So, how can you still benefit from all the previous work and benchmarks? Shouldn't a feature extractor trained on recognizing animals also perform well on recognizing faces? The classifier would certainly be different, but the visual features that are extracted from the images should be similar.

This is the idea behind **fine-tuning** pre-trained models or, more generally speaking, **transfer learning**. To fine-tune, we can simply reuse a feature extractor from a pre-trained DL model (for example, pre-trained on the ImageNet dataset, the `faces` dataset, the `CoCo` dataset, and so on) and attach a custom classifier to the end of the model. Transfer learning means that we can transfer the features from a model from one task to another task: for example, from classification to object detection. It may be a bit confusing at first regarding whether we would want to reuse features for a different task. However, if a model has been taught to identify patterns of geographical shapes in images, this same feature extractor could certainly be reused for any image-related task in the same domain.

One useful property of transfer learning is that the initial learning task doesn't necessarily need to be a supervised ML task, so it is not necessary to have annotated training data to train the feature extractor. A popular unsupervised ML technique is called auto-encoders, where an ML model tries to generate a similar-looking output, given input, using a feature extractor and an upsampling network. By minimizing the error between the generated output and the input, the feature extractor learns to efficiently represent the input data in latent space. Auto-encoders are popular for pre-training network architectures before the pre-trained weights for the actual ML task are used.

We need to make sure that the pre-trained model was trained on a dataset in the same domain. Images of biological cells look very different from faces, and clouds look very different from buildings. In general, the ImageNet dataset covers a broad spectrum of photograph-style images for many standard visual features, such as buildings, cars, animals, and more. Therefore, it is a good choice to use a pre-trained model for many computer vision tasks.

Transfer learning is not only tied to image data and modeling data for computer vision. Transfer learning has proven valuable in any domain where datasets are sufficiently similar, such as for human voices or written text. Hence, whenever you are implementing a DL model, do your research on what datasets could be used for transfer learning and to ultimately improve the model's performance.

Let's bring the theory into practice and dive into some examples. We saw a similar example earlier in this chapter, where we piped the output of the feature extractor to an SVM. In this section, we want to achieve something similar, but the result will be a single end-to-end model. Therefore, in this example, we will build a network architecture for the new model consisting of a pre-trained feature extractor and a newly initialized classification head:

1. First, we must define the number of output classes and the input shape and load the base model from Keras:

    ```
    from tensorflow.keras.applications.resnet50 \
        import ResNet50


    num_classes = 10
    input_shape = (224, 224, 3)


    # create the base pre-trained model
    base_model = ResNet50(input_shape=input_shape,
                          weights='imagenet',
                          include_top=False,
                          pooling='avg')
    ```

    In the preceding code, most of the magic for pre-training happens thanks to Keras. First, we specified the image dataset that will be used to train this model using the `weights` argument, which will automatically initialize the model weights with the pre-trained `imagenet` weights. With the third argument, `include_top=False`, we told Keras to only load the feature extractor part of the model. Using the `pooling` argument, we also specified how the last pooling operation should be performed. In this case, we chose average pooling.

2. Next, we must freeze the layers of the model by setting their `trainable` property to `False`. To do so, we can simply loop over all the layers in the model:

    ```
    for layer in base_model.layers:
        layer.trainable = False
    ```

3. Finally, we can attach any network architecture to the model that we want. In this case, we will attach the same classifier head that we used in the CNN network from the previous section. Finally, we must construct the final model class by using the new architecture and output as the classifier output layer:

```
from tensorflow.keras.models import Model
from tensorflow.keras.layers import Flatten, Dense

clf = base_model.output
clf = Dense(256, activation='relu')(clf)
clf = Dense(10, activation='softmax')(clf)

model = Model(base_model.input, clf)
```

That's it! You have successfully built a new end-to-end model that combines a pre-trained ResNet50 feature extractor on ImageNet with your custom classifier. You can now use this Keras model and plug it into your preferred optimizer and send it off to the GPU cluster. The output of the training process will be a single model that can be managed and deployed as any other custom model.

> **Important Note**
>
> You are not limited to always freezing all the layers of the original network. A common approach is to also unfreeze later layers in the network, decrease the learning rate by at least a factor of 10, and continue training. By repeating this procedure, we could even retrain (or fine-tune) all the layers of the network in a step-by-step approach with a decreasing learning rate.

Independently of your choice and use case, you should add transfer learning to your standard repertoire for training DL models. Treat it like other popular preprocessing and training techniques, such as data augmentation, which should always be used when you're training DL models.

Summary

In this chapter, we learned when and how to use DL to train an ML model on Azure. We used both a compute instance and a GPU cluster from within the Azure Machine Learning service to train a model using Keras and TensorFlow.

First, we found out that DL works very well on highly structured data with non-obvious relationships from the raw input data to the resulting prediction. Good examples include image classification, speech-to-text, and translation. We also saw that DL models are parametric models with a large number of parameters, so we often need a large amount of labeled or augmented input data. In contrast to traditional ML approaches, the extra parameters are used to train a fully end-to-end model, also including feature extraction from the raw input data.

Training a CNN using the Azure Machine Learning service is not difficult. We saw many approaches, from prototyping in Jupyter to augmenting the training data, to running the training on a GPU cluster with autoscaling. The difficult part in DL is preparing and providing enough high-quality training data, finding a descriptive error metric, and optimizing between costs and performance. We provided an overview of how to decide on the best VM and GPU size and configuration for your job, something that I recommend you do before starting your first GPU cluster.

In the next chapter, we will go one step further and look into hyperparameter tuning and automated ML, a feature in the Azure Machine Learning service that lets you train and optimize stacked models automatically.

11

Hyperparameter Tuning and Automated Machine Learning

In the previous chapter, we learned how to train **convolutional neural networks** and complex **deep neural networks**. When training these models, we are often confronted with difficult choices in terms of the various parameters we should use, such as the number of layers, filter dimensions, the type and order of layers, regularization, batch size, learning rate, the number of epochs, and many more. And this is not only the case for DNNs – the same challenges arise when we need to select the correct preprocessing steps, features, models, and model parameters in statistical ML approaches.

In this chapter, we will look at optimizing the training process to remove some of the non-optimal human choices in ML. This will help you train better models faster and more efficiently without manual intervention. First, we will explore **hyperparameter optimization** (also called **HyperDrive** in Azure Machine Learning), a standard technique for optimizing parameters in an ML process. By evaluating different sampling techniques for hyperparameter sampling, such as random sampling, grid sampling, and Bayesian optimization, you will learn how to efficiently trade model runtime for model performance.

In the second half of this chapter, we will look at model optimization by automating the complete end-to-end ML training process using **Automated Machine Learning**. This process is also often referred to as **AutoML**. Using Automated Machine Learning, we can optimize preprocessing, feature engineering, model selection, hyperparameter tuning, and model stacking all in one abstract optimization pipeline.

One benefit of Azure Machine Learning is that both parameter optimization (HyperDrive) and model optimization (Automated Machine Learning) are supported in the same generalized way. This means we can deploy both to an auto-scaling training cluster, store the best model or parameter combination on disk, and then deploy the best model to production without ever leaving our notebook environment.

The following topics will be covered in this chapter:

- Finding the optimal model parameters with HyperDrive
- Finding the optimal model with Automated Machine Learning

Technical requirements

In this chapter, we will use the following Python libraries and versions to create decision-tree based ensemble classifiers:

- `azureml-core 1.34.0`
- `azureml-sdk 1.34.0`

Similar to the previous chapters, you can run this code using either a local Python interpreter or a notebook environment hosted in Azure Machine Learning. However, all the scripts need to be scheduled in Azure Machine Learning training clusters.

All the code examples in this chapter can be found in this book's GitHub repository: `https://github.com/PacktPublishing/Mastering-Azure-Machine-Learning-Second-Edition/tree/main/chapter11`.

Finding the optimal model parameters with HyperDrive

In ML, we typically deal with either parametric or non-parametric models. Models represent the distribution of the training data to make predictions for unseen data from the same distribution. While parametric models (such as linear regression, logistic regression, and neural networks) represent the training data distribution by using a learned set of parameters, non-parametric models describe the training data distribution through other traits, such as decision trees (all tree-based classifiers), training samples (k-nearest neighbors), or weighted training samples (support vector machine).

Parametric models such as linear or logistic regression are typically defined by a constant number of parameters that are independent of the training data. These models make strong assumptions about the training data, so they often require fewer training samples. As a result, both training and inferencing are usually very fast.

In comparison, for **non-parametric models** such as decision trees or k-nearest neighbors, the number of traits usually increases with the number of training samples. While these models don't assume anything about the training data distribution, many training samples are required. This often leads to slow training and slow interference performance.

The term **hyperparameter** refers to all the parameters that are used to configure and tune the training process of parametric or non-parametric models. The following is a list of some typical hyperparameters in a neural network:

- The number of hidden layers
- The number of units per layer
- Batch size
- Filter dimensions
- Learning rate
- Regularization terms
- Dropout
- Loss metric

The number of hyperparameters and parameter values for training a simple ML model is astonishing. Have you ever caught yourself manually tweaking a parameter in your training processes, such as the number of splits in a decision-based classifier or the number of units in a neural network classifier? If so, you are not alone! However, it's very important to accept that manually tweaking parameters requires deep expertise in the specific model or model configuration. However, we can't possibly be an expert in every type of statistical modeling, ML, and optimization to tune all the possible parameters manually. Given that the number of parameter choices is enormous, it is not feasible to try all possible combinations, so we need to find a better way to optimize them.

Not only can we not possibly try all the distinct combinations of parameters manually, but in many cases, we also can't possibly predict the outcome of a tweak in a hyperparameter, even with expert knowledge. In such scenarios, we can start looking at finding the optimal set of parameters automatically. This process is called **hyperparameter tuning** or **hyperparameter search**.

Hyperparameter tuning entails automatically testing a model's performance against different sets of hyperparameter combinations and ultimately choosing the best combination of hyperparameters. The definition of the *best performance* depends on the chosen metric and validation method. For example, stratified-fold cross-validation with the f1-score metric will yield a different set of optimal parameters than the accuracy metric with k-fold cross-validation.

One reason why we are discussing hyperparameter tuning (and Automated Machine Learning later) in this book is that we have a competitive advantage from using elastic cloud computing infrastructure. While it is difficult to train hundreds of models sequentially on your laptop, it is easy to train thousands of models in parallel in the cloud using cheap auto-scaling compute. Using cheap cloud storage, we can also persist all potentially good models for later analysis. Many of the recent ML papers have shown that we can often achieve better results by using more compute power and/or better parameter choices.

Before we begin tuning hyperparameters, we want to remind you of the importance of a baseline model. For many practical ML tasks, you should be able to achieve good performance using a single tree-based ensemble classifier or a pre-trained neural network with default parameters. If this is not the case, hyperparameter tuning won't magically output parameters for a top-performing best-in-class model. In this case, it would be better to go back to data preprocessing and feature engineering to build a better baseline model first, before tuning the batch sizes, the number of hidden units, or the number of trees.

Another issue to avoid with hyperparameter tuning is overfitting and focusing on the wrong performance metric or validation method. As with any other optimization technique, hyperparameter tuning will yield the best parameter combination for a given loss function or metric. Therefore, it is essential to validate your loss function before starting hyperparameter tuning.

As with most other techniques in ML, there are multiple ways to find the best hyperparameters for a model. The most popular techniques are *grid search*, *random search*, and *Bayesian optimization*. In this chapter, we will investigate all three of them, discuss their strengths and weaknesses, and experiment with practical examples.

Sampling all possible parameter combinations using grid search

Grid search (or **grid sampling**) is a popular technique for finding the optimal hyperparameters from a parameter grid by testing every possible parameter combination of the multi-dimensional parameter grid. For every parameter (continuous or categorical), we need to define all the values or value ranges that should be tested. Popular ML libraries provide tools to create these parameter grids efficiently.

Two properties differentiate grid search from other hyperparameter sampling methods:

- All parameter combinations are assumed to be independent of each other, which means they can be tested in parallel. Therefore, given a set of 100 possible parameter combinations, we can start 100 models to test all the combinations in parallel.

- By testing all possible parameter combinations, we can ensure that we search for a global optimum rather than a local optimum.

Grid search works perfectly for smaller ML models with only a few hyperparameters but grows exponentially with every additional parameter because it adds a new dimension to the parameter grid.

Let's look at how grid search can be implemented using Azure Machine Learning. In Azure Machine Learning, the hyperparameter tuning functionality lives in the `hyperdrive` package. Here is what we are going to do:

1. Create a grid sampling configuration
2. Define a primary metric to define the tuning goal
3. Create a `hyperdrive` configuration
4. Submit the `hyperdrive` configuration as an experiment to Azure Machine Learning

Let's look at these steps in more detail:

1. First, we must create the grid sampling configuration by defining the parameter choices and ranges for grid sampling, as shown in the following code block:

```
from azureml.train.hyperdrive import \
    GridParameterSampling
from azureml.train.hyperdrive.parameter_expressions \
    import *


grid_sampling = GridParameterSampling({
    "--first-layer-neurons": choice(16, 32, 64, 128),
    "--second-layer-neurons": choice(16, 32, 64, 128),
    "--batch-size": choice(16, 32)
})
```

In the preceding code, we defined a parameter grid using discrete parameter choices along three parameter dimensions – the number of neurons in the first layer, the number of neurons in the second layer, and the training batch size.

2. The parameter names are formatted as command-line arguments because they will be passed as arguments to the training script. So, we need to make sure that the training script can configure parameters via command-line arguments. The following code shows what this could look like in your training example:

```
import argparse

parser = argparse.ArgumentParser()
parser.add_argument('--batch-size', type=int,
   default=50)
parser.add_argument('--epochs', type=int, default=30)
parser.add_argument('--first-layer-neurons', type=int,
   dest='n_hidden_1', default=100)
parser.add_argument('--second-layer-neurons',
   type=int,
   dest='n_hidden_2', default=100)
parser.add_argument('--learning-rate', type=float,
   default=0.1)
parser.add_argument('--momentum', type=float,
   default=0.9)
args = parser.parse_args()
```

With grid sampling, we can test all the possible combinations of these parameters. This will result in a total of 32 runs (*4 x 4 x 2*) that we could theoretically run in parallel, as the training runs, and the parameter configurations are independent of each other. In this case, the total number of required training runs is obvious as we are only using discrete parameter ranges. Later, we will see that this is not the case for random sampling and Bayesian optimization. For these other methods, we sample from a continuous distribution, so the number of training runs won't be bounded. We will also see that the number of parallel runs can affect the optimization process when parameter choices are not independent. So, let's appreciate the simplicity of the grid sampling solution for a small number of discrete parameters.

3. Next, we need to define a metric that measures the performance of each parameter combination. This metric can be any numeric value that is logged by the training script. Please note that this metric does not need to be the same as the loss function – it can be any measurement that you would like to use to compare different parameter pairs. Have a look at the following example. Here, we have decided to maximize the `accuracy` metric and defined the following parameters:

```python
from azureml.train.hyperdrive import PrimaryMetricGoal

primary_metric_name = "accuracy"
primary_metric_goal = PrimaryMetricGoal.MAXIMIZE
```

In the preceding code, we chose the `accuracy` metric, which is what we want to maximize. Here, you can see that we simply specified any metric name as a string. To use this metric to evaluate hyperparameter optimization runs, the training script needs to log a metric with this exact name. We saw this in the previous chapters, where we emitted metrics for an Azure Machine Learning run.

4. We must use the same metric name of `primary_metric_name` to define and log a metric that can be picked up by `hyperdrive` to evaluate the run in the training script:

```python
from azureml.core.run import Run

run = Run.get_context()
run.log("accuracy", float(val_accuracy))
```

5. Before we continue, recall the script run configuration from the previous chapters. Similar to the previous chapters, we must configure a CPU-based Azure Machine Learning training cluster defined as `aml_cluster` and an environment called `tf_env` containing all the relevant packages for running TensorFlow:

```python
src = ScriptRunConfig(source_directory="train",
    script="train.py",
    compute_target=aml_cluster,
    environment=tf_env)
```

6. Now, we can initialize the `hyperdrive` configuration, which consists of the estimator, the sampling grid, the optimization metric, and the number of runs and concurrent runs:

```
from azureml.train.hyperdrive import HyperDriveConfig

hyperdrive_run_config = HyperDriveConfig(
    run_config=src,
    hyperparameter_sampling=grid_sampling,
    primary_metric_name=primary_metric_name,
    primary_metric_goal=primary_metric_goal,
    max_total_runs=32,
    max_concurrent_runs=4)
```

In grid sampling, the number of runs should correspond with the number of possible parameter combinations. As it is a required attribute, we need to compute this value and pass it here. The maximum number of concurrent runs in grid sampling is limited only by the number of nodes in your Azure Machine Learning cluster. We are using a four-node cluster, so we have set the number to 4 to maximize concurrency.

7. Finally, we can submit the `hyperdrive` configuration to an experiment, which will execute all the concurrent child runs on the specified compute target:

```
from azureml.core.experiment import Experiment

experiment = Experiment(workspace, experiment_name)
hyperdrive_run = experiment.submit(hyperdrive_run_config)
print(hyperdrive_run.get_portal_url())
```

The preceding snippet will kick off the training process, build and register new Docker images if needed, initialize and scale up the nodes in the cluster, and finally run the training scripts on the cluster. Each script will be parameterized using a unique parameter combination from the sampling grid. The following screenshot shows the resulting experiment run. We can go to this page by clicking on the link that is returned from the preceding code snippet:

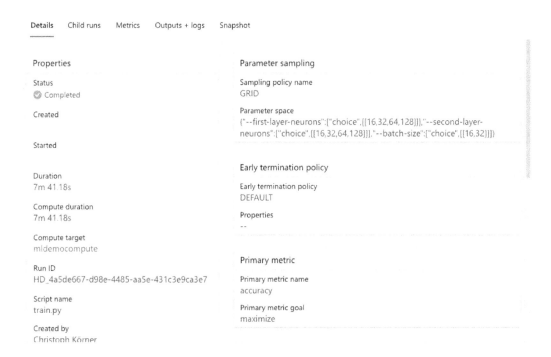

Details   Child runs   Metrics   Outputs + logs   Snapshot

Properties

Status
✓ Completed

Created

Started

Duration
7m 41.18s

Compute duration
7m 41.18s

Compute target
mldemocompute

Run ID
HD_4a5de667-d98e-4485-aa5e-431c3e9ca3e7

Script name
train.py

Created by
Christoph Körner

Parameter sampling

Sampling policy name
GRID

Parameter space
{"--first-layer-neurons":["choice",[[16,32,64,128]]],"--second-layer-neurons":["choice",[[16,32,64,128]]],"--batch-size":["choice",[[16,32]]]})

Early termination policy

Early termination policy
DEFAULT

Properties
--

Primary metric

Primary metric name
accuracy

Primary metric goal
maximize

Figure 11.1 – Grid sampling overview

Here, we can see the sampling policy's name, which is **GRID**, and the configured parameter space. These parameters will be applied as command-line arguments to the training script.

As you may have guessed already, not everything is great when you must sample all the possible parameter combinations from a multi-dimensional grid. As the number of hyperparameters grows, so do the dimensions of the grid. And each dimension of parameters adds a magnitude of new parameter configurations that need to be tested. And don't forget that testing a parameter's configuration usually means performing training, cross-validation, and test set predictions on your model, which can take a significant number of resources.

Imagine that you want to search for the best parameter combination for five parameters with 10 different values for each parameter. Let's assume the following:

- We are testing 10^5 (*10 x 10 x 10 x 10 x 10*) parameter combinations.
- One training run takes only 2 minutes.
- We are performing four-fold cross-validation.

Here, we would end up with 555 days (*2min x 4 x 10^5 = 800,000min*) of combined training time. While you could decrease the total runtime by running parameter combinations in parallel, other methods exist that are better suited for large numbers of parameters, such as random sampling. Let's see how we can limit the required runtime of the parameter optimization search by sampling parameter configurations at random.

Testing random combinations using random search

Random search is another popular hyperparameter sampling method that's similar to grid search. The main difference is that instead of testing all the possible parameter combinations, only a few combinations are randomly selected and tested. The main idea is that grid search often samples nearby parameter configurations that have little effect on model performance. Therefore, we waste a lot of time chasing similarly bad solutions where we could use our time to try diverse and hopefully more successful parameter configurations.

When you're dealing with large amounts of hyperparameters (for example, more than 5), random search will find a good set of hyperparameters much faster than grid search – however, it might not be the optimal result. Even so, in many cases, it will be a reasonable trade-off to use random search over grid search to improve prediction performance with hyperparameter tuning.

In random search, parameters are usually sampled from a continuous distribution instead of discrete parameter choices being used. This leads to a slightly different way of defining the parameter grid. Instead of providing choices for distinct values, we can define a distribution function for each parameter to draw random values from a continuous range.

Like grid search, all parameter combinations are independent if they're drawn with replacement, which means they can be fully parallelized. If a parameter grid with 10,000 distinct parameter configurations is provided, we can run and test all the models in parallel.

Let's look at random search in Azure Machine Learning:

1. As with all other hyperparameter optimization methods, we find the random sampling method in the `hyperdrive` package. As we discussed previously, we can now define probability distribution functions such as `normal` and `uniform` for each parameter instead of choosing only discrete parameters:

```
from azureml.train.hyperdrive import \
    RandomParameterSampling
from azureml.train.hyperdrive.parameter_expressions \
    import *
```

```
random_sampling = RandomParameterSampling({
    "--learning-rate": normal(10, 3),
    "--momentum": uniform(0.5, 1.0),
    "--batch-size": choice(16, 32, 64)
})
```

Using continuous parameter ranges is not the only difference in random sampling. Due to the possibility of sampling an infinite amount of parameter configurations from a continuous range, we need a way to specify the duration of the search. We can use the `max_total_runs` and `max_duration_minutes` parameters to define the expected runtime in minutes or to limit the amount of sampled parameter configurations.

2. Let's test 25 different configurations and run the hyperparameter tuning process for a maximum of 60 minutes. We must set the following parameters:

```
max_total_runs = 25
max_duration_minutes = 60
```

3. We will reuse the same metric that we defined in the previous section, namely *accuracy*. The `hyperdrive` configuration looks as follows:

```
from azureml.train.hyperdrive import HyperDriveConfig

hyperdrive_run_config = HyperDriveConfig(
    run_config=src,
    hyperparameter_sampling=random_sampling,
    primary_metric_name=primary_metric_name,
    primary_metric_goal=primary_metric_goal,
    max_total_runs=max_total_runs,
    max_duration_minutes=max_duration_minutes)
```

4. Similar to the previous example, we must submit the `hyperdrive` configuration to Azure Machine Learning from the authoring runtime, which will schedule all the optimization runs on the compute target:

```
from azureml.core.experiment import Experiment

experiment = Experiment(workspace, experiment_name)
hyperdrive_run = experiment.submit(hyperdrive_run_config)
print(hyperdrive_run.get_portal_url())
```

Random sampling is an excellent choice for testing large numbers of tunable hyperparameters or sampling values from a continuous range. However, instead of optimizing the parameter configurations step by step, we simply try all those configurations at random and compare how they perform.

In the next section, we will learn how to find a good parameter combination faster by stopping training runs early. In the subsequent section, *Optimizing parameter choices using Bayesian optimization*, we will look at a more elegant way of navigating through the parameter space in hyperparameter tuning by using optimization.

Converging faster using early termination

Both the grid and random sampling techniques test models for poor parameter choices and hence spend precious compute resources on fitting poorly parameterized models to your training data. **Early termination** is a technique that stops a training run early if the intermediate results look worse than other runs. It is a great solution for speeding up expensive hyperparameter optimization techniques.

In general, you should always try to use early termination when using either grid or random sampling. You get no benefit from training all the parameter combinations if the results are a lot worse than for some of the existing runs.

Once we understand the idea of canceling poor-performing runs, we need to find a way to specify a threshold of when a run should be canceled – we refer to this threshold as the **termination policy**. Azure Machine Learning provides the most popular termination policies, namely **bandit**, **median stopping**, and **truncation selection**. Let's take a look at them and see what their differences are.

Before we get into the details, though, let's learn how to configure early termination. In Azure Machine Learning, we can parameterize the different early termination policies with two global properties, namely `evaluation_interval` and `delay_evaluation`. These parameters control how often the early termination policy is tested. An example of using these parameters are as follows:

```
evaluation_interval = 1
delay_evaluation = 10
```

The units of both parameters are in intervals. An **interval** is defined by the training code and corresponds to one invocation of `run.log()`. For example, when you're training a neural network, an interval will equal one training epoch. The `delay_evaluation` parameter controls how many intervals we want to wait after the start to test the early termination policy for the first time. In the preceding example, we configured it as `10`, so we wait for 10 epochs before testing the early termination policy.

Then, every other policy evaluation is configured using the `evaluation_interval` parameter. It describes how many iterations need to pass until the next test. In the preceding example, we set `evaluation_interval` to 1, which is also the default value. This means that we test the early termination policy every interval after the `delay_evaluation` interval – here, every 1 iteration. Let's look into the three termination policies in more detail.

The median stopping policy

Let's start with the easiest termination policy – the **median stopping policy**. It takes no other arguments than the two default arguments, which control when and how often the policy should be tested. The median stopping policy keeps track of the running average of the primary metric across all experiment runs. Whenever the median policy is evaluated, it will test whether the current metric is above the median of all running experiments and stop those runs that are below. The following code shows how to create a median stopping early termination policy for any hyperparameter tuning script:

```
from azureml.train.hyperdrive import MedianStoppingPolicy

early_termination_policy = MedianStoppingPolicy(
    evaluation_interval=evaluation_interval,
    delay_evaluation=delay_evaluation)
```

As we can see, it's quite simple to construct a median stopping policy as it is only configured by the two default parameters. Due to its simplicity, it is a very effective method for reducing the runtime of your hyperparameter optimization script. The early termination policy is then applied to the `hyperdrive` configuration file using the `policy` parameter. Now, let's look at the truncation selection policy.

The truncation selection policy

Unlike the median stopping policy, the **truncation selection policy** will always kill runs when evaluated. It will kill a percentage of runs with the lowest primary metric. The percentage is defined using the `truncation_percentage` parameter:

```
truncation_percentage = 10
evaluation_interval = 5
delay_evaluation = 10
```

In the preceding example, we set the `truncation_percentage` value to `10`. This means that whenever the early termination policy is executed, it will kill the lowest-performing 10% of runs. We must also increase the `evaluation_interval` value to 5 as we don't want to kill runs every epoch, as shown in the following example:

```
from azureml.train.hyperdrive import TruncationSelectionPolicy
```

```
early_termination_policy = TruncationSelectionPolicy(
    truncation_percentage=truncation_percentage,
    evaluation_interval=evaluation_interval,
    delay_evaluation=delay_evaluation)
```

This early termination policy makes sense when only very few training resources are available, and we want to aggressively prune the number of runs each time the early termination policy is evaluated. Let's look at the final policy – the bandit policy.

The bandit policy

The **bandit policy** works similarly but inverse to the truncation policy. Instead of stopping a percentage of the lowest-performing runs, it kills all the runs that are worse than the best current run. In contrast to the previous policies, the bandit policy is not configured using a percentage value, but rather a `slack_factor` or `slack_amount` parameter. The `slack_factor` parameter describes the relative deviation from the best metric, whereas the `slack_amount` parameter describes the absolute deviation from the best primary metric.

Let's look at an example. Here, we will configure `hyperdrive` by configuring a `slack_factor` parameter of `0.2` and testing an accuracy value (*bigger is better*). As we did previously, we will set the `evaluation_interval` value to 5 and the `evaluation_delay` value to 10 intervals:

```
slack_factor = 0.2
evaluation_interval = 5
delay_evaluation = 10
```

```
from azureml.train.hyperdrive import BanditPolicy
```

```
early_termination_policy = BanditPolicy(
    slack_factor = slack_factor,
    evaluation_interval=evaluation_interval,
    delay_evaluation=delay_evaluation)
```

Let's say that the best-performing run yields an accuracy of 0.8 after epoch 10, which is when the early termination policy gets applied for the first time. Now, all the runs that are performing up to 20% worse than the best metric are killed. We can compute the relative deviation from an accuracy of 0.8 by using the following function:

0.8/(1 + 0.2) = 0.67

Hence, all the runs that yield a performance that's lower than 0.67 will get canceled by the early termination policy.

A HyperDrive configuration with the termination policy

To create a `hyperdrive` configuration, we need to pass the early termination policy using the `policy` parameter. Here is an example of using grid search sampling and the previously defined bandit policy:

```
from azureml.train.hyperdrive import HyperDriveConfig

hyperdrive_run_config = HyperDriveConfig(
    run_config=src,
    hyperparameter_sampling=grid_sampling,
    policy=early_termination_policy,
    primary_metric_name="accuracy",
    primary_metric_goal=PrimaryMetricGoal.MAXIMIZE)
```

The bandit policy is a good trade-off between the median stopping and the truncation selection policy that works well in many cases. You can rest assured that only a well-performing subset of all the hyperparameter configurations will be run and evaluated for multiple intervals.

Let's submit this HyperDrive configuration as an experiment to Azure Machine Learning. We can use the `RunDetails` method that we saw in the previous chapters to output additional information about the hyperparameter tuning experiment, such as scheduling and parameter information, a visualization of the training performance, and a parallel coordinate chart showing the parameter dimensions:

```
from azureml.widgets import RunDetails

hyperdrive_run = exp.submit(hyperdrive_run_config)
RunDetails(hyperdrive_run).show()
```

If you run the preceding code, it will run the hyperparameter search for the configured policies. Once the experiment is running, you will see the specified metric for the individual parameter combinations and iterations as a chart in a widget:

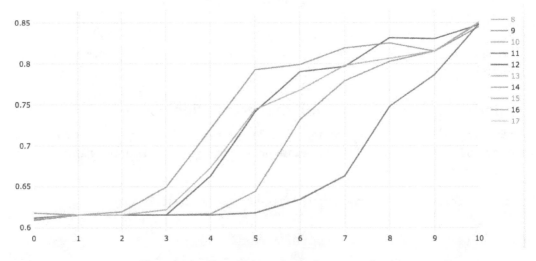

Figure 11.2 – HyperDrive – the performance of runs

Besides looking at the defined metric, you can select other visualizations that show the sampled parameters, such as on a parallel coordinates plot, or as two- and three-dimensional scatter plots. Here, you can see which parameter combinations yield high model accuracy:

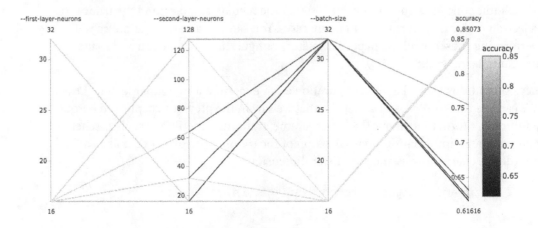

Figure 11.3 – HyperDrive – visualization of the results

In this section, you learned that applying an early termination policy to your hyperparameter optimization script is a simple but extremely effective way to reduce the number of poorly performing training runs. With just a few lines of code, we can reduce the number of training runs to a minimum and only finish those that are yielding promising results.

> **Important Note**
>
> When you're using hyperparameter optimization with random or grid sampling, *always* use an early termination policy.

Optimizing parameter choices using Bayesian optimization

In the previous examples, we evaluated different parameter configurations sampled from a grid or at random without any optimization or strategic parameter choice. This had the benefit that all the configurations were independent and could be evaluated in parallel. However, imagine using an ML model to help us find the best parameter combination for a large multi-dimensional parameter space. That's exactly what **Bayesian optimization** does in the domain of hyperparameter tuning.

The job of an optimization method is to find the optimal value (that is, a minimum or maximum) of a predefined objective function. In hyperparameter tuning, we are faced with a very similar problem: we want to find the parameter configuration that yields the best-predefined evaluation metric for an ML model.

So, how does optimization work for hyperparameter search? First, we must define a hyperplane – a multi-dimensional grid where we can sample our parameter configurations. In the following diagram, we can see such a plane for two parameters along the x and y axes. The z-axis represents the performance of the model that is being tested using the parameters at this specific location:

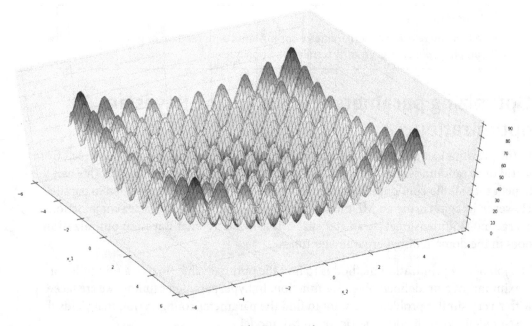

Figure 11.4 – The Rastrigin function

The preceding diagram shows the multi-dimensional Rastrigin function, as an example of something extremely hard to optimize. In hyperparameter tuning, we often face a similar problem in that finding the optimal solution is difficult – just like finding the global minimum in the Rastrigin function.

Then, we must sample points from this plane and test the first (few) parameter configurations. We assume that the parameters are not independent and that the model will have similar performance when using similar nearby parameters. However, each evaluation only yields a noisy value of the true model performance. Using these assumptions, we can use **Gaussian processes** to combine the model evaluations into a multi-variate continuous Gaussian. Next, we can compute the points for the highest expected improvements on this Gaussian. These points will yield new samples to test with our model.

Luckily, we don't have to implement the algorithm ourselves, but many ML libraries provide a hyperparameter optimization algorithm out of the box. In Azure Machine Learning, we can use the **Bayesian sampling method**, which helps us pick good parameter configurations to optimize the predefined metric.

The parameter grid is defined similarly to the random sampling technique – that is, by using a continuous or discrete parameter space for all the parameter values, as shown in the following code block:

```
from azureml.train.hyperdrive import BayesianParameterSampling
from azureml.train.hyperdrive.parameter_expressions import *


bayesian_sampling = BayesianParameterSampling({
    "--learning-rate": normal(10, 3),
    "--momentum": uniform(0.5, 1.0),
    "--batch-size": choice(16, 32, 64)
})
```

Before we continue, we need to keep one thing in mind. The Bayesian sampling technique tries to predict well-performing parameter configurations based on the results of the previously tested parameters. This means that the parameter choices and runs are not independent anymore. We can't run all the experiments in parallel at the same time as we need the results of some experiments to sample new parameters. Therefore, we need to set an additional parameter to control how many training runs should run concurrently.

We can do this using the max_concurrent_runs parameter. To let the Bayesian optimization technique converge, it is recommended to set this value to a small value, for example, in the range of 2-10. Let's set the value to 4 for this experiment and the number of total runs to 100. This means that we are using 25 iterations for the Bayesian optimization method, where we explore four parameter configurations concurrently at a time:

```
max_concurrent_runs = 4
max_total_runs = 100
```

Let's kick off the experiment with Bayesian sampling:

```
from azureml.train.hyperdrive import HyperDriveConfig
from azureml.core.experiment import Experiment


hyperdrive_run_config = HyperDriveConfig(
```

```
    estimator=estimator,
    hyperparameter_sampling=bayesian_sampling,
    primary_metric_name=primary_metric_name,
    primary_metric_goal=primary_metric_goal,
    max_total_runs=max_total_runs,
    max_concurrent_runs=max_concurrent_runs)


experiment = Experiment(workspace, experiment_name)
hyperdrive_run = experiment.submit(hyperdrive_run_config)
print(hyperdrive_run.get_portal_url())
```

Unfortunately, this technique can't be parallelized further to finish faster as all the parameter choices are dependent on the results of the previous iteration. However, due to the optimization step, it generally yields good results in a relatively short amount of time.

Another downside of Bayesian optimization or optimization for hyperparameter tuning is that the optimization requires each result of each run with the defined parameter configuration to compute the new parameter choices. Therefore, we can't use early termination together with Bayesian sampling as the training would be stopped earlier, which means no accurate metric can be computed.

> **Important Note**
> Early termination doesn't work for optimization techniques such as Bayesian optimization because it requires the final testing score to compute the parameter gradient.

Once you've played around with using ML to optimize an ML model, you may already think about taking it one step further: why should we stop at optimizing hyperparameters, and why shouldn't we optimize model choices, network structures, or model stacking altogether?

And this is a perfectly valid thought. No human can test all the variations of different ML models, different parameter configurations, and different nested models together. In the next section, we will do exactly this and optimize not just parameters but also model architecture and preprocessing steps using Automated Machine Learning

Finding the optimal model with Automated Machine Learning

Automated Machine Learning is an exciting new trend that many (if not all) cloud providers follow. The aim is to provide a service to users that automatically preprocesses your data, selects an ML model, and trains and optimizes the model to fit your training data to optimize a specified error metric. This will create and train a fully automated end-to-end ML pipeline that only needs your labeled training data and target metric as input. Here is a list of steps that Automated Machine Learning optimizes for you:

- Data preprocessing
- Feature engineering
- Model selection
- Hyperparameter tuning
- Model ensembling

While most experienced ML engineers or data scientists would be very cautious about the effectiveness of such an automated approach, it still has a ton of benefits, which will be explained in this section. If you like the idea of hyperparameter tuning, then you will find value in Automated Machine Learning.

A good way to think about Automated Machine Learning is that it performs a hyperparameter search over the complete end-to-end ML pipeline, similar to Bayesian optimization, but over a much larger parameter space. The parameters are now individual steps in the end-to-end ML pipeline, which should be automated. The great thing about Automated Machine Learning is that instead of going through the dumb sampling of all possible parameter choices, it will predict how well certain preprocessing steps and models will perform on a dataset before actually training a model. This process is called **meta-learning** and will help the optimization process yield great candidate solutions for the pipeline without spending time being evaluated.

The unfair advantage of Automated Machine Learning

Let's evaluate the advantages of Automated Machine Learning If we look at the list of automated steps we mentioned earlier, each one requires days for an experienced data scientist to explore, evaluate, and fine-tune. Even steps such as selecting the correct model, such as either LightGBM or XGBoost for gradient-based tree ensemble classification, are non-trivial as they require experience and knowledge of both tools. Moreover, we all know that those two are only a tiny subset of all the possible options for a classification model. If we look at hyperparameter tuning and model stacking, we can immediately tell that the amount of work that's required to build a great ensemble model is non-trivial.

This is not only a problem of knowledge or expertise. It's also very time-consuming. Automated Machine Learning aims to replace manual steps with automated best practices, applying continuously improving rules, and heavily optimizing every possible human choice. It's very similar to hyperparameter tuning but for the complete end-to-end process. A machine will find the best parameters much faster and much more accurately than a human by using optimization instead of manual selection.

We can also look at Automated Machine Learning from a different perspective, namely as a **machine learning as a service (MLaaS)** product: data in, model (or prediction endpoint) out. By now, you should be aware that each step of building an end-to-end ML pipeline is a thorough, complicated, and time-consuming task. Even when you can choose the correct model and tuning parameters using Bayesian optimization, the cost of building this infrastructure and operating it is significant. In this case, choosing MLaaS would provide you with an ML infrastructure for a fraction of the usual cost.

There is another reason why the idea of Automated Machine Learning is very interesting. It separates the ML part from your data-fitting problem and leaves you with what you should know best – the data. Similar to using a managed service in the cloud (for example, a managed database), which lets you focus on implementing business logic rather than operating infrastructure, Automated Machine Learning will allow you to use a managed ML pipeline built on best practices and optimization by using data instead of specific ML algorithms.

This also leads to the reason why Automated Machine Learning is still a great fit for many (mature) companies – it reduces a prediction problem to the most important tasks:

- Data acquisition
- Data cleansing
- Data labeling
- Selecting an error metric

We don't want to judge anyone, but ML practitioners often like to skip these topics and dive right into the fun parts, namely feature engineering, model selection, parameterization, stacking, and tuning. Therefore, a good start for every ML project is to start with an Automated Machine Learning baseline model, because it will force you to focus only on the data side. After achieving a good initial score, you can always go ahead and start further feature engineering and build a model if needed.

Now that we've talked about the Automated Machine Learning trend being reasonable and that you could benefit from it in one way or another, let's dive deep into some examples and code. We will look at the different capabilities of Azure Automated Machine Learning, a product of Azure Machine Learning, as applied in a standard end-to-end ML pipeline.

Before we jump into the code, let's take a look at what problem Azure Automated Machine Learning can tackle. In general, we can decide between *classification*, *regression*, and *time series forecasting* in Automated Machine Learning As we know from the previous chapters, time series forecasting is simply a variant of regression, where all the predicted values are in the future.

Hence, the most important task after choosing the correct ML task is choosing the proper error metric that should be optimized. The following list shows all the error metrics that are supported:

- **Classification**: `accuracy`, `AUC_weighted`, `average_precision_score_weighted`, `norm_macro_recall`, and `precision_score_weighted`

- **Regression and time series forecasting**: `spearman_correlation`, `normalized_root_mean_squared_error`, `r2_score`, and `normalized_mean_absolute_error`

You should be familiar with most of these metrics as they are variants of the most popular error metrics for classification and regression.

Among the supported models, there's LogisticRegression, SGD, MultinomialNaiveBayes, SVM, KNN, Random Forest, ExtremeRandomTrees, LigthtGBM, GradientBoosting, DNN, Lasso, Arima, Prophet, and more. The great thing about a managed service in the cloud is that this list will most likely grow in the future and add the most recent state-of-the-art models. However, this list should be thought of just as additional information for you, since the idea of Automated Machine Learning is that the models are automatically chosen for you. However, according to the user's preference, individual models can be allow- or deny-listed for Automated Machine Learning.

With all this in mind, let's look at a classification example that uses Automated Machine Learning

A classification example with Automated Machine Learning

When you're using new technology, it's always good to take a step back and think about what the technology could be capable of. Let's use the same approach to figure out how automated preprocessing could help us in a typical ML project and where its limitations will be.

Automated Machine Learning is great for applying best-practice transformations to your dataset: applying date/time transformations, as well as the normalization and standardization of your data when using linear regression, handling missing data or dropping low-variance features, and so on. A long list of features is provided by Microsoft that is expected to grow in the future.

Let's recall what we learned in *Chapter 7, Advanced Feature Extraction with NLP*. While Automated Machine Learning can detect free text and convert it into a numeric feature vector, it won't be able to understand the semantic meaning of the data in your business domain. Therefore, it will be able to transform your textual data, but if you need to semantically encode your text or categorical data, you have to implement that yourself.

Another thing to remember is that Automated Machine Learning will not try to infer any correlations between different feature dimensions in your training data. Hence, if you want to combine two categorical columns into a combined feature column (for example, using one-hot-encoding, mean embedding, and so on), then you will have to implement this on your own.

In Automated Machine Learning there are two different sets of preprocessors – the **simple** ones and the **complex** ones. Simple preprocessing is just referred to as **preprocessing**. The following list shows all the simple preprocessing techniques that will be evaluated during Automated Machine Learning training if the `preprocess` argument is specified. If you have worked with scikit-learn before, then most of the following preprocessing techniques should be fairly familiar to you:

- `StandardScaler`: Normalization – mean subtraction and scaling a feature to unit variance.

- `MinMaxScaler`: Normalization – scaling a feature by the minimum and maximum.

- `MaxAbsScaler`: Normalization – scaling a feature by the maximum absolute value.

- `RobustScaler`: Normalization – scaling a feature to the quantile range.

- `PCA`: Linear dimensionality reduction based on PCA.

- `TruncatedSVD`: Linear dimensionality reduction-based truncated **singular value decomposition** (**SVD**). Contrary to PCA, this estimator does not center the data beforehand.

- `SparseNormalizer`: Normalization – each sample is normalized independently.

Complex preprocessing is referred to as **featurization**. These preprocessing steps are more complicated and apply various tasks during Automated Machine Learning optimization. As a user of Azure Automated Machine Learning, you can expect this list to grow and include new state-of-the-art transformations as they become available. The following list shows the various featurization steps:

- **Drop high cardinality or no variance features**: Drops high cardinality (for example, hashes, IDs, or GUIDs) or no variance (for example, all values missing or the same value across all rows) features.

- **Impute missing values**: Imputes missing values for numerical features (mean imputation) and categorical features (mode imputation).

- **Generate additional features**: Generates additional features derived from date/time (for example, year, month, day, day of the week, day of the year, quarter, week of the year, hour, minute, and second) and text features (term frequency based on n-grams).

- **Transform and encode**: Encodes categorical features using one-hot encoding (low cardinality) and one-hot-hash encoding (high cardinality). Transforms numeric features with few unique values into categorical features.

- **Word embeddings**: Uses a pre-trained embedding model to convert text into aggregated feature vectors using mean embeddings.

- **Target encodings**: Performs target encoding on categorical features.

- **Text target encoding**: Performs target encoding on text features using a bag-of-words model.

- **Weight of evidence**: Calculates the correlation of categorical columns to the target column through the weight of evidence and outputs a new feature per column per class.

- **Cluster distance**: Trains a k-means clustering model on all the numerical columns and computes the distance of each feature to its centroid before outputting a new feature per column per cluster.

Let's start with a simple Automated Machine Learning classification task that also uses preprocessing.

We will start by defining a dictionary containing the Automated Machine Learning configuration. To enable standard preprocessing such as scaling, normalization, and PCA/SVD, we need to set the `preprocess` property to `true`. For advanced preprocessing and feature engineering, we need to set the `featurization` property to `auto`. The following code block shows all these settings:

```
automl_settings = {
  "experiment_timeout_minutes": 15,
  "n_cross_validations": 3,
  "primary_metric": 'accuracy',
  "featurization": 'auto',
  "preprocess": True,
  "verbosity": logging.INFO,
}
```

Using this configuration, we can now load a dataset using `pandas`. As shown in the following snippet, we are loading the `titanic` dataset and specifying the target column as a string. This column is required later for configuring Automated Machine Learning:

```
import pandas as pd

df = pd.read_csv("train.csv")
target_column = "survival"
```

> **Important Note**
>
> When you're using Automated Machine Learning and the local execution context, you can use a pandas DataFrame as the input source. However, when you execute the training process on a remote cluster, you need to wrap the data in an Azure Machine Learning dataset.

Whenever we use a black-box classifier, we should also hold out a test set to verify the test performance of the model to validate generalization. Therefore, we must split the data into training and test sets:

```
from sklearn.model_selection import train_test_split

df_train, df_test = train_test_split(df, test_size=0.2)
```

Finally, we can supply all the required parameters to the Automated Machine Learning configuration constructor. In this example, we are using a local execution target to train the Automated Machine Learning experiment. However, we can also provide an Azure Machine Learning dataset and submit the experiment to our training cluster:

```
from azureml.train.automl import AutoMLConfig

automl_config = AutoMLConfig(
    task='classification',
    debug_log='debug.log',
    compute_target=aml_cluster,
    training_data=df_train,
    label_column_name=target_column,
    **automl_settings)
```

Let's submit the Automated Machine Learning configuration as an experiment to the defined compute target and wait for completion. We can output the run details:

```
from azureml.widgets import RunDetails

automl_run = experiment.submit(automl_config,
    show_output=False)
RunDetails(automl_run).show()
```

Similar to `HyperDriveConfig`, we can see that `RunDetails` for Automated Machine Learning shows a lot of useful information about your current experiment. Not only can you see all of your scheduled and running models, but you also get a nice visualization of the trained models and their training performance. The following screenshot shows the accuracy of the first 14 runs of the Automated Machine Learning experiment:

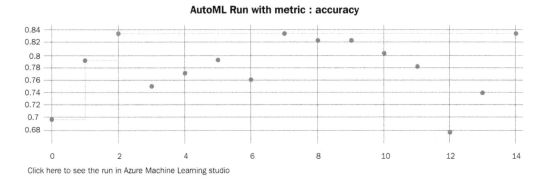

Figure 11.5 – Automated Machine Learning – visualization of the results

Finally, after 15 minutes, we can retrieve the best ML pipeline from the Automated Machine Learning run. From now on, we will refer to this pipeline simply as the **model**, as all the preprocessing steps are packed into the model, which itself is a pipeline of operations. We can use the following code to retrieve the pipeline:

```
best_run, best_model = remote_run.get_output()
```

The resulting fitted pipeline (called `best_model`) can now be used exactly like a scikit-learn estimator. We can store it on disk, register it to the model store, deploy it to a *container instance*, or simply evaluate it on the test set. We will see this in more detail in *Chapter 14, Model Deployment, Endpoints, and Operations*. Finally, we want to evaluate the best model. To do so, we will take the testing set that we separated from the dataset beforehand and predict the output on the fitted model:

```
from sklearn.metrics import import accuracy_score

y_test = df_test[target_column]
X_test = df_test.drop(target_column, axis=1)
y_pred = fitted_model.predict(X_test)

accuracy_score(y_test, y_pred)
```

In the preceding code, we used the `accuracy_score` function from scikit-learn to compute the accuracy of the final model. These steps are all you need to perform classification on a dataset using automatically preprocessed data and fitted models.

Summary

In this chapter, we introduced hyperparameter optimization through **HyperDrive** and model optimization through **Automated Machine Learning** Both techniques can help you efficiently retrieve the best model for your ML task.

Grid sampling works great with classical ML models, and also when the number of tunable parameters is fixed. All the values on a discrete parameter grid are evaluated. In **random sampling**, we can apply a continuous distribution for the parameter space and select as many parameter choices as we can fit into the configured training duration. Random sampling performs better on a large number of parameters. Both sampling techniques can/should be tuned using an **early stopping criterion**.

Unlike random and grid sampling, **Bayesian optimization** probes the model performance to optimize the following parameter choices. This means that each set of parameter choices and the resulting model performance are used to compute the next best parameter choices. Therefore, Bayesian optimization uses ML to optimize parameter choices for your ML model. Since the underlying Gaussian process requires the resulting model performance, early stopping does not work with Bayesian optimization.

We also learned that Automated Machine Learning is a generalization of Bayesian optimization on the complete end-to-end ML pipeline. Instead of choosing only hyperparameters, we also choose pre-processing, feature engineering, model selection, and model stacking methods and optimize those together. Automated Machine Learning speeds up this process by predicting which models will perform well on your data instead of blindly trying all possible combinations. Both techniques are essential for a great ML project; Automated Machine Learning lets you focus on the data and labeling first, while hyperparameter tuning lets you optimize a specific model.

In the next chapter, we will look at training DNNs where the data or the model parameters don't fit into the memory of a single machine anymore, and therefore distributed learning is required.

12
Distributed Machine Learning on Azure

In the previous chapter, we learned about hyperparameter tuning through search and optimization, using HyperDrive as well as Automated Machine Learning as a special case of hyperparameter optimization, involving feature engineering, model selection, and model stacking. Automated Machine Learning is **machine learning as a service (MLaaS)**, whereby the only input is your data, an ML task, and an error metric. It's hard to imagine running all experiments and parameter combinations for Automated Machine Learning on a single machine or a single CPU/GPUwe are looking into ways to speed up the training process through parallelization and distributed computing.

In this chapter, we will look into distributed and parallel computing algorithms and frameworks for efficiently training ML models in parallel. The goal of this chapter is to build an environment in Azure where you can speed up the training process of classical ML and deep learning models by adding more machines to your training environment, thereby scaling out the cluster.

First, we will take a look at the different methods and fundamental building blocks for **distributed ML**. You will grasp the difference between training independent models in parallel, as done in HyperDrive and Automated Machine Learning, and training a single model ensemble on a large dataset in parallel by partitioning the training data. We will then look into distributed ML for single models and discover data-distributed and model-distributed training methods. Both methods are often used in real-world scenarios for speeding up or enabling the training of large deep neural networks.

After that, we will discover the most popular frameworks for distributed ML and how they can be used in Azure and in combination with Azure Machine Learning compute. The transition between execution engines, communication libraries, and functionality for distributed ML libraries is smooth but often hard to understand. However, after reading this chapter, you will understand the difference between running Apache Spark in Databricks with MLlib and using Horovod, Gloo, PyTorch, and TensorFlow parameter servers.

In the final section, we will take a look at two practical examples of how to implement the functionality we'll be covering in Azure and integrate it with Azure Machine Learning compute.

This chapter covers the following topics:

- Exploring methods for distributed ML
- Using distributed ML in Azure

Technical requirements

In this chapter, we will use the following Python libraries and versions to create decision-tree-based ensemble classifiers:

- `azureml-core 1.34.0`
- `azureml-sdk 1.34.0`
- `horovod 0.23.0`
- `tensorflow 2.6.0`
- `pyspark 3.2.0`
- `numpy 1.19.5`
- `pandas 1.3.2`
- `scikit-learn 0.24.2`

Similar to previous chapters, you can execute this code using either a local Python interpreter or a notebook environment hosted in Azure Machine Learning.

All code examples in this chapter can be found in the GitHub repository for this book, found at `https://github.com/PacktPublishing/Mastering-Azure-Machine-Learning-Second-Edition/tree/main/chapter12`.

Exploring methods for distributed ML

The journey of implementing ML pipelines is very similar for a lot of users and is often similar to the steps described in the previous chapters. When users start switching from experimentation to real-world data or from small examples to larger models, they often experience a similar issue: training large parametric models on large amounts of data—especially DL models—takes a very long time. Sometimes, epochs last hours, and training takes days to converge.

Waiting hours or even days for a model to converge means precious time wasted for many engineers, as it makes it a lot harder to interactively tune the training process. Therefore, many ML engineers need to speed up their training process by leveraging various distributed computing techniques. The idea of distributed ML is as simple as speeding up a training process by adding more compute resources. In the best case, the training performance improves linearly by adding more machines to the training cluster (scaling out). In this section, we will take a look at the most common patterns of distributed ML and try to understand and reason about them. In the next section of this chapter, we will also apply them to some real-world examples.

Most modern ML pipelines use some of the techniques discussed in this chapter to speed up the training process once their data or models become larger. This is similar to the need for big data platforms—such as Spark, Hive, and so on—for data preprocessing, once the data gets large. Hence, while this chapter seems overly complex, we would recommend revisiting it whenever you are waiting for your model to converge or want to produce better results faster.

There are generally three patterns for leveraging distributed computing for ML, as presented here:

- Training independent models on small data in parallel
- Training copies of a model in parallel on different subsets of the data
- Training different parts of the same model in parallel

Let's take a look at each of these methods.

Training independent models on small data in parallel

We will first look at the easiest example: training (small) independent models on a (small) dataset. A typical use case for this parallel training is performing a hyperparameter search or the optimization of a classic ML model or a small neural network. This is very similar to what we covered in *Chapter 11, Hyperparameter Tuning and Automated Machine Learning*. Even Automated Machine Learning—where multiple individual independent models are trained and compared—uses this approach under the hood. In parallel training, we aim to speed up the training of multiple independent models with different parameters by training these models in parallel.

The following diagram shows this case, where instead of training the individual models in sequence on a single machine, we train them in parallel:

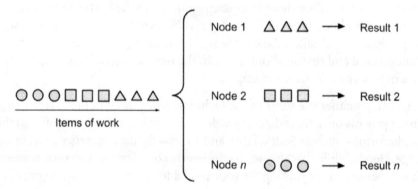

Figure 12.1 – Parallel processing

You can see that no communication or synchronization is required during the training process of the individual models. This means that we can train either on multiple CPUs/GPUs on the same machine or on multiple machines.

When using Azure Machine Learning for hyperparameter tuning, this parallelization is easy to achieve by configuring an Azure Machine Learning compute target with multiple nodes and selecting the number of concurrent runs through the `max_concurrent_runs` parameter of the HyperDrive configuration. In Azure Machine Learning HyperDrive, all it takes is to specify an estimator and `param_sampling`, and submit the HyperDrive configuration as an experiment in order to run the individual task in parallel, as shown here:

```
from azureml.train.hyperdrive import HyperDriveConfig
hyperdrive_run_config = HyperDriveConfig(
    estimator=estimator,
    hyperparameter_sampling=param_sampling,
    primary_metric_name="accuracy",
```

```
    primary_metric_goal=PrimaryMetricGoal.MAXIMIZE,
    max_total_runs=100,
    max_concurrent_runs=4)
```

```
from azureml.core.experiment import Experiment
experiment = Experiment(workspace, experiment_name)
hyperdrive_run = experiment.submit(hyperdrive_run_config)
```

Here are some formulas to compute the value for `max_concurrent_runs` for HyperDrive or any other distributed computing setup:

- For CPU-based training, the maximal number of concurrent training runs is limited by the number of available CPUs and compute nodes. The available physical memory is also a limitation, but swapping to virtual memory allow us to consume more memory than is physically available.

- For GPU-based training, the maximal number of concurrent training runs is limited by the number of available GPUs and compute nodes, as well as the amount of available GPU memory. Typically, one training run is pinned to one physical GPU, but through GPU virtualization we can also train multiple models on a single physical GPU if enough GPU memory is available.

Here is a guide to how to estimate how much memory a single model will consume:

Size of a single parameter:

- Half-precision float: 16 bits (2 bytes).
- Single-precision float: 32 bits (4 bytes)—this is often the default.
- Double-precision float: 64 bits (8 bytes).

Number of parameters required for a model:

- Parametric model: Sum of all parameters
- Non-parametric model: Number of representations (for example, decision trees) * number of a representation's parameters

Then, you multiply additional factors, as follows:

- Models using backpropagation: overall memory * 2
- Models using batching: overall memory * batch size
- Models using (recurrent) states: memory per state * number of recurrent steps

While this use case seems very similar, let's move on to the next use case where we are given a large dataset that cannot be copied onto every machine.

Training a model ensemble on large datasets in parallel

The next thing we will discuss is a very common optimization within ML, particularly when training models on large datasets. In order to train models, we usually require a large amount of data that rarely all fits into the memory of a single machine. Therefore, it is often required to split the data into chunks and train multiple individual models on the different chunks.

The following screenshot shows two ways of splitting data into smaller chunks—by splitting the rows horizontally (left) or by splitting the columns vertically (right):

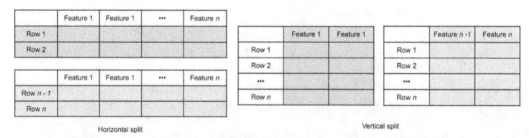

Figure 12.2 – Data split: horizontal (row-wise) versus vertical (column-wise)

You could also mix both techniques to extract a subset from your training data. Whenever you are using tools from the big data domain—such as MapReduce, Hive, or Spark—partitioning your data will help you to speed up your training process or enable training over huge amounts of data in the first place.

A good example of performing data-distributed training is to train a massive tree ensemble of completely separate decision-tree models, also called a random forest. By splitting the data into many thousands of randomized chunks, you can train one decision tree per chunk of data and combine all trained trees into a single ensemble model. Apache Hivemall is a library based on Hive and Spark that does exactly this on either of the two execution engines. Here is an example of training multiple XGBoost multi-class ensemble models on Hive using **Hive Query Language** (**HiveQL**) and Apache Hivemall:

```
-- explicitly use 3 reducers
-- set mapred.reduce.tasks=3;

create table xgb_softmax_model as
```

```
select
  train_xgboost(features, label,
    '-objective multi:softmax -num_class 10 -num_round 10')
    as (model_id, model)
from (
  select features, (label - 1) as label
  from data_train
  cluster by rand(43) -- shuffle data to reducers
) data;
```

In the preceding function, we use the `cluster` keyword to randomly move rows of data to the reducers. This will partition the data horizontally and train an XGBoost model per partition on each reducer. By defining the number of reducers, we also define the number of models trained in parallel. The resulting models are stored in a table where each row defines the parameters of one model. In a prediction, we would simply combine all individual models and perform an average-voting criterion to retrieve the final result.

Another example of this approach would be a standard Spark pipeline that trains multiple independent models on vertical and horizontal data partitions. When we've finished training the individual models, we can use an average-voting criterion during inference to find the optimal result for a prediction task. Here is a small example script for training multiple models on horizontally partitioned data in parallel using Python, PySpark, and scikit-learn:

```
from pyspark.sql import SparkSession
spark = SparkSession.builder \
    .appName("Distributed Training") \
    .master("local") \
    .getOrCreate()


# read the input data
df = spark.read.parquet("data/")


# define your training function
from sklearn.ensemble import RandomForestClassifier
def train_model(data):
    clf = RandomForestClassifier(n_estimators=10)
    return clf.fit(data['train_x'], data['train_y'])
```

```
# split your data into partitions and train models
num_models = 100
models = df.rdd.repartition(num_models) \
  .mapPartitions(train_model) \
  .collect()
```

In the preceding function, we can now load almost any amount of data and repartition it such that each partition fits into the local memory of a single node. If we have 1 **terabyte (TB)** of training data, we could split it into 100 partitions of 10-**gigabyte (GB)** chunks of data, which we distribute over 10 12-core worker nodes with 128 GB **random-access memory (RAM)** each. The training time will, at most, take a couple of seconds for the training of the 100 models in parallel. Once all the models are trained, we use the `collect()` method to return all trained models to the head node.

We could have also decided to just store the models from each individual worker on disk or in a distributed filesystem, but it might be nicer to just combine the results on a single node. In this example, you see we have the freedom to choose either of the two methods because all models are independent of each other. This is not true for cases where the models are suddenly dependent on each other—for example, when minimizing a global gradient or splitting a single model over multiple machines, which are both common use cases when training DNNs in the same way. In this case, we need some new operators to steer the control flow of the data and gradients. Let's look into these operators in the following section.

Fundamental building blocks for distributed ML

As we saw in the previous example, we need some fundamental building blocks or operators to manage the data flow in a distributed system. We call these operators **collective algorithms**. These algorithms implement common synchronization and communication patterns for distributed computing and are required when training ML models. Before we jump into distributed training methods for DNNs, we will have a quick look at these patterns to understand the foundations.

The most common communication patterns in distributed systems are listed here:

- One-to-one
- One-to-many (also called *broadcast* or *scatter* patterns)
- Many-to-one (also called *gather* or *reduce* patterns)
- Many-to-many (also called *all-gather* or *all-reduce* patterns)

The following screenshot gives a great overview of these patterns and shows how the data flows between the individual actors of a system:

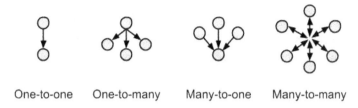

One-to-one   One-to-many   Many-to-one   Many-to-many

Figure 12.3 – Communication patterns in distributed systems

We can immediately think back to the hyperparameter optimization technique of Bayesian optimization. First, we need to **broadcast** the training data from the master to all worker nodes. Then, we can choose parameter combinations from the parameter space on the master and broadcast those to the worker nodes as well. Finally, we perform training on the worker nodes, before then **gathering** all the model validation scores from the worker nodes on the master. By comparing the scores and applying Bayes' theorem, we can predict the next possible parameter combinations and repeat broadcasting them to the worker nodes.

Did you notice something in the preceding algorithm? How can we know that all worker nodes finished the training process, and gather all scores from all worker nodes? To do this, we will use another building block called synchronization, or **barrier synchronization**. With barrier synchronization, we can schedule the execution of a task such that it needs to wait for all other distributed tasks to be finished. The following screenshot shows a good overview of the synchronization pattern in multiprocessors:

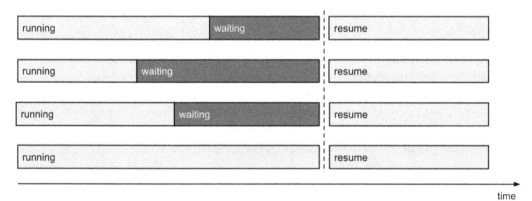

time

Figure 12.4 – Synchronization mechanism

As you can see, we implicitly used these algorithms already in the previous chapter, where they were hidden from us behind the term *optimization*. Now, we will use them explicitly by changing the optimizers in order to train a single model over multiple machines.

As you might have already realized, these patterns are not new and are used by your operating system many times per second. However, in this case, we can take advantage of these patterns and apply them to the execution graph of a distributed training process, and through specialized hardware (for example, by connecting two GPUs together using **InfiniBand (IB)**).

In order to use this collective algorithm with a different level of hardware support (GPU support and vectorization), you need to select a communication backend. These backends are libraries that often run as a separate process and implement communication and synchronization patterns. Popular libraries for collective algorithms include **Gloo, Message Passing Interface (MPI)**, and **NVIDIA Collective Communications Library (NCCL)**.

Most DL frameworks, such as PyTorch or TensorFlow, provide their own higher-level abstractions on one of these communication backends—for example, PyTorch **Remote Procedure Call (RPC)** and a TensorFlow **parameter server (PS)**. Instead of using a different execution and communication framework, you could also choose a general-purpose framework for distributed computing, such as Spark.

> **Important Note**
>
> The PyTorch documentation has an up-to-date guide on when to use which collective communication library: `https://pytorch.org/docs/stable/distributed.html#which-backend-to-use`.

As you can see, the list of possible choices is endless, and multiple combinations are possible. We haven't even talked about Horovod, a framework used to add distributed training to other DL frameworks through distributed optimizers. The good part is that most of these frameworks and libraries are provided in all Azure Machine Learning runtimes as well as being supported through the Azure ML SDK. This means you will often only specify the desired backend, supply your model to any specific framework, and let Azure Machine Learning handle the setup, initialization, and management of these tools. We will see this in action in the second half of this chapter.

Speeding up deep learning with data-parallel training

Another variation of distributed data-parallel training is very common in DL. In order to speed up the training of larger models, we can run multiple training iterations with different chunks of data on distributed copies of the same model. This is especially crucial when each training iteration takes a significant amount of time (for example, multiple seconds), which is a typical scenario for training large DNNs where we want to take advantage of multi-GPU environments.

Data-distributed training for DL is based on the idea of using a **distributed gradient descent (DGD)** algorithm, as follows:

1. Distribute a copy of the model to each node.
2. Distribute a chunk of data to each node.
3. Run a full pass through the network on each node and compute the gradient.
4. Collect all gradients on a single node and compute the average gradient.
5. Send the average gradient to all nodes.
6. Update all models using the average gradient.

The following diagram shows this in action for multiple models, running the forward/backward pass individually and sending the gradient back to the parameter server:

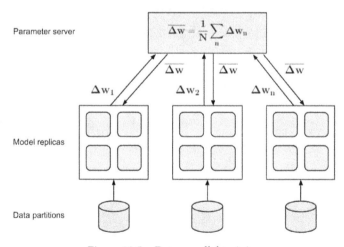

Figure 12.5 – Data-parallel training

As seen here, the server computes the average gradient, which is sent back to all other nodes. We can immediately see that, suddenly, communication is required between the worker nodes and a primary node (let's call it the *parameter server*), and that synchronization is required too while waiting for all models to finish computing the gradient.

A great example of this use case is speeding up the training process of DL models by parallelizing the backpropagation step and combining the gradients from each node to an overall gradient. TensorFlow currently supports this distribution mode using a so-called parameter server. The *Horovod* framework developed at Uber provides a handy abstraction for distributed optimizers and plugs into many available ML frameworks or distributed execution engines, such as TensorFlow, PyTorch, and Apache Spark. We will take a look at practical examples of using Horovod and Azure Machine Learning in the *Horovod – a distributed DL training framework* section.

Training large models with model-parallel training

Lastly, another common use case in DL is to train models that are larger than the provided GPU memory of a single GPU. This approach is a bit trickier as it requires the model execution graph to be split among different GPUs or even different machines. While this is not a big problem in CPU-based execution and is often done in Spark, Hive, or TensorFlow, we also need to transfer the intermediate results between multiple GPU memories. In order to do this effectively, extra hardware and drivers such as **Infiniband** (GPU-to-GPU communication) and **GPUDirect** (efficient GPU memory access) are required.

The following diagram displays the difference between computing multiple gradients in parallel (on the left) and computing a single forward pass of a distributed model (on the right):

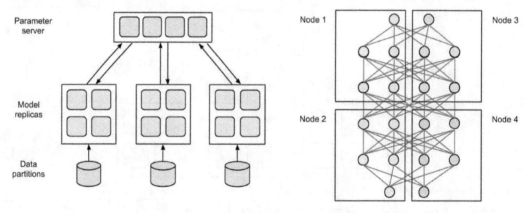

Figure 12.6 – Model-parallel training

The latter is a lot more complicated as data has to be exchanged during forward and backward passes between multiple GPUs and/or multiple nodes.

In general, we choose between two scenarios: multi-GPU training on a single machine and multi-GPU training on multiple machines. As you might expect, the latter is a lot more difficult, as it requires communication between and the synchronization of multiple machines over a network.

In the following script, we create a simple model running distributed on two GPUs using PyTorch. Using `.to('cuda:*')` methods throughout the model, we define the GPU on which an operation should be performed. In addition, we also need to add the same annotation to the input data for these computations:

```python
import torch
import torch.nn as nn
import torch.optim as optim


class ParallelModel(nn.Module):
    def __init__(self):
        super(ParallelModel, self).__init__()
        self.net1 = torch.nn.Linear(10, 10).to('cuda:0')
        self.relu = torch.nn.ReLU()
        self.net2 = torch.nn.Linear(10, 5).to('cuda:1')

    def forward(self, x):
        x = self.relu(self.net1(x.to('cuda:0')))
        return self.net2(x.to('cuda:1'))
```

As we can see in the preceding code, we configure the network to compute the first fully connected layer on GPU 0 whereas the second fully connected layer is computed on GPU 1. When configuring forward steps, we also need to configure the inputs to both layers accordingly.

Training the model using a built-in optimizer and loss function is not very different from non-distributed models. The only difference is that we also have to define the target GPU for the training labels so that the loss can be computed, as follows:

```python
model = ParallelModel()
loss_fn = nn.MSELoss()
optimizer = optim.SGD(model.parameters(), lr=0.001)

optimizer.zero_grad()
outputs = model(torch.randn(20, 10))
```

```
labels = torch.randn(20, 5).to('cuda:1')
loss_fn(outputs, labels).backward()
optimizer.step()
```

As you can see, we have split individual layers to run on multiple GPUs, while the data between these layers needs to be transferred during forward and backward passes. We have to apply code changes to the model itself in order to specify which parts of the model should run on which GPU.

> **Important Note**
> Please note that we could also make this split dynamic, such that we split the model into x consecutive subgraphs that are executed on x GPUs.

It's interesting to note that many of the techniques discussed in this chapter can be combined. We could, for example, train one multi-GPU model per machine, while partitioning the data into chunks and computing multiple parts of the gradient on multiple machines—hence adopting a data-distributed model-parallel approach.

In the next section, we will learn how to put these concepts into practice.

Using distributed ML in Azure

The *Exploring methods for distributed ML* section contained an overwhelming amount of different parallelization scenarios, various communication backends for collective algorithms, and code examples using different ML frameworks and even execution engines. The amount of choice when it comes to ML frameworks is quite large, and making an educated decision is not easy. This choice gets even more complicated as some frameworks are supported out of the box in Azure Machine Learning while others have to be installed, configured, and managed by the user.

In this section, we will go through the most common scenarios, learn how to choose the correct combination of frameworks, and implement a distributed ML pipeline in Azure.

In general, you have three choices for running distributed ML in Azure, as follows:

- The first obvious choice is using Azure Machine Learning, the notebook environment, the Azure Machine Learning SDK, and Azure Machine Learning compute clusters. This will be the easiest solution for many complex use cases. Huge datasets can be stored on Azure Blob Storage, and models can be trained as data-parallel and/ or model-parallel models with different communication backends. Everything is managed for you by wrapping your training script with an estimator abstraction.

- The second choice is to use a different authoring and execution engine for your code instead of Azure Machine Learning notebooks and Azure Machine Learning compute clusters. A popular option is Azure Databricks with integrated interactive notebooks and Apache Spark as a distributed execution engine. Using Databricks, you can use the pre-built ML images and auto-scaling clusters, which provides a great environment for running distributed ML training.

- The third choice is to build and roll out your own custom solution. To do so, you need to build a separate cluster with virtual machines or Kubernetes and orchestrate the setup, installation, and management of the infrastructure and code. While this is the most flexible solution, it is also—by far—the most complex and time-consuming to set up.

For this book, we will first look into Horovod optimizers, Azure Databricks, and Apache Spark before diving deeper into Azure Machine Learning.

Horovod – a distributed deep learning training framework

Horovod is a framework for enabling **distributed DL** and was initially developed and made open source by Uber. It provides a unified way to support the distributed training of existing DL training code for the following supported frameworks—TensorFlow, Keras, PyTorch, and Apache MXNet. The design goal was to make the transition from single-node training to data-parallel training extremely simple for any existing project, and hence enable these models to train faster on multiple GPUs in a distributed environment.

Horovod is an excellent choice as a drop-in replacement for optimizers in any of the supported frameworks for data-parallel training. It integrates nicely with the supported frameworks through initialization and update steps or update hooks, by simply abstracting the GPUs from the DL code. From a user's perspective, only minimal code changes have to be done to support data-parallel training for your model. Let's take a look at an example using Keras and implement the following steps:

1. Initialize Horovod.
2. Configure Keras to read GPU information from Horovod.
3. Load a model and split training data.
4. Wrap the Keras optimizer as a Horovod distributed optimizer.
5. Implement model training.
6. Execute the script using `horovodrun`.

The detailed steps are listed here:

1. The first step is the same for any script using Horovod—we first need to load horovod from the correct package and initialize it, as follows:

```
import horovod.keras as hvd
hvd.init()
```

2. Next, we need to perform a custom setup step, which varies depending on the framework used. This step will set up the GPU configuration for the framework, and ensure that it can call the abstracted versions through Horovod. The code is illustrated in the following snippet:

```
from tensorflow.keras import backend as K
import tensorflow as tf


# pin GPU to be used to process local rank.
# one GPU per process
config = tf.ConfigProto()
config.gpu_options.allow_growth = True
config.gpu_options.visible_device_list = str(hvd.local_
rank())
K.set_session(tf.Session(config=config))
```

3. Now, we can simply take our single-node, single-GPU Keras model and define all parameters and the training and validation data. There is nothing special required during this step, as we can see here:

```
# standard model and data
batch_size = 10
epochs = 100
model = load_model(...)
x_train, y_train = load_train_data(...)
x_test, y_test = load_test_data(...)
```

4. Finally, we arrive at the magical part, where we wrap the framework optimizer—in this case, Adadelta from Keras—as a Horovod distributed optimizer. For all subsequent code, we will simply use the distributed optimizer instead of the default one. We also need to adjust the learning rate to the number of used GPUs, as the resulting gradient will be averaged from the individual changes. This can be done using the following code:

```
from tensorflow.keras.optimizers import Adadelta
```

```
# adjust learning rate based on number of GPUs
opt = Adadelta(1.0 * hvd.size())


# add Horovod Distributed Optimizer
opt = hvd.DistributedOptimizer(opt)
```

5. The remaining part looks fairly simple. It involves compiling the model, fitting the model, and evaluating the model, just as with the single-node counterpart. It's worth mentioning that we need to add a callback to initialize all gradients during the training process. The code is illustrated in the following snippet:

```
model.compile(loss=keras.losses.categorical_crossentropy,
              optimizer=opt,
              metrics=['accuracy'])
callbacks = [
  hvd.callbacks.BroadcastGlobalVariablesCallback(0)
]
model.fit(x_train,
          y_train,
          batch_size=batch_size,
          callbacks=callbacks,
          epochs=epochs,
          verbose=1 if hvd.rank() == 0 else 0,
          validation_data=(x_test, y_test))
score = model.evaluate(x_test, y_test)
print('Test loss:', score[0])
print('Test accuracy:', score[1])
```

When looking at the preceding code, it's fair to say that Horovod is not over-promising on making it easy to extend your code for distributed execution using a data-parallel approach and distributed gradient computation. If you have looked into the native TensorFlow or PyTorch versions, you will have seen that this requires far fewer code changes and is a lot more readable and portable than a parameter server or RPC framework.

6. The Horovod framework uses a communication based on MPI to handle collective algorithms under the hood, and usually requires one running process per GPU per node. However, it can also run on top of the Gloo backend or a custom MPI backend through a configuration option. Here is a sample snippet of how to use the `horovodrun` command to start a training process on two machines, `server1` and `server2`, each using four separate GPUs:

```
horovodrun -np 8 -H server1:4,server2:4 python train.py
```

Running and debugging Horovod on your own cluster can still be painful when you only want to speed up your training progress by scaling out your cluster. Therefore, Azure Machine Learning compute provides a wrapper that does all the heavy lifting for you, requiring only a training script with Horovod annotations. We will see this in the *Training models with Horovod on Azure Machine Learning* section.

Model-parallel training can be combined with Horovod by using the model-parallel features of the underlying framework and using only one Horovod process per machine instead of per GPU. However, this is a custom configuration and is currently not supported in Azure Machine Learning.

Implementing the HorovodRunner API for a Spark job

In many companies, ML is an additional data processing step on top of existing data pipelines. Therefore, if you have huge amounts of data and you are already managing Spark clusters or using Azure Databricks to process that data, it is easy to also add distributed training capabilities.

As we have seen in the *Exploring methods for distributed ML* section of this chapter, we can simply train multiple models using parallelization or by partitioning the training data. However, we could also train DL models and benefit from distributed ML techniques to speed up the training process.

When using the Databricks ML runtime, you can leverage Horovod for Spark to distribute your training process. This functionality is available through the `HorovodRunner` API and is powered by Spark's barrier-mode execution engine to provide a stable communication backend for long-running jobs. Using `HorovodRunner` on the head node, it will send the training function to the workers and start the function using the MPI backend. This all happens under the hood within the Spark process.

Again, this is one of the reasons why Horovod is quite easy to use, as it is literally just a drop-in replacement for your current optimizer. Imagine that you usually run your Keras model on Azure Databricks using the PySpark engine; however, you would like to add Horovod to speed up the training process by leveraging other machines in the cluster and splitting the gradient descent over multiple machines. In order to do so, you would have to add literally only two lines of code to the example from the previous section, as seen here:

```
hr = HorovodRunner(np=2)

def train():
    # Perform your training here..
    import horovod.keras as hvd
    hvd.init()
    ...

hr.run(train)
```

In the preceding code snippet, we observe that we only need to initialize `HorovodRunner()` with the number of worker nodes. Calling the `run()` method with the training function will automatically start the new workers and the MPI communication backend and will send the training code to the workers, executing the training in parallel. Therefore, you can now add data-parallel training to your long-running Spark ML jobs.

Training models with Horovod on Azure Machine Learning

One of the benefits of moving to a cloud service is that you can consume functionality as a service rather than managing infrastructure on your own. Good examples are managed databases, lambda functions, managed Kubernetes, or container instances, where choosing a managed service means that you can focus on your application code while the infrastructure is managed for you in the cloud.

The Azure Machine Learning service sits in a similar spot where you can consume many of the different functionalities through an SDK (such as model management, optimization, training, and deployments) so that you don't have to maintain an ML cluster infrastructure. This brings a huge benefit when it comes to speeding up DNNs through distributed ML. If you have stuck with Azure Machine Learning compute until now, then moving to data-parallel training is as difficult as adding a single parameter to your training configuration—for any of the various choices discussed in this chapter.

Let's think about running the Keras training script in data-parallel mode using a Horovod optimizer in a distributed environment. You need to make sure all the correct versions of your tools are set up (from **Compute Unified Device Architecture (CUDA)** to **CUDA Deep Neural Network (cuDNN)**, GPUDirect, MPI, Horovod, TensorFlow, and Keras) and play together nicely with your current operating system and hardware. Then, you need to distribute the training code to all machines, start the MPI process, and then call the script using Horovod and the relevant command-line argument on every machine in the cluster. And we haven't even talked about authentication, data access, or auto-scaling.

With Azure Machine Learning, you get an ML environment that just works and will be kept up to date for you. Let's take a look at the previous Horovod and Keras training script, which we stored in a `train.py` file. Now, similar to the previous chapters, we create an estimator to wrap the training call for the Azure Machine Learning SDK. To enable multi-GPU data-parallel training using Horovod and the MPI backend, we simply add the relevant parameters. The resulting script looks like this:

```
from azureml.core import ScriptRunConfig
from azureml.core.runconfig import MpiConfiguration

run_config = get_run_config(aml_cluster, [
    'numpy', 'pandas', 'scikit-learn', 'joblib',
    'tensorflow', 'horovod'])

distr_config = MpiConfiguration(process_count_per_node=1,
                                node_count=2)

src = ScriptRunConfig(source_directory=script_folder,
                      script='train.py',
                      run_config=run_config,
                      arguments=script_params
                      distributed_job_config=distr_config)
```

Using the `use_gpu` flag, we can enable GPU-specific machines and their corresponding images with precompiled binaries for our Azure Machine Learning compute cluster. Using `node_count` and `process_count_per_node`, we specify the level of concurrency for the data-parallel training, where `process_count_per_node` should correspond with the number of GPUs available per node. Finally, we set the `distributed_backend` parameter to `mpi` to enable the MPI communication backend for this estimator. Another possible option would be using `ps` to enable the TensorFlow `ParameterServer` backend.

Finally, to start up the job, we simply submit the experiment, which will automatically set up the MPI session on each node and call the training script with the relevant arguments for us. I don't know how you feel about this, but for me, this is a really big step forward from the previous manual examples. The following line of code shows how you can submit the experiment:

```
run = experiment.submit(src)
```

Wrapping your training as part of an Azure Machine Learning estimator gives you the benefit of fine-tuning your training script configuration for multiple environments, be it multi-GPU data-parallel models for distributed gradient descent training or single-node instances for fast inference. By combining distributed DL with Azure Machine Learning compute auto-scaling clusters, you can get the most from the cloud by using pre-built managed services instead of manually fiddling with infrastructure and configurations.

Summary

Distributed ML is a great approach to scaling out your training infrastructure in order to gain speed in your training process. It is applied in many real-world scenarios and is very easy to use with Horovod and Azure Machine Learning.

Parallel execution is similar to hyperparameter searching, while distributed execution is similar to Bayesian optimization, which we discussed in detail in the previous chapter. Distributed executions need methods to perform communication (such as one-to-one, one-to-many, many-to-one, and many-to-many) and synchronization (such as barrier synchronization) efficiently. These so-called collective algorithms are provided by communication backends (MPI, Gloo, and NCCL) and allow efficient GPU-to-GPU communication.

DL frameworks build higher-level abstractions on top of communication backends to perform model-parallel and data-parallel training. In data-parallel training, we partition the input data to compute multiple independent parts of the model on different machines and add up the results in a later step. A common technique in DL is distributed gradient descent, where each node performs gradient descent on a partition of the input batch, and a master collects all the separate gradients to compute the overall average gradient of the combined model. In model-parallel training, you distribute a single model over multiple machines. This is often the case when a model doesn't fit into the GPU memory of a single GPU.

Horovod is an abstraction on top of existing optimizers of other ML frameworks, such as TensorFlow, Keras, PyTorch, and Apache MXNet. It provides an easy-to-use interface to add data-distributed training to an existing model without many code changes. While you could run Horovod on a standalone cluster, the Azure Machine Learning service provides good integration by wrapping its functionality as an estimator object. You learned how to run Horovod on an Azure Machine Learning compute cluster to speed up your training process through distributed ML with a few lines of Horovod initialization and a wrapper over the current optimizer.

In the next chapter, we will use all the knowledge from the previous chapters to train recommendation engines on Azure. Recommendation engines often build on top of other NLP feature extraction or classification models and hence combine many of the techniques we have learned about so far.

13
Building a Recommendation Engine in Azure

In the previous chapter, we discussed distributed training methods for ML models, and you learned how to train distributed ML models efficiently in Azure. In this chapter, we will dive into traditional and modern recommendation engines, which often combine technologies and techniques covered in the previous chapters.

First, we will take a quick look at the different types of recommendation engines, what data is needed for each type, and what can be recommended using these different approaches. This will help you understand when to choose from non-personalized, content-based, or rating-based recommenders.

After this, we will dive into content-based recommendations, namely item-item and user-user recommenders, based on feature vectors and similarity. You will learn about cosine distance to measure the similarity between feature vectors and feature engineering techniques to avoid common pitfalls while building content-based recommendation engines.

Subsequently, we will discuss rating-based recommendations that can be used once enough user-item interaction data has been collected. You will learn the difference between implicit and explicit ratings, develop your own implicit metric function, and think about the recency of user ratings.

In the section following this, we will combine content- and rating-based recommenders into a single hybrid recommender and learn about state-of-the-art techniques for modern recommendation engines. You will implement two recommenders using Azure Machine Learning, one using Python and one using Azure Machine Learning designer – the graphical UI of Azure Machine Learning.

In the last section, we will look into an online recommender system as a service using reinforcement learning – Azure Personalizer. Having understood both content- and rating-based methods, you will learn how to improve your recommendations on the fly using a fitness function and online learning.

The following topics will be covered in this chapter:

- An introduction to recommendation engines
- A content-based recommender system
- Collaborative filtering – a rating-based recommender system
- Combining content and ratings in hybrid recommendation engines
- Automatic optimization through reinforcement learning

Technical requirements

In this chapter, we will use the following Python libraries and versions to create content- and rating-based recommendation engines, as well as hybrid and online recommenders:

- `azureml-core 1.34.0`
- `azureml-sdk 1.34.0`
- `numpy 1.19.5`
- `scipy 1.7.1`
- `pandas 1.3.2`
- `scikit-learn 0.24.2`
- `lightgbm 3.2.1`
- `pyspark 3.2.0`
- `azure-cognitiveservices-personalizer 0.1.0`

Similar to previous chapters, you can run this code using either a local Python interpreter or a notebook environment hosted in Azure Machine Learning.

For the Matchbox recommender example, you need to use Azure Machine Learning designer in your Azure Machine Learning workspace. For Azure Personalizer, you need to set up an Azure Personalizer resource in the Azure portal.

All code examples in this chapter can be found in the GitHub repository for this book: `https://github.com/PacktPublishing/Mastering-Azure-Machine-Learning-Second-Edition/tree/main/chapter13`.

Introduction to recommendation engines

In today's digital world, recommendation engines are ubiquitous among many industries. Many online businesses, such as streaming, shopping, news, and social media, rely at their core on recommending the most relevant articles, news, and items to their users. How often have you clicked on a suggested video on YouTube, scrolled through your Facebook feed, listened to a personalized playlist on Spotify, or clicked on a recommended item on Amazon?

If you ask yourself what the term *relevant* means for the different services and industries, you are on the right track. In order to recommend relevant information to the user, we need to first define a relevancy metric, and a way to describe and compare different items and their similarity. These two properties are the key to understanding the different recommendation engines. We will learn more about this in the following sections of this chapter.

While the purpose of a recommendation engine is clear to most people, the different approaches are usually not. Hence, in order to better understand this, in this chapter, we will compare the different types of recommender systems and give some examples of them that you might have seen in your daily life. It's also worth mentioning that many services implement more than one of these approaches to produce great recommendations.

The easiest recommendation engines and methods are *non-personalized* recommendations. They are often used to show global interest (for example, Twitter global trends, popular Netflix shows, and a news website's front page) or trends where no user data is available. A good example is the recommendations of any streaming service that appear when you register and log into the service for the first time.

Once you log into a web service and start using it moderately, you are usually confronted with *content-based recommendations*. Content-based recommenders look for similar items or items of similar users, based on the item and user profile features. User profile items can contain many personality-based or socio-demographic traits including the following:

- Age
- Gender
- Nationality
- Country of residence
- Mother tongue

Imagine logging into Amazon without having bought anything there yet. Most recommended items will be similar to the ones you just viewed or the ones matching your demographics and location.

Once enough interaction data is available, you will start seeing *rating-based recommendations*, a method that is also called collaborative filtering. In rating-based recommenders, the users' interactions with items are transformed into explicit or implicit ratings. Based on these ratings, recommendations are made based on similar recommendations given by other users. Rating a movie on Netflix is an explicit rating, while watching a full 20-minute documentary on YouTube is an implicit rating. Therefore, a user will be shown movies liked by other people who also liked the movie that you just rated. And similarly, YouTube will show videos watched by other users who also watched the video you just saw.

> **Important Note**
>
> Microsoft provides many different implementations for popular recommendation engines in their GitHub repository at `https://github.com/Microsoft/Recommenders/`. This makes it easy to get started, pick the right algorithm, and implement, train, and deploy a recommendation engine on Azure.

The next natural step is to combine both content- and rating-based recommenders into a single *hybrid recommendation engine* that can deal with both user ratings and cold-start users, who are users without ratings. The benefit of this approach is that both recommender systems are optimized together and create a combined recommendation. Azure Machine Learning Studio (classic) and Azure Machine Learning designer provide the building blocks to train and deploy the Matchbox recommender, an online Bayesian hybrid recommendation engine built by Microsoft Research.

Another exciting new development in the past year was the introduction of hybrid online recommender optimization based on reinforcement learning. By providing a fitness function for the user rating, the algorithm can continuously learn to optimize this function. In the last section of this chapter, we will take a look at Azure Personalizer, a reinforcement learning-based recommendation engine as a service.

Let's dive right into the methods discussed and develop some example solutions for scalable recommendation engines in Azure.

A content-based recommender system

We first start with content-based recommendations, as they are the most similar to what we previously discussed in this book. The term *content* refers to the usage of only an item's or user's content information in the shape of a (numeric) feature vector. The way to arrive at a feature vector from an item (an article in a web shop) or a user (a browser session in a web service) is through data mining, data pre-processing, and feature engineering – skills you learned in the previous chapters.

Using users' and items' feature vectors, we can divide content-based recommendations into roughly two approaches:

- Item-item similarity
- User-user similarity

Hence, recommendations are based on the similarity of items or the similarity of users. Both approaches work great in cases where little to no interaction data between user and items is available (for example, a user with no purchase history on Amazon, no search history on YouTube, or no movies yet watched on Netflix – the so-called cold-start problem).

You will always have to deal with the cold-start problem the moment you decide to roll out recommendations or the moment a new user starts using your service. In both cases, you don't have sufficient user-item interactions (so-called ratings) available and need to recommend items based on content only.

For the first approach, we design a system that recommends similar items to the one a user currently interacts with. When a user looks at an item, the recommender returns the most similar items. The item similarity is based on the similarity of the item's feature vectors – we will see in the subsequent section how to compute this similarity. This approach can be used when no or little user interaction data is available. *Figure 13.1* visualizes this approach of recommending similar items based on content features and a single user interaction:

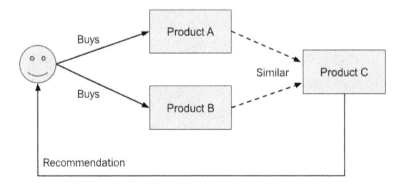

Figure 13.1 – Finding similar products using a content-based recommendation

Creating a playlist on Spotify will yield a box with recommended songs at the bottom, as shown in *Figure 13.2*. We can see that the recommended songs are based on the songs in the playlist; hence, it is similar content:

Figure 13.2 – Spotify's recommended songs

We can see songs listed that are similar to the ones in the playlist – similar in terms of genre, style, artists, and many more features.

Clicking on a product on Amazon will yield a box with related products at the bottom of the page, as shown in *Figure 13.3*. Again, similar products mean it is a content-based recommendation:

Shop Related Products

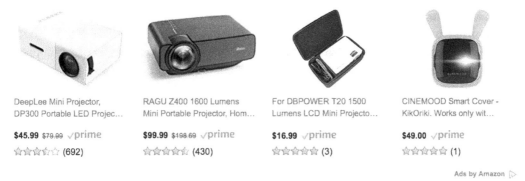

DeepLee Mini Projector,
DP300 Portable LED Projec…

$45.99 ~~$79.99~~ ✓prime

⭐⭐⭐⭐☆ (692)

RAGU Z400 1600 Lumens
Mini Portable Projector, Hom…

$99.99 ~~$198.69~~ ✓prime

⭐⭐⭐⭐☆ (430)

For DBPOWER T20 1500
Lumens LCD Mini Projecto…

$16.99 ✓prime

⭐⭐⭐⭐⭐ (3)

CINEMOOD Smart Cover -
KikOriki. Works only wit…

$49.00 ✓prime

⭐⭐⭐⭐⭐ (1)

Figure 13.3 – Amazon's recommended products

This recommendation has nothing to do with your previous shopping experience and can be displayed even when no user-purchase history is found.

In the second approach, the system recommends similar users based on a user profile. From those similar users, we can then select the favorite items and present them as a recommendation. Please note that in digital systems, the user profile can be implicitly defined via location (for example, through an IP address), language, demographic, and device fingerprinting. This technique can be used when user-item interaction data is available from other users but not for the current user. *Figure 13.4* visualizes this recommendation of the purchases of a similar user based on content features:

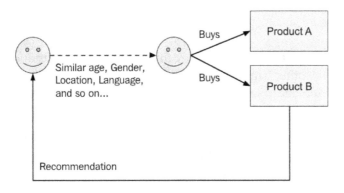

Figure 13.4 – Finding similar users using a content-based recommendation

From a user's perspective, it is usually hard to distinguish between this kind of recommendation and a non-personalized recommendation (for example, the top products in your location for your demographic or your language – all properties that can be extracted from your browser's fingerprint).

Measuring the similarity between items

The crucial part of training a content-based recommendation engine is to specify a metric that can measure and rank the similarity between two items. A popular choice is to use the **cosine similarity** or **cosine distance** between the items' feature vectors to measure the similarity between two items. The *cosine similarity* is computed as the cosine of the angle between two vectors where a vector is an observation in the dataset. The *cosine distance* is computed as 1 minus the cosine similarity. *Figure 13.5* shows two numeric feature vectors and the cosine distance between the feature vectors:

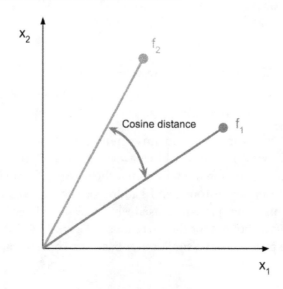

Figure 13.5 – Cosine distance

We can see in the figure that if both vectors are the same, the cosine distance between the two vectors is 0. On the other hand, the cosine similarity yields 1 when both vectors are pointing in the same direction, and 0 when both vectors are orthogonal to each other; hence, there is no similarity between the observations.

If you are unsure, you can always compute the cosine distance or similarity between two feature vectors using the following code (make sure that your DataFrame (df) has no additional id column and all columns are numeric):

```
from scipy import spatial
f1 = df.iloc[0, :]
f2 = df.iloc[1, :]

# compute the cosine distance between the first 2 rows
```

```
cosine_distance = spatial.distance.cosine(f1, f2)
print(cosine_distance)

# compute the cosine similarity between the first 2 rows
cosine_similarity = 1 - spatial.distance.cosine(f1, f2)
print(cosine_similarity)
```

Looking at the preceding snippet, I recommend you pick a few rows from your dataset, estimate their similarity (1 if they are the same or 0 if they are completely different), and then compute the cosine similarity using the aforementioned approach. If your guess and the computed approach are very different and you don't understand the reason, you'd better go back to data pre-processing and feature engineering. In the next section, you will learn the most common mistakes in feature engineering for recommender systems.

Feature engineering for content-based recommenders

Training a content-based recommendation engine is very similar to training a classical ML model. For end-to-end ML pipelines, all the steps, such as data preparation, training, validation, optimization, and deployment, are the same and use very similar or even the same tools and libraries as any traditional embedding, clustering, regression, or classification technique.

As for most other ML algorithms, great feature engineering is the key to good results from a recommendation engine. The difficulty for clustering-based recommenders is that most embeddings and similarity metrics only work in numeric space. While other techniques, such as tree-based classifiers, give you more freedom in the structure of input data, many clustering techniques require numeric features.

Another important factor for training content-based recommenders is the semantic meaning of categorical features. Therefore, you most likely want to use advanced natural language processing methods to embed categorical features into numerical space to capture this semantic meaning and provide it for the recommendation engine. The reason for the effect of categorical features in recommendation systems is based on the way similarity is measured.

As we discussed in the previous section, a similarity is often expressed/measured as the cosine similarity and, hence, computing the cosine between two feature vectors. Therefore, even if there is only a single different character between two categorical values, those categorical values would yield a similarity of 0 using one-hot encoding – although they are semantically very similar. Using simple label encoding, the results are even less obvious. With label encoding, the resulting similarity is now not only 0 but a non-interpretable value different from 0.

Therefore, we recommend semantic embedding of nominal/textual variables in order to capture their semantic meaning in numeric space and avoid common pitfalls, with categorical embeddings leaking into the similarity metric.

In general, there are two possible ways to implement content-based recommenders. If you are looking for a pure similarity, you can use any non-supervised embedding and clustering technique for finding similar items or users. The second possibility is to implement the recommender as a regression or classification technique. With this, you can predict a discrete or continuous value of relevance for all items, only considering item features or combinations of an item and user features. We will take a look at an example method in the subsequent section.

Content-based recommendations using gradient boosted trees

For our content-based model, we will use the *Criteo dataset* to predict the **Click-Through Rate (CTR)** per article, based on article features. We will use the predicted CTR to recommend articles with the highest predicted CTR. As you can see, it's very simple to formulate a content-based recommendation engine as a standard classification or regression problem.

For this example, we will use a gradient-boosted tree regressor from LightGBM. The model to predict the CTR is very similar to any regression model previously trained in this book. Let's get started:

1. First, we define the parameters for the LightGBM model:

```
params = {
    'task': 'train',
    'boosting_type': 'gbdt',
    'num_class': 1,
    'objective': "binary",
    'metric': "auc",
    'num_leaves': 64,
```

```
    'min_data': 20,
    'boost_from_average': True,
    'feature_fraction': 0.8,
    'learning_rate': 0.15,
}
```

2. Next, we define the training and test set as LightGBM datasets:

```
lgb_train = lgb.Dataset(x_train,
                        y_train.reshape(-1),
                        params=params)
lgb_test = lgb.Dataset(x_test,
                       y_test.reshape(-1),
                       reference=lgb_train)
```

3. Using this information, we can now train the model:

```
lgb_model = lgb.train(params,
                      lgb_train,
                      num_boost_round=100)
```

4. Finally, we can evaluate the model performance by predicting the CTR and computing the area under the ROC curve as an error metric:

```
y_pred = lgb_model.predict(x_test)
auc = roc_auc_score(np.asarray(y_test.reshape(-1)),
                    np.asarray(y_pred))
```

Great! You have learned to create recommendations based on item similarities. However, these recommendations have a poor diversity and will only recommend similar items. Therefore, they can be used when no user-item interaction data is available but will perform poorly once the user is active on your service. A better recommendation engine would recommend a variety of different items to help users explore and discover new and unrelated items they might like. This is exactly what we will do with collaborative filtering in the next section.

Collaborative filtering – a rating-based recommender system

By recommending only similar items or items from similar users, your users might get bored of the recommendations provided due to the lack of diversity and variety. Once a user starts interacting with a service (for example, watching videos on YouTube, reading and liking posts on Facebook, or rating movies on Netflix), we want to provide them with great personalized recommendations and relevant content to keep them happy and engaged. A great way to do so is to provide a good mix of similar content and new content to explore and discover.

Collaborative filtering is a popular approach for providing such diverse recommendations by comparing user-item interactions, finding other users who interact with similar items, and recommending items that those users also interacted with. It's almost as if you were to build many custom stereotypes and recommend other items consumed from by same stereotype. *Figure 13.6* illustrates this example:

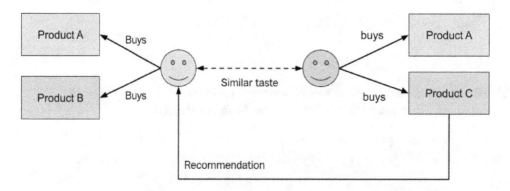

Figure 13.6 – Finding similar user ratings using collaborative filtering

As the person on the left buys similar items to the person on the right, we can recommend a new item to the person on the left that the person on the right bought. In this case, the user-item interaction is a person buying a product. However, in recommender language, we speak about ratings as a term summarizing all possible interactions between a user and an item. Let's look at building such a rating function (also called a feedback function).

One great example of amazing rating-based recommendations are the personalized recommended playlists in Spotify, as shown in *Figure 13.7*. In contrast to the previous Spotify recommendation at the bottom of each playlist, these recommendations are personalized based on my interaction history and feedback:

Figure 13.7 – Spotify's rating-based song recommendation

These playlists contain songs similar to the ones I listened to and that are also listened to by other people with my taste. Another nifty extension is that the song recommendations are categorized by genre into these six playlists.

What is a rating? Explicit feedback versus implicit feedback

A **feedback function** (or rating) quantifies the interaction between a user and an item. We differentiate between two types of feedback – explicit ratings (or non-observable feedback) and implicit ratings (or directly observable feedback). An **explicit rating** would be leaving a five-star review of a product on Amazon, whereas an **implicit rating** is buying the said product. While the former is a biased decision of the user, the latter can be objectively observed and evaluated.

The most obvious form of rating is to explicitly ask the user for feedback – for example, to rate a certain movie, song, article, or the helpfulness of a support document. This is the method most people think about when first implementing recommendations engines. In the case of an explicit rating, we cannot directly observe the user's sentiment but must rely on the user's ability to quantify their sentiment with a rating, such as rating a movie on an ordinal scale from one to five.

There are many problems with explicit ratings – especially on ordinal scales (for example, stars from one to five) – that we should consider when building our feedback function. Most people will have a bias when rating items on an ordinal scale – for example, some users might rate a movie 3/5 if they are unsatisfied and 5/5 if they liked the movie, while other users might rate 1/5 for a bad movie, 3/5 for a good one, and only very rarely 5/5 for an exceptional one.

Therefore, the ordinal scales either need to be normalized across users or you'll need to use a binary scale (such as thumbs up/thumbs down) to collect binary feedback. Binary feedback is usually much easier to handle, as we can remove the user bias from the feedback function, simplify the error metric, and therefore provide better recommendations. Many popular streaming services nowadays collect binary (thumbs up/thumbs down, star/unstar, and so on) feedback.

Here is a little snippet to help normalize user ratings. It applies a normalization across each group of user ratings:

```python
import numpy as np


def normalize_ratings(df,
                      rating_col="rating",
                      user_col="user"):
    groups = df.groupby(user_col)[rating_col]

    # computes group-wise mean/std
    mean = groups.transform(np.mean)
    std = groups.transform(np.std)
    return (df[rating_col] - mean) / std


df["rating_normalized"] = normalize_ratings(df)
```

Another popular way to train recommender systems is to build an implicit feedback function based on the direct observation of an implicit user rating. This has the benefit that the user feedback is unbiased. Common implicit ratings include the user adding an item to the cart, the user buying the item, the user scrolling to the end of the article, and the user watching the full video to the end.

One additional problem to consider is that the way a user interacts with items will change over time. This could be due to a user's habit due to consuming more and more items on the service or changing user preferences. Recommending a video to you that you once liked in your childhood might not be helpful to another adult. Similar to this user drift, the popularity of items will also change over time. Recommending the song *Somebody That I Used to Know* to a user today might not lead to the same CTR as in 2011. Therefore, we also must model time and account for temporal drift in our item ratings and feedback function.

The time drift of explicit or implicit ratings can be modeled using exponential time decay on the numeric rating. Depending on the business rules, we can, for example, use explicit ratings with a binary scale [1, -1] and exponentially decay these ratings with a half-life time of 1 year. Hence, after 1 year, a rating of 1 becomes 0.5; after 2 years, it becomes 0.25, and so on. Here is a snippet to exponentially decay your ratings:

```python
import numpy as np


def cumsum_days(s, duration='D'):
    diff = s.diff().astype('timedelta64[%s]' % duration)
    return diff.fillna(0).cumsum().values


def decay_ratings(df,
                  decay=1,
                  rating_col="rating",
                  time_col="t"):
    weight = np.exp(-cumsum_days(df[time_col]) * decay)
    return df[rating_col] * weight


half_life_t = 1
decay = np.log(2) / half_life_t
df["rating_decayed"] = decay_ratings(df, decay=decay)
```

We learned that the choice of a proper feedback function matters greatly and is as important for designing a rating-based recommendation engine as feature engineering is for content-based recommenders.

Predicting the missing ratings to make a recommendation

By collecting user-item ratings, we generate a sparse user-item-rating matrix that looks similar to *Figure 13.8*. However, in order to make a recommendation, we first need to fill the unknown ratings displayed red in the diagram. Collaborative filtering is about filling the blank rows or columns of the user-item-ratings matrix, depending on the prediction use case:

	Titanic	Matrix	...	Terminator
Alice	5		...	3
Bob		4	...	5
...	...	...	...	...
Chris	3		...	

Figure 13.8 – The user-item-ratings matrix

To recommend the best movie for Alice, we only need to compute the first row of the rating matrix, whereas to compute the best candidates for Terminator, we only need to compute the last column of the matrix. It is important to know that we don't have to compute the whole matrix all the time, which helps to significantly improve the recommendation performance.

You can also probably already guess that this matrix will get really, really large as the number of users and/or items grows. Therefore, we need an efficient parallelizable algorithm for computing the blank ratings in order to make a recommendation. The most popular method to solve this problem is to use matrix factorization and, hence, decompose the matrix into a product of two lower dimensional matrices. These two matrices and their dimensions can be interpreted as user trait and item trait matrices; by way of analogy, the dimension refers to the number of different distinct traits – the so-called latent representation.

Once the latent representation is known, we can fill the missing ratings by multiplying the correct rows and columns from the latent trait matrices. A recommendation can then be made by using the top *n* highest computed ratings. But that's enough of the theory – let's look at an example using the **Alternating Least Square** (**ALS**) method to perform the matrix factorization in PySpark. Apart from the method, everything else in the pipeline is the same as in a standard ML pipeline.

Similar to all previous pipelines, we also compute a training and testing set for validating the model performance using a grouped selection algorithm (for example, `LeavePGroupsOut` and `GroupShuffleSplit`), performing training, optimizing the hyperparameters, validating the model test performance, and eventually, stacking multiple models together. As in many other methods, most models are trained using gradient descent. We can also use a standard regression loss function, such as the **RMSE**, to compute the fit of our recommendations on the test set. Let's dive into the example.

Scalable recommendations using ALS factorization

To train a large collaborative filtering model using matrix factorization, we need an algorithm that is easily distributable. The ALS algorithm of the Spark `MLlib` package is an excellent choice – however, many other algorithms for factorizing matrices are available, such as *Bayesian personalized ranking*, FastAI's *EmbeddingDotBias*, or *neural collaborative filtering*.

> **Important Note**
>
> A summary of example applications using the preceding methods can be found on Microsoft's GitHub repository at `https://github.com/Microsoft/Recommenders`.

By using Spark, or more precisely PySpark – the Python bindings for Spark and its libraries – we can take advantage of the distributed computing framework of Spark. While it's possible to run Spark on a single-node, single-core process locally, it can be easily distributed to a cluster with hundreds and thousands of nodes. Hence, it is a good choice, as your code automatically becomes scalable if your input data scales and exceeds the memory limits of a single node:

1. Let's first create and parametrize an ALS estimator in PySpark using `MLlib`, the standard ML library of Spark. We will find `ALS` in the recommendation package of `MLlib`:

```
import pyspark
from pyspark.ml.recommendation import ALS
sc = pyspark.SparkContext('local[*]')
n_iter = 10
rank = 10
l2_reg = 1
```

```
als = ALS() \
    .setMaxIter(n_iter) \
    .setRank(rank) \
    .setRegParam(l2_reg)
```

In the preceding code, we initialize the ALS estimator and define the number of iterations for gradient descent optimization, the rank of the latent trait matrices, and the L2 regularization constant.

2. Next, we fit the model using this estimator:

```
model = als.fit(train_data)
```

3. That's all we have to do. Once the model is successfully trained, we can now predict the ratings for the test set by calling the transform method on the trained model:

```
y_test = model.transform(test_data)
```

4. To compute the performance of the recommendations, we use a regression evaluator and the rmse metric as a scoring function:

```
from pyspark.ml.evaluation import RegressionEvaluator

scoring = RegressionEvaluator(metricName="rmse",
                              labelCol="rating",
                              predictionCol="y")
```

5. To compute the rmse score, we simply call the evaluate method on the scoring object:

```
rmse = scoring.evaluate(y_test)
```

Congratulations! You successfully implemented a rating-based recommendation engine with a collaborative filtering approach by factorizing the user-item-ratings matrix. Have you realized that this approach is similar to finding the eigenvectors of a matrix and that they can be interpreted as user stereotypes (or user tastes, traits, and so on)? While this approach is great for creating diverse recommendations, it requires the availability of (many) user-item ratings. Therefore, it would work great in a service with a lot of user interaction and poorly with completely new users (the cold-start problem).

Combining content and ratings in hybrid recommendation engines

Instead of seeing rating-based recommenders as a successor to content-based recommenders, you should consider them as a different recommender after having acquired enough user-item interaction data to provide rating-only recommendations. In most practical cases, a recommendation engine will exist for both approaches – either as two distinct algorithms or a single hybrid model. In this section, we will look into training such a hybrid model.

To build a state-of-the-art recommender using the **Matchbox recommender**, open Azure Machine Learning designer and add the building blocks for the Matchbox recommender to the canvas, as shown in the following diagram. As we can see, the recommender can now take ratings and user and item features as input to create a hybrid recommendation model:

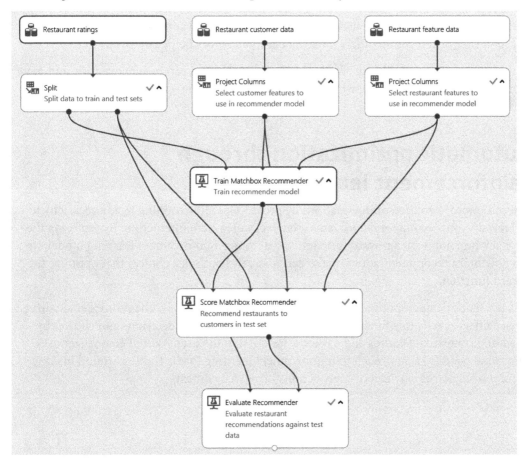

Figure 13.9 – The Matchbox recommender in Azure Machine Learning designer

In order to configure the Matchbox recommender, we need to configure the number of traits and, hence, the dimensions of the latent space matrices. We set this value to 10. Similar to the content-based recommender, instead of feeding raw unprocessed feature vectors into the recommender, we should pre-process the data and encode categorical variables using advanced NLP techniques.

Once you have built the recommendation engine in Azure Machine Learning designer, you simply press **Run** to train the model. You can also pull-request input and output blocks to the canvas to deploy this model as a web service.

Currently, the Matchbox recommender is only available through the graphical interface. However, you can use other hybrid models, such as Extreme Deep Factorization Machines and Wide and Deep, to train hybrid recommenders from Python.

Hybrid recommenders are very powerful, as they help avoid the cold-start problem but refine recommendations based on ratings once a user provides item ratings. However, the additional ratings are only used to refine predictions, and similar to all previous techniques, hybrid recommenders have to be trained before being deployed.

In the next section, we will take a look at recommenders that can be deployed without any user ratings and trained online while users interact with items – recommenders based on reinforcement learning.

Automatic optimization through reinforcement learning

You can improve your recommendations by providing online training techniques, which will retrain your recommender systems after every user-item interaction. By replacing the feedback function with a reward function and adding a reinforcement learning model, we can now make recommendations, make decisions, and optimize choices that optimize the reward function.

This is a fantastic new approach to training recommender models. The Azure Personalizer service offers exactly this functionality – to make and optimize decisions and choices by providing contextual features and a reward function to the user. Azure Personalizer uses contextual bandits, an approach to reinforcement learning that is framed around making decisions or choices between discrete actions in a given context.

> **Important Note**
>
> Under the hood, Azure Personalizer uses the Vowpal Wabbit (`https://github.com/VowpalWabbit/vowpal_wabbit/wiki`) learning system from Microsoft Research to provide high-throughput and low-latency optimization for the recommendation system.

From a developer's perspective, Azure Personalizer is quite easy to use. The basic recommender API consists of two main requests, the rank request and the reward request. During the rank request, we send the user features of the current user, plus all possible item features, to the API which returns a ranking of those items and an event ID in the response.

Using this response, we can present the items to the user who will then interact with these items. Whenever the user creates implicit feedback (for example, they click on an item or scroll to the end of the item), we make a second call to the service, this time to the reward API. In this request, we only send the event ID and the reward (a numeric value) to the service. This will trigger another training iteration using the new reward and the previously submitted user and item features. Hence, with each iteration and each service call, we optimize the performance of the recommendation engine.

Azure Personalizer SDKs are available for many different languages and are mainly wrappers around the official REST API. In order to install the Python SDK, run the following command in your shell:

```
pip install azure-cognitiveservices-personalizer
```

Now, go to the Azure portal and deploy an instance of Azure Personalizer from your portal and configure the **Rewards** and **Exploration** settings, as discussed in the following paragraphs.

> **Important Note**
>
> You can find more information about Azure Personalizer configurations in the official documentation at `https://docs.microsoft.com/en-us/azure/cognitive-services/personalizer/how-to-settings`.

First, you need to configure how long the algorithm should wait to collect rewards for a certain event, as shown in *Figure 13.10*. Up to this time, rewards are collected and aggregated by the reward aggregation function. You can also define the model update frequency, which allows you to train your model frequently when requiring recommendations for quick-changing user behaviors. It makes sense to set the reward time and model update frequency to the same value – for example, 10 minutes:

Rewards

After a Personalizer API Rank call, your application will call the Reward API with a score that is used to train the service.

Read more about setting rewards

Reward wait time ⓘ

Days	Hours	Minutes	Seconds
0	0	10	0

Default reward ⓘ

0

Reward aggregation ⓘ

Sum	⌄

Figure 13.10 – Rewards settings

In the preceding figure, we can also select the aggregation function for rewards collected on the same event during the reward wait time. The possible options are **Earliest** and **Sum** – hence, using only the first reward or a sum of all rewards in the reward period.

The **Exploration** setting makes the algorithm explore alternative patterns over time, which is very helpful in discovering a diverse set of items through exploration. It can be set through the percentage of rank calls used for exploration, as shown in *Figure 13.11*:

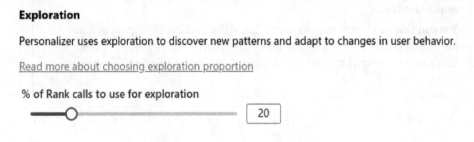

Exploration

Personalizer uses exploration to discover new patterns and adapt to changes in user behavior.

Read more about choosing exploration proportion

% of Rank calls to use for exploration

20

Figure 13.11 – Exploration settings

Hence, in 20% of the calls, the model won't return the highest ranked item but will randomly explore new items and their rewards. It sounds reasonable that the value for exploration should be greater than 0% to let the reinforcement algorithm try variations of items over time and set lower than 100% to avoid making the algorithm completely random.

Let's embed a recommendation engine in your application using Python:

1. Let's grab your resource key, open a Python environment, and start implementing the rank and reward calls. First, we define the API URLs for both calls:

```
personalization_base_url =
    "https://<name>.cognitiveservices.azure.com/"
resource_key = "<your-resource-key>"
rank_url = personalization_base_url \
    + "personalizer/v1.0/rank"
reward_url = personalization_base_url \
    + "personalizer/v1.0/events/"
```

2. Next, we create a unique `eventid` function and an object containing the user features of the current user and the item features of all possible actions. Once the request is constructed, we can send it to the rank API:

```
eventid = uuid.uuid4().hex
data = {
    "eventid": eventid,
    "contextFeatures": user_features,
    "actions": item_features
}
response = requests.post(rank_url,
                         headers=headers,
                         json=data)
```

3. The response contains the ranking of the possible items/actions and a probability value, as well as the winning item under the `rewardActionId` property:

```
{
    "result": {
        "ranking": [
            {
                "id": "ai-for-earth",
```

```
            "probability": 0.664000034
        }, ...
    ],
    "eventId": "482d82bc-2ff8-4721-8e92-607310a0a415",
    "rewardActionId": "ai-for-earth"
    }
}
```

4. Let's parse `rewardActionId` from `response` – this contains the winning item and, hence, the recommended action for the user:

```
action_id = response.json()["rewardActionId"]
prediction = json.dumps(action_id).replace('"','')
```

5. Using this ranking, we can return the winning item to the user based on `rewardActionId`. We now give the user some time to interact with the item. Finally, we use this ID to return the tracked implicit feedback as a reward value to the reward API:

```
reward_url = reward_url + eventid + "/reward"
response = requests.post(reward_url,
                         headers=headers,
                         json = {"value": reward})
```

That's all you need to embed a fully online self-training recommendation engine in your application using Python and Azure Personalizer. It's that simple. As previously mentioned, other SDKs that wrap the API calls are available for many other languages.

> **Important Note**
>
> A demo of Personalizer to test the reward function, as well as the request and response of the service, can be found at `https://personalizationdemo.azurewebsites.net/`.
>
> Detailed up-to-date examples for other languages are provided on GitHub at `https://github.com/Azure-Samples/cognitive-services-personalizer-samples`.

Summary

In this chapter, we discussed the need for different types of recommendation engines, from non-personalized ones to rating- and content-based ones, as well as hybrid models.

We learned that content-based recommendation engines use feature vectors and cosine similarity to compute similar items and users based on content alone. This allows us to make recommendations via *k-means clustering* or *tree-based regression* models. One important consideration is the embedding of categorical data, which, if possible, should use semantic embedding to avoid confusing similarities based on one-hot or label encodings.

Rating-based recommendations or collaborative filtering methods rely on user-item interactions, so-called ratings, or feedback. While explicit feedback is the most obvious possibility for collecting user ratings through ordinal or binary scales, we need to make sure that those ratings are properly normalized.

Another possibility is to directly observe the feedback through implicit ratings – for example, a user bought a product, clicked on an article, scrolled a page until the end, or watched a whole video until the end. However, these ratings will also be affected by user preference drift over time, as well as item popularity over time. To avoid this, you can use exponential time decay to decrease ratings over time.

Rating-based methods are great for providing diverse recommendations but require a lot of existing ratings for a good performance. Hence, they are often combined with content-based recommendations to fight this cold-start problem. Therefore, popular state-of-the-art recommendation models often combine both methods in a single hybrid model, of which the *Matchbox recommender* is one such example.

Finally, you learned about the possibility of using reinforcement learning to optimize the recommender's feedback function on the fly. *Azure Personalizer* is a service that can be used to create hybrid online recommenders.

In the next chapter, we will look into deploying our trained models as batch or real-time scoring systems directly from the Azure Machine Learning service.

Section 4: Machine Learning Model Deployment and Operations

In this final section, we will bring our models into production by deploying them to a cluster for batch scoring or to endpoints for online scoring and we will learn how to monitor these deployments. Furthermore, we will discuss specialized deployment targets and available integrations with other Azure services. Bringing everything we learned together, we will then learn how to operate enterprise-grade end-to-end **Machine Learning** (**ML**) projects using MLOps concepts and Azure DevOps. Finally, we will end the book with a summary of what we learned, having a look at what can and will change and gaining an understanding of our responsibility when building ML models and working with data.

This section comprises the following chapters:

- *Chapter 14, Model Deployment, Endpoints, and Operations*
- *Chapter 15, Model Interoperability, Hardware Optimization, and Integrations*
- *Chapter 16, Bringing Models into Production with MLOps*
- *Chapter 17, Preparing for a Successful ML Journey*

14

Model Deployment, Endpoints, and Operations

In the previous chapter, we learned how to build efficient and scalable recommender engines through feature engineering, natural language processing, and distributed algorithms.

In this chapter, we will tackle the next step after training a **recommender engine** or any machine learning model; we are going to deploy and operate the ML model. This will require us to package and register the model, build an execution runtime, build a web service, and deploy all components to an execution target.

First, we will take a look at all the required preparations to deploy ML models to production. You will learn the steps that are required in a typical deployment process, how to package and register trained models, how to define and build inferencing environments, and how to choose a deployment target to run the model.

In the next section, we will learn how to build a web service for a real-time scoring service, similar to Azure Cognitive Services, but using custom models and custom code. We will look into model endpoints, controlled rollouts, and endpoint schemas so that the models can be deployed without downtime and can be integrated into other services. Finally, we will also build a batch-scoring solution that can be scheduled or triggered through a web service or pipeline.

In the last section, we will focus on how to monitor and operate your ML scoring services. In order to optimize performance and cost, you need to keep track not only of system-level metrics but also of telemetry data and scoring results to detect model or data drift. By the end of this section, you will be able to confidently deploy, tune, and optimize your scoring infrastructure in Azure.

In this chapter, you will cover the following topics:

- Preparations for model deployments
- Deploying ML models in Azure
- ML operations in Azure

Technical requirements

In this chapter, we will use the following Python libraries and versions to create model deployments and endpoints:

- `azureml-core 1.34.0`
- `azureml-sdk 1.34.0`
- `scikit-learn 0.24.2`
- `joblib 1.0.1`
- `numpy 1.19.5`
- `tensorflow 2.6.0`
- `pandas 1.3.3`
- `requests 2.25.1`
- `nvidia-smi 0.1.3`

Similar to previous chapters, you can run this code using either a local Python interpreter or a notebook environment hosted in Azure Machine Learning. However, all scripts need to be scheduled to execute in Azure.

All code examples in this chapter can be found in the GitHub repository for this book: `https://github.com/PacktPublishing/Mastering-Azure-Machine-Learning-Second-Edition/tree/main/chapter14`.

Preparations for model deployments

Throughout this book, we have learned how to experiment with, train, and optimize various ML models to perform classification, regression, anomaly detection, image recognition, text understanding, and recommendations. Having successfully trained our ML model, we now want to package and deploy this model to production with tools in Azure.

In this section, we will learn about the most important preparation steps that are required to deploy a trained model to production using Azure Machine Learning. We will discuss the different components involved in a standardized deployment, customizing a deployment, auto-deployments, and how to choose the right deployment target. Let's delve into it.

Understanding the components of an ML model

Independent of the use case, there are similar preparation steps required for putting an ML model to production. First, the trained model needs to be registered in the model registry. This will allow us to track the model version and binaries and fetch a specific version of the model in a deployment. Second, we need to specify the deployment assets (for example, the environment, libraries, assets, and scoring file). These assets define exactly how the model is loaded and initialized, how user input is parsed, how the model is executed, and how the output is passed back to the user. Finally, we need to choose a compute target to run the model.

When using Azure Machine Learning for deployments, there is a well-defined list of things you need to specify in order to deploy and run an ML model as a web service. This list includes the following components:

- **A trained model**: The model definition and parameters
- **An inferencing environment**: A configuration describing the environment, for example, as a Docker file
- **A scoring file**: The web service code to parse user inputs and outputs and invoke the model
- **A runtime**: The runtime for the scoring file, for example, Python or PySpark
- **A compute target**: The compute environment to run the web service, for example, **Azure Kubernetes Service** (**AKS**) or **Azure Container Instances** (**ACI**)

Let's look into these five components in more detail:

1. First, we need a trained model. A model (depending on the framework, libraries, and algorithm used) consists of one or multiple files storing the model parameters and structure. In scikit-learn, this could be a pickled estimator; in **LightGBM**, this could be a serialized list of decision trees; and in Keras, this could be a model definition and a binary blob storing the model weights. We call this the *model*, and we store and version it in Blob storage. At the startup time of your scoring service, the model will be loaded into the scoring runtime.

2. Besides the model, we also need an execution environment, which can be defined via `InferenceConfig`. In Azure Machine Learning deployments, the environment will be built into a *Docker* image and stored in your private Docker registry. During the deployment process, Azure Machine Learning will automatically build the Docker image from the provided environment configuration and load it into the private registry in your workspace.

   In Azure Machine Learning deployments, you can select predefined ML environments or configure your own environments and Docker base images. On top of the base image, you can define a list of Python *Pip* or *Conda* dependencies, enable GPU support, or configure custom Docker steps. The environment, including all required packages, will automatically be provided during runtime and set up on the Docker image. On top of this, the environment can be registered and versioned by the Azure Machine Learning service. This makes it easy to track, reuse, and organize your deployment environments.

3. Next, we need a so-called scoring file. This file typically loads the model and provides a function to score the model when given some data as input. Depending on the type of deployment, you need to provide a scoring file for either a (real-time) synchronous scoring service or an asynchronous batch-scoring service. The scoring files should be tracked in your version control system and will be mounted in the Docker image.

4. To complete `InferenceConfig`, we are missing one last but important step: the Python runtime, used to run your scoring file. Currently, Python and PySpark are the only supported runtimes.

5. Finally, we need an execution target that defines the compute infrastructure that the Docker image should be executed on. In Azure, this is called the compute target and is defined through the deployment configuration. The compute target can be a managed Kubernetes cluster (such as AKS), a container instance (such as ACI), **Azure Machine Learning Compute** (**AmlCompute**), or one of the many other Azure compute services.

> **Important Note**
>
> The preceding components are only required for managed deployments within Azure Machine Learning. Nothing prevents you from fetching the model binaries in another environment or running an inferencing environment (the Docker image) on your on-premises compute target.

If you simply want to deploy a standard model file, such as scikit-learn, **ONNX**, or TensorFlow models, you can also use the built-in *auto-deployment* capabilities in Azure Machine Learning. Instead of providing all the preceding components, auto-deployment requires only the name and version of the used framework and a resource configuration, for example, the number of CPUs and the amount of RAM to execute. Azure Machine Learning will do the rest; it will provide all the required configurations and deploy the model to an ACI. This makes it easy to deploy standard models with no more than one line of code – great for development, debugging, and testing.

Now that we know the basic deployment components in Azure Machine Learning, we can move on and look at an example of registering a model to prepare it for deployment.

Registering your models in a model registry

The first step of the deployment process should happen during or after the training and optimization process, namely *registering* the best model from each run in the Azure Machine Learning model registry. Independent of whether your training script produces a single model, a model ensemble, or a model combined with multiple files, you should always store the training artifacts and register the best model from each run in your Azure Machine Learning workspace.

It takes one additional line of code in your training script to store a model and register it in Azure Machine Learning and, therefore, never lose your training artifacts and models. The Blob storage and model registry are directly integrated with your workspace and so the process is tightly integrated into the training process. Once a model is registered, Azure Machine Learning provides a convenient interface to load the model from the registry.

Let's take a quick look at what this means for your training script:

1. Let's define the run context and train the `sklearn` classifier:

```
Run = Run.get_context()
exp = run.experiment

# train your model
clf, test_acc = train_sklearn_mnist()
```

2. Next, we write a small helper function that returns the best test accuracy metric from all previous runs. We will use this metric to check whether the new model performs better than all previous runs:

```
Def get_metrics(exp, metric):
  for run in Run.list(exp, status='Completed'):
    yield run.get_metrics().get(metric)


m_name = 'Test accuracy'
best_acc = max(get_metrics(exp, m_name), default=0)
```

3. Next, we check whether the model has better performance than all previous runs and register it in the model factory as a new version:

```
Import joblib


# serialize the model and write it to disk
joblib.dump(clf, 'outputs/model.pkl')


if test_acc > best_acc:
  model = run.register_model(
    model_name='sklearn_mnist',
    model_path='outputs/model.pkl')
  print(model.name, model.id, model.version, sep='\t')
```

In the preceding code block, we first use the `joblib.dump()` function to serialize and store a trained classifier to disk. We then call the `run.model_register()` function to upload the trained model to the default datastore and register the model to the disk. This will automatically track and version the model by name and link it to the current training run.

4. Once your model is stored in the model registry of your Azure Machine Learning workspace, you can use it for deployments and retrieve it by name in any debugging, testing, or experimentation step. You can simply request the latest model by name, for example, by running the following snippet on your local machine:

```
import joblib
from azureml.core.model import Model


model_path = Model.get_model_path('sklearn_mnist')
model = joblib.load(model_path)
```

All we did in the preceding code is run `Model.get_model_path()` to retrieve the latest version of a model by name. We can also specify a version number to load a specific model from the registry.

A built-in model registry is one of the functionalities of the Azure Machine Learning workspace that gets you hooked and makes you never want to miss a model registry, experiment run, and metrics tracking in the future. It gives you great flexibility and transparency when working with model artifacts in different environments and during different experiments.

In the preceding example, we didn't provide any metadata about the trained model and, therefore, Azure Machine Learning couldn't infer anything from the model artifact. However, if we provide additional information about the model, Azure Machine Learning can autogenerate some of the required deployment configurations for you to enable auto-deployments. Let's take a look at this in the next section.

Auto-deployments of registered models

If you stick to the standard functionality provided in scikit-learn, TensorFlow, or ONNX, you can also take advantage of auto-deployments in Azure Machine Learning. This will allow you to deploy registered models to testing, experimentation, or production environments without defining any of the required deployment configurations, assets, and service endpoints.

> **Important Note**
> Azure Machine Learning model auto-deployment will automatically make your model available as a web service. If you provide model metadata during training, you can invoke auto-deployment using a single command, `Model.deploy()`.

Let's take a look at how we need to change the previous example to take advantage of auto-deployments:

1. First, we define the resource configuration of the model as shown in the following code block:

```
From azureml.core.resource_configuration import \
    ResourceConfiguration

resource_config = ResourceConfiguration(
    cpu=1, memory_in_gb=2.0, gpu=0)
```

2. Next, we need to define the framework and framework version when registering the model. To do so, we need to add this additional information to the model by extending the `Model.register()` arguments, as shown in the following snippet:

```
From azureml.core import Model

model = run.register_model(
    model_name='sklearn_mnist',
    model_path='outputs/model.pkl',
    model_framework=Model.Framework.SCIKITLEARN,
    model_framework_version='0.24.2',
    resource_configuration= resource_config)
```

In the preceding code, we added the framework and framework version to the model registry, as well as the resource configuration for this specific model. The model itself is stored in a standard format in one of the supported frameworks (scikit-learn, ONNX, or TensorFlow). This metadata is added to the model in the model registry. This is all the configuration required to auto-deploy this model as a real-time web service in a single line of code.

3. Finally, we call the `Model.deploy()` function to start the deployment process. This will build the deployment runtime as a Docker image, register it in your container registry, and start the image as a managed container instance, including the scoring file, REST service abstraction, and telemetry collection:

```
Service_name = 'my-sklearn-service'
service = Model.deploy(ws, service_name, [model])
```

4. To retrieve the URL of the scoring service once the deployment is finished, we run the following code:

```
service.wait_for_deployment(show_output=True)
print(service.state)
print("Scoring URL: " + service.scoring_uri)
```

If you want more granular control over the execution environment, endpoint configuration, and compute target, you can use the advanced inference, deployment, and service configurations in order to customize your deployment. Let's now take a look at customized deployments.

Customizing your deployment environment

As you have seen in the previous chapters, the number of libraries, frameworks, and customization steps to transform data with an ML model is huge. Azure Machine Learning gives us enough flexibility to configure ML scoring services that can reflect these customizations. In this section, we will learn how to customize the deployment to include libraries and frameworks. Let's dive a bit deeper into these individual deployment steps.

In the Azure Machine Learning service, you use an execution environment to specify a base Docker image, Python runtime, and all the dependent packages required to score your model. Like models, environments can also be registered and versioned in Azure, so both the Docker artifacts and the metadata are stored, versioned, and tracked in your workspace. This makes it simple to keep track of your environment changes, figure out which environment was used for a specific run, jump back and forth between multiple versions of an environment, and share an environment for multiple projects.

Perform the following steps to build and package your deployment in Docker:

1. Let's start by writing a helper function to create environments on the fly. This snippet is very useful when creating environments programmatically based on a list of packages. We will also automatically add the `azureml-defaults` package to each environment:

```python
From azureml.core import Environment
from azureml.core.conda_dependencies import \
  CondaDependencies

def get_env(name="my-env", packages=None):
  packages = packages or []
  packages += ['azureml-defaults']
  conda_deps = CondaDependencies.create(
    pip_packages=packages)
  env = Environment(name=name)
  env.python.conda_dependencies = conda_deps
  return env
```

As you can see in the preceding code block, we first initialize an `Environment` instance and then add multiple conda packages. We assign the conda dependencies by overriding the `env.python.conda_dependencies` property with the `conda_deps` dependencies. Using the same approach, we can also override Docker, Spark, and any additional Python settings using `env.docker` and `env.spark`, respectively.

2. Next, we can define a custom environment to use for experimentation, training, or deployment:

```
myenv = get_env(name="PythonEnv",
                packages=["numpy",
                          "scikit-learn",
                          "tensorflow"])
```

3. In the next step, you can now register the environment using a descriptive name. This will add a new version of the current environment configuration to your environment with the same name:

```
myenv.register(ws, name="PythonEnv")
```

4. You can also retrieve the environment from the registry using the following code. This is also useful when you have registered a base environment that can be reused and extended for multiple experiments:

```
myenv = Environment.get(ws, name="PythonEnv")
```

5. As with the model registry, you can also load environments using a specified version as an additional argument. Once you have configured an execution environment, you can combine it with a scoring file to an InferenceConfig object. The scoring file implements all functionalities to load the model from the registry and evaluate it given some input data. The configuration can be defined as follows:

```
from azureml.core.model import InferenceConfig

inference_config = InferenceConfig(
    entry_script="score.py",
    environment=myenv)
```

We can see, in the preceding example, that we simply specify a relative path to the scoring script in the local authoring environment. Therefore, you first have to create this scoring file; we will go through two examples of batch and real-time scoring in the following sections.

6. To build an environment, we can simply trigger a build of the Docker image:

```
from azureml.core import Image

build = myenv.build(ws)
build.wait_for_completion(show_output=True)
```

7. The environment will be packaged and registered as a Docker image in your private
container registry, containing the Docker base image and all specified libraries. If
you want to package the model and the scoring file, you can package the model
instead. This is done automatically when deploying the model or can be forced
by using the `Model.package` function. Let's load the model from the previous
section and package and register the image:

```
model_path = Model.get_model('sklearn_mnist')
package = Model.package(ws, [model], inference_config)
package.wait_for_creation(show_output=True)
```

> **Important Note**
>
> The Azure ML SDK documentation contains a detailed list of possible
> configuration options, which you can find at `https://docs.`
> `microsoft.com/en-us/python/api/azureml-core/`
> `azureml.core.environment(class)`.

The preceding code will build and package your deployment as a Docker image. In the
next section, we will find out how to choose the best compute target to execute your
ML deployment.

Choosing a deployment target in Azure

One of the great advantages of Azure Machine Learning services is that they are tightly
integrated with many other Azure services. This is extremely helpful with deployments
where we want to run Docker images of the ML service on a managed service within
Azure. These compute targets can be configured and leveraged for automatic deployment
through Azure Machine Learning.

If your job is to productionize ML training and deployment pipelines, you might not
necessarily be an expert in Kubernetes. If that's the case, you might come to enjoy the tight
integration of the management of Azure compute services in the Azure Machine Learning
SDK. Similar to creating training environments, you can create GPU clusters, managed
Kubernetes clusters, or simple container instances from within the authoring environment
(for example, the Jupyter notebook orchestrating your ML workflow).

We can follow a general recommendation for choosing a specific service, similar to
choosing a compute service for regular application deployments; so, we trade off
simplicity, cost, scalability, flexibility, and operational expense between the compute
services that can easily start a web service from a Docker image.

Here are recommendations of when to use each Azure compute service:

- For quick experiments and local testing, use Docker and local deployment targets in Azure Machine Learning.

- For testing and experimentation, use ACI. It is easy to set up and configure, and it is made to run container images.

- For deployments of scalable real-time web services with GPU support, use AKS. This managed Kubernetes cluster is a lot more flexible and scalable, but also a lot harder to operate.

- For batch deployments, use Azure Machine Learning clusters, the same compute cluster environment we already used for training.

For quick experiments, you can deploy your service locally using `LocalWebservice` as a deployment target. To do so, you can run the following snippet on your local machine, providing the scoring file and environment in the inferencing configuration:

```
From azureml.core.webservice import LocalWebservice

deployment_config = LocalWebservice.deploy_configuration(
    port=8890)

service = Model.deploy(ws,
    name=service_name,
    models=[model],
    inference_config=inference_config,
    deployment_config=deployment_config)

service.wait_for_deployment(show_output=True)
print(service.state)
```

As you can see, once your model is registered, you can deploy it to multiple compute targets depending on your use case. While we have covered a few different configuration options, we haven't yet discussed multiple deployment options and scoring files. We will do this in the next section.

Deploying ML models in Azure

Broadly speaking, there are two common approaches to deploying ML models, namely deploying them as synchronous real-time web services and as asynchronous batch-scoring services. Please note that the same model could be deployed as two different services, serving different use cases. The deployment type depends heavily on the batch size and response time of the scoring pattern of the model. Small batch sizes with fast responses require a horizontally scalable real-time web service, whereas large batch sizes and slow response times require horizontally and vertically scalable batch services.

The deployment of a text-understanding model (for example, an entity recognition model or sentiment analysis) could include a real-time web service that evaluates the model whenever a new comment is posted to an app, as well as a batch scorer in another ML pipeline to extract relevant features from training data. With the former, we want to serve each request as quickly as possible, and so we will evaluate a small batch size synchronously. With the latter, we are evaluating large amounts of data, and so we will evaluate a large batch size asynchronously. Our aim is that, once the model is packaged and registered, we can reuse it for either a task or use case.

In this section, we will take a look at these deployment approaches and build one service for real-time scoring and one for batch-scoring. We will also evaluate different options to manage and perform deployments for scoring services.

Building a real-time scoring service

In this section, we will build a real-time scoring service in Azure Machine Learning. We will look into the required scoring file that will power the web service, as well as the configuration to start the service on an AKS cluster.

For this example, we will train an NLP Hugging Face transformer model to perform sentiment analysis on user input. Our aim is to build our own Cognitive Services Text Analytics API that uses a custom model that is trained or fine-tuned on a custom dataset.

To do so, we will train a sentiment analysis pipeline, save it, and register it as a model in Azure Machine Learning, as shown in the following snippet:

```
clf = train(name="sentiment-analysis")
clf.save_pretrained("outputs/sentiment-analysis")

model = Model.register(ws,
   model_name='sentiment-analysis',
   model_path='outputs/sentiment-analysis')
```

Once we have the model, we start building the web service by taking a look at the scoring file. The scoring file will be loaded when the web service starts and gets invoked for every request to the ML service. Therefore, we use the scoring file to load the ML model, parse the user data from a request, invoke the ML model, and return the results of the ML model. To do so, you need to provide the `init()` and `run()` functions in the scoring file, where the `run()` function is run once when the service starts, and the `run` method is invoked with user inputs for every request. The following example shows a simple scoring file:

scoring_file_example.py

```python
def init():
    print("Initializing service")
def run(data):
    print("Received a new request with data: ", data)
```

Now that we have the trained model and we know the structure of the scoring file, we can go ahead and build our custom web service:

1. Let's start with the initialization of the service. We first define a global model variable, and then fetch the model path from the AZUREML_MODEL_DIR environment variable. This variable contains the location of the model on the local disk. Next, we load the model using the Hugging Face AutoModel transformer:

Scoring_file.py

```python
from transformers import AutoModel
from azureml.core import Model

def init():
    global model
    model_path = os.getenv("AZUREML_MODEL_DIR")
    model = AutoModel.from_pretrained(model_path,
                                      from_tf=True)
```

2. Next, we tackle the actual inferencing part of the web service. To do so, we need to parse incoming requests, invoke the NLP model, and return the prediction to the caller:

Scoring_file.py

```
import json

def run(request):
    try:
        data = json.loads(request)
        text = data['query']
        sentiment = model(text)
        result = {'sentiment': sentiment}
        return result
    except Exception as e:
        return str(e)
```

In the `run()` function, we are provided with a `request` object. This object contains the body of the request sent to the service. As we expect JSON input, we parse the request body as a JSON object and access the input string via the `query` property. We expect a client to send a valid request that contains exactly this schema. Finally, we return a prediction that will be automatically serialized into JSON and returned to the caller.

3. Let's deploy the service to an ACI compute target for testing purposes. To do so, we need to update the deployment configuration to contain the ACI resource configuration:

```
from azureml.core.webservice import AciWebservice

deploy_config = AciWebservice.deploy_configuration(
    cpu_cores=1,
    memory_gb=1)
```

> **Important Note**
> You can find more information about Azure Container Instance in the official documentation at `https://docs.microsoft.com/en-us/azure/container-instances/container-instances-overview`.

4. Next, we pass the environment and scoring file to the inferencing configuration:

```
from azureml.core.model import InferenceConfig

env = get_env(name="sentiment-analysis",
              package=["tensorflow", "transformers"])

inference_config = InferenceConfig(
    environment=env,
    source_directory="code",
    entry_script="scoring_file.py",
)
```

5. Having all the required components, we can finally pass the model, the inferencing configuration, and the deployment configuration to the `Model.deploy` method and start the deployment:

```
service_name = "sentiment-analysis"

service = Model.deploy(ws,
    name=service_name,
    models=[model],
    inference_config=inference_config,
    deployment_config=deploy_config)

service.wait_for_deployment(show_output=True)
print(service.state)
```

6. Once the service is up and running, we can try a test request to the service to make sure everything is working properly. By default, Azure Machine Learning services use key-based (primary and secondary) authentication. Let's retrieve the key from the service and send some test data to the deployed service:

```
import requests
import json
from azureml.core import Webservice

service = Webservice(ws, name="sentiment-analysis")
```

```
scoring_uri = service.scoring_uri

# If the service is authenticated
key, _ = service.get_keys()

# Set the appropriate headers
headers = {"Content-Type": "application/json"}
headers["Authorization"] = f"Bearer {key}"

data = {"query": "AzureML is quite good."}
resp = requests.post(scoring_uri,
                     data=json.dumps(data),
                     headers=headers)
print(resp.text)
```

The preceding snippet fetches the service URL and access key and sends the JSON encoded data to the ML model deployment as a POST request.

That's it! You have deployed your sentiment analysis model successfully and tested it from Python. However, using the service endpoint and token, you can also send requests from any other programming language or HTTP client to your service.

Deploying to Azure Kubernetes Services

We have successfully deployed our sentiment analysis model to ACI. As a next step, however, we want to deploy it to AKS. While ACI is fantastic for quickly getting Docker containers deployed, AKS is a service for complex container-based production workloads. Among other features, AKS supports authentication, autoscaling, GPU support, replicas, and advanced metrics and logging.

> **Important Note**
>
> You can find more information about Azure Kubernetes Services in the official documentation at https://docs.microsoft.com/en-us/azure/aks/intro-kubernetes.

Let's now deploy this service to an AKS cluster so we can take advantage of the GPU acceleration and autoscaling:

1. First, we need to define our required infrastructure:

```
from azureml.core.compute import AksCompute, \
  ComputeTarget


# Configure AKS cluster with NVIDIA Tesla P40 GPU
prov_config = AksCompute.provisioning_configuration(
  vm_size="Standard_ND6s")


aks_name = 'aks-ml-prod'
# Create the cluster
aks_target = ComputeTarget.create(ws,
  name=aks_name,
  provisioning_configuration=prov_config)


# Wait for the create process to complete
aks_target.wait_for_completion(show_output=True)
```

In the preceding code, we created an AKS configuration and a new AKS cluster as an Azure Machine Learning compute target from this configuration. All this happens completely within your authoring environment.

2. If you already have an AKS cluster up and running, you can simply use this cluster for Azure Machine Learning. To do so, you have to pass the resource group and cluster name to the AksCompute.attach_configuration() method. Then, set the resource group that contains the AKS cluster and the cluster name:

```
resource_group = 'my-rg'
cluster_name = 'aks-ml-prod'

attach_config = AksCompute.attach_configuration(
  resource_group = resource_group,
  cluster_name=cluster_name)

aks_target = ComputeTarget.attach(ws,
  cluster_name,
  attach_config)
```

3. Once we have a reference to the cluster, we can deploy the ML model to the cluster. This step is similar to the previous one:

```
deploy_config = AksWebservice.deploy_configuration(
    cpu_cores=1,
    memory_gb=1,
    gpu_cores=1)

service = Model.deploy(ws,
    service_name,
    [model],
    inference_config,
    deploy_config,
    aks_target)

service.wait_for_deployment(show_output=True)
print(service.state)
print(service.get_logs())
```

As you can see in the preceding example, apart from attaching the AKS clusters as a target to Azure Machine Learning, the model deployment is identical to the example using ACI.

Defining a schema for scoring endpoints

In the previous example, we parse the user input from JSON and expect it to contain a `query` parameter. To help users and services consuming your service endpoint, it would be useful to tell users which parameters the service is expecting. This is a common problem when building web service APIs.

To solve this, Azure Machine Learning provides an innovative way to autogenerate an **OpenAPI Specification** (**OAS**), previously called the **Swagger Specification**. This specification can be accessed by consumers of the API through the schema endpoint. This provides an automated standardized way to specify and consume the service's data format and can be used to autogenerate clients. One example is **Swagger Codegen**, which can be used to generate Java and C# clients for your new ML service.

You can enable automatic schema generation for pandas, NumPy, PySpark, and standard Python objects in your service through annotations in Python. First, you need to include `azureml-defaults` and `inference-schema` as PIP packages in your environment. Then, you can autogenerate the schema by providing sample input and output data for your endpoint, as shown in the following example:

scoring_file.py

```python
import numpy as np


input_sample = np.array([[10, 9, 8, 7, 6, 5, 4, 3, 2, 1]])
output_sample = np.array([3726.995])


@input_schema('data', NumpyParameterType(input_sample))
@output_schema(NumpyParameterType(output_sample))
def run(data):
    # data is a np.array
    pass
```

In the preceding example, we defined the schema for a NumPy-based model through sample data and annotations in the `run()` method.

We can also pick up the sentiment analysis model and allow it to receive multiple input queries. To do this, we can deserialize the user input into a pandas DataFrame object and return an array of predictions as a result, as shown in the following example. Note that this basically adds batch prediction capabilities to our real-time web service:

scoring_file.py

```python
import numpy as np
import pandas as pd


input_sample = pd.DataFrame(data=[
    {'query': "AzureML is quite good."}])
output_sample = np.array([np.array(["POSITIVE", 0.95])])


@input_schema('data', PandasParameterType(input_sample))
@output_schema(NumpyParameterType(output_sample))
```

```
def run(data):
  # data is a pd.DataFrame
  pass
```

Defining example inputs and outputs is everything that is required to autogenerate an API specification that your clients can use to validate endpoints and arguments or to autogenerate clients. This is also the same format that can be used to create ML services that can be automatically integrated into Power BI, as shown in *Chapter 15, Model Interoperability, Hardware Optimization, and Integrations*.

Managing model endpoints

Each model deployment contains a URL to send requests to the model; online scoring services provide a URL to process online predictions, and batch-scoring services provide a URL to trigger batch predictions. While this makes it easy to spin up and query a service, one big problem remains during a deployment, namely, that the service URL changes with each deployment. This leads to the issue that we can't control which service a user request will hit.

To solve this problem, we need to hide model deployment URLs behind a fixed service URL and provide a mechanism to resolve a user request to a specific service. In Azure Machine Learning, the component that fulfills this is called an **endpoint**, which can expose multiple deployments under a fixed endpoint URL.

The following figure shows the concept of endpoints and deployments. Customers send requests to the endpoint, and we configure the endpoint to route the request to one of the services. During a deployment, we would add the new model version behind the same scoring endpoint, and incrementally start service requests from the new **(green)** version instead of the previous **(blue)** version:

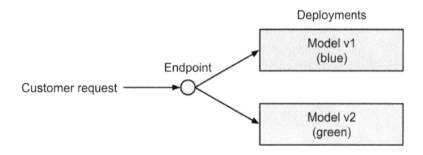

Figure 14.1 – Azure Machine Learning endpoints and deployments

This type of deployment is also called blue-green deployment. First, you serve all traffic from the old service and start the new service. Once the new service is up and running, and the health checks have finished successfully, the service is registered under the endpoint, and it will start serving requests. Finally, if there are no active requests left on the old service, you can shut it down.

This process is a very safe way to update stateless application services with zero or minimal downtime. It also helps you to fall back on the old service if the new one doesn't deploy successfully.

Azure Machine Learning provides multiple types of endpoints, depending on the model deployment mechanism:

- **Online endpoints**: For real-time online deployments:

  - **Managed online endpoints**: For managed Azure Machine Learning deployments
  - **Kubernetes online endpoints**: For managed AKS deployments

- **Batch endpoints**: For batch-scoring deployments

On the top level, we distinguish between online and batch endpoints. While online endpoints are used for synchronous scoring based on web service deployments, batch endpoints are used for asynchronous scoring based on pipeline deployments.

For online endpoints, we distinguish based on the deployment target between managed and Kubernetes-based online endpoints. This is an analog to the different compute targets and features for online scoring.

Let's take a look at how to configure endpoints for AKS:

1. First, we configure the endpoint details as shown in the following snippet:

```
from azureml.core.webservice import AksEndpoint

endpoint_config = AksEndpoint.deploy_configuration(
  version_name="version-1",
  tag'={'modelVersion':'1'},
  namespace="nlp",
  traffic_percentile=100)
```

The endpoint configuration serves as a deployment configuration for the AKS compute target.

2. Next, we provide both the endpoint configuration and the compute target to the
   `Model.deploy` method:

```
endpoint_name"= "sentiment-analysis"

endpoint = Model.deploy(ws,
    endpoint_name,
    [model],
    inference_config,
    endpoint_config,
    aks_target)

endpoint.wait_for_deployment(show_output=True)
print(endpoint.state)
```

The deployment will return an endpoint that can now be used to connect to the service
and add additional configuration. In the next section, we will look at more use cases of
endpoints and will see how to add additional deployments to the AKS endpoint.

Controlled rollouts and A/B testing

Another benefit of endpoints is to perform controlled rollouts and incremental testing of
new model versions. ML model deployments are similar to deployments of new features in
application development. We might not want to roll out this new feature to all users at once,
but first, test whether the new feature improves our business metrics for a small group
of users.

New ML model deployments should never be uncontrolled or based on personal feelings
or preferences; a deployment should always be based on hard metrics and real evidence.
The best and most systematic way to test and roll out changes to your users is to define a
key metric, roll out your new model to one section of the users (group B), and serve the
old model to the remaining section of the users (group A). Once the metrics for the users
in group B exceed the metrics from group A over a defined period, you can confidently
roll out the feature to all your users.

This concept is called **A/B testing** and is used in many tech companies to roll out new services and features. As you can see in the following diagram, you split your traffic into a control group and a challenger group, where only the latter is served the new model:

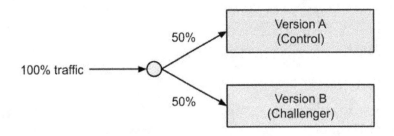

Figure 14.2 – A/B testing using endpoints

A/B testing and blue-green deployments work very well together, as they are really similar approaches. Both require the deployment of a fully functional service that is accessible to a subset of your users through routing policies. If you use Azure Machine Learning for your deployment and rollout strategy, you are very well covered. First, all deployments through Azure Machine Learning to ACI or AKS are blue-green deployments, which makes it easy for you to fall back on a previous version of your model.

Azure Machine Learning deployments on AKS support up to six model versions behind the same endpoint to implement either blue-green deployments or A/B testing strategies. You can then define policies to split the traffic between these endpoints; for example, you can split traffic by percentage. Here is a small code example of how to create another version on an AKS endpoint that should serve another version of your model to 50% of the users:

1. Let's first update the original deployment to serve as the control version and serve 50% of the traffic:

```
endpoint.update_version(
    version_name="version-1",
    traffic_percentile=50,
    is_default=True,
    is_control_version_type=True)
```

2. Next, we add the challenger version, which is a deployment of `test_model`. As you can see in the following snippet, you can also supply a different inference configuration to the new deployment:

```
endpoint.create_version(
  version_name="version-2",
  inference_config=inference_config,
  models=[test_model],
  tags={'modelVersion':'2'},
  description="my second version",
  traffic_percentile=50)
```

3. Finally, we start the deployment of the updated endpoints:

```
endpoint.wait_for_deployment(show_output=True)
print(endpoint.state)
```

In the preceding code, we show the preview feature of controlled rollouts for Azure Machine Learning and AKS. We use a different combination of model and inference configuration to deploy a separate service under the same endpoint. The traffic splitting now happens automatically through routing in Kubernetes. However, in order to align with a previous section of this chapter, we can expect this functionality to improve in the future as it gets used by many customers when rolling out ML models.

Implementing a batch-scoring pipeline

Operating batch-scoring services is very similar to the previously discussed online-scoring approach; you provide an environment, compute target, and scoring script. However, in your scoring file, you would rather pass a path to a Blob storage location with a new batch of data instead of the data itself. You can then use your scoring function to process the data asynchronously and output the predictions to a different storage location, back to the Blob storage, or push the data asynchronously to the calling service.

It is up to you how you implement your scoring file, as it is simply a Python script that you control. The only difference in the deployment process is that the batch-scoring script will be deployed as a computation on an Azure Machine Learning cluster, scheduled periodically through a pipeline, or triggered through a REST service. Therefore, it is important that your scoring script can be configured through command-line parameters. Remember that what makes batch scoring different is that we don't send the data to the scoring script, but instead, we send a path to the data and a path to write the output asynchronously.

A batch-scoring script is typically wrapped in a pipeline step, deployed as a pipeline, and triggered from a REST service or batch-scoring endpoint. The pipeline can be configured to use an Azure Machine Learning cluster for execution. In this section, we will reuse all of the concepts we have previously seen in *Chapter 8, Azure Machine Learning Pipelines*, and apply them to a batch-scoring pipeline step. Let's build a batch-scoring pipeline that scores images using the Inception v3 **DNN** model:

1. First, we define a configurable batch size. In both the pipeline configuration and the scoring file, you can take advantage of parallelizing your work in the Azure Machine Learning cluster:

```
from azureml.pipeline.core.graph import \
    PipelineParameter

batch_size_param = PipelineParameter(
    name="param_batch_size",
    default_value=20)
```

2. Next, we define a pipeline step that will call the batch-scoring script:

```
from azureml.pipeline.steps import PythonScriptStep

batch_score_step = PythonScriptStep(
    name="batch_scoring",
    script_name="batch_scoring.py",
    arguments=[
      "--dataset_path", input_images,
      "--model_name", "inception",
      "--label_dir", label_dir,
      "--output_dir", output_dir,
      "--batch_size", batch_size_param],
    compute_target=compute_target,
    inputs=[input_images, label_dir],
    outputs=[output_dir],
    runconfig=amlcompute_run_config)
```

3. Finally, we wrap the pipeline step in a pipeline. To test the batch-processing step, we submit the pipeline as an experiment to the Azure Machine Learning workspace:

```
from azureml.core import Experiment
from azureml.pipeline.core import Pipeline

pipeline = Pipeline(ws, steps=[batch_score_step])
exp = Experiment(ws, 'batch_scoring')
pipeline_run = exp.submit(pipeline,
    pipeline_params={"param_batch_size": 20})
```

4. Using this pipeline configuration, we call our scoring script with the relevant parameters. The pipeline is submitted as an experiment in Azure Machine Learning, which gives us access to all the features in runs and experiments in Azure. One feature would be that we can simply download the output from the experiment when it has finished running:

```
pipeline_run.wait_for_completion(show_output=True)
step_run = list(pipeline_run.get_children())[0]
step_run.download_file("./outputs/result-labels.txt")
```

5. If the batch-scoring file produces a nice CSV output containing names and predictions, we can now display the results using the following pandas functionality:

```
import pandas as pd

df = pd.read_csv(
    "./outputs/result-labels.txt",
    delimiter=":",
    header=None)
df.columns = ["Filename", "Prediction"]
df.head()
```

6. Let's go ahead and publish the pipeline as a REST service:

```
published_pipeline = pipeline_run.publish_pipeline(
    name="Inception_v3_scoring",
    description="Batch scoring using Inception v3",
    version="1.0")
```

```
published_id = published_pipeline.id
rest_endpoint = published_pipeline.endpoint
```

7. To run the published pipeline as a service through HTTP, we now need to use token-based authentication:

```
from azureml.core.authentication import \
  AzureCliAuthentication

cli_auth = AzureCliAuthentication()
aad_token = cli_auth.get_authentication_header()
```

8. Having retrieved the authentication token, we can now run the published pipeline:

```
import requests

# Specify batch size when running the pipeline
response = requests.post(
  rest_endpoint,
  headers=aad_token,
  json={
    "ExperimentName": "batch_scoring",
    "ParameterAssignments": {
      "param_batch_size": 50
    }
  })

run_id = response.json()["Id"]
```

That's it! You can now trigger your batch-scoring pipeline using the REST endpoint. The data will be processed, and the results will be provided in a file that can be consumed programmatically or piped into the next pipeline step for further processing.

Running a batch-scoring pipeline on an Azure Machine Learning service is a bit different from running a synchronous scoring service. While the real-time scoring service uses Azure Machine Learning deployments and AKS or ACI as popular compute targets, batch-scoring models are usually deployed as published pipelines on top of AmlCompute. The benefit of a published pipeline is that it can be used as a REST service, which can trigger and parameterize the pipeline.

ML operations in Azure

You successfully registered a trained model, an environment, a scoring file, and an inference configuration in the previous section. You optimized your model for scoring and deployed it to a managed Kubernetes cluster. You autogenerated client SDKs for your ML services. So, can you finally lean back and enjoy the success of your hard work? Well, not yet! First, we need to make sure that we have all our monitoring in place so that we can observe and react to anything happening to our deployment.

First, the good points: with Azure Machine Learning deployments and managed compute targets, you will get many things included out of the box with either Azure, Azure Machine Learning, or your service used as a compute target. Tools such as the **Azure Dashboard** on the Azure Portal, **Azure Monitor**, and **Azure Log Analytics** make it easy to centralize log and debug information. Once your data is available through Log Analytics, it can be queried, analyzed, visualized, alerted, and/or used for automation using Azure Automation. A great deployment and operations process should utilize these tools integrated with Azure and the Azure services.

The first thing that should come to mind when operating any application is measuring software and hardware metrics. It's essential to know the memory consumption, CPU usage, I/O latency, and network bandwidth of your application. Particularly for an ML service, you should always have an eye on performance bottlenecks and resource utilization for cost optimization. For large GPU-accelerated DNNs, it is essential to know your system in order to scale efficiently. These metrics allow you to scale your infrastructure vertically, and so move to bigger or smaller nodes when needed.

Another monitoring target for general application deployments should be your users' telemetry data (how they are using your service, how often they use it, and which parts of the service they use). This will help you to scale horizontally and add more nodes or remove nodes when needed.

The final important portion to measure from your scoring service, if possible, is the user input over time and the scoring results. For optimal prediction performance, it is essential to understand what type of data users are sending to your service, and how similar this data is to the training data. It's relatively certain that your model will require retraining at some point, and monitoring the input data will help you to define a time that this is required (for example, through a data drift metric).

Let's take a look at how we can monitor the Azure Machine Learning deployments and keep track of all these metrics in Azure.

Profiling models for optimal resource configuration

Azure Machine Learning provides a handy tool to help you evaluate the required resources for your ML model deployment through model profiling. This will help you estimate the number of CPUs and the amount of memory required to operate your scoring service at a specific throughput.

Let's take a look at the model profile of the model that we trained during the real-time scoring example:

1. First, you need to define `test_data` in the same format as the JSON request for your ML service; so, have `test_data` embedded in a JSON object under the `data` root property. Please note that if you defined a different format in your scoring file, then you need to use your own custom format:

    ```
    import json
    test_data = json.dump'({'data': [
        [1,2,3,4,5,6,7,8,9,10]
    ]})
    ```

2. Then, you can use the `Model.profile()` method to profile a model and evaluate the CPU and memory consumption of the service. This will start up your model, fire requests with `test_data` provided to it, and measure the resource utilization at the same time:

    ```
    profile = Model.profile(ws,
      service_name,
      [model],
      inference_config,
      test_data)


    profile.wait_for_profiling(True)
    print(profile.get_results())
    ```

3. The output contains a list of resources, plus a recommended value for the profiled model, as shown in the following snippet:

    ```
    {'cpu': 1.0, 'memoryInGB': 0.5}
    ```

It is good to run the model profiling tool before doing a production deployment, and this will help you set meaningful default values for your resource configuration. To further optimize and decide whether you need to scale up or down, vertically or horizontally, you need to measure, track, and observe various other metrics. We will discuss monitoring and scaling more in the last section of this chapter.

Collecting logs and infrastructure metrics

If you are new to cloud services, or Azure specifically, log and metric collection can be a bit overwhelming at first. Logs and metrics are generated in different layers in your application and can be either infrastructure- or application-based and collected automatically or manually. Then, there are diagnostic metrics that are emitted automatically but need to be enabled manually. In this section, we will briefly discuss how to collect this metric for the three main managed compute targets in the Azure Machine Learning service: ACI, AKS, and AmlCompute.

By default, you will get access to infrastructure metrics and logs through Azure Monitor. It will automatically collect Azure resources and guest OS metrics and logs, and provide metrics and query interfaces for logs based on Log Analytics. Azure Monitor should be used to track resource utilization (for example, CPU, RAM, disk space, disk I/O, and network bandwidth), which then can be pinned to dashboards or alerted on. You can even set up automatic autoscaling based on these metrics.

Metrics are mostly collected as distributions over time and reported back at certain time intervals. So, instead of seeing thousands of values per second, you are asked to choose an aggregate for each metric, for example, the average of each interval. For most monitoring cases, I would recommend you either look at the 95th percentile (or maximum aggregation, for metrics where lower is better) to avoid smoothing any spikes during the aggregation process. In AKS, you are provided with four different views of your metrics through Azure Monitor: clusters, nodes, controllers, and containers.

More detailed resource, guest, and virtualization host logs of your Azure Machine Learning deployment can be accessed by enabling diagnostic settings and providing a separate Log Analytics instance. This will automatically load the log data into your Log Analytics workspace, where you can efficiently query all your logs, analyze them, and create visualization and/or alerts.

It is strongly recommended to take advantage of the diagnostic settings, as they give you insights into your Azure infrastructure. This is especially helpful when you need to debug problems in your ML service (for example, failing containers, non-starting services, crashes, application freezes, and slow response times). Another great use case for Log Analytics is to collect, store, and analyze your application log. In AKS, you can send the Kubernetes master node logs, *kubelet* logs, and API server logs to Log Analytics.

One metric that is very important to track for ML training clusters and deployments, but is unfortunately not tracked automatically, is the GPU resource utilization. Due to this problem, GPU resource utilization has to be monitored and collected at the application level.

The most effective way to solve this for AKS deployments is to run a GPU logger service as a sidecar with your application, which collects resource statistics and sends them to **Application Insights (App Insights)**, a service that collects application metrics. Both App Insights and Log Analytics use the same data storage technology under the hood: Azure Data Explorer. However, default integrations for App Insights provide mainly application metrics such as access logs, while Log Analytics provides system logs.

In AmlCompute, we need to start a separate monitoring thread from your application code to monitor GPU utilization. Then, for Nvidia GPUs, we use a wrapper around the `nvidia-smi` monitoring utility, for example, the `nvidia-ml-py3` Python package. To send data to App Insights, we simply use the Azure SDK for App Insights. Here is a tiny code example showing you how to achieve this:

```
from applicationinsights import TelemetryClient
import nvidia_smi


nvidia_smi.nvmlInit()


# Get handle for card id 0
dev_handle = nvidia_smi.nvmlDeviceGetHandleByIndex(0)
res = nvidia_smi.nvmlDeviceGetUtilizationRates(dev_handle)


# Submit GPU metrics to AppInsights
tc = TelemetryClient("<insert appinsights key")
tc.track_metric("gpu", res.gpu)
tc.track_metric("gpu-gpu-mem", res.memory)
```

In the preceding code, we first used the `nvidia-ml-py3` wrapper on top of `nvidia-smi` to return a handle to the current GPU. Please note that when you have multiple GPUs, you can also iterate over them and report multiple metrics. Then, we used the `TelemetryClient` API from App Insights to report these metrics back to a central place, where we can then visualize, analyze, and alert on these values.

Tracking telemetry and application metrics

We briefly touched on Azure App Insights in the previous section. It is a great service for automatically collecting application metrics from your services, for example, Azure Machine Learning deployments. It also provides an SDK to collect any user-defined application metric that you want to track.

To automatically track user metrics, we need to deploy the model using Azure Machine Learning deployments to AKS or ACI. This will not only collect the web service metadata but also the model's predictions. To do so, you need to enable App Insights' diagnostics, as well as data model collection, or enable App Insights via the Python API:

```
from azureml.core.webservice import Webservice


aks_service= Webservice(ws, "aks-deployment")
aks_service.update(enable_app_insights=True)
```

In the preceding snippet, we can activate App Insights' metrics directly from the Python authoring environment. While this is a simple argument in the service class, it gives you an incredible insight into the deployment.

Two important metrics to measure are data drift coefficients for both training data and model predictions. We will learn more about this in the next section.

Detecting data drift

One important problem in ML is when to retrain your models. Should you always retrain when new training data is available, for example, daily, weekly, monthly or yearly? Do we need to retrain at all, or is the training data still relevant? Measuring **data drift** will help to answer these questions.

By automatically tracking the user input and the model predictions, you can compare a statistical variation between the training data and the user input per feature dimension, as well as the training labels with the model prediction. The variation of the training data and actual data is what is referred to as data drift and should be tracked and monitored regularly. Data drift leads to model performance degradation over time, and so needs to be monitored. The best case is to set up monitoring and alerts to understand when your deployed model differs too much from the training data and so needs to be retrained.

Azure Machine Learning provides useful abstractions to implement data drift monitors and alerts based on registered **datasets**, and can automatically expose data drift metrics in Application Insights. Computing the data drift requires two datasets: a baseline, which is usually the training dataset, and a target dataset, which is usually a dataset constructed from the inputs of the scoring service:

1. First, we define the target and baseline datasets. These datasets must contain a column that represents the date and time of each observation:

```
from azureml.core import Workspace, Dataset
from datetime import datetime


ws = Workspace.from_config()
ds_target = Dataset.get_by_name(ws, 'housing-data')
ds_baseline = ds_target.time_before(
    datetime(2022, 1, 1))
```

2. Next, we can set up email alerting for the monitor. This can be done in many different ways, but for the purpose of this example, we set up an email alert directly on the data drift monitor:

```
from azureml.datadrift import AlertConfiguration


alert_config = AlertConfiguration(
    email_addresses=['<insert email address>'])
```

3. Now, we can set up the data drift monitor providing all the previous details. We configure the monitor for three specific features ['a', 'b', 'c'], to measure drift on a monthly cadence with a delay of 24 hours. An alert is created when the target dataset drifts more than 25% from the baseline data:

```
from azureml.datadrift import DataDriftDetector


monitor = DataDriftDetector.create_from_datasets(ws,
    "data-drift-monitor",
    ds_baseline,
    ds_target,
    compute_target=compute_target,
    frequency='Month',
    feature_list=['a', 'b', 'c'],
```

```
    alert_config=alert_config,
    drift_threshold=0.25,
    latency=24)
```

4. Finally, we can enable the monitor schedule to run periodically:

```
monitor.enable_schedule()
```

Data drift is an essential operational metric to look at when operating ML deployments. Setting up monitors and alarms will help you get alerted early when the distribution of your data deviates too much from the training data and, therefore, requires you to retrain the model.

Summary

In this chapter, we learned how to take a trained model and deploy it as a managed service in Azure through a few simple lines of code. To do so, we learned how to prepare a model for deployment and looked into Azure Machine Learning auto-deployments and customized deployments.

We then took an NLP sentiment analysis model and deployed it as a real-time scoring service to ACI and AKS. We also learned how to define the service schema and how to roll out new versions effectively using endpoints and blue-green deployments. Finally, we learned how to integrate a model in a pipeline for asynchronous batch scoring.

In the last section, we learned about monitoring and operating your models using Azure Machine Learning services. We proposed to monitor CPU, memory, and GPU metrics as well as telemetry data. We also learned how to measure the data drift of your service by collecting user input and model output over time. Detecting data drift is an important metric that allows you to know when a model needs to be retrained.

In the next chapter, we will apply the learned knowledge and take a look at model interoperability, hardware optimization, and integration into other Azure services.

15

Model Interoperability, Hardware Optimization, and Integrations

In the previous chapter, we discovered how to deploy our machine learning scoring either as a batch or real-time scorer, what endpoints are and how we can deploy them, and finally, we had a look at how we can monitor our deployed solutions. In this chapter, we will dive deeper into additional deployment scenarios for ML inferencing, possible other hardware infrastructure we can utilize, and how we can integrate our models and endpoints with other Azure services.

In the first section, we will have a look at how to provide model interoperability by converting ML models into a standardized model format and an inference-optimized scoring framework. **Open Neural Network Exchange** (**ONNX**) is a standardized format to serialize and store ML models and acyclic computational graphs and operations efficiently. We will learn what the ONNX framework is, how we can convert ML models from popular ML frameworks to ONNX, and how we can score ONNX models on multiple platforms using ONNX Runtime.

Following that, we will take a look at alternative hardware targets, such as **field-programmable gate arrays** (**FPGAs**). We will understand how they work internally and how they can lead to higher performance and better efficiency compared to standard hardware or even GPUs.

Finally, we will have a look at how we can integrate ML models and endpoints into other services. We will get a deeper understanding of the process to deploy ML to edge devices, and we will integrate one of our previously set up endpoints with Power BI.

In this chapter, we will cover the following topics:

- Model interoperability with ONNX
- Hardware optimization with FPGAs
- Integrating ML models and endpoints with Azure services

Technical requirements

In this chapter, you will require access to a Microsoft Power BI account. You can get one either through your place of work or by creating a trial account here: `https://app.powerbi.com/signupredirect?pbi_source=web`.

All code examples in this chapter can be found in the GitHub repository for this book: `https://github.com/PacktPublishing/Masthttps://github.com/PacktPublishing/Mastering-Azure-Machine-Learning-Second-Edition/tree/main/chapter15`.

Model interoperability with ONNX

In the previous chapter, we learned how to deploy ML models as web services for online and batch scoring. However, many real-world use cases require you to embed a trained ML model directly into an application without the use of a separate scoring service. The target service is likely written in a different language than the language used for training the ML model. A common example is that a simple model trained in Python using scikit-learn needs to be embedded into a Java application.

Model interoperability gives you the flexibility to train your model with your language and framework of choice, export it to a common format, and then score it in a different language and platform using the shared format. In some cases, using a native runtime optimized for scoring on the target environment even achieves a better scoring performance than running the original model.

First, we will take a look at the ONNX initiative, consisting of the specification, runtime, and ecosystem, and how it helps to achieve model interoperability across a large set of support languages, frameworks, operations, and target platforms.

Then, we will look into converting ML models from popular frameworks to ONNX (called ONNX frontends) and executing ONNX models in a native inferencing runtime using ONNX Runtime, one of the multiple ONNX backends. Let's delve into it.

What is model interoperability and how can ONNX help?

As an IT organization grows, so does the amount of tooling, development, and deployment platforms and choices. In ML, this problem is even more present as there are multiple ML frameworks as well as model serialization formats. Therefore, once the organization grows, it becomes a near-impossible challenge to align every scientist and engineer on the same tooling, frameworks, and model formats that also need to support all your target environments. Does your XGBoost model run on iOS? Does your PyTorch model work in Java? Can your scikit-learn model be loaded in a browser-based JavaScript application? One way to solve this problem of model interoperability is to ensure that trained ML models can be ported to a standardized format that can be executed natively across all target platforms. This is exactly what ONNX is about.

ONNX is a joint initiative from major IT companies such as Microsoft, Facebook, Amazon, ARM, and Intel to facilitate ML model interoperability. It allows organizations to choose different languages, frameworks, and environments for ML training, as well as different languages, environments, and devices for inferencing. As an example, ONNX enables an organization to train deep learning models using PyTorch and TensorFlow and traditional ML models using LightGBM and XGBoost, and deploy these models to a Java-based web service, an Objective-C-based iOS application, and a browser-based JavaScript application. This interoperability is enabled through three key ingredients:

- **ONNX specification**: A data format for *efficient serialization and deserialization* for model definitions and model weights using **Protocol Buffers** (**Protobuf**). To represent a wide range of ML models, the ONNX specification is comprised of a definition of an extensible computation graph model, as well as definitions of standard data types and built-in operators. With the ONNX specification, many ML models consisting of a variety of supported architectures, building blocks, operations, and data types can be efficiently represented in a single file, which we call the *ONNX model*.

- **ONNX Runtime**: An efficient *native inferencing engine* with bindings to many higher-level languages, such as C#, Python, JavaScript, Java/Kotlin (Android), and Objective-C (iOS). This means that with the ONNX Runtime bindings for one of these languages, we can load, score, and even train ONNX models. It also provides built-in GPU acceleration using DirectML, TensorRT, **Deep Neural Network Library** (**DNNL**), nGraph, CUDA, and the **Microsoft Linear Algebra Subprograms** (**MLAS**) library, and weight quantization and graph optimization to run efficiently on various compute targets, such as Cloud Compute, Jupyter kernels, mobile phones, and web browsers.

- **ONNX ecosystem**: A *collection of libraries* that facilitate conversion from and to ONNX. ONNX libraries can be broadly categorized into ONNX frontends (*to ONNX*) and ONNX backends (*from ONNX*). While *ONNX frontend* libraries help to convert arbitrary computations into ONNX models (models following the ONNX specification), *ONNX backend* libraries provide support to execute ONNX models or to convert ONNX models into a specific framework runtime. ONNX is widely used within Microsoft as well as other large companies and, therefore, supports a wide range of frameworks and languages. Many popular libraries are officially supported frontends, such as traditional ML algorithms, scikit-learn, LightGBM, XGBoost, and CatBoost, as well as modern DL frameworks, such as TensorFlow, Keras, PyTorch, Caffe 2, and CoreML.

ONNX is a great choice for providing model interoperability to allow an organization to decouple model training, model serialization, and model inferencing. Let's learn about popular ONNX frontends and backends in action in the next section.

Converting models to ONNX format with ONNX frontends

ONNX frontends are packages, tools, or libraries that can convert existing ML models or numeric computations into ONNX models. While popular ML frameworks used to implement ONNX export out of the box (similar to the PyTorch `torch.onnx` module), most frameworks today support ONNX through a separate conversion library. The most popular ONNX frontends at the time of writing are as follows:

- `skl2onnx`: Converts scikit-learn models to ONNX

- `tf2onnx`: Converts TensorFlow models to ONNX

- `onnxmltools`: Converts XGBoost, LightGBM, CatBoost, H2O, libsvm, and CoreML models to ONNX

- `torch.onnx`: Converts PyTorch models to ONNX

Once, the ONNX frontend libraries are installed, the conversion to ONNX specification is often simply done by running a single command. Let's see this in action with TensorFlow as an example:

1. First, we will save a Keras model using the TensorFlow `SaveModel` format. We can achieve this by calling `model.save()` and providing the path to serialize the `SaveModel` model to disk:

train.py

```
model = create_model()
model.fit(X_train, y_train)
model.save('tf_model')
```

2. We can then use the `tf2onnx` library to convert the `SaveModel` model into an ONNX model, as shown in the following snippet:

convert.sh

```
python -m tf2onnx.convert \
    --saved-model tf_model \
    --output model.onnx
```

As we see in the preceding example, all we need is a single command to convert TensorFlow models into ONNX models. Once we have an ONNX model, we can use ONNX backends to score them, as shown in the following section.

Native scoring of ONNX models with ONNX backends

Once a model is exported as an ONNX model, we can load it using an ONNX-compatible backend. The reference implementation for the ONNX backend is called **ONNX Runtime**, and is a native implementation with bindings in many high-level languages.

First, we can load, analyze, and check an ONNX model using the onnx library, as shown in the following example:

```python
import onnx
model = onnx.load("model.onnx")
onnx.checker.check_model(model)
```

However, if we want to score the model, we need to use the onnxruntime backend library. First, we need to load the model for an inferencing session; this means we can load the optimized model and don't need to allocate any buffers for storing gradients. In the next step, we can score the model by executing run(output_names, input_feed, run_options=None). The output_names argument refers to the named output layer we want to return from the model, whereas input_feed represents the data we want to pass to the model. The scoring properties, such as the log level, can be configured through the run_options argument. The following example shows how to score the model and return the last layer's output from an ONNX model:

```python
import onnxruntime as rt


session = rt.InferenceSession("model.onnx")
outputs = session.run(None, {'input': X.values})
```

In the preceding code, we load the ONNX model optimized for inferencing, pass data to the model's input parameter, and return the last layer's output using the ONNX Runtime Python API. You can access the layer information, as well as names of inputs and outputs, using the helper method, session.get_modelmeta().

In this section, we learned about ONNX, how to create an ONNX model from trained ML models using ONNX frontends, and how to score an ONNX model using ONNX Runtime, the reference implementation for an ONNX backend. While we looked only at the Python API of ONNX Runtime, many other high-level bindings are available.

Hardware optimization with FPGAs

In the previous section, we exported a model to ONNX to take advantage of an inference-optimized and hardware-accelerated runtime to improve the scoring performance. In this section, we will take this approach one step further to deploy on even faster inferencing hardware: FPGAs.

But, before we talk about how to deploy a model to an FPGA, let's first understand what an FPGA is and why we would choose one as a target for DL inference instead of a GPU.

Understanding FPGAs

Most people typically come across a specific variety of **integrated circuit** (**IC**), called an **application-specific integrated circuit** (**ASIC**). ASICs are purpose-built ICs, such as the processor in your laptop, the GPU cores on your graphics card, or the microcontroller in your washing machine. These chips share the fact that they have a fixed hardware footprint optimized to support a specific task. Often, like any general processor, they operate with a specific **instruction set**, allowing certain commands to be run. When you program something with a higher-level language, such as Java, C++, or Python, the compiler or interpreter will translate this high-level code into machine code, which is the set of commands the processor understands and is able to run.

The strength of an ASIC is that the underlying chip architecture can be optimized for the specific workload, resulting in the most optimal design for the hardware in terms of the area it requires. The weakness of an ASIC is that it is only good for performing the specific task it was designed for, and its design is fixed, as the underlying hardware cannot be altered.

Even though we can run any task on a standard processor, for something very specific, such as the computation and backtracking for thousands of nodes in a neural network, they might not be optimal. Therefore, a lot of these calculations are now run on a GPU instead, as its chip architecture leans more toward running the same calculations in parallel, which leans more toward the ingrained structure of a neural network algorithm than a standard CPU would.

FPGAs are defined by a different concept than their ASIC counterparts. FPGAs trade in the most optimal design, especially when it comes to the used area on a chip, for the freedom of *re-programmability*. This main feature allows a user to purchase an FPGA and then build themselves their own processor, a hardware switch, a network router, or anything else, and change the underlying hardware design any time they feel like it.

As hardware in the end is something physical made up of some form of binary logic gates, registers, and wires, this capability of FPGAs might sound like magic. Then again, we are using flash drives daily that can store data and can erase data again. For example, modern **NAND flash drives** are erased through a process called **field electron emission**, which allows a charge to move through a thin layer of insulation to *reset* the setting of bits or, to be more precise, blocks of bits.

Remembering this, let's have a look at the basic building blocks of an FPGA, called **logic elements**. *Figure 15.1* shows the general concept of these building blocks. Different manufacturers tweak different aspects of these, but the base concept remains the same:

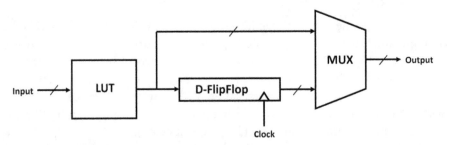

Figure 15.1 – Structure of a logic element in an FPGA

A logic element is typically made up of the following components:

- **Input/output (I/O)**: Denotes the interconnection with other logical elements or with external I/O (think of Ethernet and USB, for example).

- **Lookup table (LUT)**: Holds the main logical function performed in this logic element. Any logic in a digital circuit can be broken down to a **Boolean function** that maps a certain number of binary inputs to a certain number of binary outputs.

- **D-FlipFlop (Register)**: Stores the input value of the current **clock cycle** for the next clock cycle, the length of which is the inverse of the **frequency** of the running circuit. The idea to store something for the next round is the basic principle of all digital hardware and a necessity to be able to do hardware pipelining. The maximum processing time between any adjacent registers in the circuit defines the maximum frequency the circuit can run at.

- **Multiplexer (MUX)**: Chooses which of its inputs are shown as the output. In this case, it either shows the current result from the Boolean function, or the one from the previous clock cycle.

Through the LUT, any Boolean function (and through a register, any multi-layered hardware logic) can be realized. In addition, the LUT can be erased and reset, which enables the reprogrammable nature of FPGAs.

The full schematic structure of an FPGA is shown in *Figure 15.2*. Just understand that a normal-sized FPGA will have upward of 500,000 logic elements:

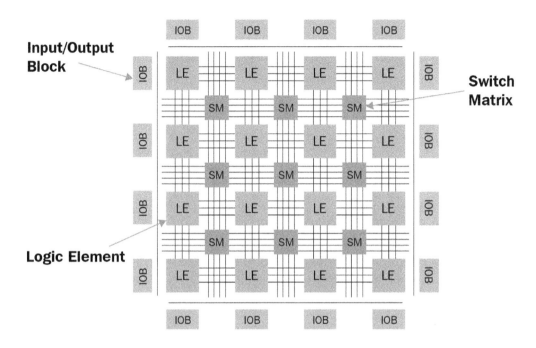

Figure 15.2 – Schematic structure of an FPGA

In addition to logic elements, *Figure 15.2* shows **switch matrices** and **I/O blocks**. Switch matrices are the last piece of the puzzle and allow the setting and resetting of the required connections among logic elements, and between them and the I/O blocks. With their help, it is possible to fully reprogram the circuit structure on an FPGA.

Finally, to facilitate the programming of an FPGA, a so-called **hardware description language** (HDL) is used. There are two major languages used for hardware design (be it for FPGAs or ASICs), **SystemVerilog** and **VHDL**. When you see code written in these languages, it might look like a high-level programming language, but in reality, you are not programming anything; you are instead *describing* the desired hardware architecture. In a sense, you give the machine a picture of a circuit in the form of code, and it tries to map this onto the given elements on the FPGA. This step is called **synthesis**. After this step, a binary is sent to the FPGA that populates the required logic elements with the correct Boolean functions and sets all the interconnections accordingly.

Besides this logical structure, you will find a lot of other integrated systems in modern FPGAs, combining the strength of ASICs and FPGAs. You might even find a processor such as an **ARM Cortex** on the IC itself. The idea is to let anything that would be extremely time-consuming to build from scratch on the FPGA fabric run on the processor instead while using the FPGA to host your custom hardware designs. For example, it would take a lot of time to build the lower layers of the Ethernet protocol on an FPGA, as TCP requires a highly sophisticated hardware circuit. Therefore, outsourcing this part into a processor can speed up development time immensely.

Now that we have a general idea of what an FPGA is and how it works, let's discuss why they might be more useful for DL than GPUs.

Comparing GPUs and FPGAs for deep neural networks

As we discussed in the previous section, the underlying hardware structure of a GPU supports deep neural networks for training and inference. The reason for this is that they are designed with 3D image rendering in mind and, therefore, have a lot of logic on board to facilitate matrix multiplications, a task that is extremely time-consuming on CPUs and crucial for DNNs. Through GPUs, the processing time can typically be lowered from days to mere hours. The same can be said for FPGAs, as we can basically build any specialized circuit we require to optimize the speed and power consumption of any tasks we want to perform.

Therefore, both are options that are far superior for DNNs than general CPUs. But, which one should we choose and why? Let's now go through a list of aspects to consider and how each of these two options fares in both cases:

- **Complexity to implement**: GPUs typically offer a software-level language (for example, CUDA) to disconnect the programmer from the underlying hardware. For FPGAs, the programmer must understand the hardware domain and how to design for it. Therefore, building the correct circuit for an FPGA is far more complicated than just using another library in a high-level programming language. But, there is work being done to abstract this layer as much as possible with specialized tooling and converters.

- **Power consumption**: GPUs produce a lot of heat and require a lot of cooling and electricity. This is because of the additional complexity of the hardware design in order to facilitate software programmability, in turn supporting the base hardware stack of RAM, CPU, and GPU. FPGAs, on the other hand, do not require this stack to operate and, therefore, in most cases, have a low to medium power output, through which they are 4 to 10 times more power-efficient than GPUs.

- **Hardware stack**: GPUs are dependent on the whole memory management of the standard hardware stack (CPU cache, RAM, and GPU memory), and require an external system to control them. This leads to an inefficient but required hardware design for GPUs to facilitate the connection layers to the standard hardware stack, which makes it less performant. FPGAs, on the other hand, have all the required elements (such as high-speed memory) on board the IC and, therefore, can run completely *autonomously* without pulling any data from system memory or any other place.

- **Latency and interconnectability**: While GPUs are connected to a standard hardware stack and only have a few actual hardware ports at the back of it (HDMI and DisplayPort), which are often only outputs, an FPGA can connect to anything. This means it can support vastly different input and output standards at the same time, making it extremely flexible and adaptable to any given situation. In addition, it can process data with very low latency, as no data needs to pass through the system memory, CPU, or SW layer, making it far superior for applications such as real-time video processing.

- **Flexibility**: Even though GPUs have a parallel hardware architecture, you might not be able to use it effectively. The specific DNN algorithm must be mapped to the underlying hardware, and this might be neither perfect nor even feasible. It falls into the same problem class as distributing processes among CPU cores. In addition, GPUs are designed to handle 32-bit or 64-bit standard data types. If you are using a very specialized data type or a custom one, you might not be able to run it on a GPU at all. FPGAs, on the other hand, allow you to define whatever data size or data type you want to work with and, on top of that, allow even a so-called *partial reconfiguration* during runtime, which it uses to reprogram parts of the logic during runtime.

- **Industry readiness**: In a typical industrial scenario, be it defense, manufacturing, smart cities, or any other, the hardware deployed must be compact, must have a long lifespan, should have low power consumption, should survive the environment it is positioned in (dust, heat, humidity), and in some scenarios, needs to have *functional safety*, which means it must follow certain compliance standards and protocols. A GPU is a bad choice for any of these circumstances, as it is very power-hungry, has a lifespan of 2 to 5 years, requires massive amounts of cooling, does not survive hostile environments, and does not have functional safety. FPGAs were designed with industrial settings in mind and, therefore, are typically built for long life (10 to 30 years) and safety, while having a low footprint on power and required space.

- **Costs**: If you've ever bought a GPU for your PC, you might have an idea of the cost of such an extension card. FPGAs, on the other hand, can be expensive but are typically cheaper to obtain for comparable setup requirements.

Taking all these points into consideration, FPGAs are technically superior in most ways and often cheaper, but have the major problem that they require developers to understand hardware design. This problem led to the creation of toolkits helping bridge the gap between hardware and ML development, some of which are as follows:

- **Vitis AI for Xilinx FPGAs**: A development kit for ML inferencing utilizing pre-designed **Deep Learning Processor Units (DLUs)**. More information can be found here: `https://www.xilinx.com/products/design-tools/vitis/vitis-ai.html`. In addition, you can find some information on how to use this with the NP VM series in Azure here: `https://github.com/Xilinx/Vitis-AI/tree/master/docs/azure`.

- **OpenVINO for Intel FPGAs**: A development kit for DL and ML inferencing. More information can be found here: `https://www.intel.com/content/www/us/en/artificial-intelligence/programmable/solutions.html`.

- **Microsoft Project Brainwave**: A development platform for DL and ML inferencing for computer vision and NLP. More information can be found here: `https://www.microsoft.com/en-us/research/project/project-brainwave`.

These are just a few options to support the deployment and acceleration of ML models through FPGAs.

> **Important Note**
> FPGAs are a very exceptional technology, but they require an ample understanding of hardware design to be used efficiently and successfully in any project, or a very sophisticated toolkit for abstracting the hardware layer.

Now that we know why we might prefer to take an FPGA for DNNs, let's have a brief look at how FPGAs can be utilized in that regard with Azure Machine Learning.

Running DNN inferencing on Intel FPGAs with Azure

As discussed in the previous section, building a hardware design for an FPGA is not an easy task. You could certainly do this from scratch utilizing one of the Azure VMs sporting an FPGA (`https://docs.microsoft.com/en-us/azure/virtual-machines/np-series`), or with your own FPGA development kit. Another option is to use the hardware-accelerated Python package that is available in the Azure Machine Learning Python SDK. This package gives you an abstraction layer through a generic hardware design supporting a subset of models and options to use, specifically ones for DNN inferencing. Through this, you have access to the **Azure PBS VM family**, which has an Intel FPGA attached and is only available through Azure Machine Learning. This machine type is deployable in East US, Southeast Asia, West Europe, and West US 2.

The general approach is very similar to ONNX; you take a trained model and convert it to a specific format that can be executed on FPGAs. In this case, your model must be either ResNet, DenseNet, VGG, or SSD-VGG, and must be written in TensorFlow in order to fit the underlying hardware design. Furthermore, we will use quantized 16-bit float model weights converted to ONNX models, which will be run on the FPGA. For these models, FPGAs give you the best inference performance in the cloud.

To enable hardware acceleration through FPGAs, we require a few extra steps compared to the ONNX example. The following list shows what steps need to be performed:

1. Pick a supported model featurizer.

2. Train the supported model with a custom classifier.

3. Quantize the model featurizer's weights to 16-bit precision.

4. Convert the model to an ONNX format.

5. (Optional) Register the model.

6. Create a compute target (preferably Azure Kubernetes Service) with PBS nodes.

7. Deploy the model.

> **Important Note**
>
> As the code is cluttered and hard to interpret, we will skip the code examples in this section. However, you can find detailed examples of FPGA model training, conversion, and deployments on Azure's GitHub repository at `https://github.com/Azure/MachineLearningNotebooks/tree/master/how-to-use-azureml/deployment/accelerated-models`.

Let's discuss these steps in some more detail.

From the DNN layers we discussed in *Chapter 10, Training Deep Neural Networks on Azure*, only the feature extractor layers (**featurizers**) will be hardware-accelerated for inferencing. In order to run a model on an FPGA, you need to pick a supported model from the `azureml.accel.models` package (`https://docs.microsoft.com/en-us/python/api/azureml-accel-models/azureml.accel.models`). You can attach any classification or regression head (or both) on top using TensorFlow or Keras, but they will not be hardware-accelerated, similar to running only certain operations on GPUs. The designers opted here to deploy only the most time-consuming parts onto the FPGA.

In the next step, you can train the model, consisting of a predefined feature extractor and a custom classification head, using your own data and weights, or by fine-tuning, for example, provided ImageNet weights. This should happen with 32-bit precision, as convergence will be faster during training.

Once the training is finished, you need to quantize the weights of the featurizer into half-precision floats, using the quantized models provided in the `azureml.accel.models` package. This step needs to be done because the designers opted here for a fixed data size of 16-bit in order to make the hardware design as generic and reusable as possible.

For the next step, you convert the whole model into an ONNX model, using the `AccelOnnxConverter` method from the same Azure package. In addition, the `AccelContainerImage` class helps you to define `InferenceConfig` for the FPGA-based compute targets.

Finally, you can register your model using the Azure Machine Learning model registry, and you can create an AKS cluster using the `Standard_PB6s` nodes. Once the cluster is up and running, you use your `Webservice.deploy_from_image` method to deploy the web service.

> **Important Note**
> You can find a detailed example of the deployment steps in the Azure Machine Learning documentation here: `https://docs.microsoft.com/en-us/azure/machine-learning/how-to-deploy-fpga-web-service`.

The workflow to deploy a model through Azure Machine Learning to an FPGA-based compute target is a bit different from simply deploying ONNX models, as you have to consider the limited supported selection of models right from the beginning. Another difference is that, while you choose a predefined supported model for FPGA deployment, you can only accelerate the feature extractor part of the model. This means you have to attach an additional classification or regression head—a step that is not immediately obvious. Once you understand this, it will make more sense that you only quantize the feature extractor to half-precision floats after training.

While this process seems a bit difficult and customized, the performance and latency gain, especially when dealing with predictions on image data, is huge. But, you should take advantage of this optimization only if you are ready to adapt your training processes and pipelines to this specific environment, as shown throughout the section.

Now that we have a good understanding of what FPGAs are and how we can utilize them through Azure Machine Learning, let's have a look in the next section at what other Azure services we can integrate with our models.

Integrating ML models and endpoints with Azure services

Relying on the Azure Machine Learning service either for experimentation, performing end-to-end training, or simply registering your trained models and environments brings you a ton of value. In *Chapter 14, Model Deployment, Endpoints, and Operations*, we covered two main scenarios, a real-time scoring web service through automated deployments and batch scoring through a deployed pipeline. While these two use cases are quite different in requirement and deployment types, they show what is possible once you have a trained model and packaged environment stored in Azure Machine Learning. In this section, we will discuss how to use and integrate these models or their endpoints in other Azure services.

In many scenarios, abstracting your batch-scoring pipeline from the actual data processing pipeline to separate concerns and responsibilities makes a lot of sense. However, sometimes your scoring should happen directly during the data processing or querying time and in the same system. Once your ML model is registered and versioned with Azure Machine Learning, you can pull out a specific version of the model anywhere using the Azure ML SDK, either in Python, C#, the command line, or any other language that can make a call to a REST service.

This makes it possible to pull trained and converted ONNX models from a desktop application, either during build time or at runtime. You can load models while running a Spark job, for example, on Azure Databricks or Azure Synapse. Through that, you can avoid transferring TBs of data to a separate scoring service.

Other services, such as Azure Data Explorer, allow you to call models directly from the service through a Python extension (`https://docs.microsoft.com/en-us/azure/data-explorer/kusto/query/pythonplugin`). Azure Data Explorer is an exciting managed service for storing and querying large amounts of telemetry data efficiently. It is used internally at Azure to power Azure Log Analytics, Azure Application Insights, and Time Series Insights. It has a powerful Python runtime with many popular packages available, and so provides the perfect service for performing anomaly detection or time-series analysis based on your custom models. In addition, it allows you to access its time-series data during ML modeling through a Python extension called **Kqlmagic** (`https://docs.microsoft.com/en-us/azure/data-explorer/kqlmagic`).

> **Important Note**
> When using Azure Machine Learning for model deployments, you can take advantage of all the Azure ecosystem and can expect to see model or endpoint integration with more and more Azure services over time.

Closing this chapter, we will dive deeper into two other integration options in the upcoming sections. We will have a look at deploying ML models through **Azure IoT Edge** to a gateway or device in the field, and we will look at how to utilize ML endpoints for data augmentation in **Power BI**.

Integrating with Azure IoT Edge

So far, we have discussed different ways to make our models run on systems in the cloud, be it on machines with CPUs, GPUs, or FPGAs, either as a batch-scoring process or as a real-time endpoint. Now, let's discuss another interesting deployment scenario, deploying real-time scorers to one to up to hundreds of thousands of devices in the field. The control of such devices and the processing of gathered telemetry and events fall under the topic of the so-called **Internet of Things** (**IoT**), which enables us to react in near real time to changes and critical problems in any sort of environment.

In these scenarios, the integration of ML allows us to distribute a model to a multitude of systems and devices simultaneously, allowing these so-called **edge devices** to execute the model on the local runtime in order to react to the result of the ML processing accordingly. This could be a local camera system that performs ML-powered image processing to react to intruders and send out alarms or any other scenario you might imagine.

To get a base understanding of how to achieve this utilizing the Azure platform, let's first have a look at how IoT scenarios are realized through the help of **Azure IoT Hub** and other services, and then discuss how this can be integrated with Azure Machine Learning and our trained models.

Understanding IoT solutions on Azure

The basis for any IoT architecture in Azure is Azure IoT Hub. This serves as a cloud gateway to communicate with devices and other gateways in the field and offers the ability to control them to a certain extent. On the one hand, it runs Azure Event Hubs underneath to be able to handle a huge amount of incoming telemetry through a distributed structure, not too different from Apache Kafka. On the other hand, it serves as a control instrument serving the following functions:

- **Device cataloging**: The ledger of all devices registered to Azure IoT Hub. Any device connected receives its own device name and connection configuration, defining how the direct connection between hub and device is secured, which happens using either a rotating key or a device certificate.

- **Device provisioning**: A service that allows devices to automatically register themselves to IoT Hub to obtain either a connection string with a key or a certificate. Useful if more than a handful of devices must be registered.

- **Device twin**: A configuration file that defines important properties for the device, which can be set or requested. In between the stream of telemetry, the device is asked to send this file sporadically, updating the state of the device in the cloud gateway. Therefore, the device twin always holds the most recent state of the device. This functionality is automatically implemented when using the **Azure IoT device SDK** on the device.

- **Command and control**: This is enabled through the **Azure IoT Service SDK**. Commands from a console or an external application can be used to either send new desired properties to single devices, define configurations for a group of devices, or send a predefined command that the device needs to understand and implement. This could be a request to restart the device or flash its firmware.

- **Monitoring and diagnostics**: A diagnostic view on any incoming and outgoing messaging from and to IoT Hub. It can be used to understand the throughput of incoming telemetry, understand any control plane information exchanged, and warn if a device is unreachable and malfunctioning.

In addition to this cloud gateway, Azure offers a device runtime on the edge called Azure IoT Edge, which can be installed on a device or gateway. It is powered by the Moby Docker runtime (`https://mobyproject.org/`), which allows users to deploy Docker containers to a device in the field. The setup of any solution operating in this runtime is defined by a **deployment manifest** that is set up for an edge device through a device twin configuration file in IoT Hub. This manifest defines the following components:

- **IoT Edge agent**: Verifies and instantiates modules, checks their state during runtime, and reports back any configuration or runtime problem utilizing the device twin configuration file. It is the main module of the runtime and is *required*.

- **IoT Edge hub**: Enables the IoT Edge runtime to mimic IoT Hub for additional devices connecting to this local edge device. This enables any form of complex hierarchy, while devices can use the same protocol communicating with an IoT Edge device as they would with IoT Hub. This module is *required*.

- **Container modules**: Defines the container images to be copied to the edge runtime. This is done by defining a link to the source files stored in Azure Container Registry. Besides any user-defined container that can be deployed in this manner, there are also a bunch of containerized versions of Azure services that can be sent to the runtime. This list includes Blob storage, an Azure Function app, certain Cognitive Services, and even a small, optimized version of a SQL server called **SQL Edge**.

- **Local communication via routing**: Defines the first option to connect modules together by setting direct connections between inputs and outputs of the various modules defined before.

- **Local communication via an MQTT broker**: Defines the second option to connect modules together. Instead of setting direct connections, a broker is used to which modules can subscribe. This broker also offers connections to external devices that understand how to talk to an MQTT broker.

These are the main components and options to consider when defining the deployment manifest.

> **Important Note**
>
> The greatest strength that Azure IoT Edge brings to the table is the ability to define, manage, and version containers in the cloud, and deploy them to thousands of devices. With the help of device configurations, we can group devices and only target a certain group for a new test update, thus enabling best practices for DevOps in an IoT setting.

Now, let's briefly have a look at an example. *Figure 15.3* shows a simple setup for scoring a containerized ML model on incoming telemetry through Azure IoT Edge and its connection with Azure IoT Hub:

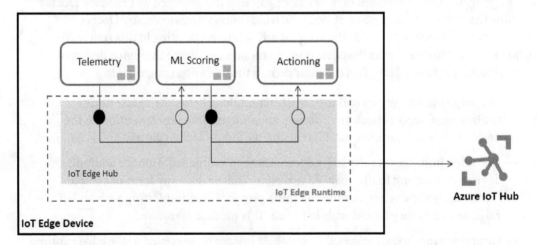

Figure 15.3 – Azure IoT Hub connecting to the edge runtime

The connections in *Figure 15.3* show the internal routing between containers, including actioning that takes place locally, while any insights from the ML scoring and any initial telemetry are sent additionally to the cloud for further analysis. This is the typical scenario for any ML model operating on the edge.

With this knowledge in mind, let's now have a look at how to integrate Azure Machine Learning in such an IoT architecture.

Integrating Azure Machine Learning

In *Chapter 3*, *Preparing the Azure Machine Learning Workspace*, we learned that every Azure Machine Learning workspace comes with its own Azure Container Registry. We can now use this registry to achieve our goal. *Figure 15.4* shows an example of an end-to-end solution for ML on the edge:

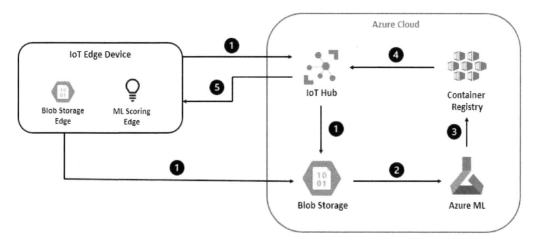

Figure 15.4 – End-to-end ML on Azure IoT Edge scenario

It depicts the following steps:

1. Collecting telemetry in a storage account, either through routing single messages from IoT Hub or through a batch upload from the Blob storage on the edge to the storage account in the cloud

2. Training an ML model on the captured data as we learned previously

3. Registering a container including the trained model and dependencies in the existing Azure Container Registry of the Azure Machine Learning workspace

4. Creating an IoT Edge deployment manifest defining an ML module sourced fromAzure Container Registry

5. Deploying the created configuration through Azure IoT Hub to the edge device

Through this setup, we are now able to deploy and control an ML model on the edge, enabling vast scenarios for running low-latency ML solutions on external devices.

> **Important Note**
> If you are interested to try this out, feel free to follow the tutorial for setting up an example ML model on Azure IoT Edge, found here: `https://docs.microsoft.com/en-us/azure/iot-edge/tutorial-machine-learning-edge-01-intro`.

Finally, if you are interested in further options for ML solutions on the edge, have a look at one of the newest additions to the Azure IoT space, called **Azure Percept** (`https://azure.microsoft.com/en-us/services/azure-percept/`). It offers a ready-made hardware development kit for video and audio inferencing that works together with Azure IoT Hub and Azure Machine Learning.

Now that we've had a glimpse into the world of IoT and scenarios for ML on the edge, let's have a look at how to utilize real-time ML endpoints with Power BI.

Integrating with Power BI

One of the most interesting integrations from an enterprise perspective is the Azure Machine Learning integration with Power BI. It allows us to utilize our ML endpoints to apply our models to data columns from the comfort of the built-in **Power Query editor**. Think for a second how powerful this concept of rolling out ML models to be used by data analysts in their BI tools is.

Let's try this out by utilizing the `sentiment-analysis-pbi` endpoint we created in *Chapter 14*, *Model Deployment, Endpoints, and Operations*, by following these steps:

1. If you haven't done so already, download the Power BI Desktop application (`https://powerbi.microsoft.com/en-gb/desktop/`) to your machine, run it, and log in.

2. Download the `sentiment_examples.csv` file from the chapter repository, and select **Get Data** | **Text/CSV** to load the content of this local file into an in-memory dataset in Power BI.

3. The Power Query editor will open and will show you an icon of the file with the name and size. Right-click on that, and select **Text**.

4. You should be greeted by a table with one column. Rename the column `Phrases`, as shown in *Figure 15.5*:

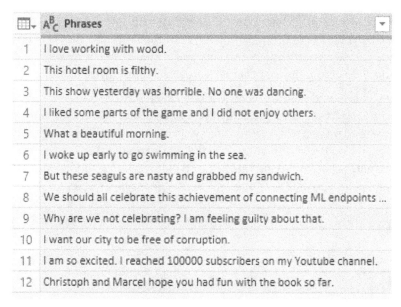

Figure 15.5 – Sample phrases for sentiment analysis

5. The editor gives you a lot of possibilities to apply transformations to this data. Looking at the menu, you should see a button on the far-right side called **Azure Machine Learning**. Click on it.

6. If you are logged in correctly, you should see all available endpoints in all the Azure Machine Learning workspaces you have access to. Select our previously created endpoint, `AzureML.sentiment-analysis-pbi`. In the **query** field, select the `Phrases` column. This will be the input for our ML endpoint. *Figure 15.6* shows what this should look like:

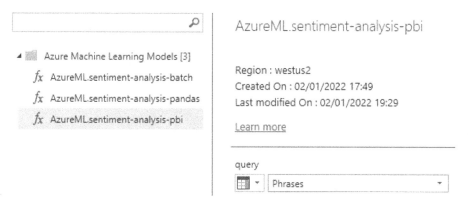

Figure 15.6 – Choosing the right ML endpoint in Power BI

7. Click on **OK**. Power BI will now start sending the request to the endpoint. Please be aware that you might get a warning in one of the Power BI windows concerning data privacy, as we are sending potentially private data to another service. Please accept this by selecting the first checkbox, so the action can be performed.

8. As a result, you should now see a new column called `AzureML.sentiment-analysis-pbi`, with a lot of fields denoted as `Record`. As our endpoints send more than one output, we receive a record. You can now click on each record individually, or you can click on the small button showing two arrows next to the column header name. This allows you to expand this `Record` column into multiple ones. Select all column names and press **OK**. *Figure 15.7* shows the result you should see:

A^B_C Phrases	AzureML.sentiment-analysis-pbi.label	AzureML.sentiment-analysis-pbi.score
1 I love working with wood.	POSITIVE	0.999274552
2 This hotel room is filthy.	NEGATIVE	0.999582946
3 This show yesterday was horrible. No one was dancing.	NEGATIVE	0.99976474
4 I liked some parts of the game and I did not enjoy others.	NEGATIVE	0.999073267
5 What a beautiful morning.	POSITIVE	0.9998774711
6 I woke up early to go swimming in the sea.	POSITIVE	0.93852514
7 But these seaguls are nasty and grabbed my sandwich.	NEGATIVE	0.976354241
8 We should all celebrate this achievement of connecting ML endpoints ...	POSITIVE	0.999759853
9 Why are we not celebrating? I am feeling guilty about that.	NEGATIVE	0.996743381
10 I want our city to be free of corruption.	POSITIVE	0.99303484
11 I am so excited. I reached 100000 subscribers on my Youtube channel.	POSITIVE	0.998908997
12 Christoph and Marcel hope you had fun with the book so far.	POSITIVE	0.99969101

Figure 15.7 – Power BI sentiment results

As we can see, the model gives a label for each sentence (`NEGATIVE` or `POSITIVE`) and a confidence value score, denoting how sure the ML model is about the label given. The results are reasonably accurate, except perhaps for the fourth phrase.

9. You can now click **Close & Apply** in the upper left-hand corner, which will result in Power BI creating an ML-enhanced dataset, with which you could now build visuals in a report and eventually publish a report to the Power BI service in the cloud.

As you can see for yourself, integrating with Power BI is a quick and easy way to empower everyone to utilize your deployed ML endpoints with their business data, while not understanding much about the inner workings of the ML services.

Feel free to add some of your own phrases to play around with.

Summary

In this chapter, we learned how to convert ML models into a portable and executable format with ONNX, what an FPGA is, and how we can deploy a DNN featurizer to an FPGA VM through Azure Machine Learning. In addition, we learned how to integrate our ML models into various Azure services, such as Azure IoT Edge and Power BI.

This concludes our discussion through the previous two chapters on the various options to deploy ML models for batch or real-time inferencing.

In the next chapter, we will bring everything we learned so far together to understand and build an end-to-end MLOps pipeline, enabling us to create an enterprise-ready and automated environment for any kind of process that requires the addition of ML.

16

Bringing Models into Production with MLOps

In the previous chapter, we looked into model interoperability using ONNX, hardware optimization using FPGAs, and the integration of trained models into other services and platforms. So far, you have learned how to implement each step in an end-to-end machine learning pipeline with data cleansing, preprocessing, labeling, experimentation, model training, optimization, and deployment. In this chapter, we will connect the bits and pieces from all the previous chapters to integrate and automate them in a build and release pipeline. We will reuse all these concepts to build a version-controlled, reproducible, automated ML training and deployment process as a **continuous integration and continuous deployment** (**CI/CD**) pipeline in Azure. In analogy to the **DevOps** methodology in software development, we will refer to this topic as **MLOps** in ML.

First, we will take a look at how to produce reproducible builds, environments, and deployments for ML projects. We will cover version control for code, as well as the versioning/snapshotting of data and building artifacts.

Next, we will learn how to automatically test our code and validate our code quality with a focus on ML projects. To do this, we will see how unit, integration, and end-to-end tests can be adapted for ensuring good quality of training data and ML models.

Finally, you will build your own MLOps pipeline. First, you will learn how to set up Azure DevOps as your orchestration and coordination layer for MLOps, and then you will implement a build (CI) and release (CD) pipeline.

In this chapter, we will cover the following topics:

- Ensuring reproducible builds and deployments
- Validating the code, data, and models
- Building an end-to-end MLOps pipeline

Technical requirements

In this chapter, we will use the following Python libraries and versions to create MLOps pipelines in Azure DevOps:

- `azureml-core 1.34.0`
- `azureml-sdk 1.34.0`
- `pandas 1.3.3`
- `tensorflow 2.6.0`
- `pytest 7.1.1`
- `pytest-cov 3.0.0`
- `mock 4.0.3`
- `tox 3.24.5`

Most of the scripts and pipelines discussed in this chapter need to be scheduled to execute in Azure DevOps.

All code examples in this chapter can be found in the GitHub repository for this book: `https://github.com/PacktPublishing/Mastering-Azure-Machine-Learning-Second-Edition/tree/main/chapter16`.

Ensuring reproducible builds and deployments

DevOps has many different meanings but is usually about enabling rapid and high-quality deployments when the source code changes. One way of achieving high-quality operational code is by guaranteeing reproducible and predictable builds. While it seems obvious that the compiled binary will look and behave similarly for application development with only a few minor configuration changes, the same is not true for the development of ML pipelines.

ML engineers and data scientists face many problems that make building reproducible deployments very difficult:

- The development process is often performed in notebooks and so it is not always linear.

- Refactoring notebook code often breaks older notebooks.

- There are mismatching library versions and drivers.

- Source data can be changed or modified.

- Non-deterministic optimization techniques can lead to completely different outputs.

We discussed interactive notebooks (such as Jupyter, Databricks, Zeppelin, and Azure notebooks) in the first few chapters of this book, and you have probably seen them in a lot of places when implementing ML models and data pipelines. While interactive notebooks have the great advantage of executing cells to validate blocks of models iteratively, they also often encourage a user to run cells in a non-linear order. The main benefit of using a notebook environment becomes a pain when trying to productionize or automate a pipeline.

The second issue that is common in ML is ensuring that the correct drivers, libraries, and runtimes are installed. While it is easy to run a small linear model based on scikit-learn in Python 2, it makes a big difference for deep learning models if the deployed CUDA, cuDNN, libgpu, Open MPI, Horovod, TensorFlow, PyTorch, and similar libraries match the versions from development. Containerization via Docker or similar technologies helps to build reproducible environments, but it's not straightforward to use them throughout the experimentation, training, optimization, and deployment processes.

Another challenge faced by data scientists is that often data changes over time. Either a new batch of data is added during development or data is cleaned, written back to the storage, and reused as input for other experiments. Data, due to its variability in format, scale, and quality, can be one of the biggest issues when producing reproducible models. Versioning data similar to version-controlling code is essential, not only for reproducible builds but also for auditing purposes.

One more challenge that makes reproducible ML builds difficult is that they often contain an optimization step, as discussed in *Chapter 11, Hyperparameter Tuning and Automated Machine Learning*. While optimization is an essential step for ML (for example, for model selection, training, hyperparameter tuning, or stacking), it can add non-deterministic behavior to the training process. Let's find out how we can fight these problems step by step.

Version-controlling your code

Version-controlling source code is a best practice, not only for software development but also for data engineering, data science, and machine learning As an organization, you have the option to set up your own internal source code repository or use an external service. **GitHub**, **GitLab**, **Bitbucket**, and **Azure DevOps** are popular services for managing source control repositories. The benefit of these services is that some of them offer additional features, such as support for CI workers and workflows. We will use the CI runner integration of Azure DevOps later in this chapter.

Using version control for your code is more important than the version control system you use. Yes, **Git** works pretty well, but so does **Mercurial** and **Subversion** (**SVN**). For our example MLOps pipeline, we will use Git as it is the most widely used and supported. It's essential that you make yourself familiar with the basic workflows of the version control system that you choose. You should be able to create commits and branches, submit **pull requests** (**PRs**), comment on and review requests, and merge changes.

The power of version-controlling source code is to document changes. On each such change, we want to trigger an automatic pipeline that tests your changes, validates the code quality, and when successful and merged, trains your model and automatically deploys it to staging or production. Your commit and PR history will not only become a source of documenting changes but also triggering, running, and documenting whether these changes were tested and ready for production.

In order to work effectively with version control, it is essential that you try to move business logic out of your interactive notebooks as soon as possible. Notebooks store the code and output of each cell in custom data formats – for example, serialized to JSON files. This makes it very difficult to review changes in the serialized notebook. A good trade-off is to follow a hybrid approach, where you first test your code experiments in a notebook and gradually move the logic to a module that is imported into each file. Using auto-reload plugins, you can make sure that these modules get automatically reloaded whenever you change the logic, without needing to restart your kernel.

Moving code from notebooks to modules will not only make your code reusable for all other experiments (no need to copy utility functions from notebook to notebook) but it will also make your commits much more readable. When multiple people change a few lines of code in a massive JSON file (that's how your notebook environment stores the code and output of every cell), then the changes made to the file will be almost impossible to review and merge. However, if those changes are made in a module (a separate file containing only executable code), then these changes will be a lot easier to read, review, reason about, and merge.

Before we continue looking into the versioning of training data, this would be a good opportunity to brush up on your Git skills, create a (private) repository, and experiment with your version control features.

Registering snapshots of your data

Your ML model is the output of your training code and your training data. If we version-control the training source code to create reproducible builds, we also need to version the training data. While it sounds reasonable to check small, text, non-binary, and non-compressed files into the version control system together with your source code, it doesn't sound reasonable for large binary or compressed data sources. In this section, we will discuss a solution on how to deal with the latter.

Let's re-iterate the idea of reproducible builds: regardless of when the training is executed – it could run today, or a year from now – the output should be identical. This means that any modifications to the training data should create a new version of the dataset, and training should use a specific version of the dataset. We differentiate between operational transactional data and historical data. While the former is usually stateful and mutable, the latter is often immutable. Sometimes, we also see a mix of both, for example, mutable historical event data.

When working with mutable data (for example, an operational database storing customer information), we need to create snapshots before pulling in the data for training. For ML, it's easier to use full snapshots than incremental snapshots, as each snapshot contains the complete dataset. While incremental snapshots are often created to save costs, full snapshots can also be stored cost-efficiently using column-compressed data formats and scalable blob storage systems (such as Azure Blob storage), even if you have multiple TBs of data.

When dealing with historical or immutable data, we don't usually need to create full snapshots, since the data is partitioned—that is, organized in directories where directories correspond to the values of the partition key. Historical data is often partitioned by processing date or time, such as the time when the data ingestion was executed. Date or time partitions make it easier to point your training pipelines to a specific range of partitions instead of pointing to a set of files directly.

There are multiple ways to take snapshots of your training data. However, when working with the Azure Machine Learning workspace, it is recommended to wrap your data in Azure Machine Learning datasets, as discussed in *Chapter 4, Ingesting Data and Managing Datasets*. This makes it easy to take data snapshots or version your data. When processing and modifying data in Azure Machine Learning, you should make a habit of incrementing the dataset's version. In addition, you should pass a specific version of the dataset when fetching the data in the training script.

Whenever you pass parameters to your training scripts, it is helpful to parameterize the pipeline using deterministic placeholders. Parameters such as dates and timestamps should be created in the pipeline scheduling step rather than in the code itself. This ensures you can always re-run failed pipelines with historical parameters, and it will create the same outputs.

So, make sure your input data is registered and versioned and your output data is registered and parameterized. This takes a bit of fiddling to set up properly but is worth it for the whole project life cycle.

Tracking your model metadata and artifacts

Moving your code to modules, checking it into version control, and versioning your data will help to create reproducible models. If you are building an ML model for an enterprise, or you are building a model for your start-up, knowing which model version is deployed and with which dataset it was trained is essential. This is relevant for auditing, debugging, or resolving customers' inquiries about the predictions of your service.

We have seen in the previous chapters that a few simple steps can enable you to track model artifacts and model versions in a model registry. Versioning the model artifacts is an essential step for continuous deployments. The model consists of artifacts, files that are generated while training, and metadata. Model assets contain the definition of the model architecture, parameters, and weights, whereas model metadata contains the dataset, commit hash, experiment and run IDs, and more of the training run.

Another important consideration is to specify and version-control the seed for your random number generators. During most training and optimization steps, algorithms will use pseudo-random numbers based on a random seed to shuffle data and parameter choices. So, in order to produce the same model after running your code multiple times, you need to ensure that you set a fixed random seed for every operation that uses randomized behaviors.

Once you understand the benefit of source code version control for your application code and versioning your datasets, you will understand that it makes a lot of sense for your trained models as well. However, instead of readable code, you now store the model artifacts (binaries that contain the model weights and architecture) and metadata for each model.

Scripting your environments and deployments

Automating every operation that you perform during the training and deployment process will increase the initial time of development, testing, and deployment, but ultimately save you a ton of time when these steps have to be executed again. The benefit of cloud services, such as Azure Machine Learning and Azure DevOps, is that they provide you with all the necessary tools to automate every step of the development and deployment process.

If you haven't already done so, you should start organizing your Python in virtual environments. Popular options are `requirements`, `pyenv`, `Pipenv`, or `conda` files that help you to track development and test dependencies. This helps you to specify dependencies as part of the virtual environment and not rely on global packages or the global state of the development machine.

Azure DevOps and other CI runners will help you define dependencies because running integration tests will install all the defined dependencies automatically during the test. This is usually one of the first steps in a CI pipeline. Then, whenever you check in new code or tests to your version control system, the CI pipeline is executed and also tests the installation of your environment automatically. Therefore, it is good practice to add integration tests to all of your modules, so that you can never miss a package definition in your environment. If you miss declaring a dependency, the CI build will fail.

Next, you also need to script, configure, and automate all your infrastructure. If you have followed the previous chapters in this book, you might have figured out by now why we did all the infrastructure automation and deployments through an authoring environment in Python. If you have scripted these steps previously, you can simply run and parameterize these scripts in your CI pipelines.

If you run a CI pipeline that generates a model, you most likely want to spin up a fresh Azure Machine Learning cluster for this job so you don't interfere with other releases, build pipelines, or experimentation. While this level of automation is very hard to achieve on on-premises infrastructures, you can do this easily in the cloud. Many services, such as YAML files in Azure Machine Learning, ARM templates in Azure, or Terraform from HashiCorp, provide full control over your infrastructure and configuration.

The last part is to automate deployments within Azure Machine Learning. Performing deployments through code doesn't take much longer than through the UI but it gives you the benefit of a repeatable and reproducible deployment script. You will often be confronted to do the same operation in multiple ways; for example, deploying an ML model from Azure Machine Learning via the CLI, Python SDK, YAML, the Studio, or a plugin in Azure DevOps. It is recommended to pick whatever works for you, stick with one way of doing things, and perform all automation and deployments in the same way. Having said this, using Python as the scripting language for deployments and checking your deployment code in version control is a good and popular choice.

The key to reproducible builds and CI pipelines is to automate the infrastructure and environment from the beginning. In the cloud, especially in Azure, this should be very easy as most tools and services can be automated through the SDK. The Azure Machine Learning team put a ton of work into the SDK so that you can automate each step –from ingestion to deployment – from within Python.

Next, let's take a look into the validation of code and assets to ensure the code and trained model work as expected.

Validating the code, data, and models

When implementing a CI/CD pipeline, you need to make sure you have all the necessary tests in place to deploy your newly created code with ease and confidence. Once you are running a CI or CI/CD pipeline, the power of automated tests will become immediately visible. It not only helps you to detect failures in your code, but it also helps to detect future issues in the whole ML process, including the environment setup, build dependencies, data requirements, model initialization, optimization, resource requirements, and deployment.

When implementing a validation pipeline for our ML process, we can take inspiration from traditional software development principles (for example, unit testing, integration testing, and end-to-end testing). We can translate these techniques directly to steps during the ML process, such as input data, models, and the application code of the scoring service. Let's understand how we can adapt these testing techniques for ML projects.

Testing data quality with unit tests

Unit tests are essential to writing good-quality code. A unit test aims to test the smallest unit of code (a function) independently of all other code. Each test should only test one thing at a time and should run and finish quickly. Many application developers run unit tests either every time they change the code, or at least every time they submit a new commit to version control.

Here is a simple example of a unit test written in Python using the `unittest` module provided by the standard library in Python 3:

```python
import unittest


class TestStringMethods(unittest.TestCase):
  def test_upper(self):
    self.assertEqual('foo'.upper(), 'FOO')
```

As you can see in the code snippet, we run a single function and test whether the outcome matches a predefined variable. We can add more tests as additional methods to the test class.

In Python and many other languages, we differentiate between test frameworks and libraries that help us to author and organize tests, and libraries to execute tests and create reports. `pytest` and `tox` are great libraries to execute tests; `unittest` and `mock` help you to author and organize your tests in classes and mock out dependencies on other functions.

When you write code for your ML model, you will also find units of code that can, and probably should, be unit tested on every commit. However, ML engineers, data engineers, and data scientists now deal with another source of errors in their development cycle: the data. Therefore, it is a good idea to rethink what unit tests could mean in terms of data quality.

Once you get the hang of it, you will quickly understand the power of using unit tests to measure data quality. You can interpret feature dimensions of your input data as a single testable unit and write tests to ensure each unit is fulfilling the defined requirements. This is especially important when new training data is collected over time and it is planned to retrain the model in the future. In such a case, we always want to ensure that the data is clean and matches our assumptions before we start the training process.

Here are some examples of what your unit tests can test in the training data:

- Number of unique/distinct values
- Correlation of feature dimensions
- Skewness
- Minimum and maximum values
- Most common value
- Values containing zero or undefined values

Let's put this into practice and write a unit test that ensures that the minimum value of a dataset is 0. This simple test will ensure that your CI/CD pipeline will fail if your dataset contains unexpected values:

```python
import unittest
import pandas as pd


class TestDataFrameStats(unittest.TestCase):
    def setUp(self):
```

```
    # initialize and load df
    self.df = pd.DataFrame(data={'data': [0,1,2,3]})
  def test_min(self):
    self.assertEqual(self.df.min().values[0], 0)
```

In the preceding code, we use `unittest` to organize the tests in multiple functions within the same class. Each class corresponds to a specific data source, and in each class, we can test all feature dimensions. Once set up, we can install `pytest` and simply execute it from the command line to run the test.

In Azure DevOps, we can set up `pytest` or `tox` as a simple step in our build pipeline. For a build pipeline step, we can simply add the following block to the `azure-pipelines.yml` file:

```
- displayName: 'Testing data quality'
  script: |
    pip install pytest pytest-cov
    pytest tests --doctest-modules
```

In the preceding code, we first installed `pytest` and `pytest-cov` to create a `pytest` coverage report. In the next line, we executed the tests, which will now use the dataset and compute all the statistical requirements. If the requirements are not met according to the tests, the tests will fail, and we will see these errors in the UI for this build. This adds protection to your ML pipeline, as you can now make sure no unforeseen problems with the training data make it into the release without you noticing.

Unit testing is essential for software development, and so is unit testing for data. As with testing in general, it will take some initial effort to be implemented, which doesn't immediately turn into value. However, you will soon see that having these tests in place will give you good peace of mind when deploying new models faster, as it will catch errors with the training data at build time and not when the model is already deployed.

Integration testing for ML

In software development, integration testing verifies individual so-called components often made up of multiple smaller units. You normally use a test driver to run the test suite and mock or stub other components in your tests that you don't want to test. In graphical applications, you could test a simple visual component while imitating the modules the component is interacting with. In the backend code, you test your business logic module while mocking all dependent persistence, configuration, and UI components.

Integration tests, therefore, help you to detect critical errors when combining multiple units together, without the expense of scaffolding the whole application infrastructure. They are placed between unit testing and end-to-end testing and are typically run per commit, branch, or PR on the CI runtime.

In ML, we can use the concept of integration testing to test the training process of an ML pipeline. This can help your training run to find potential bugs and errors during the build phase. Integration testing allows you to test whether your model, pre-trained weights, a piece of test data, and optimizer can yield a successful output. However, different algorithms require different integration tests to test whether something is wrong in the training process.

When training a **DNN** model, you can verify a lot of aspects of the model with integration tests. Here is a non-exhaustive list of steps to verify:

- Weights initialization
- Default loss
- Zero input
- Single batch fitting
- Default activations
- Default gradients

Using a similar list, you can easily identify and catch cases where all activations are capped at the maximum value in a forward pass, or when all gradients are 0 during a backward pass. Theoretically, you can run any experiment, test, or check you would do manually before working with a fresh dataset and your model, continuously in your CI runtime. So, any time your model gets retrained or fine-tuned, these checks run automatically in the background.

A more general assumption is that when training a regression model, the default mean should be close to the mean prediction value. When training a classifier, you could test the distribution of the output classes. In both cases, you can detect issues due to modeling, data, or initialization error already, before starting the expensive training and optimization process.

In terms of the runner and framework, you can choose the same libraries as used for unit testing because, in this case, integration testing differs only in the components that are tested and the way they are combined. Therefore, choosing `unittest`, `mock`, and `pytest` is a popular choice to scaffold your integration testing pipeline.

Integration testing is essential for application development and for running end-to-end ML pipelines. It will save you a lot of time and lowers your operational costs, if you can detect and avoid such problems automatically.

End-to-end testing using Azure Machine Learning

In end-to-end testing, we want to verify all components involved in a request to a deployed and fully functional service. To do so, we need to deploy the complete service all together. End-to-end testing is critical for catching errors that are triggered only when combining all the components together and running the service in a staging or testing environment without mocking any of the other components.

In ML deployments, there are multiple steps where a lot of things can go very wrong if not tested properly. Let's discard the easy ones where we need to make sure that the environment is correctly installed and configured. A more critical piece of the deployment in Azure Machine Learning is the code for the application logic itself: the scoring file. There is no easy way to test the scoring file, the format of the request, and the output together without a proper end-to-end test.

As you might imagine, end-to-end tests are usually quite expensive to build and operate. First, you need to write code and deploy applications to only test the code, which requires extra work, effort, and costs. However, this is the only way to truly test the scoring endpoint in a production-like end-to-end environment.

The good thing is that by using Azure Machine Learning deployments, end-to-end testing becomes so easy that it should be part of everyone's pipeline. If the model allows it, we could even do a no-code deployment where we don't specify the deployment target. If this is not possible, we can specify an Azure Container Image as a compute target and deploy the model independently. This means taking the code from the previous chapter, wrapping it in a Python script, and including it as a step in the build process.

End-to-end testing is usually complicated and expensive. However, with Azure Machine Learning and automated deployments, a model deployment and sample request could just be part of the build pipeline.

Continuous profiling of your model

Model profiling is an important step during your experimentation and training phase. This will give you a good understanding of the resources your model will require when used as a scoring service. This is critical information for designing and choosing a properly sized inference environment.

Whenever training and optimization processes run continuously, the model requirements and profile evolve over time. If you use optimization for model stacking or automated ML, your resulting models could grow bigger to fit the new data. So, it is good to keep an eye on your model requirements to account for deviations from your initial resource choices.

Luckily, Azure Machine Learning provides a model profiling interface that you can feed with a model, scoring function, and test data. It will instantiate an inferencing environment for you, start the scoring service, run the test data through the service, and track the resource utilization. Let's bring all the pieces together and set up an end-to-end MLOps pipeline.

Building an end-to-end MLOps pipeline

In this section, we want to set up an end-to-end MLOps pipeline. All required training code should be checked into version control, and the datasets and model will be versioned as well. We want to trigger a CI pipeline to build the code and retrain the model when the code or training data changes. Through unit and integration tests we will ensure that the training and inferencing code works in isolation and that the data and model fulfill all requirements and don't deviate from our initial assumptions. Therefore, the CI pipeline will be responsible for automatic continuous code builds, training, and tests.

Next, we will trigger the CD pipeline whenever a new model version is ready. This will deploy the model and inferencing configuration to a staging environment and run the end-to-end tests. After the tests have been completed successfully, we automatically want to deploy the model to production. Therefore, the CD pipeline will be responsible for the automatic deployment.

The separation of the pipeline into CI and CD parts makes it easy to decouple the process of building assets from deploying assets. However, you can also combine both parts into a single CI/CD pipeline, and so build, train, optimize, and deploy it all with a single pipeline. It's up to you and your organization how to model the CI and CD components of your pipeline, and how to set up any triggers and (manual) approvals. You can choose between either deploying every commit to production or deploying a number of commits each day or week after manual approval.

In this section, we will use Azure DevOps to author and execute the CI/CD pipelines and, therefore, to set up triggers, run the build, training, and testing steps, and handle the deployment of the trained model. Azure DevOps has built-in functionalities to automate the end-to-end CI/CD process. In general, it lets you run pieces of functionality, called tasks, grouped together in pipelines on a compute infrastructure that you define. You can either run pipelines that are triggered automatically through a new commit in your version control system or trigger them through a new revision of a build artifact or a button, for example, for semi-automated deployments. The former is called a **code pipeline** and refers to CI, while the latter is called a **release pipeline** and refers to CD.

Let's start setting up an Azure DevOps project.

Setting up Azure DevOps

Azure DevOps will be the container for authoring, configuring, triggering, and executing all our CI/CD pipelines. It provides useful abstractions to work with version-controlled resources, such as code repositories and a connection to Azure and the Azure Machine Learning workspace, and lets you collaboratively access runners, pipelines, and build artifacts.

> **Important Note**
> **Azure DevOps** refers to the managed Azure DevOps Services accessible via `https://dev.azure.com/`. There also exists an on-premises offering for similar CI/CD integration capabilities called **Azure DevOps Server**, which was formerly known as Visual Studio **Team Foundation Server (TFS)**.

As a first step, we are going to set up the Azure DevOps workspace, so that we can author and execute Azure MLOps pipelines. Let's start by setting up the organization and projects.

Organization and projects

First, you need to set up your organization. An organization is a workspace to manage similar projects and collaborate with a group of people. You can create an organization by either using your Microsoft account, GitHub account, or even connecting to **Azure Active Directory** (**AAD**). To create an organization, you need to log into Azure DevOps (`https://dev.azure.com/`), provide the slug name for your organization, and select a region to host your organization's assets.

The following figure shows the screen for creating a new Azure DevOps organization:

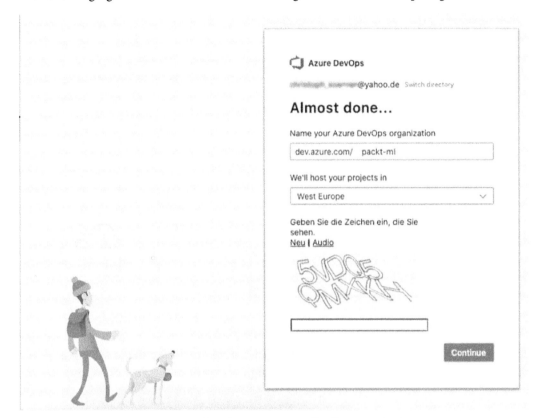

Figure 16.1 – Creating a new Azure DevOps organization

Next, you can set up projects in your organization; we will start with one project that will contain the configuration and code to run your MLOps pipelines. A project is a place to keep all assets for a specific ML project logically grouped. You will be able to manage your code repositories, sprint boards, issues, PRs, build artifacts, test plans, and CI/CD pipelines within an Azure DevOps project.

The following figure shows the process of creating a new Azure DevOps project. This will be the container for our pipelines, as well as testing and deployment configuration:

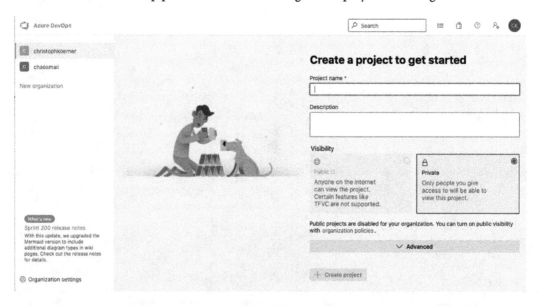

Figure 16.2 – Creating a new Azure DevOps project

Once we have the organization and project set up, we need to add the Azure Machine Learning capabilities to Azure DevOps by installing the appropriate Azure DevOps extension.

Azure Machine Learning extension

Next, it is recommended to install the Azure Machine Learning extension for your Azure DevOps organization. This will tightly integrate your Azure Machine Learning workspace into Azure DevOps so that you can do the following things within Azure DevOps:

1. Assign automatic permissions to access your Azure Machine Learning workspace resources automatically through Azure Resource Manager.

2. Trigger release pipelines for new model revisions.

3. Run Azure Machine Learning pipelines as tasks.

4. Set pre-configured tasks for model deployment and model profiling.

It's fair to say that all the preceding things can also be set up manually using custom credentials and the Azure ML Python SDK, but the tight integration makes it a lot easier to set up.

> **Important Note**
>
> You can install the Azure Machine Learning extension for Azure
> DevOps from `https://marketplace.visualstudio.com/`
> `items?itemName=ms-air-aiagility.vss-services-`
> `azureml`.

Next, we will use the extension to set up the service connections and access permissions
for your Azure and Azure Machine Learning workspace accounts.

Service connections

You might remember from previous code examples that interacting with Azure and Azure
Machine Learning resources requires the appropriate permissions, tenants, and subscriptions
to be configured. Permissions to access these services and resources are often defined
through **service principals**. In Azure DevOps, we can set up permissions for our Azure
DevOps pipelines to access Azure and Azure Machine Learning resources, create compute
resources, and submit ML experiments through **service connections**.

In your Azure DevOps project, go to **Settings | Service connections** and configure a new
Azure service connection with service principal authentication for your Azure Machine
Learning workspace. The following figure shows how to set this up in Azure DevOps:

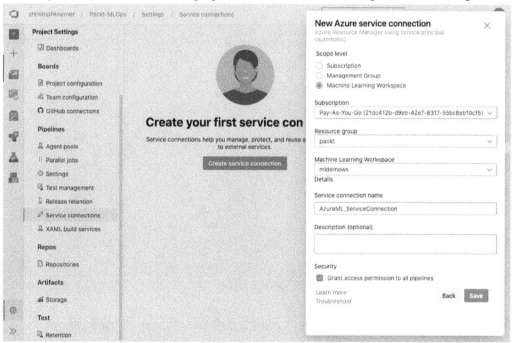

Figure 16.3 – Creating an Azure DevOps service connection

Similarly, you can also permit Azure DevOps pipelines to manage resources in an Azure resource group programmatically. It is recommended that you create both permissions through service principals and note the name of both newly created connections.

Secrets

In the next step, we want to store and manage all the variables and credentials outside of the actual CI/CD pipelines. We don't want to embed credentials or configuration parameters (such as subscription ID, workspace name, and tenant ID) into the pipeline, but pass them as parameters to the running pipeline.

In Azure DevOps, you can achieve this by using **variable groups** and **secure files**. You can even connect a variable group to an Azure Key Vault instance to manage your secrets for you.

It is recommended that you navigate to **Pipelines | Library** to set up a variable group that contains your subscription ID, tenant ID, names of your service connections, and so on as variables, so that they can be reused in pipelines. You can always come back later and add more variables if you need them. The following figure shows a sample variable group definition that can be included in your pipelines:

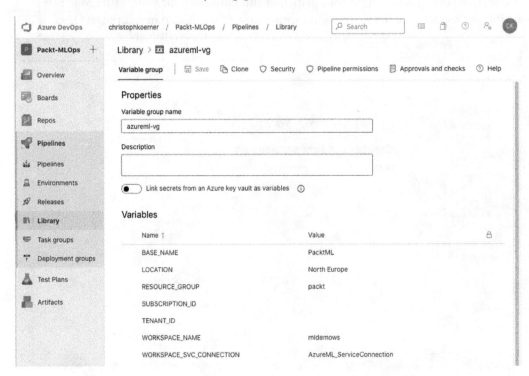

Figure 16.4 – Creating an Azure DevOps variable group

Next, we will set up a repository and write a code pipeline.

Agents and agent pools

Your CI and CD tasks will eventually check out the project, build it, train the model, run the tests, and deploy it. To do all this (and more), you need a compute infrastructure to run the CI/CD jobs. In Azure DevOps, these compute resources are called **agents**.

Azure DevOps Services provides Microsoft-hosted agents, which will execute your pipeline jobs either in VMs or Docker images. Both compute resources are ephemeral and torn down after each pipeline job.

When using Azure DevOps with public projects, Azure Pipelines is free and provides you with Microsoft-hosted agents for your CI/CD pipeline jobs. This allows you to run 10 parallel jobs for up to 6 hours each. For private projects, you are limited to one parallel job for up to 1 hour each with at most 30 hours per month.

> **Important Note**
>
> To prevent abuse, all free pipeline resources need to be requested for an organization via this form: `https://aka.ms/azpipelines-parallelism-request`.

If more capacity is needed, we can either run self-hosted agents via Azure DevOps Server and/or Azure VM scale set agents or purchase additional Microsoft-hosted agents through Azure DevOps Services. For the purpose of this book, you should be able to start experimenting comfortably with the free capacity on private repositories.

Continuous integration – building code with pipelines

Now, we can start to set up an automatic build, test, and training pipeline for our ML model using Azure DevOps pipelines. Conceptually, we will create or import a Git repository to Azure DevOps that serves as a container for our ML project and will contain the CI pipeline definitions. By convention, we will store the pipelines in the `.pipeline/` directory.

The following figure shows how to set up or import a repository in Azure DevOps:

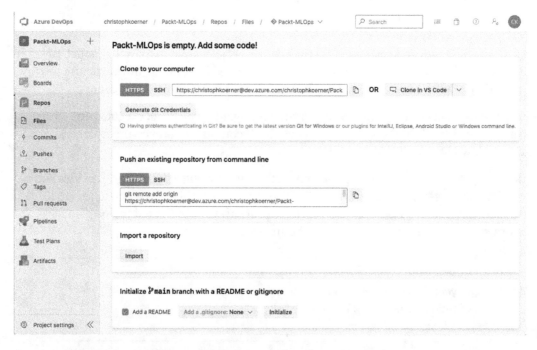

Figure 16.5 – Cloning or importing a repository

Next, we open Visual Studio Code and start authoring our pipeline. Instead of constructing the CI pipeline from widgets and plugins, we will choose YAML to author the pipeline code. This is very similar to how GitHub CI or Jenkins workflows are written.

A pipeline contains a linear series of tasks to be executed to build, test, and train the ML model that can be triggered by a condition in the repository. In the Azure DevOps pipeline, tasks are organized in the following hierarchy:

- Stage A:

  - Job 1:

    - Step 1.1
    - Step 1.2

  - Job 2:

    - Step 2.1

Therefore, a pipeline is made up of stages, where each stage contains multiple jobs. Each job can contain multiple tasks called steps. Besides stages and jobs, the pipeline can contain the following sections:

- Pipeline definition:

  - `name`: The name of the pipeline

- Pipeline triggers:

  - `schedules`: Scheduling-based pipeline trigger configuration
  - `trigger`: Code-based pipeline trigger configuration
  - `pr`: PR-based pipeline trigger configuration

- Pipeline compute resources:

  - `resources`: Containers and repository configuration
  - `pool`: Agent pool configuration for pipeline compute resources

- Pipeline customization:

  - `variables`: Pipeline variables
  - `parameters`: Pipeline parameters

- Pipeline job definition:

  - `stages`: Grouping of pipeline jobs, can be skipped if the pipeline contains only a single stage
  - `jobs`: Pipeline jobs to be executed

As you can see in the preceding list, the Azure DevOps pipeline YAML schema allows you to customize pipeline triggers, compute resources, variables, and configurations, and lets you define the tasks to run in the pipeline. Azure DevOps pipelines also understand the concept of templating. You can use the `template` directive for stages, pipelines, jobs, steps, parameters, and variables to reference files from the template.

> **Important Note**
> You can find the documentation of the pipeline's YAML schema in the Microsoft documentation at `https://docs.microsoft.com/en-us/azure/devops/pipelines/yaml-schema/`.

Let's use these step definitions and construct a simple pipeline to test the model code and start model training:

---

ci-pipeline.yaml

```yaml
trigger:
- main

pool:
  vmImage: ubuntu-latest

stages:
- stage: CI
  jobs:
  - job: Build
    steps:
    - script: pytest tests --doctest-modules

- stage: Train
  jobs:
  - job: Train
    steps:
    - script: python train.py
```

In the preceding pipeline, we define the trigger to start the pipeline for new commits on the main branch. For execution, we run each job on the Microsoft-hosted free agent pool using an Ubuntu VM. Then, we group the tasks into two stages: CI and Train. The former will build and test the code and datasets, whereas the latter will train the ML model and create a new version of the model in the model registry.

Now, we can add a commit to the repository and merge it to the main branch, and the CI pipeline will be triggered and train a new model version. You can use the preceding pipeline definition as a starting point to add additional steps, tests, configurations, and triggers to fully customize your CI pipeline.

> **Important Note**
>
> You can find an up-to-date example of an MLOps pipeline in the Microsoft GitHub repository at `https://github.com/microsoft/MLOpsPython`.
>
> You can find more examples for MLOps starting points on the Azure MLOps repository `https://github.com/Azure/mlops-v2`

Next, we will take a look at a CD pipeline to deploy the trained model to production.

Continuous deployment – deploying models with release pipelines

An additional benefit of tracking model artifacts in a model registry (for example, in Azure Machine Learning) is that you can automatically trigger release pipelines in Azure DevOps when the artifacts change. Any artifact, such as a new ML model or version, can be configured to trigger a release in Azure DevOps. Therefore, code changes trigger CI build pipelines, and artifact changes trigger CD release pipelines. In this section, we will create a CD pipeline for our model and automatically roll the model out into staging and production.

While the triggering mechanism for release pipelines is different from build pipelines, most of the concepts for pipeline execution are very similar. Release pipelines also have pipeline stages, whereas each stage can have multiple tasks. One additional feature of release pipelines, since they deal with the deployment of artifacts, is that each stage can have additional **triggers**, as well as **pre-deployment** and **post-deployment conditions**, such as **manual approval** and **gates**.

Triggers will allow you to continue the pipeline execution during a specified schedule only. Manual approvals will halt the pipeline until it is approved by the defined user or user group, whereas gates will halt the pipeline for a predefined time before executing a programmatic check. Multiple stages, triggers, and pre- and post-deployment conditions are often combined to safely deploy artifacts to different environments.

If you have the Azure Machine Learning plugin installed, you can select triggers and deployment tasks specifically for Azure Machine Learning, such as artifacts based on ML model versions and Azure Machine Learning model deployment and profiling tasks. In this section, we will choose both the ML model artifact trigger and the ML model deployment task.

> **Important Note**
> You can find the available Azure DevOps tasks in the Microsoft documentation
> at `https://docs.microsoft.com/en-us/azure/devops/`
> `pipelines/tasks/`.

The following figure shows you an Azure DevOps release pipeline, where we select an ML model as an artifact for the release pipeline trigger. We configure the pipeline with two stages, a deployment to staging and a deployment to production. In addition, we add a manual approval as a post-deployment condition of the staging deployment:

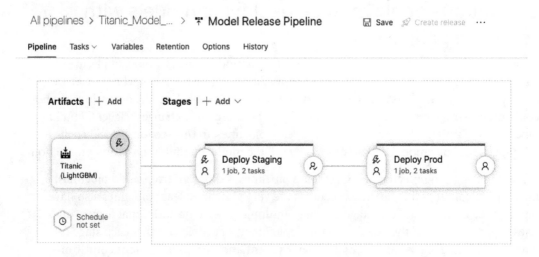

Figure 16.6 – Defining an Azure DevOps Release Pipeline

By default, the release pipeline will require a user to create a release by pressing the **Create release** button in the top-right corner. This mode is intended to create releases only when an operator decides to trigger a deployment, and helps us avoid any automated deployments while configuring the release pipeline. However, once the operator is confident that the pipeline and release process are working as intended, we can enable automated deployments by toggling the flash icon on the asset in the release pipeline. This will enable the CD trigger and, therefore, trigger a release and deployment whenever the asset has changed. As a final task in this chapter, you can go ahead and activate the CD trigger to fully automate your CD pipeline.

Summary

In this chapter, we introduced MLOps, a DevOps-like workflow for developing, deploying, and operating ML services. DevOps stands for a quick and high-quality way of making changes to code and deploying these changes to production.

We first learned that Azure DevOps gives us all the features to run powerful CI/CD pipelines. We can run either build pipelines, where steps are coded in YAML, or release pipelines, which are configured in the UI. Release pipelines can have manual or multiple automatic triggers (for example, a commit in the version control repository or if the artifact of a model registry was updated) and create an output artifact for release or deployment.

Version-controlling your code is necessary, but it's not enough to run proper CI/CD pipelines. In order to create reproducible builds, we need to make sure that the dataset is also versioned and pseudo-random generators are seeded with a specified parameter. Environments and infrastructure should also be automated, and deployments can be done from the authoring environment.

In order to keep the code quality high, you need to add tests to the ML pipeline. In application development, we differentiate between unit, integration, and end-to-end tests, where they test different parts of the code, either independently or together with other services. For data pipelines with changing or increasing data, unit tests should test the data quality as well as units of code in the application. Integration tests are great for loading a model or performing a forward or backward pass through a model independently from other components. With Azure Machine Learning, writing end-to-end tests becomes a real joy as they can be completely automated with very low effort and costs.

Now, you have learned how to set up continuous pipelines that can retrain and optimize your models and then automatically build and redeploy the models to production. In the last chapter, we will look at what's next for you, your company, and your ML services in Azure.

17
Preparing for a Successful ML Journey

Congratulations, you've made it – what an incredible journey you've been on! By now, you should have learned how to preprocess data in the cloud, experiment with **ML** models, train deep learning models and recommendation engines on auto-scaling clusters, optimize models, and deploy them wherever you want. And you should know how to add a cherry to the top of the cake by operationalizing all of these steps through **MLOps**.

In this last chapter, we will recap some important revelations we learned during this journey. It's easy to get lost or overwhelmed by technological and algorithmic choices. You could dive deep into modeling, infrastructure, or monitoring without getting any closer to having a good predictive model.

In the first section, we will remind you that ML is mostly about data. Artificial intelligence should probably be called data cleansing and labeling, but of course, this doesn't sound as good as AI. You will come to understand that your data is key to great performance, so it's what you should care about the most. Your data is all that matters!

In the following section, we will show you how to start your ML projects. We will do this by providing you with some guidance and making a point about the importance of a clean base infrastructure and thoughtful monitoring.

After that, we will reiterate the importance of automation and how new technologies will take us further into the world of **machine learning as a service (MLaaS)**. It is always great to understand where technology is heading and in the case of ML, it is meta-learning and systems that already automatically suggest fitting models and stack them to achieve good predictive performance. And what is left when modeling is fully automated? Exactly – your data!

Following that, we will talk about the constant change and evolution of cloud services while focusing on PaaS offerings. We will look at why PaaS solutions are built and what their foundation is. This will help you understand how best to prepare for change and why you are still betting on the right foundation, despite ever-changing services.

Finally, we will talk about a topic we have mostly ignored throughout this book. We will talk about some questions you should think about before starting any ML project: Should you do it? Will the results of your model have a grave impact on people's lives? You may have guessed it: we will talk about **ethics** in terms of data processing. With a more and more connected world, you shouldn't misuse the personal data of others, you shouldn't build models that are extremely biased toward certain groups of people, and you shouldn't influence people's lives negatively with your deployed solution.

The following topics will be covered in this chapter:

- Remembering the importance of data
- Starting with a thoughtful infrastructure
- Automating recurrent tasks
- Expecting constant change
- Thinking about your responsibility

Remembering the importance of data

Many algorithmic problems for predictions and model fitting are hard to model, compute, and optimize using classic optimization algorithms or complex heuristics. Supervised machine learning provides a powerful new way to solve the most complex problems using optimization and a ton of labeled training data.

Some may think you just should throw a metric ton of data at a model. Imagine that you have thousands of pictures of the same bird from every possible angle. A trained model based on those pictures would probably not be very predictive for classifying different bird families.

> **Choosing the Right Data Samples for Your Model**
>
> A trained model will increase in quality when it's using highly distinct data samples and data samples that are useful in the context of what your model should predict.

So, when you're working with ML algorithms, you need to remember that models are powered by the training data you provide them with, as well as their training labels. Good data is the key to good performance.

Knowing this, let's reiterate the key takeaways when it comes to working with data and training ML models:

- **Spend most of your time wrangling the data**: As we discussed at the beginning of this book, in most ML projects, you'll spend about 80% of your time on data analysis, preprocessing, and feature engineering. Understanding your data inside and out is critical to developing a successful predictive model. Think about it this way: the only thing that makes you stand out from your competition is your data. Most likely, your competitors have access to a similar set of algorithms, optimizations, and compute infrastructure that you do. The only thing they don't have is your data and your skill to take apart this data (hopefully). Hence, this is where your secret to success lies: in interpreting, cleaning, modeling, and preparing your data for high-quality predictions.

- **Emphasize the engineering of your features**: The biggest opportunity you get to increase the predictive baseline performance of any of your models is to improve your underlying dataset through better feature engineering or by adding more predictive features. Don't get lost trying to tune and stack the model. Rather, spend most of your time and resources on data preprocessing and feature engineering. Feature engineering is where you can shine and win the prediction game. Are you dealing with dates? Pull in other data sources, such as local and global holidays, and nearby events; add relative dates, such as days before a holiday, days before a weekend, and so on. Are you dealing with locations, cities, or countries? Here, you should pull in demographic data, political data, or geographic data. You get the point.

- **Do not get sidetracked with model tuning**: There is only so much that your model can do. Yes, you can stack multiple models, tune and optimize them, optimize for different metrics, and so on. However, your biggest leverage is your data. A good plan for any ML model is to start with a very simple baseline model. Are you working with categorical data? If so, choose a gradient-boosted tree ensemble and stick with the default parameters. Are you predicting continuous values? If so, choose a logistic regression model. Start small and make sure you get your data right before you start to fiddle with your model.

- **Always start with a baseline model**: Use a baseline model and start to build all your automation, infrastructure, and metrics around it. It's worth noting that a baseline model should perform better than a random approach. Once the pipeline has finished, you can dive into the data, add new data, perform better feature engineering, deploy again, test, and re-iterate. Reducing your model to a primitive baseline model is a difficult step, but it will help you succeed in managing your priorities during the first phase of the project. Why is the baseline model approach so important? Because it sets your mindset for an iterative project, where you constantly measure, add data, retrain, and improve your model. Your model will require retraining and you need to measure when this is the case. To retrain, you will need new training data.

- **Continuously collect new, relevant data samples**: In a perfect setup, you would install a continuous data collection pipeline that collects new training data and training labels directly from your current product. Does your model predict search relevance? Collect search queries and the clicked results. Does your model predict fraud? Collect new data and the results of manually verified fraud cases. Does your model predict hashtags? Track the predictions and let your users change them if they're not accurate. In all these examples, we continuously track relevant training data that we can use for constant retraining and fine-tuning. Having this constant stream of training data could be the competitive advantage for your business that sets you up for success. Hence, when you oversee an ML project, think about how you are going to retrain the model in the future.

Besides following these technical rules to handle an ML project, it is of utmost importance to understand the business side of your company. Such a project typically requires an interdisciplinary team of people to succeed. Therefore, it is vital to get C-level buy-in for a complete company data strategy. Data is your fuel, and it is typically distributed throughout the company in a vast amount of data silos, controlled by different departments. As you probably need access to a lot of these sources to implement and improve ML models, it is of utmost importance to have the authority to access and use that data.

This often requires a mental shift in most companies, as data from different departments needs to be combined and analyzed to be used in predictions. Hence, data quality matters, data lineage is important so that you can understand where it came from, timeliness is important, and correctness is essential. So, make sure that data is a first-class citizen in your company that gets the support, love, and care it deserves.

Now that we've reiterated these important facts about data processing, let's talk about the environment you are working with.

Starting with a thoughtful infrastructure

Successfully applied ML projects depend on an iterative approach to tackle data collection, data cleansing, feature engineering, and modeling. After a successful deployment and rollout, you should go back to the beginning, keep an eye on your metrics, and collect more data. By now, it should be clear that you will repeat some of your development and deployment steps in the life cycle of your ML project.

Getting the infrastructure and environment for your ML project right from the beginning will save you a lot of trouble down the road. One key to a successful infrastructure is automation and versioning, as we discussed in the previous chapter. So, we recommend that you take a few extra days to set up your infrastructure and automation and register your datasets, models, and environments from within Azure Machine Learning.

The same can be said for monitoring. To make educated decisions about whether your model is working as intended, whether the training data is still accurate, or whether the resource utilization is high enough, you need accurate metrics. Adding metrics to a project after deployment is quite tricky. Therefore, you should be aware of what you want to measure and what you want to be alerted on beforehand. Take some extra time at the beginning of your project to think about the metrics that you are going to track.

Finally, prioritizing infrastructure while working on the data and models is hard. If you can afford the luxury to split these into separate teams for ML infrastructure, modeling, and data, then this may not be at the top of your mind. However, this is often not the case. To avoid this prioritization issue, we recommend starting with a simple baseline model and defining your infrastructure automation based on this simple model.

Let's look at the steps you should perform when you're starting your ML project:

1. **Choose a baseline model**: Pick the simplest model with default parameters for your use case, a small set of training data, and the most important engineered features.

2. **Build a simple pipeline**: Put all these model training steps into a pipeline that builds your model automatically and deploys it into a staging environment. The great thing about this approach is that you automatically prioritize infrastructure and always output a deployed scoring service. This will set you up for success.

3. **Dive into the data**: Make sure you understand the data and its quality, how to fill in missing values, and how to pre-process features. You can add additional data and work on feature engineering to turn your raw input data into interpretable data. If you pick a good baseline model, this work should greatly improve the performance of the baseline and give your colleagues a scoring service API to use with the new service.

4. **Experiment with more complex models**: Once you are confident that you have built a solid data pipeline, you can tackle modeling, including model selection, training, validation, optimization, and stacking. Again, you should be able to see incremental improvements that can be measured and continuously deployed to any QA environment. Once your performance is good enough, roll out the service to your customers and start collecting metrics and more training data.

5. **Monitor cloud usage**: When you develop using compute infrastructure in the cloud, it is easy to quickly spend a few thousand dollars for a couple of unused or underutilized virtual machines. We recommend that you regularly check the number of machines and their utilization. If something is not being used anymore, scale or shut it down. Remember that the cloud's number-one benefit is scalable infrastructure. So, please take advantage of it.

Following this guidance will help you set up a clean and monitored infrastructure that you can evolve along the way.

Now that we've talked about the base infrastructure you should set up, let's talk about automation again.

Automating recurrent tasks

Training an ML model is a complex iterative process that includes data preparation, feature engineering, model selection, optimization, and deployment. Above all, an enterprise-grade end-to-end ML pipeline needs to be reproducible, interpretable, secure, and automated, which poses an additional challenge for most companies in terms of know-how, costs, and infrastructure requirements.

In the previous chapters, we learned the ins and outs of this process, so we can confirm that there is nothing simple or easy about it. Tuning a feature engineering approach will affect model training; the missing value strategy during data cleansing will influence the optimization process.

Above all, the information that's captured by your model is rarely constant, so most ML models require frequent retraining and deployments. This leads to a whole new requirement for MLOps: a DevOps pipeline for ML to ensure continuous integration and continuous deployment of your data, pipelines, and models.

Automated ML helps simplify this complex iterative process by automating many of these challenges. Instead of manually tuning the input data, then selecting, optimizing, and deploying an ML model manually, an automated service just requires the input data, as well as a few business-related configurations, such as the type of prediction to train.

Therefore, using tools such as Azure DevOps and Azure Machine Learning pipelines greatly reduces errors and system downtime and frees the user from performing a bunch of manual tasks. In addition, services such as Azure Automated Machine Learning allows users to optimize ML training and even stack multiple models to improve prediction performance. The biggest benefit of this is that the user can focus on the most important part of the ML process: understanding, acquiring, and cleaning the data.

In many cases, automated ML services will outperform manually trained models while requiring significantly less in terms of training and operation costs. The reason for this is that many tasks, such as choosing the correct categorical embedding, handling imbalanced data, selecting the best model, finding the best parameters, and combining multiple models to improve performance, can be systematically optimized as opposed to being chosen manually.

Every major cloud provider offers mature services so that you can perform automated ML in the cloud and functionalities to deploy these models conveniently. Automated ML is a great way to save time and costs while providing your existing employees with the tools needed for training complex end-to-end ML pipelines. This makes automated ML a real service – MLaaS.

Speaking about tooling, let's talk about the changes you need to keep up with when you're working with modern cloud systems.

Expecting constant change

Everything is in a constant state of change. 15 years ago, only a few people ever heard about neural networks and machine learning. Today, you have access to a vast amount of ML libraries, programs, and cloud services. Every day, new progress is made to automate ML tasks and improve ML modeling. Just think about the voice assistants you may use and what is happening with self-driving vehicles.

Due to this, you are in for a whole bunch of constant changes being made to ML libraries and their tooling. This is especially true in a cloud environment, where updates can quickly be pushed out to the userbase compared to licensed software. As we learned previously, looking at the big cloud providers, their services can typically be divided into the following categories:

- **Infrastructure as a Service (IaaS)**: IaaS services are all-infrastructure abstractions such as virtual machines (compute), disks (storage), and networking.

- **Platform as a Service (PaaS)**: PaaS services are platforms built on top of these components with additional functionality that exposes a service while hiding the underlying infrastructure and operating system.

- **Software as a Service (SaaS)**: SaaS services, in contrast, are exposed through a UI and don't give you any access to the underlying software and hardware stack.

Azure Machine Learning is a great example of a PaaS offering as it combines different infrastructure services, UIs, and SDKs to give you great new features and full access to the underlying services, such as blob storage, training clusters, and container registries while putting the operating system out of sight in most cases. On your monthly Azure bill, you will see that you spend most of your money on infrastructure services when using a PaaS solution.

While the underlying infrastructure builds the foundation for all cloud services, they are not likely to change drastically over the next few years. New improvements will make their way to the market that typically concentrate on throughput levels and network security. Still, you shouldn't expect major changes to be made to the existing APIs. In addition, these offerings are not likely to be discontinued since they are the backbone of many services.

The same is not true for PaaS services. They are designed to answer the requests of customers regarding an abstracted solution so that they are freed from implementing tons of boilerplate code and handling the lower-level infrastructure details of a solution. How many times have you seen a feature of Azure Machine Learning and thought, *Hey, I could easily implement this on my own*? This is certainly true, but you may want someone else to solve this simple thing so that you can concentrate on the complex problems you are trying to solve. And that's why PaaS exists in the first place.

However, the downside with customer-driven needs is that those needs and usage patterns are constantly evolving. New use cases are cropping up (such as MLOps) that ask for new services or extensions to existing services to be supported. Hence, you should always expect that PaaS will change over time.

If you were to look at the first version of this book, you would find that nearly half of the code and features that were shown in that version were either deprecated, replaced by something new, or merged with other parts of the Azure Machine Learning service. Depending on when you are reading this book, you may have found discrepancies between the features or APIs that we are describing here and the current APIs and features in Azure.

If you were understandably confused and asked yourself how this book could already be out of date, we want to assure you that what we are presenting is the right technology to bet on. PaaS offerings in general and MLaaS offerings specifically undergo massive changes and improvements all the time. Expect change!

Let's look at some possible changes you may encounter over time:

- **Expect names to change**: This is probably the most common change. Companies are notoriously bad at naming products, and Azure and all other cloud providers are no exception. This may look like a big change or inconvenience, but it is nothing more than changing the name of a service or component or hiding it somewhere else in the cloud platform. In the past few years, a lot of changes were made to ML regarding Azure. There was a service called **Azure Machine Learning Studio (classic)**, which mostly survived as the **Designer** in Azure Machine Learning. There were – and still are – services called **Azure Batch**, **Azure BatchAI**, and **AML Compute**, which offered mostly the same functionality as the compute cluster for batch inference you will now find in Azure Machine Learning. Simply put, do not let yourself get distracted by this. Expect some interesting new names to pop up for the functionality that you know and love.

- **Expect the UIs to change**: This is the most visible change and is quite common in cloud offerings of late. Many services get revamped UIs, some get integrated into the Azure UI, and some get placed in a separate application. Expect some functionality to be exposed only in one UI and not another. Most often, however, a new UI means that just the same or similar functionality is accessible through a new interface. This is one of the reasons why we trained you to work so much with the Python API or the Azure CLI instead of the graphical interface.

- **Expect classes and packages to change in the SDKs**: Most APIs of most cloud providers for ML solutions are constantly evolving. Azure has invested a lot of money in its ML service, so change is inevitable. A good way to prepare for this change is to abstract code into specific implementations that can be swapped out easily with new functionality. Another good practice is to be cautious with library updates, but also don't stay behind the most recent version for too long.

Do you agree that change is the only constant, given all these circumstances? Just keep in mind that all PaaS solutions are ultimately built on an underlying infrastructure, which provides a rock-solid foundation for your computing, storage, and networking.

So, remember: despite the constant change, you are building on the right foundation!

Having talked about most of the things you should consider while using a cloud platform for ML, let's talk about something far more important: data ethics.

Thinking about your responsibility

In this final section of this book, we want to take a step back from models, deployments, and optimization to talk about a much more important topic: ethics when it comes to handling data or what is today known as **responsible AI/ML**.

In *Chapter 1*, *Understanding the End-to-End Machine Learning Process*, we talked about **bias** in data, how it can be introduced willingly or unwillingly into a dataset, and what you have to look out for. This is but one small piece of the puzzle to reflect how you are gathering data and how your trained model can negatively influence other people's lives.

Imagine that you are training an ML model to suggest to a bank teller that the customer in front of him is allowed to receive a loan and what kind of interest rate the customer is allowed to have on that loan. Using an automated system to make this decision can be a blessing or a curse. If there is an inherent bias in most of the bank tellers of a company and you build a fair model, then this will probably be a blessing. However, if your model is based on the previous decisions of those bank tellers, you must be on the lookout for a lot of bias in your data. If not, you may create an even more unfair world because now, your ML system is in charge. A fair teller giving out the loan, even though they may understand that there is a bias in your ML system, is now probably not allowed to overrule it.

There are far worse examples than this one, but this should give you a good idea of what we want to talk about.

Generally speaking, we can group the responsibilities you have into the following categories:

- **Interpretability**: How well can you explain your model and the results it generates?

- **Fairness**: How well can you ensure fairness by eliminating bias in the data?

- **Privacy**: How well are the **personally identifiable information** (**PII**) of individuals being safeguarded in your underlying data and model? Who has access to it?

- **Compliance**: How well documented is everything you work with and have access to? How do you track who is using your data or model?

Let's have a more detailed look at what you have to watch out for and what tooling is offered through Azure Machine Learning to accommodate you while you're doing this.

Interpreting a model

Any deployed ML model is a black box. We send input and receive output in the form of a prediction or classification through the model. Therefore, it is hard for stakeholders to understand why and why not a system makes certain decisions. To alleviate this situation, you can apply new tooling to explain your model.

But before we talk about tooling and approaches to explain an ML model, let's group models into two categories:

- **Black-box models**: Models where the calculations are so complex that we do not know how the decision came to be.

- **Glass-box models**: Models where the result can be relatively easily explained and calculated. Think about linear regression models, for example.

Glass-box models tend to be simpler, so the trade-off seems to be between explainability and complexity (and therefore, possibly accuracy). But if your model handles a whole bunch of personal information, you will want to know how the model comes to its conclusion.

Therefore, the need for an explainer arises that can interpret black-box models, called the **Black Box Explainer**. The following are the two most well-known explainers:

- **Shapley Additive Explanations (SHAP)**: This is a game theory approach that's applied to ML models and is used primarily for explainability. This family of methods assumes every feature in a model as a **player** in a game. Based on this assumption, you can use the so-called **Shapley values** to calculate the average contribution of a feature value to a prediction. Simply put, this is done by adding and removing features from **coalitions**, which in game theory is the group of players cooperating. SHAP can be used for any type of model, but it is well defined for linear regression, trees, ensemble trees, and deep learning with TensorFlow or Keras. Furthermore, it can explain individual predictions, not only explanations on a global scale. You can read more about SHAP in its open source release (https://github.com/slundberg/shap).

- **Local Interpretable Model-agnostic Explanations** (**LIME**): This is a method that creates a so-called surrogate glass-box model based on any black-box classifier model. A surrogate model tries to mimic the behavior of an underlying model while reducing its complexity. This is done by training a linear model in the vicinity of a particular instance. Users can then look at this newly created glass-box model to understand the black-box model's outputs for this neighborhood or subset of predictions. Therefore, LIME can explain individual predictions of the black-box model. You can read more about LIME in its open source release (`https://github.com/marcotcr/lime`).

These are the techniques you can use to interpret black-box models. To alleviate the situation with glass-box models a bit, Microsoft Research is working on an ML model called **Explainable Boosting Machine** (**EBM**) that is as accurate as gradient boosting while still being completely explainable. Their original paper can be found at `https://arxiv.org/abs/2106.09680`.

To try out these explainers, you can either use these packages directly in your project or you can use the `azureml-interpret` package (`https://docs.microsoft.com/en-us/python/api/azureml-interpret`) from the Azure ML SDK. This package gives you access to the **Interpret Community SDK** (`https://github.com/interpretml/interpret-community`). Have a read through the explainer that's available on that package.

If you want to try this out, have a look at the following guide: `https://docs.microsoft.com/en-us/azure/machine-learning/how-to-machine-learning-interpretability-aml`. When you were looking at the Azure Machine Learning studio pages throughout all the hands-on exercises in this book, you may have noticed a tab called **Explanations** in the training runs and models. When you're using this package, you can add the results of the explainers to your training runs and view the visuals online afterward.

For further reading, have a look at the **InterpretML** project (`https://interpret.ml/docs/intro.html`), which provides an overview of the different types of explainers.

Now that we have an idea of how to interpret the results of our models, let's look at fairness.

Fairness in model training

One of the major tools for analyzing the fairness of a model is called **Fairlearn** (`https://fairlearn.org/`). To define if a model behaves fairly, the algorithms and metrics in the Fairlearn package look for two types of harm that can be done, as follows:

- **Allocation harm**: A model or system withholds opportunities, resources, or information. This would fit our previous example, where we discussed an ML system giving out loans to individuals.

- **Quality-of-service harm**: A model or system that does not withhold something but behaves differently toward different groups.

To assess the fairness in a given model, two constructs are used, assessment metrics and mitigation algorithms. These can be classified as follows:

- **Assessment metrics**: Metrics can be calculated for a single model by comparing multiple models and for models that have been created through the mitigation algorithms. They span from simple metrics calculating the recall rate of a model up to adding grouping information to the mix to analyze the model results. Further information is available here: `https://fairlearn.org/main/user_guide/assessment.html`.

- **Reduction algorithms**: These build a new standard black-box model from a re-weighted training dataset after the assessment. Users can tweak this through different model runs to find the optimum trade-off between accuracy and fairness. Further information is available here: `https://fairlearn.org/main/user_guide/mitigation.html#reductions`.

- **Post-processing algorithms**: These algorithms take the original model and the sensitive feature to calculate a transformation to be applied to the prediction of the model. Through this process, we avoid retraining the original model.

Be aware that packages such as Fairlearn are still in development. Since deciding on fairness is not a simple topic, do not only rely on such tooling. When you're thinking about the types of biases you can introduce, be reflective on what you are doing and use tools like these to get more insights. The developers of Fairlearn pointed the following out:

> *"Fairness is fundamentally a sociotechnical challenge. Many aspects of fairness, such as justice and due process, are not captured by quantitative fairness metrics. Furthermore, there are many quantitative fairness metrics which cannot all be satisfied simultaneously. Our goal is to enable humans to assess different mitigation strategies and then make trade-offs appropriate to their scenario."*

For a guide on how to use the Fairlearn package with Azure Machine Learning and how to upload your results, go to `https://docs.microsoft.com/en-us/azure/machine-learning/how-to-machine-learning-fairness-aml`.

Finally, let's learn how to handle privacy and compliance with Azure Machine Learning.

Handling PII data and compliance requirements

With the dawn of legislation such as the **General Data Protection Regulation** (**GDPR**) in Europe and the **California Consumer Privacy Act** (**CCPA**) in California, businesses are now in a predicament. Besides having clear instructions on how PII data can be utilized, they are also often required to store audit trails of any action that involved this data, from a user up to an employee of the company accessing this data.

Therefore, it is very important to have the tooling to support this effort. Most Azure services have security measures in place to deal with external intruders and to build multi-tenant applications, helping customers avoid seeing the PII data of others. Still, the ones administrating the system have access to this clear text data in most organizations. And the same is true for someone building an ML model. In addition, databases on Azure can typically log any access and build an audit trail for review. But what about the ML modeling pipeline or deployment pipeline? Who can see the data in which form and at which point?

All these questions need to be answered. Let's look at some of the available tooling and research that's being done in this area:

- **Differential privacy**: This mechanism is used to add noise or randomness to data to make the data of a person unidentifiable. In doing so, we can still build an accurate model on a slightly changed dataset. Be aware that this is not referring to obvious PII data, such as your name or email address. To give you something to think about: you can likely be identified directly by the version of the browser and the installed browser add-ons you are using. This method was implemented in a package called **SmartNoise** (`https://github.com/opendp/smartnoise-core`), which you can use in your ML projects. Additional information about this topic can be found here: `https://docs.microsoft.com/en-us/azure/machine-learning/concept-differential-privacy`.

- **Homomorphic encryption**: This allows computation to be done on encrypted data without allowing access to a decryption key. Only the results of the computation need to be decrypted with a secret key. So far, even using encrypted data and decrypting it with a key was bothersome, since running encryption on TBs of data was time-consuming. Now, this technology, which has been researched by Microsoft, is available through the **Microsoft SEAL** project (`https://www.microsoft.com/en-us/research/project/microsoft-seal/`). Furthermore, you can learn how to use this method with an inferencing web service by following the guide at `https://docs.microsoft.com/en-us/azure/machine-learning/how-to-homomorphic-encryption-seal`.

- **Datasheets for models**: This provides guidelines for documenting ML assets and their life cycles. To be compliant with regulations and also just to work cleanly, a guideline called **ABOUT ML** (`https://partnershiponai.org/paper/about-ml-reference-document/`) can be adapted. A view of how to adapt this guideline in the context of Azure Machine Learning can be found here: `https://github.com/microsoft/MLOps/blob/master/pytorch_with_datasheet/model_with_datasheet.ipynb`.

Keep an eye on these topics as they develop since failure to comply with these regulations can have dire consequences.

As you have seen, all the packages we've discussed in this section are still in alpha or beta stages since the topics of interpretability, fairness, and privacy are relatively new in the context of ML. For a decade, ML was more of a research topic than a real-life production environment. Nowadays, solutions that build on ML have found their way into our daily lives. Therefore, we need to take a step back and start asking if we can let machines decide for us without questioning their validity.

So, when you're running your next ML project that is bound for production, bring these topics into the discussion since they need to be handled from the beginning.

Summary

In this chapter, we looked at a few things from a much higher level by covering data, infrastructure, monitoring, automation, change management, and ethics. We hope that our coverage of these topics made sense to you after reading this book.

It is important to understand that your data will control and influence everything, so making data a first-class citizen in your company is the first important step. Hiring a *VP of Data* and defining standards on data quality, lineage, and discoverability are just a few of the measures you can take.

Looking at automatization, we saw that Automated Machine Learning will run the world in a couple of years. The idea is quite simple: a trained meta-model will always be better at proposing, training, optimizing, and stacking models for higher predictive performance than humans. This makes total sense. It is just another parameter optimization step that also includes the model architecture. Another interesting thought is that Automated Machine Learning will offer true MLaaS to users who aren't ML-savvy. Maybe a prediction column will be provided in Excel, or an ML transformation step in Power BI, meaning regular Office users can suddenly harness the power of ML through spreadsheet applications.

We also mentioned that change is inevitable when working with PaaS in the cloud. This is because PaaS solutions are designed to implement typical customer solutions and drive you toward consuming more infrastructure services. As customer needs evolve, so do these PaaS offerings. Hence, a good takeaway is to not get too attached to product names, UIs, or SDK packages.

Finally, we understood the importance of ethics in data handling. We discussed the topics of building models that can be explained, assessing the fairness of our models, and how we can safeguard the personal data of individuals from ourselves and others.

We hope you have enjoyed this book and learned how to master ML and Azure Machine Learning. However, the rabbit hole is far deeper than this book. So, keep on learning, as we also will. Reach out to us on social media and tell us what you've learned, what you liked, and what could be improved in this book. We would love to hear your feedback.

Until then, happy machine learning!

Index

`Packt.com`

Subscribe to our online digital library for full access to over 7,000 books and videos, as well as industry leading tools to help you plan your personal development and advance your career. For more information, please visit our website.

Why subscribe?

- Spend less time learning and more time coding with practical eBooks and Videos from over 4,000 industry professionals

- Improve your learning with Skill Plans built especially for you

- Get a free eBook or video every month

- Fully searchable for easy access to vital information

- Copy and paste, print, and bookmark content

Did you know that Packt offers eBook versions of every book published, with PDF and ePub files available? You can upgrade to the eBook version at `packt.com` and as a print book customer, you are entitled to a discount on the eBook copy. Get in touch with us at `customercare@packtpub.com` for more details.

At `www.packt.com`, you can also read a collection of free technical articles, sign up for a range of free newsletters, and receive exclusive discounts and offers on Packt books and eBooks.

Other Books You May Enjoy

If you enjoyed this book, you may be interested in these other books by Packt:

Azure Data Scientist Associate Certification Guide

Andreas Botsikas, Michael Hlobil

ISBN: 978-1-80056-500-5

- Create a working environment for data science workloads on Azure
- Run data experiments using Azure Machine Learning services
- Create training and inference pipelines using the designer or code
- Discover the best model for your dataset using Automated ML
- Use hyperparameter tuning to optimize trained models
- Deploy, use, and monitor models in production
- Interpret the predictions of a trained model

Engineering MLOps

Emmanuel Raj

ISBN: 978-1-80056-288-2

- Formulate data governance strategies and pipelines for ML training and deployment
- Get to grips with implementing ML pipelines, CI/CD pipelines, and ML monitoring pipelines
- Design a robust and scalable microservice and API for test and production environments
- Curate your custom CD processes for related use cases and organizations
- Monitor ML models, including monitoring data drift, model drift, and application performance
- Build and maintain automated ML systems

Packt is searching for authors like you

If you're interested in becoming an author for Packt, please visit authors.packtpub.com and apply today. We have worked with thousands of developers and tech professionals, just like you, to help them share their insight with the global tech community. You can make a general application, apply for a specific hot topic that we are recruiting an author for, or submit your own idea.

Share Your Thoughts

Now you've finished *Mastering Azure Machine Learning*, we'd love to hear your thoughts! Scan the QR code below to go straight to the Amazon review page for this book and share your feedback or leave a review on the site that you purchased it from.

https://packt.link/r/1-803-23241-2

Your review is important to us and the tech community and will help us make sure we're delivering excellent quality content.

Printed in the USA
CPSIA information can be obtained
at www.ICGtesting.com
LVHW011803121023
760795LV00008B/125

9 781803 232416